ELEMENTARY ECONOMICS

ELEMENTARY ECONOMICS

J. HARVEY, B.Sc. (ECON.)

LECTURER IN ECONOMICS, UNIVERSITY OF READING

FOURTH EDITION

MACMILLAN EDUCATION

First edition 1957
Reprinted 1958, 1960, 1962
Second edition 1965
Reprinted 1966, 1968, 1969 (with corrections)
Third edition 1971
Reprinted 1972, 1973
Fourth edition 1976
Reprinted 1976, 1977 (twice)

Published by
MACMILLAN EDUCATION LIMITED
Houndmills Basingstoke Hampshire RG21 2XS
and London
Associated companies in Delhi Dublin
Hong Kong Johannesburg Lagos Melbourne
New York Singapore and Tokyo

Printed in Hong Kong by
DAI NIPPON PRINTING CO. (H.K.) LTD.

PREFACE TO THE FIRST EDITION

THE primary aim of this textbook is to meet the needs of persons who are undertaking a study of economics for the first time. While it covers, in particular, the G.C.E. ('O' level) syllabuses of the various Examining Boards, it should also prove helpful in the 'A' level course and to those university students who are looking for preliminary reading in the subject. For the general reader who is seeking guidance in analysing current economic problems, the book provides a simple groundwork in the methods used by economists.

Much of the book is descriptive, but whenever it seems helpful, subjects have been approached historically. Moreover, where, in the opinion of the writer, simple theory is essential to the full understanding of economic problems and policy, such theory has been introduced. Indeed, demand and supply analysis has been covered fairly thoroughly and many examples of its application have been included in order to show how such analytical tools can be used.

It must be pointed out, however, that the book is elementary and therefore limited in its scope. Hence, either because it is too abstract or too difficult, much theory has had to be omitted. The result is that certain practical problems, which can be analysed adequately only by the use of such theory, have similarly had to be excluded. Moreover, the analysis of some topics has been somewhat simplified, and on occasions this has led to slight inaccuracies for which the writer craves the tolerance of the teacher. Apology must also be made for the fact that certain terms current in everyday speech, such as 'monopoly', 'factors of production', 'terms of trade', etc., are used without definition in the earlier chapters. This is done in order to avoid interrupting the flow of the main argument by lengthy explanations which can be fitted in more appropriately later in the book.

Nevertheless, in those subjects with which it does deal, the book aims at being informative and, above all, stimulating. An effort has been made to examine analytically and at some length many present-day economic aspects and problems of the United Kingdom's economy. To this end, much use has been made of current official statistics, the main source chosen being the Annual Abstract of Statistics. No doubt many readers will be aware of better statistics to be found in other publications, but the merit of concentrating on one volume is that figures are easily accessible when they have to be brought up to date later. Where any other source has been used, it is given at the foot of the appropriate table.

PREFACE TO THE SECOND EDITION

FACTS have been brought up to date and the functions of various institutions amended in order to bring the text into line with current practice.

Some theory has also been added. As a result, the book now covers the syllabuses of the Intermediate Examinations in Economics of bodies such as the Chartered Institute of Secretaries, the Institute of Bankers, the Institute of Chartered Accountants and the Institute of Cost and Works Accountants.

PREFACE TO THE THIRD EDITION

TABLES and facts have been brought up to date and prices have been converted into decimal currency. The upward trend of prices, means, however, that in time figures of prices are liable to be somewhat understated.

PREFACE TO THE FOURTH EDITION

WITH this new edition the opportunity has been taken to bring facts and the working of institutions up to date.

A chapter has been added on the European Economic Community, and a new section on retail outlets has been added to Chapter 7.

Chapters 11, 14, 21 and 22 have been extensively re-written.

CONTENTS

VI. FACILITIES TO EXCHANGE

VII. GOVERNMENT FINANCE

VIII. FULL EMPLOYMENT

MAPS

TABLES

FIGURES

PART I

INTRODUCTORY

CHAPTER I

SCARCITY: THE ECONOMIC PROBLEM

LET us suppose that Edwards Minor, a schoolboy aged fourteen years, is willing to allow us to ask him some questions regarding the spending of his pocket-money. It is probable that our conversation would go something like this:

Questioner: How much pocket-money per week do you have?
Edwards: A pound.
Questioner: How do you spend it?
Edwards: On an average week as follows:

Cinema	30
Sweets and ice-cream	20
Comics	10
Fares	15
Saving towards a new bicycle . .	25
	—
	100

Questioner: Is a pound enough?
Edwards: Certainly not. I would like to be able to buy a new football, a model yacht and more sweets; but a pound does not run to that.
Questioner: Quite. But because it is not enough what do you do?
Edwards: Well, I spend it on what I consider are the most important things. They are the things above— cinema, sweets, comics and so on.
Questioner: I understand. Thank you very much indeed for the information you have given me.

If we put the same sort of questions to a housewife regarding her housekeeping money, we should, without much doubt, obtain somewhat similar replies. When we ask her what she does because her housekeeping money is insufficient, she

might even say: 'I try to spend it as economically as possible.'
Let us set out the conversation from there.

Questioner: Could I ask you what exactly you mean by spending money 'as economically as possible'? For instance, would you go without fires in the winter?

Mrs. Jones: Certainly not. That would be mere stinginess and absolutely ridiculous because we might catch cold with all the extra discomfort involved. What I really mean is that I try to obtain the best possible value from every penny that I spend. For instance, when new potatoes come on the market at 15p per lb. I do not buy them immediately because the old potatoes are still only 3p per lb. However, as the price of the new potatoes falls, I consider carefully how much nicer they would be and how little waste there is. When the price is round about 8p per lb, I think new potatoes are better value than old ones at 3p per lb. So I start buying the new potatoes in place of the old.

Questioner: Thank you very much. I understand now what you mean.

We could go on questioning other people and we should obtain similar replies. From all our investigations, two important points would emerge:

(1) Every person's income is insufficient to buy all the things he would like.
(2) Because this income is insufficient, people have to spend it on the more important things first and in such a way that they get the best possible value from it or, in other words, so that it 'goes as far as possible'.

However, you might be arguing that the reason why everyone in the United Kingdom, for example, cannot buy as much as he likes, is simply because he hasn't enough money. Therefore, all that need be done is for the government to mint or print more money and distribute it to everybody. But would this solve the problem, and allow people to obtain more of the goods they wanted? Let us see. Assume that in the whole of the United Kingdom the total amount of all 'goods' is represented by X, and that the total amount of money which the people have to spend on the 'goods' is represented by £Y. Then we can say that the average price per 'good' is $£\frac{Y}{X}$. Assume, too, that there is no unemployment. Now suppose that the government prints some more bank-notes and gives them away until everybody has exactly twice as much money to spend as before. What happens? Now £2Y are being spent on X 'goods'; therefore the average price per 'good' is $£2\frac{Y}{X}$. In other words, prices of goods have doubled and, as no more goods can be bought than formerly, we are no nearer a solution. As we shall see later in this book, money is simply a device to help us carry out our exchanges of goods more easily. It is the goods themselves which actually satisfy our wants, not money. Do you remember Ben Gunn, who had been left behind by Captain Flint on Treasure Island? He found the treasure, and so had a superabundance of money. But it was of no use to him, for it could not satisfy any of his desires— above all, the desire to leave the island and return to England. If we want to be better off, that is to satisfy more of our wants, then we must have more goods.

We can see this more easily if we look back into history and consider a community, such as the medieval village, where money was not used to any great extent. The peasant himself grew the grain he and his family ate, reared the beasts which provided him with his meat, built his own house, and so on. Thus his yearly income consisted of the rye, wheat and oats he grew and the few pigs and beasts he reared in the course of the year. If he wanted to increase his income, he had to work harder and longer, either in tilling the ground better or by improving the tools he used, so that eventually he would be able to do the work more quickly, leaving him more time to do other necessary jobs. But since he was already working during most of the hours of daylight the amount of the extra work he could do was limited. Moreover, he was also limited in what he could produce by the natural fertility of the soil. Thus there would be no spectacular increase in his income, any increase coming about very slowly indeed. Much, of course, would depend on the weather, but even if this were favourable, his income would still be restricted by the limits imposed by his own efforts and the fertility of the land. Therefore, since it would increase so slowly, we can say that, for any particular year, the villager's total possible income was fixed.

This meant that he, too, had to face up to the second problem —of allocating his labour and land to produce those goods which he required most. If he wanted more oxen, he had to give them more of the limited grazing ground at his disposal, with a consequent reduction in the number of sheep and pigs he could keep. If he wanted more rye, then he had to spend more time tilling and weeding his rye strips and less on his strips in the oat-field. If he wished to gather more wood for the winter, then he had to forgo some of his leisure or leave other jobs undone.

THE NATIONAL INCOME

So far we have spoken about the incomes of individual persons. Today, however, there is much talk about 'national income'. What exactly does that mean? Later on (Chapter 19) we give a detailed explanation, but for the time being we can say that the 'national income' is simply the total of the incomes of all the persons comprising the particular nation under review, say the United Kingdom. Suppose in the Middle Ages the King had wanted to know the 'national income' for England. Since England at the time consisted primarily of a number of fairly self-sufficient villages, he probably first of all would have required each villager to give to the lord of the manor the figure of his total yearly produce. Then by adding up this figure for the whole of the village, and also from the demesne land in the particular village, the lord of the manor would have been able to furnish the King with a figure showing total income of the village. The King would then have totalled the incomes for every village—so many quarters of wheat, rye and oats, so many oxen, pigs, sheep and chickens reared in the course of the year, so many goods made and so on—and this would have given him a figure showing the 'national income' of England. (In fact, William I did carry out such a national survey for 1086, though it was chiefly of the total land and labour available, what today we would call 'capital', and the results are recorded in the Domesday Book.)

Roughly, we follow a similar procedure today when we wish to find the total income per annum of the United Kingdom. We simply add, though for convenience the sum has to be done in money values, the total production of everyone in the United Kingdom in the year. And like the income of Edwards Minor, Mrs. Jones and the medieval peasant (which is insufficient to satisfy all their wants), the national income is limited and is insufficient to satisfy the wants of the nation, i.e. the people of the United Kingdom. In other words, many of our wants have to go unsatisfied. Today we want more schools and more hospitals—but both make demands on the limited amount of materials which we can devote to each. Similarly, we want more teachers, more scientists, more engineers and more policemen—but all make demands on our limited supply of manpower. So we could go on—we want more animals for meat, and more playing-fields—but both make demands on our limited supply of land. There is no end to these problematic situations.

We can increase our income, first by working harder, either by working longer hours, or by inducing more people to work. Examples of the latter are the housewives who do part-time work in offices, factories, and schools, and the students who, during their vacations, take jobs on building sites, etc. Or, secondly, we can reorganise our methods to increase output. Workers, for instance, may be more efficient if they are employed on a profit-sharing basis than on a weekly wage basis, or if they have canteen and sports-ground facilities. And finally, but most important, we can improve and increase the machines which help us in our work. A combine harvester, for example, will, with two men, cut and thrash as much wheat in one day, as one hundred years ago was cut and thrashed by six men working for four full days (which equals 24 men for 1 day). In other words, twenty-two men are now saved on that particular job each day and they can be used to produce other goods, such as houses, cars, radio and television sets, thereby increasing our national income.

But as with the medieval villager who tried to improve his tools, modern machines still take time to make and their production involves taking away men and materials from the production of goods for our immediate use—houses, washing machines, defence equipment, etc. Thus, the increase in our national income is only very gradual—just as it was in the Middle Ages. We are faced with a limited national income, whereas our wants are unlimited. The two together give us the 'economic problem', the problem produced, in a word, by 'scarcity'. So, like the medieval peasant, Edwards Minor, and Mrs. Jones, we must first determine what things we want most of, and secondly, arrange that our means of obtaining these goods and services go as far as possible. If, for example, we want more houses, then men, building materials and land must be taken away from building roads, government offices, schools, etc., and we must be sure that they are employed in the best possible way. In other words, we must allocate our limited land, machines and manpower so as to obtain what we think is the best possible value from them.

It is the task of economics to examine the methods by which the limited means of production are allocated to provide the desired goods and services, and to assess the efficiency achieved.

FIG. 1.—The Economic Problem

QUESTIONS WHICH HAVE TO BE ANSWERED IN SOLVING THE 'ECONOMIC PROBLEM'

As we have seen, the solution to the 'economic problem' which arises is along two lines:

(a) The wants must be placed in some order of importance and the more important satisfied first. No ethical judgment is involved in this arranging of wants. Economists accept 'wants' as they are, and if a man prefers a glass of beer to a loaf of bread they do not question the moral implications of his choice.

Of course, some wants can be satisfied more easily than others because some goods take more of the scarce means of production than other goods. Allowances must be made for this in the way in which production is organised. For example, if a person wants a car only twice as much as he wants a motor cycle, but its real cost (that is, in terms of the factors of production used) is eight times as much, then probably he will have to be content with the motor cycle and his want for the car must go unsatisfied.

(b) The limited factors of production must be used as effectively as possible, without waste.

In the first place, waste occurs if these factors are allowed to stand idle. If, for instance, many persons are unable to obtain work, then we are not making full use even of the limited amount of labour which we do possess. The same applies if we allow good land and machinery to stand idle.

Secondly, waste in the use of the factors of production occurs if they are not related to wants; that is, if they are employed in making things which are not really wanted. This relating of production to wants has become more difficult with the increased complexity of the economic system. At one time most of the population of the United Kingdom consisted of peasant farmers and each peasant produced to satisfy the wants of his family. He knew roughly how much wheat, barley, meat, etc., his family would need in the course of the year and he could plan the distribution of his productive resources accordingly. But the population of the United Kingdom today is different. Men specialise in the work they do. (We shall see why later.) A builder, for instance, builds houses for others than himself and, therefore, in some way or other he has to estimate the strength of the 'want' for houses. Again, each day in London, the bank manager and the office boy, the bus conductor and the motor salesman, the tinker, the tailor, the soldier, the sailor all go about their respective tasks. While they are working in their own chosen occupations, somebody else is baking the bread and others are growing the potatoes they will eat. At the same time the lorry-driver is bringing to town the milk they will drink in their cup of tea at breakfast the next morning. But our system must provide answers to a multitude of questions. How many suits shall the tailor make? Have we got the right number of bank managers? How much bread shall the baker bake? How much milk shall the farmer send to town? If too much bread is baked it will go stale, if too much milk is sent to town it will simply be left to turn sour and it would have been better if, instead of sending it away, the farmer had turned the surplus into cheese. Over-production involves waste, and waste means that the factors could have been used to satisfy some of our other 'wants'. Clearly then, any organisation of production requires a method by which estimates of the size of wants can be made.

Thirdly, waste in the use of the factors of production occurs if the organisation of production is faulty. This takes place, for instance, when many small firms are producing a good which could be made by a few large firms with the use of fewer factors of production. It happens, too, when the layout of the factory has not been planned with care so that men have to spend unnecessary time in passing from one particular machine to another. Likewise, the organisation may be defective in that processes are not fully integrated—as occurs when steel ingots are allowed to cool before being rolled into steel sheets, for then fuel is wasted in re-heating them. Nor must we ignore the possibility of the centre of production being badly chosen. If a blast furnace, for instance, were situated without regard to its accessibility to supplies of iron ore, coke and limestone, waste would result because extra factors of production would have to be used to transport those materials to the blast furnace. Finally, for full efficiency, the organisation of production must be continually revised to allow for new techniques, new processes and new power supplies.

Any economic system adopted must solve the problem along these two lines. Stated in everyday language, it means that such a system has to provide answers to the following questions:

> (1) What is to be produced?
> (2) How much is to be produced?
> (3) How is it to be produced?
> (4) Where is it to be produced?
> (5) How are the factors of production to be rewarded?

Later in this book we shall examine these questions in more detail showing how, in the United Kingdom in particular, the answers to them are arrived at. Our immediate task, however, is to conduct a simplified and broad survey of two different systems, each of which seeks to answer the problems in an alternative way.

CHAPTER 2

ECONOMIC SYSTEMS

BROADLY speaking, and with much simplification, we can classify the systems which have set out to answer these questions into two groups. Variations exist within each group, but the broad, abstract principles underlying each are the same. These systems are: (1) Collectivism, in which we can include Communism, Socialism and a Controlled Economy; (2) Capitalism, in which we include *laissez-faire*, Private Enterprise, and an Uncontrolled Economy. (In future, we shall refer to Capitalism used in this sense with a capital 'C', in order to distinguish it from 'capitalism', the term which is generally used in economics to describe the method of production using capital equipment—factories, machinery, etc.)

I. COLLECTIVISM

Here the State assumes responsibility for estimating people's wants. It owns the factors of production and then directs them into the production of the goods and services decided upon. Thus, whether or not resources are employed efficiently depends very largely on how accurately wants are estimated and resources allocated. Here we may mention four criticisms of the system.

First, the difficulties in estimating the size of all the various wants of a population are enormous. With goods which satisfy the basic necessities of life, estimation is not too difficult, for, within certain limits, most people want so much bread, butter, meat, potatoes, overcoats, houses and so on. But with comforts and luxuries there are so many variations that estimating accurately the demand for each is a well-nigh impossible task. At least in its early years, the demand for the National Giro, for example, has fallen far short of that estimated. Moreover, particularly with luxury goods and services, demand is changing continually. The State, for instance, would have to decide how much extra ice-cream should be produced in a sudden heat-wave, how many boys would want model tanks for their Christmas presents, and so on. Russia soon discovered this difficulty under Communism, and eventually she had to fall back on a price system to obtain an indication of wants and changes in them.

Secondly, many officials are required to estimate wants and to direct factors of production. Inasmuch as such officials are avoidable in a Capitalist economy, they represent wasted factors of production, for they could be employed to satisfy more wants. Moreover, the use of officials may give rise to bureaucracy—excessive form-filling, an addiction to 'red tape', slowness in coming to a decision and an impersonal approach to individual members of the community. At times, too, though not so much in the United Kingdom as elsewhere, officialdom has been accompanied by corruption.

Thirdly, even when wants have been decided upon, there arise the difficulties of co-ordination. On the one hand, wants have to be dovetailed and awarded priorities. On the other, factors have to be combined in the best proportions for producing those wants. Collectivism usually plans co-ordination through numerous committees, directed at the top by a Central Planning Committee. Yet members of this Committee would be first and foremost politicians and may have little ability in administration. And even if they were the most able administrators available, they would still have to encounter the difficulties of managing a large organisation (see page 67).

Fourthly, it is argued that State ownership of the factors of production, by lessening incentives, diminishes effort and initiative. Direction of labour may mean that persons are dissatisfied with their allotted jobs. Even though not deliberately slacking, they may, through psychological reactions, not work so hard as when they are allowed to choose their own jobs. It must be questioned, too, whether State ownership of factors of production achieves as great an output as private ownership. Apart from the incentive of working for private profit, the necessity of making State activity accountable to the public (chiefly through Parliament) has the inherent disadvantage of encouraging cautious policies. This is due to the fact that officials find it easier to earn 'brickbats' than 'bouquets' (see page 91).

II. CAPITALISM

Under Capitalism the emphasis is laid on the freedom of the individual, both as a consumer and as the owner of a factor or factors of production.

As a consumer he expresses his wants through the price system which, as we shall see in Chapter 8, so operates that those wants are registered and satisfied. As the owner of a factor of production, he so conducts his affairs that he obtains as large a profit as possible, either from the sale of that factor or from the production of a commodity. For many persons, the workers, the factor of production for sale is their labour, but the same general rule still applies. Once again the price system comes into use—this time to calculate profit. We see, therefore, that a price system is an integral part of an economy based on Capitalism.

But this use of the price system based on the profit motive as a means of solving the economic problem has both advantages and disadvantages. We will deal with the latter first, for it is largely from the defects of the Capitalist system that the arguments in favour of Collectivism stem.

In the first place, Capitalism leads to great inequalities of wealth, for the rule ' to him that hath shall be given ' seems to apply fairly generally in the accumulation of wealth. It is much easier, for instance, to make £1,000 once £1,000 is already possessed than when you have to start from nothing. By allocating the fruits of the productive effort according to need, a more equitable distribution is achieved. Such a distribution is carried out directly under Collectivism. Connected closely with inequalities in wealth is the inequality in power which results, a power sometimes translated into political action by the few possessing it to build up still greater power. Occasionally, too, economic concessions are obtained by a large class of voters which are nevertheless harmful to the community as a whole. Thus even today, the United States Government pays its farmers many millions of dollars in order to encourage them *not* to produce certain goods.

Secondly, disadvantages follow because profit is the dominant motive in production. Those goods are produced which yield the greatest money profit. This may be injurious when incomes are very unequal. Persons who spend the most money carry most weight in saying what is to be produced—and this may lead to the production of luxury goods for the wealthy to the exclusion of necessities for the poor. For instance, large mansions may be built instead of houses for working men. We must be careful, however, not to over-emphasise this point; 70 per cent of personal income, even before the deduction of tax, still goes to wage- and salary-earners. Another disadvantage is that, through intensive advertising and high-pressure salesmanship, the public may be deceived into buying certain goods at a price which is many times the cost of production.

Thirdly, if left entirely to private enterprise, some goods and services would not be produced at all or would be produced so inefficiently that the total supplied would be quite inadequate. We could not, for instance, leave the provision of such vital services as justice, police administration and defence of the realm to free enterprise and the profit incentive. Indeed, most advanced communities have considered that it is the duty of the State to provide for other basic needs, such as education, medical attention, and insurance against sickness, industrial accident and unemployment (see page 432).

Fourthly, certain forms of competition may themselves lead to waste and inefficiency in the use of the factors of production. An industry may be divided into small units of production when really co-ordination is desirable in order to secure the advantages of producing on a large scale. Furthermore, resources may be wasted in competitive advertising. Above all, insufficient capital may be invested in the industry. This may come about because an individual firm is uncertain regarding the size of future demand for its product or the policies of its rivals. Or it may result from the fact that modern techniques necessitate production on a vast scale. On the other hand, it may arise simply because the owners prefer to take out quick profits rather than use them for the development of the business. The State, however, which has a much longer existence than the private individual, must take a long-term view and see that sufficient resources are devoted to the maintenance and improvement of machinery in order to ensure that standards of living do not drop catastrophically in the future. (These technical inefficiencies of private enterprise are dealt with in more detail in Chapter 6.)

It is obvious that in an economy where the State decides what to produce, the defects of the last paragraph can be avoided. The State not only has to estimate the wants of consumers but, when deciding what to produce, has, very often, to modify those wants. It tells its citizens, in effect, that though they think they know what they want, they are to some extent misguided because they lack the superior knowledge possessed by the State. Had they this knowledge, then, without doubt, they would modify their wants in the way in which the State does it for them. And so, for instance, the State sees that working-class flats and fewer large houses are built, more guns and less butter are provided, and, instead of building football stadiums, the labour and materials are used in the construction of nuclear power plants.

Fifthly, in practice, the competition upon which the efficiency of the Capitalist system depends is liable to break down. An employer may be the *only* buyer of a certain type of labour in a locality. If so, he is in a strong position when fixing wage-rates with a number of independent and unorganised workers. The State must, therefore, often protect the individual worker. Similarly, on the selling side, the consumer's position may be weak. If there is only one seller of the good, custom cannot be taken elsewhere. Later we shall discuss monopolies in more detail. Here we need only note that where they result in inefficiency and the restriction of supplies, they are harmful to the community. Thus before the war, fish was dumped back into the sea even in the United Kingdom. Of course, under a Collectivist system, the State represents one big monopoly but the supposition is that it would not act contrary to the interests of the people.

Sixthly, it is necessary to draw attention to a fact which the *laissez-faire* advocates seem to ignore—that the motive of private profit does not ensure that public wealth, as distinct from private, will be maximised. A manufacturer building a factory does not consider the soot which falls from his factory chimney on the nearby washing-lines. It is not a cost to him, but it is a cost to the community who live in the neighbourhood. Or, if he spends £50 advertising his products on a hideous hoarding in the middle of a beautiful stretch of country, the £50 is the limit of the cost to him. But that hoarding might be such an eyesore to passers-by that its ' public cost ' may be far greater than £50. On the other hand, there may exist certain 'public benefits' which are not allowed for by the individual producer in calculating the return to his outlay. Thus, when considering the building of a passenger liner, he merely estimates whether receipts from fares will exceed costs. The fact that the liner is a reserve troop transport and therefore of defence value does not enter his calculations. Under Collectivism, the State can allow for such 'public costs' and 'public benefits' when planning production.

Lastly, and most important of all, under Capitalism, where individuals decide what to produce, there occur periods when factors of production are allowed to stand idle because producers as a whole consider that the prospects of making a profit are poor. Under Collectivism, on the other hand, the people who decide which wants shall be satisfied are also the people who direct labour and other factors into the production of the necessary goods and services. All factors, therefore, are fully employed.

The advantages of Capitalism similarly correspond very closely to the defects of the Collectivist system. In the first place, wants are easily gauged and changes of wants are reflected by changes in prices, other things being equal. Consumers are able to express their own particular tastes because the way they spend their incomes influences prices. Thus it is the individual who has the final say under Capitalism. Hence it is directly opposed to Collectivism, where the State decides what the people want and often produces what it considers is good for the people. There is much in favour of letting the individual decide. It has been said that the most terrible form of tyranny throughout history has been forcing on people what is believed to be good for them! In any case most people would rather go to the devil in their own way than be directed to a paradise of the government's making. ' What's one man's meat is another man's poison '—and it is only the individual who can distinguish between the two.

Secondly, because owners wish to obtain the greatest return possible from the factors of production, they take them to where profit is highest. Thus production responds to changes in demand. Moreover, in order to obtain a high profit, they use enterprise, initiative and new methods to keep ahead of rivals. Yet, it is important to note, this efficient production for wants is secured without any direction of labour. People are free to work wherever they choose. Efficiency is achieved simply by using the incentive of private profit.

Lastly, because the price system registers wants and arranges the allocation of factors of production automatically, it operates without hosts of officials. Thus a larger labour force can be employed in the production of goods and services to satisfy wants.

Unfortunately, in our survey so far, we have had to put far more stress on the disadvantages of Capitalism than on those of Collectivism. This has been partly necessary in order to lay the foundations for our future study of the United Kingdom's economy. It does not mean, however, that because fewer disadvantages of Collectivism than of Capitalism have been pointed out, the former is the better system. One big disadvantage of Collectivism has remained unstated. It arises from the fact that, once individuals have given power to the State to prescribe what is good for them, to own all the factors of production and to direct labour, it may not be long before the State has usurped absolute political power in addition to its economic power and the people are at the mercy of a dictatorship. Individuals then exist for the State, and not the State for the individual. In short, we are in George Orwell's *1984*. Thus the ultimate decision as to whether a Capitalist economy is to be preferred to a Collectivist economy (in their extreme forms) really hinges on the question whether you are prepared to run the risk of being ruled by a dictator or whether you would rather be left in freedom to choose your own job and to suffer such defects of the Capitalist system as the risk of unemployment, the possibility of inadequate provision for future production, and the existence of wide variations in wealth.

III. BRITAIN'S 'MIDDLE WAY'

No one country today can boast a purely Collectivist or a purely Capitalist economic system. Probably Russia, which nevertheless has to make use of a price system and private incentives, comes the closest to the first and the U.S.A. to the second. The United Kingdom has followed a 'middle way', and her system makes use of both methods in an attempt, as it were, to get the best of both worlds. In the main, however, production is still carried on under a Capitalist system, for the government is directly responsible (through the nationalised industries, Civil Service, local government, etc.), for only one-quarter of the total production of the economy.

The other three-quarters of the economy is carried on under a Capitalist system, but the government interferes in an effort to offset the disadvantages of that system. From a political point of view, the Labour Party leans towards the adoption of a system whereby a large proportion of the economy is run under the Collectivist system, while there is a greater interference by the government in the rest of the economy. The sympathies of the Conservative Party are in the opposite direction.

Consequently, interference by the government of the United Kingdom has one or more of the following objects:

(1) To produce those goods and services which would either not be provided by private enterprise, or might be provided very indifferently (see Chapter 22).

(2) To take over the production of certain goods and services because they can be produced more efficiently by the resources of the State than by the resources of private enterprise. Under this heading we are thinking principally of the nationalised industries, but it also applies to roads, libraries, and other goods and services provided by local authorities.

(3) To overcome great inequalities in the distribution of wealth and to ensure:
   (a) a minimum standard of life for all;
   (b) equality of opportunity for all.

(4) To protect the individual, both as a consumer and a worker, from the operations of powerful interests, such as monopolies.

(5) To overcome frictions, e.g. to the movement of labour, which hamper the efficient operation of the price system.

(6) To modify the full operation of the price system when shortages, e.g. in housing, would entail hardships.

(7) To control the entrepreneur—where public costs may be incurred outside the costs assessed by him or where public benefits are derived additional to his receipts.

(8) To regulate the economy in order to secure full employment.

(9) To obtain a balanced regional development.

(10) To maintain a stable level of prices.

(11) To improve the balance of payments in order that:
  (a) foreign currency reserves may be strengthened;
  (b) aid may be given to underdeveloped countries.

(12) To ensure a steady growth of national production.

Here we have merely stated various objectives. No attempt has been made to enunciate the practical lines of action to be taken by the government. Sometimes interference is direct, as with rent control, town planning, the investigation of monopolies and mergers, nationalisation and so on. In other cases the interference is less obtrusive, working perhaps, as the redistribution of income does, through a public finance policy. We have to allow for these variations in the methods of interference. Often, as we go along, we shall direct attention to government action in the particular sphere under discussion. At other times, we shall discuss government policy specifically and in more detail, as with interference in the price system, nationalisation, the localisation of industry, the control of monopoly, the regulation of international trade, the promotion of employment and the maintenance of a stable currency.

We can now return to our consideration of the 'economic problem' as it affects the United Kingdom. We commence by an examination of the population in order to see more specifically the nature of the consumers, whose wants are unlimited, and of the producers, who form the limited labour force.

CHAPTER 3

THE POPULATION AS CONSUMERS AND PRODUCERS*

I. THE GROWTH OF POPULATION

1. EARLY HISTORY

TODAY, in order to obtain accurate knowledge of the size, composition and distribution of the population, we take a 'census'. This means that, on a certain day, we count all persons who are resident in the United Kingdom. Normally the census is taken every ten years; the last was in 1971. All persons resident in the United Kingdom on the night of 25th/26th April, 1971, were included, plus persons in all vessels in port or at anchor at census midnight (other than ships of foreign navies) and all persons in boats on fishing and coastwise voyages. It did not include members of the Armed Forces stationed abroad, or merchant seamen and civilians overseas.

Because the first official census for Great Britain was not taken until 1801, we have to make use of indirect sources for our knowledge of the population before that date. Thus from the Domesday Survey in 1086, we judge that the population of Great Britain at the end of the eleventh century was of the order of two million, roughly two-thirds living south-east of a line joining the Wash and the Bristol Channel.

The Black Death in 1349 took a heavy toll of the people, for it is probable that between one-third and one-half perished. When, some thirty years later, Richard II instituted a 'poll tax', it appears that the population was somewhere in the region of two and a half million. In spite of the meagre information, therefore, we can say one very important thing about

* Owing to difficulty in obtaining comparable figures for Northern Ireland most of the discussion which follows refers to Great Britain only. The basic conclusions, however, are equally applicable to the United Kingdom.

the population of the Middle Ages—it grew very slowly indeed.

Our evidence after this date becomes even more scanty. It is probable that the unsettled conditions in England during the fifteenth century restricted the rate at which the population grew. During Elizabeth's reign, however, the population did increase more rapidly, but only to slacken off again in the seventeenth century owing to political and religious tension, the Civil War and the 1665 plague of London and the Home Counties.

The most important work on population during the period 1400–1700 was that of Gregory King in 1690. He estimated the population of England and Wales at five and a half million, while Scotland's was put at about one million. It is known that after 1690, particularly during the second half of the eighteenth century, the population increased rapidly, so much so that it became an important subject for discussion by politicians and thinkers of the day. Malthus's first essay on ' The Principle of Population as it affects the future improvement of Society', with his gloomy predictions as to the effect of the rapid increase, preceded the first census only by three years. Population and its growth had now become a matter of government policy.

2. Growth of Population, 1801 onwards

The figures show that in every decade there has been an increase in the population of approximately two million and this is reflected in the continuous upward trend of the graph in Fig. 2. Underlying this steady upward trend, however, we must note a very important change. From 1811 to 1821 there was an increase of just over two million; and between 1921 and 1931 there was an almost identical increase. But there is an essential difference between the increase in these two decades. Between 1811 and 1821 it was a population of 12 million which grew by two million; between 1921 and 1931 it was a population of nearly 43 million. In other words, the *rate* at which the population was increasing at the beginning of the nineteenth century was very different from what it was a hundred years later.

TABLE 1.—*Population (in ooo's) 1801–1971*

Date	Great Britain (England, Wales and Scotland)	Northern Ireland
1801	10,501	—
1811	12,006	—
1821	14,092	1,380
1831	16,264	1,574
1841	18,534	1,649
1851	20,816	1,443
1861	23,129	1,396
1871	26,072	1,359
1881	29,710	1,305
1891	33,028	1,236
1901	37,000	1,237
1911	40,831	1,251
1921	42,769	1,258
1931	44,795	1,243
1941 Estimate	46,605	1,308
1951	48,854	1,371
1961	51,250	1,425
1971	53,979	1,536

Table 2 shows the *rate* of increase (per cent) in the population between each census date.

TABLE 2.—*Inter-censal Rate of Increase 1801–1971, Great Britain*

Date	Inter-censal rate of increase per cent
1801–11	14·3
1811–21	17·4
1821–31	15·4
1831–41	14·0
1841–51	12·3
1851–61	11·1
1861–71	12·7
1871–81	14·0
1881–91	11·2
1891–1901	12·0
1901–11	10·4
1911–21	4·7
1921–31	4·7
1931–41	4·0
1941–51	4·8
1951–61	5·0
1961–71	5·3

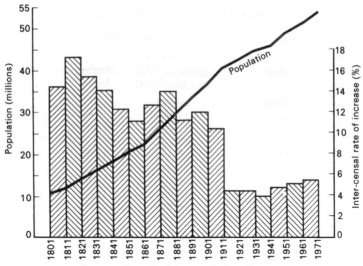

Fig. 2.—Growth of the population 1801–1971

We can see from the above figures that a high rate of increase, averaging 13·2 per cent per decade, was maintained until 1911. But then it fell suddenly, remaining below 5 per cent for each decade until 1951. It will be convenient, therefore, if we examine the growth of population separately over the periods (*a*) 1801–1911, (*b*) 1911–1941, (*c*) 1941 to the present, and then conclude with a look at the future. First, however, we must dispose of some preliminary definitions.

An increase or decrease of population during any period depends upon what has happened as regards (*a*) births, (*b*) deaths, (*c*) migration. The excess of births over deaths we call *the natural increase of population*. *Migration* represents the net balance between emigration (leaving the country) and

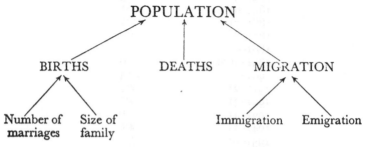

Fig. 3.—The factors affecting population

immigration (coming into the country). There are many statistical methods of measuring the rate of births and deaths, but for our purposes the *crude rates* will be sufficient. The *crude birth rate* is the number of births per year expressed as so many per thousand of the total population. For example, if the total population is 50 million and the number of births in the year is one million then the crude birth rate equals 20. Similarly *the crude death rate* is the number of deaths per year per thousand of the population.

3. POPULATION 1801–1911

The feature of this period was the rapid increase in the population from $10\frac{1}{2}$ million to 41 million, with an average rate of increase of 13 per cent every ten years. Some explanation of this is necessary.

1. *Migration*

TABLE 3.—*Net Migration, Great Britain 1861–1971 (000's)*

	Net gain (+) or loss (−)		Net gain (+) or loss (−)
1861–71	− 193	1921–31	− 562
1871–81	− 257	1931–41	+ 650
1881–91	− 817	1941–51	− 144
1891–1901	− 122	1951–61	+ 97
1901–11	− 756	1961–71	− 365
1911–21	− 858		

Source: Royal Commission on Population Report, 1949, and Annual Abstract of Statistics

Table 3 shows that, in every decade from 1861 to 1911, Great Britain lost by net outward migration an average of just under half a million persons. But the loss varied considerably from decade to decade.

People emigrate for a variety of reasons. These include the love of adventure and desire for change; the wish to escape from political, religious or racial persecution; the offer of lucrative posts abroad, particularly in undeveloped countries, as technicians, engineers, administrators, and teachers; the belief that a developing country offers greater prospects of economic improvement than their homeland. This latter is the most important reason, but because economic prospects vary from decade to decade, the volume of emigration also varies.

Since Great Britain lost by migration in each decade, it affords no explanation of the rapid increase in the population. The increase, therefore, must be a natural one, due either to a rise in the number of births or to a fall in the number of deaths.

2. Births

From such inaccurate estimates which have been made, it appears that the rapid increase in the population was not due to any great increase in the birth rate. Although there was plenty of employment available for young children, it is very doubtful whether they were ever reared by their parents for their usefulness as wage-earners. It must be remembered that the employment of children was no new phenomenon, for even under the old domestic system, children at an early age could be found tasks which would relieve their parents of the burden of their upbringing. Judged by modern standards, the birth rate remained high for the whole of this period, exceeding 35 until about 1872, from which date it began to decline (Table 4).

3. Deaths

The rise in the natural increase in the population was due primarily to a fall in the death rate. The crude death rate at the middle of the eighteenth century was probably about 33; by 1851 it had fallen to 22·7, and in 1911 it was 13·8.

A variety of causes contributed to this fall, though not all were operative throughout the whole of the period. Among the most important are:

(a) the establishment of general hospitals, lying-in hospitals and dispensaries (although recent research suggests that, during the eighteenth century, the lack of hygiene in hospitals increased the chances of a patient dying—by disease caught from another patient!);

(b) the virtual ending of bubonic plague as the black rat died out;

(c) the reimposition of the tax on gin in 1751;

(d) improved medical knowledge and practice, which

reduced considerably infant mortality and deaths from smallpox, typhus and typhoid fever;

(e) improvements in water supply and sanitary arrangements, particularly after the cholera epidemic of 1847;

(f) general advances in the standard of living largely as a result of the cheaper clothes and fresher foods which followed the inventions and discoveries of the Industrial and Agricultural Revolutions.

4. POPULATION 1911–1941

Although the population continued to increase, the *rate* at which it increased fell. Between 1801 and 1911 the rate of increase had averaged 13 per cent every ten years; in the decade 1911–21 it suddenly dropped to 4·7 per cent and remained at or below this figure until 1941. To find the cause we must examine again the three factors on which population depends.

1. *Migration*

Until 1931 Great Britain continued to lose population by migration. Between 1911 and 1921 there was a net loss of 858,000 and in the next decade the net loss was 562,000.

In 1931, however, there was a sudden reversal of the trend of the previous century—in 1931–41 Great Britain had a net gain of 650,000. Special factors, however, were probably at work to bring this about. Many people who had migrated some years previously returned home because of the world depression; immigration was being restricted by the U.S.A.; political and Jewish refugees were fleeing from Germany to Britain; and, after the collapse of the Continent in 1940, many French, Polish, Norwegian, and Czechoslovak service-men came to England.

The effect of migration is greater in 1931 than in 1871. 1871–1901 migration averages a little less than 10 per cent of the natural increase; between 1921 and 1931 it is just under 20 per cent. And of the actual increase in the population 1931–41, over 30 per cent is represented by net inward migration. Yet though migration has thus, especially during the latter part of this period, played quite an important part, the fall in the rate of growth of the population was due to factors operating on the natural increase.

2. Deaths

The death rate continued to fall, though the rate of fall slackened off. This is not surprising, for medical science had successfully combated the most virulent diseases, such as smallpox, cholera and typhus, and therefore less spectacular results were forthcoming when the comparatively minor ones were tackled. Even so the fall continued as further progress took place in medical science, more hospitals were built, new standards of cleanliness to prevent disease were laid down, improved transport brought cheaper and more varied food from abroad, better housing and increased leisure raised still further the standard of living, and the social services were developed.

But the fact that the death rate continued to fall at a slower rate does not offer sufficient explanation of the large fall in the rate at which the population was increasing. We must look for this in the third section.'

3. Births

TABLE 4.—*Crude Birth Rate, England and Wales, 1872-1973*

Date	Crude birth rate for year (or annual average)
1870–72	35·5
1880–82	34·1
1890–92	30·8
1900–02	28·7
1910–12	24·5
1920–22	22·8
1930–32	15·8
1933	14·4
1938	15·1
1947	20·5
1950	15·9
1961	17·6
1971	16·0
1973	13·7

The figures show that, within this period, the birth rate

dropped fairly rapidly until 1941. In fact the drop began during the last quarter of the nineteenth century; it was particularly rapid during the 1920's. This is the real reason for the fall in the rate of increase in the population and therefore needs explanation.

Since the great majority of births are to married women, the number of births depends almost entirely on (a) the number of married couples; (b) the size of the family they have. We shall consider each of these in turn.

(a) *The number of marriages.* Statistics show that the proportion of persons marrying by the age of 54 throughout this period continued very stable, within the limits of 88·2 and 88·5 per cent. People remained just as inclined to marry. Nevertheless, between the period 1881 and 1931 they did postpone marriage to an older age—though this cannot explain the considerable fall in the birth rate.

(b) *The size of family.* The cause lies in the rapid decrease in the size of the family. In mid-Victorian times there were on the average 5·5–6 children in the completed family. From then onwards the size fell, at first gradually, then more rapidly, with the result that persons marrying between 1925 and 1929 had an average of only 2·17 children. The mid-Victorian family had been reduced by 60 per cent. Table 5 enables us to see the change in a slightly different way.

TABLE 5.—*Changes in Distribution of Families by Size*

	Marriages taking place in:	
Number of children born	*1860*	*1925*
o children - - - -	1 in 10	1 in 6
5 or more children - - -	6 in 10	1 in 10
10 or more children - - -	1 in 6	1 in 330

Source: Royal Commission on Population Report, 1949

Thus, whereas for the 1860 marriages, a family of five or more children was the rule, by 1925 it was the exception; in fact, at the latter date, 67 per cent had two or less children. Moreover, the reduction in the size of the family was greatest among the professional classes. The judgment of the Royal Commission on Population, 1949, was: 'The fall in the size of the family over the last 70 years is the salient fact in the modern history of population in Great Britain.' What are the causes of this fall?

At the outset it must be emphasised that we cannot explain it simply by saying 'birth control'. Improved methods have provided the means for the prevention of conception, and thus it is by birth control that families have been limited. More-over, the repercussions of Darwin's theory of natural selection, the publicity given to birth control by the Bradlaugh–Besant trials of 1877–78, and increased propaganda for birth control (often by commercial interests) may have broken down the psychological barriers to its use. By 1918 voluntary clinics were in existence to give advice to women on family planning. But this provides no explanation of *why* people should wish to limit their family. A variety of factors, it seems, contributed to this:

- (i) the increased economic burden of parenthood due, for instance, to the gradual raising of the school-leaving age to 14 years;
- (ii) the higher standards which parents generally set them-selves for their children's welfare;
- (iii) the growth of competing alternatives to children, such as holidays, foreign travel, the cinema and motor car, available particularly for those not inconvenienced or financially handicapped by children;
- (iv) the emancipation of women, politically, economically and socially, with the consequent desire to be free from home ties;
- (v) the momentum which social example, smaller houses and advertisement provided when once the movement towards smaller families had started.

5. 1941 TO THE PRESENT

1. *Births*

Table 4 shows a remarkable fact—that the crude birth rate, after reaching a bottom in 1941, commenced to rise. More-over, from 1942 onwards, there is a marked increase in the number of annual births compared with the previous decade. Once again we have to look at the number of marriages and the size of family in order to account for this change.

(a) *The number of marriages.* In spite of the fact that there was no increase in the size of the population available for marriage, the number of marriages each year, with the exception of the period 1942–44, has been considerably higher than the yearly average of the 1930's. This increase resulted from a rise in the marriage rates due primarily to the fact that people were getting married younger, though we cannot ignore the possibility of an increase in the actual proportion of the people who eventually marry through the greater equality between the sexes. We must note, however, that earlier marriages increase the number of marriages only over a year or so, unless the trend of still earlier marriages continues. In short, it represents borrowing married couples from the future.

Reasons for this tendency for persons to marry younger include: (i) the economic prosperity of the post-war years in which young persons as a group gained relatively to other age-groups; (ii) the increased possibilities of work for women after marriage.

(b) *The size of the family.* Many of the births in the late 1940's were undoubtedly due to the reunion of families separated during the war. But it now seems that there has also been a long-term change in attitude to the size of family (Table 6).

TABLE 6.—*Average family size, Great Britain*

Date	Completed family size
1925–9	2·17
1935–9	2·07
1945–9	2·22
1955–9	2·38

Source: Social Trends, 1974

It can be seen that there has been an increase in the average size of the completed family. Various reasons can be suggested for this new and important departure:

(i) Younger marriages increase the possibility of a larger family.

(ii) Present-day luxuries, such as the car, television set, and holidays, are complementary to, rather than competitive with, children.

(iii) The small family has probably gone 'out of fashion'. Much has been written in recent years regarding the disadvantages of the one-child family, both to the child and to the parents. This discussion may have discouraged such families. Moreover, whereas the couples married prior to 1925 had come from large families and would wish to avoid the disadvantages of such, the couples marrying from 1937 onwards probably came from the small family and had experienced that this, too, had its disadvantages.

(iv) Greater economic prosperity, which makes it easier to keep children.

(v) The possibility of mothers being able to return to work while their children are still fairly young.

(vi) Increased government help to the man with a family. This help is both direct and indirect. It is afforded by means of family allowances; income-tax reliefs; family income supplements; a comprehensive National Health Scheme which covers the whole of a family although a single man pays the same contribution as a married man; welfare services for expectant and nursing mothers and their babies; subsidies on food and housing, with priority for the latter given to persons with large families; free secondary education and more generous grants for higher education; cheap meals and free milk at school. Such help redistributes the real income of the community in favour of parents, and thus tends to offset the material disadvantages which formerly weighed so heavily against the large family.

2. Deaths

Factors previously mentioned as being responsible for the fall in the death rate (improvements in the standard of living, advances in the educational level of the community, progress in medical knowledge, and the expansion and improvement in the health services) have continued to bring down the death rate, but more slowly. Their effect has been most marked in the case of babies, where health and welfare services for infants and expectant mothers have been extended and improved. During the period 1941–73 the infant mortality rate (that is, the deaths of infants under one year of age per thousand live births) for England and Wales fell from 60·0 to 16·9.

But we must remember that old people, too, have better care and will have enjoyed a more comfortable childhood and middle-age than their predecessors. Their old age is healthier, and so there is a good possibility of the death rate falling still further.

3. *Migration*

After the outward rush of Britons to Australia, New Zealand and Canada immediately after the war, there was some falling off in the number of such emigrants. On the other hand, considerable immigration took place from Northern Ireland and Eire and the newer members of the Commonwealth, particularly the West Indies. This produced a net gain from migration of 97,000 during the decade ending in 1961. Subsequent controls on immigration have resulted in a net outward flow since 1961.

6. THE FUTURE POPULATION

When we come to discuss the future population of Great Britain, we soon enter the realms of speculation. All we can do is to make the most reasonable assumptions regarding births, deaths and migration, bearing in mind the present trends.

The projections in Table 7 are based on the following assumptions:

(i) Death rates at the outset are based on recent experience. For ages under 40 for males and under 50 for females they are assumed to decline progressively until at the end of 40 years they are about half the present rate.

(ii) Births are assumed to be 816,000 mid-1974, increasing gradually to 1,015,000 in 1991, and falling to 992,000 at the end of the century.

(iii) Net outward migration of 50,000 a year for all future years.

TABLE 7.—*Estimated Future Total Population of the United Kingdom*

Mid-year estimates
(*000's*)

1981	57,263
1991	59,768
2001	62,400

II. THE AGE DISTRIBUTION OF THE POPULATION

Through the decline in the birth rate and in the rate of increase of the population, there has been a big change in the age composition of the population of Great Britain over the last hundred years. This is shown in Table 8 and Fig. 4.

TABLE 8.—*Age Distribution of the Population of Great Britain 1851–1971*

	Under 15		15–64		Over 65	
	Population (millions)	% of total	Population (millions)	% of total	Population (millions)	% of total
1851	7·4	35·5	12·5	59·8	1·0	4·7
1911	12·6	30·8	26·1	63·9	2·1	5·3
1939	10·0	21·4	32·4	69·7	4·2	8·9
1971	12·9	23·9	33·9	62·8	7·2	13·3

Source: Compiled from Royal Commission on Population Report, 1949, and Annual Abstract of Statistics.

The figures show a much older composition of the population. In 1851 approximately one-third of the population was under 15 years of age; by 1971 only one-quarter was under 15—and this in spite of the fact that during the years 1957–64 the number of births was rising. On the other hand, whereas in 1851 less than one-twentieth of the population was over 65 years of age, in 1971 one-eighth was in this age-group.

We can look at this in a slightly different way, for this same trend of an ageing population is reflected in the average age of the population. In 1891 the average age was 27 years; in 1971 it was 37 years. The two factors which have brought this about are:

(*a*) the lengthening of life due to the various factors which have led to a fall in the death rate;

(*b*) the fall in the birth rate at the end of the nineteenth century and the consequent fall in the number of births each year between 1911 and 1941.

The change in the percentage of the 15–64 age-group, which contains roughly two out of every three persons, has not been proportionately so large. Owing to the increasing number of births up to 1911, the older people in the group will continue to increase until 1975, and this will roughly offset the reduced intake (due to the considerable drop in the number of births

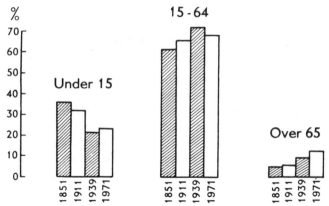

FIG. 4.—Changes in the age distribution of the population of Great Britain 1851–1971

between the wars) of younger people. But as the pre-1911 high-birth years move into the over-65 group, the 'working' group will decline, for the increase in births since 1942 is still insufficient to offset the loss. By 1981 the working group will form about 63 per cent of the population (using the same assumptions upon which Table 7 is based).

What is likely to be the future position of the other two groups? The population over 65 years will, until the end of this century, consist of survivors of people already born.

Therefore we can make reasonably accurate predictions regarding its size. Until the end of the century the percentage it forms of the total population will increase because:

  (a) more persons who were born in those years during which the number of births was high will be coming into this class; and

  (b) mortality will probably fall still further.

Thus it is probable that by 1981 the 65 + age-group will form 14 per cent, one in seven, of the population. By then the average age of Great Britain's population will be about 38 years.

The percentage formed by the under-15 age-group depends very much on the size of the family in the future. But if the present increase in size is maintained, the group will form about 23 per cent of the population in 1981.

THE RESULTS OF THIS CHANGING
AGE DISTRIBUTION

Before considering the economic results of this ageing population a word of warning is necessary. As has already been pointed out, much of the trend results from the fall in mortality and is therefore a normal development. Hence our attitude to it must not be entirely one of prevention but rather of acceptance, with an effort to readjust ourselves as far as possible to the changing circumstances.

1. *An increased dependence of old people on the working population*

The saying that 'with every mouth God sends a pair of hands' is only partly true, for in the United Kingdom, people do not start to earn a living until they leave school, the minimum age for which is 16 years, and cease to earn their living when they retire, at about 65 years of age. The result is that, whereas all the population are consumers and have wants to be satisfied, only about two-thirds of the population (that is approximately those contained in the 16–64 age-group), are producers, and this includes housewives and the sick and un-employed of this group. In effect, then, somewhat less than two-thirds of the population are producers. The proportion of producers to consumers could be increased by encouraging people to go on working after reaching 65 years of age or by reducing the school-leaving age to say 14 years, though the latter would be a very short-sighted policy, for it would probably lower the quality of the producers and so result very quickly in a net loss in total production. It is obvious that the scope for such action is limited. Indeed we are back to the 'economic problem'—the number of workers, like the amount of land and machinery at their disposal, is very limited compared with wants.

Thus where the population is ageing, fewer workers have to maintain more children at school and more old persons. Even though the latter are living on pensions and savings, it means that they are drawing on the goods and services which are being produced currently by the workers. Whereas in 1851 there were over 12 workers to every person over 65 years of age, in 1951 there were only 6, and by 1981 the number will have fallen to just over 3! The result is shown in the increased burden of retirement pensions. In 1945 there were approximately 16 pensioners to every 100 contributors; in 1998 it is estimated that there will be 34 pensioners to every 100 contributors. Thus over this period the annual real cost of retirement pensions is likely to double and the greater part of this increased cost will have to be met from taxation.

2. *A changing pattern of consumption*

When discussing the nature of 'wants', attention was drawn to the fact that one of the chief factors influencing their composition was the age and sex distribution of the population. An ageing population means, to take extreme examples, that bath-chairs will be wanted in place of prams, walking-sticks in place of hockey-sticks, tea in place of milk. But for many of these new 'wants' provision has to be made well in advance. For instance, the increase in the over-65 age-group means that we must make provision for aged couples without families when planning a housing programme. Similarly the rise in the number of births in recent years has meant that more primary schools have had to be built; and, as these children grow older, different kinds of schools will be required. We could multiply these examples indefinitely.

3. *Increased difficulty in shifting labour from one industry to another*

Increased difficulty will be experienced in shifting labour from one industry to another. Such shifts are necessary when tastes change, when technical processes change or when new discoveries, such as petro-chemicals and North Sea oil, cause new industries to arise. In the past it has not usually been necessary for the older persons to uproot themselves and to learn new techniques. The expanding industries have been supplied by new trainees who are leaving the university, college or school, and just starting their working lives, while the decaying industries have declined fairly quietly by failing to recruit new entrants to replace the workers who retire on account of old age.

Until 1980, the number of workers over 55 years of age will be increasing. This creates difficulties when the structure of industry is changing. Expanding industries, such as oil-refining and electrical equipment, have to draw on older workers from the declining industries, such as ship-building, to meet their labour requirements. This involves some dislocation—teaching the old persons new techniques and removing them to new areas.

4. *The possibility that the community will become less progressive*

We must remember that, while older people are more patient, more experienced and more broadminded than younger people, the latter excel in energy, enterprise, enthusiasm and the ability to adapt themselves to learn new things. There is thus a danger that where the proportion of young people in the community is diminishing, the community may become unprogressive. For example, since the older people own the larger share of the nation's capital, it may be that an over-cautious investment policy could result.

III. THE SEX DISTRIBUTION

In 1971 the population of the United Kingdom was 53,979,000 of whom 26,198,000 were males and 27,781,000 were females. Thus females outnumbered males by 1,583,000. This fact influences the pattern of consumption, the nature of the labour force, and may affect the number of births.

We have seen that, since the great majority of children are born to married mothers, the number of births depends considerably on the number of marriages. But where the sexes are unequal, especially where they are unequal between the usual ages of marriages, that is 16–49 years, the proportion of persons likely to get married will be smaller. When, for instance, as in 1951, women exceeded men in the age-group 15–49 by 460,000, at least this number of women will probably remain spinsters—and this provided that all the men marry. Even if the men marry women in a slightly younger age-group than their own (as they usually do), it still means that women in their own age-group have gone unmarried. The balance of males to females is thus a matter to which we must give some attention.

The proportion of male to female births does not vary a great deal from 106:100. Yet, as Table 9 shows, in the 15–49 years age-group, females have, until recently, formed a higher proportion than males.

TABLE 9.—*Proportion of Females to Males,*
15–49 Age-Group, Great Britain

Date	Percentage
1851	107
1891	109
1911	108
1921	113
1931	110
1939	106
1951	104
1961	100·4
1971	97·9

Source: Royal Commission on Population Report, 1949,
and Annual Abstract of Statistics.

How can we account for this reversal of the preponderance of males at birth within the 15–49 age-group?

In the first place, at each age, mortality is heavier among males than among females. Even so, unless there were some other factors at work, mortality would not equalise the size of the sexes until the 50-year age-group. For younger age-groups there would still be an excess of men. (Before we consider these other factors we might note that after 50 years the relative mortality of males to females increases considerably, so much so, in fact, that in the 85+ group females outnumber males by nearly 3 to 1.)

The second factor which reduces the proportion of men is emigration. Particularly before 1914 more men emigrated than women. Moreover, many men go abroad, not as permanent emigrants, but to spend much of their working lives as colonial administrators, soldiers, traders, engineers, technicians, planters and so on. Such persons while away would not be included in census returns of Great Britain. Often the areas to which they go are not so healthy as Great Britain, or the nature of the work (often pioneering) involves risk to life and health with resulting high mortality.

Thirdly, in wartime casualties are higher amongst men than amongst women. We can see, for example, the effect of the heavy casualties of the 1914–18 war by the sudden increase in the proportion of women in 1921.

What of the future? Since the high proportion of females in 1921, the percentage figure has steadily fallen. This has been due to various causes. In the first place, the generation affected by the war casualties of 1914–18 has been passing out of the age-group. Moreover, casualties were not nearly so heavy in the 1939–45 war, and in any case a higher proportion of women were killed than in the 1914–18 war. Secondly, from 1931 and until the end of the war, there was no net emigration. In fact, as we have already seen, the trend was reversed and there was a net inward movement. The majority of the immigrants during this period were men.

Is this trend likely to continue in the future? We cannot give a definite answer without knowing whether or not there will be war, the numbers of men who go abroad for their working lives and the scale of migration. But if we ignore the first two, we can make estimates which do have some value. If we assume no net migration and that the mortality rates are constant at the present level, in 1977 the ratio of women to men will be 97·6 per cent. This is the 'normal' ratio and it should remain at this level thereafter. If mortality is assumed to decline, then the ratio is 96·6 per cent, for such a decline would probably benefit men the most.

Thus it seems that the proportion of women to men in the

15–49 age-group will in the future be more equal. Hence a slight increase in the proportion of persons who eventually marry may occur.

IV. THE DISTRIBUTION OF THE WORKING POPULATION

1. WHAT DO WE MEAN BY THE 'WORKING POPULATION'?

Great Britain's population in 1973 was estimated to be 54,386,000 persons. Of these, 24,909,000 persons (15,745,000

TABLE 10.—*Industrial Distribution of the Working Population 1841–1973*

	Percentage Distribution			Numbers (000's)
	England and Wales (1) 1841	Great Britain (2) 1901	(3) 1973	G.B. (4) 1973
Agriculture, forestry and fishing	22·8	9·0	1·7	421
Mining and quarrying . .	3·0	5·8	1·4	361
Construction	6·1	8·1	5·4	1,338
Manufacture (including gas, electricity and water supply)	35·4	32·6	32·1	8,000
Transport and communication.	2·9	9·3	6·0	1,501
Distributive trades . . . } Insurance, banking and finance }	5·7	11·0	{ 10·8 { 4·2	2,691 1,043
Public administration . .	0·6	1·4	6·2	1,543
Professional and scientific services	2·8	4·4	12·7	3,171
Catering and domestic services	18·7	14·3	3·2	784
Miscellaneous services . .	1·2	2·0	5·3	1,329
Employers and self-employed persons	—	—	7·3	1,820
H.M. Forces and Women's Services	0·8	1·1	1·5	361
Registered unemployed . .	—	—	2·2	546
TOTALS . . .	100·0	100·0	100·0	24,909

Sources: Cols. (1) and (2) compiled from Colin Clark, 'Conditions of Economic Progress' (quoting Booth, Journal of Royal Statistical Society, 1856). Cols. (3) and (4) compiled from Annual Abstract of Statistics.

males and 9,165,000 females), are described by the Department of Employment as 'the working population'.

The working population is defined as persons, over 16 years of age, 'who work for pay or gain or register themselves as available for such work'. It therefore includes all persons who are: (a) in civil employment, even if they are over retirement age or are working only part-time; or (b) in the Armed Forces or on release leave; or (c) registered as unemployed. Excluded by the definition are: (a) children under 16 years of age and students above 16 years of age who are receiving full-time education; (b) persons, such as housewives, who do not work for pay or gain; (c) persons who, having private means, e.g. from investments or gifts, do not need to work; (d) retired persons.

2. Changes in the Distribution of the Working Population since 1841

From Table 10 we can see that the chief changes in the distribution of the working population since 1841 are:

(a) A large decrease in the percentage of the population employed in agriculture, forestry and fishing, and in catering and domestic services.

(b) An increase in the percentage of the population employed in commerce (insurance, banking, finance and the distributive trades), professional and miscellaneous services, public administration, transport and communication, and the Armed Forces.

(c) A decrease from 1901, after an increase in the previous 60 years, of the percentage of the population engaged in mining and quarrying, construction, transport and communication.

3. Causes of these Changes

In looking for the causes of the changes in the distribution of the working population, two of the above groups can be selected as being of special significance. The decline in the importance of agriculture is so fundamental and so rapid that it is indicative of far-reaching developments elsewhere. These developments occurred in the industrial field and are usually referred to as 'the Industrial Revolution'. The increase in the importance of public administration is indicative of a change in thought regarding the extent to which the State should interfere in the life of the citizens of the country. It is these two main factors—the Industrial Revolution and the increase in the importance of the State in the life of the nation —which we must examine more closely.

While the term 'the Industrial Revolution' usually refers to the period 1760–1830, it must be remembered that the process of industrial advance has continued fairly rapidly since then; in fact it is still continuing today. This advance has produced a large increase in the real income per head of the population. ('Real income' is income measured in terms of the actual goods and services received, as opposed to 'money income', which is income measured in terms of money.) While the population increased by nearly three times between 1841 and 1971, the total real national income increased at least nine times. Hence, real income per head more than trebled. This has been accompanied by a more equal distribution of the national income. The improved standard of living which has resulted from these two factors is reflected in the fact that while Eden's 'State of the Poor' investigation in 1797 showed that a labourer could scarcely afford the bare necessities of life, by 1885 newspapers and periodicals were included in his annual budget, while bicycles were a luxury within the reach of all. Today we would include among such luxuries television sets and motor cars. Now, as income increases, so a person tends to spend a smaller proportion of it on food, for 'the capacity of the human stomach is limited'. Instead, the increase is largely directed to the purchase of the comforts of life and eventually of luxuries. In 1797, for example, the average labourer spent at least 70 per cent of his annual income on food; by 1904 it had fallen to 60 per cent and in 1973 it was 25 per cent. But the distribution of labour between industries is largely a reflection of the way in which people spend their incomes. So, with the increase in real income, we should expect a lower percentage of the population to be engaged in producing food and a greater percentage engaged in producing those other goods which afford extra comforts after the necessities of life (food, shelter and clothing) have been provided for. Thus we should expect a rise in the proportion of people engaged in transport and communications, manufacturing, and professional and miscellaneous services (such as entertainments, hairdressers, etc.). In short, as agriculture declined in importance, so workers moved into the rapidly rising new industries.

Nevertheless, the fall in the relative importance of agriculture cannot be fully explained by the increase in real income. Agriculture itself has been particularly affected by the very factors which brought about the overall increase in production. Of these factors, the most important are the improvement in techniques and the application of machinery. Improved techniques came with the Agricultural Revolution of the eighteenth century and have been further developed in recent years. But the large increase in the output of British agriculture, especially over the last twenty years, has been chiefly due to the introduction of machinery, notably the tractor. Whereas in 1913 basic crop production in Great Britain was 7 tons per man, by 1974 it had risen to over 50 tons. In short, compared with the beginning of the century, more food is produced today by a labour force which is approximately only one-tenth the size.

The Industrial Revolution was also accompanied by a revolution in transport. During the period 1840–1900 we had a rapid development of the new means of locomotion, the steam engine. In the second half of the century, too, we had the development of the steel ship propelled by steam power, the United Kingdom's merchant fleet almost trebling in tonnage. After World War I the railways were supplemented, and often replaced, especially for local transport, by motor vehicles. Taken together with the growth of the postal, telegraph and the wireless services, these developments explain the increase in proportion of persons engaged in transport and communications.

The importance of transport and communications has declined relatively since 1901, although in actual fact its peak probably occurred nearer 1930. The chief reason for this decline is that the same services can be operated by a smaller labour force, though we must also remember that nowadays many people use their own motor cars.

The transport revolution resulted in an increase in the size of the market, for it now became much cheaper to send goods over long distances. Thus the cotton goods of Lancashire were distributed all over the world, while wheat was brought from Canada and the U.S.A. Hence the volume of goods exchanged increased and trade, both internal and international, became continuous instead of intermittent. In place of the weekly market, permanent shops could be established serving the needs of consumers throughout the week and thus we can account for the increase in the importance of the distributive trades. The increase in international trade led to the development of the United Kingdom's financial, banking and insurance activities. These she carried out, not only for herself, but for many other countries.

But the purpose of international trade is to make the best use of the factors of production which a country has in relative abundance. The United Kingdom thus became the 'workshop of the world', improving her standard of living by exchanging manufactured goods for the foodstuffs and raw materials which she required. Thus agriculture declined more than it otherwise would have done were there no other influence except the rise in real income. Countries which are roughly in the same stage of economic development as the United Kingdom find that they require about 20 per cent of the total labour force to be engaged on agriculture if they are to be self-supporting. Great Britain has less than 2 per cent, thereby showing how heavily she specialises on manufactures, services, etc.

The expansion and concentration in the industrial and commercial fields during the period 1841–1973 was accompanied by changes in thought concerning the influence which the State should exert in the economic life of the nation. By the middle of the eighteenth century the Mercantilist policy, with variations, had been in operation for over 200 years. In 1776, however, regulation of trade and restrictions on the free movement of labour were devastatingly criticised by Adam Smith in his 'Enquiry into the Nature and Causes of the Wealth of Nations'. The book sounded the death-knell of Mercantilism. By 1850 the United Kingdom was a free-trade country and her economic system was almost completely organised according to *laissez-faire* principles. This meant that industry was to be left free to expand under private enterprise unfettered by State interference. Hence few government employees were required.

Nevertheless, towards the end of the nineteenth century, small voices of protest were beginning to be heard regarding this absence of State control. These pointed out that wealth is not synonymous with welfare and that some State control of industry is necessary. It was also realised that certain services could be provided better by the State than by private enterprise, while some security should be given to the worker against unemployment, sickness and old age. In many ways, these new theories were connected with the rise of a new political party, the Labour Party, and, from the end of the nineteenth century onwards, Socialist ideas began to have an increasing influence on the overall organisation of the economy of the United Kingdom. The growth of State interference resulted in an expansion of the Civil Service and in the number of local government officials.

It was also considered that welfare could be increased by redistributing wealth and income on a more equal basis. This was also a function of the State. The effect of this redistribution of wealth, however, was the virtual elimination of very high incomes. This, together with the raising of their wages as they were attracted to new industries, has led to the decline in the relative importance of domestic servants in the economy.

The relative decline of mining and quarrying since 1901 is largely due to the almost complete elimination of coal exports since that date. Whereas in 1901, 230 million tons of coal were mined, in 1973 the figure was only 130 million tons. This, together with the increased output per man resulting from mechanisation, has led to a decline in the absolute number of miners.

A similar decline has occurred since 1901 in the importance of the construction industry. Capital construction has proceeded rapidly during the twentieth century, but against this increased mechanisation must be taken into account.

PART II

HOW TO PRODUCE

CHAPTER 4

ECONOMIES OF SCALE

WE have seen that, under a Capitalist system, people produce
goods if they expect to make a profit. To make a profit, the
cost of producing a good must be less than the price at which
it is sold. Where, however, the amount of the good he supplies
is only a small fraction of the total put on the market (as is
usual with most goods produced), the producer is unable to
influence the price. Thus, in order to fulfil his aim of making
as large a profit as possible, he must tackle the problem from
the costs of production side and keep these costs as low as
possible. (We shall contrast this situation with monopoly
later.)

The cost of production depends on three things: (a) the
cost of the materials (labour, machinery, buildings, land and
other factors of production) which he uses; (b) the way in
which he combines these factors of production; (c) the various
techniques he adopts when he sets them to work. As regards
(a), the cost of these factors is governed by the price they themselves fetch in the market and, unless the producer is buying a
very large part of the total market supply, he cannot influence
that price. With (b), however, he is at liberty to combine the
factors of production in whatever way he chooses (subject to
technical limitations). If he is a builder, for instance, he can
have more men and fewer concrete mixers, or less men and
more concrete mixers—it is for the builder to decide, and he will
be guided by the relative prices he has to pay for them, together
with a consideration of the scale on which he will produce.
Thus, even if concrete mixers were cheap relative to the cost
of labour, it would hardly pay a builder to buy one if, for the
job he was doing, the mixer were used only half an hour each
week.

The producer also has to decide on how the factors of production are to be set to work. His chances of making a profit
may rest on the fact that he intends to make use of a new

invention or process. Or he may be able to keep his costs lower by paying piece-rates instead of time-rates. Above all, and especially with the production of modern goods, such as motor cars, radio and television sets, steel sheeting, sewing machines and so on, the total profit margin might be greatest when he is producing on a large scale. Here we are not thinking of the fact that doing so may render him the sole seller of a commodity (that is, a 'monopolist'), thereby enabling him to push home bargaining advantages. This represents no gain to the community. What we really have in mind are the real advantages of large-scale production. Because it allows goods to be produced more cheaply, there is a definite gain to the community.

It is necessary, therefore, to undertake a study of these advantages. But since they depend so much on the principle of specialisation as applied to men and machines, it is desirable to begin by examining this principle separately. We do so under the traditional title of 'the division of labour'.

I. THE DIVISION OF LABOUR

Table 10 gives a classification of the working population in broad industrial groups. Each of these groups, however, can be fairly easily subdivided. For instance, 'mining' includes coal, iron-ore, lead, tin and copper mines, stone and slate quarries, and clay, sand, gravel and chalk pits; 'manufacturing industries' includes, among others, chemicals, textiles, engineering, shipbuilding, clothing, tobacco, food and drink processing, water, gas, and electricity supply, paper and printing; 'public administration' covers both central and local government.

Usually it is not difficult to carry this process of subdivision one stage further. Thus 'chemicals' includes explosives, paint, varnish, red lead, soap, ink, and matches; 'distributive trades' includes wholesalers and retailers of both foodstuffs and non-foodstuffs, coalmen and newspaper-sellers. Indeed, the workers themselves can be classified into different occupations. Railway transport, for instance, could be divided into train-drivers, porters, guards, inspectors, signalmen, plate-layers, booking-clerks and so on; coal-mining into hewers, shot-firers, winding-men and others; retailing into managers, shop assistants, cashiers, liftmen, delivery men, etc.

This analysis of the working population brings out a very significant fact—that nearly all people, like the drivers and signalmen on the railway, or the winding-men or shot-firers in coal-mines, earn their living by doing one particular job only. Instead of trying to satisfy his various wants by producing all the goods himself, the train driver, for instance, specialises in one small portion of the task of conveying people from one place to another. For his work he receives a wage with which he purchases the goods and services he desires. These goods and services have likewise been produced by many persons who themselves have specialised in some small part of the production.

This characteristic of modern production—persons producing goods (and often services) by each specialising in a certain part of the general task—is known as the division of labour. Its importance was emphasised by Adam Smith, who devoted the first chapter of his *Wealth of Nations* to an analysis of it. But the general principle of specialisation of which it forms a part is much older. It is probable that the early cave dwellers so organised their families that, while the father concentrated on the hunting, the mother did the cooking and the children collected the fuel. We know that, in the Middle Ages, while the peasant produced for himself most of the food his family required, there were some specialists—the miller, the wheelwright, the priest—in particular trades. And, as the town developed, so the amount of specialisation increased, the specialists grouping themselves together in a 'guild'. The principle was carried one stage further in the early West of England cloth industry, for now the division of labour began to be applied to different processes. Here the master clothier bought wool from the sheep farmer, passed it on to people who spun it in their homes, collected the yarn and once more passed it on to weavers who wove it into cloth. Finally he collected the cloth and found a purchaser for it. But the big change came with the Industrial Revolution. Employers now had to concentrate their workers in factories because larger and more expensive machines were being used in the manufacture of most goods. One person would learn how to operate a particular

machine; another person would have the task of bringing him
the raw materials. Even if little machinery was used, as in
Adam Smith's example of pin-making, the whole process would
still be split up with each worker concentrating on a particular
part of it. Adam Smith describes how, in pin-making, 'one
man draws out the wire, another straightens it, a third cuts it,
a fourth points it, a fifth grinds it at the top for receiving the
head; to make the head requires two or three distinct operations; to put it on is a peculiar business, to whiten the pins is
another; it is even a trade by itself to put them into the paper;
and the important business of making a pin is, in this manner,
divided into about eighteen distinct operations, which, in some
manufactories, are all performed by distinct hands, though in
others, the same man will sometimes perform two or three of
them.'

Modern methods of mass-production have extended the
division of labour still further. The building of a motor car,
for example, has been broken down into thousands of separate
operations. The usual method of assembling the car is for men
to build it up gradually as it passes along a moving belt. The
men themselves remain stationary and, as each vehicle passes
before them, so they add their own particular part.

As we shall see later, the localisation of industry with its
resulting inter-regional and international trade, is really only
an extension of the principle of division of labour—instead of
men specialising in one particular part of the production process, whole regions and even countries concentrate to a large
degree on the production of one particular type of good.

1. The Advantages of the Division of Labour

Why is production so organised that people specialise rather
than produce directly for themselves?

The main reason is that increased production results. In the
first place, the worker can be employed in that job where his
particular ability has the greatest relative advantage or, in
everyday language, where his superiority is most marked. We
can show this best by means of a very simple arithmetical
example. Let us suppose that, in one day, Smith can make
either 10 walking-sticks or 10 wicker baskets, while Brown can
make either 8 walking-sticks or 4 wicker baskets. Let us further

suppose that the walking-sticks and baskets are of equal value. If Smith divides his time equally between making walking-sticks and baskets, he will make 5 of each, while if Brown similarly divides his time, he will make 4 walking-sticks and 2 baskets. The combined production in a day, therefore, is 9 walking-sticks and 7 baskets, equalling 16 units. When specialisation takes place, and Smith spends his day making only baskets while Brown spends it producing walking-sticks, the total production of walking-sticks is 8, while the total production of baskets is 10, equalling 18 units. Specialisation has thus increased production by 2 units, that is, by $12\frac{1}{2}$ per cent.

Thus it is through the division of labour that full use is made of exceptional skills, in particular those of research workers, professional men and highly-skilled technicians. The above example explains why it is better for the surgeon to spend his time in the operating theatre rather than at a bench making his own furniture in spite of the fact that he may be an excellent carpenter. It explains, too, why a good all-round athlete still concentrates on one particular distance.

Particular ability can come about in many different ways and in varying degrees; but because in modern production the most complicated work is divided up into a series of simple operations, these varying abilities can be used to the full. Most firms, for instance, are able to find a proportion of suitable jobs for disabled persons; indeed, those employing over twenty are required by the Disabled Persons Act, 1944, to do so.

Secondly, when persons are continually performing a single operation, they improve in dexterity and skill. The average person takes a long time to fit a cycle tube and tyre compared with an employee at the Raleigh factory, where a rim tape, inner tube and outer cover is fitted, the tyre inflated and the dust cap screwed on in 45 seconds! It can all be summed up in the phrase 'practice makes perfect'. Moreover, familiarity with the job makes the workers familiar with the difficulties of their jobs. If a car goes wrong, a skilled mechanic can very quickly diagnose the fault by carrying out a few simple tests. An employer recognises the value of experience in a particular job when he engages new staff. Closely connected with this increase in skill is the fact that the worker may find a method of improving the machinery. Hence the division of labour stimulates invention. Thus Joseph Lucas, Ltd. has a 'suggestion scheme' which gives cash awards to employees who submit ideas for improving efficiency. In fact, men working in the same occupation often form themselves into associations or unions, where they compare methods of work and spread new ideas or suggest improvements through their own trade journals.

Thirdly, the division of labour assists the mobility of labour. Where a process is broken down into a number of specialised jobs, less time is taken in learning one of those jobs. Moreover, the barrier between different industries is lowered because there is no need to learn all the different processes involved. For example a lorry driver, a lathe worker or an electrician can all move easily from a factory making motor cars to one making sewing machines.

Fourthly, where a man in making a good performs all the tasks himself, much time is spent in switching from one process to another. Tools, for example, have to be put away or reset. This is avoided when he uses one tool all the time.

Fifthly, if one man does all the job, only the tool or machine he is using at the particular moment is occupied; the rest are standing idle. With the division of labour, however, all tools are in use. One man saws, another planes, and so on. As a result they can be given specialised tools—a circular saw, a mechanical plane, etc., particularly if the demand is sufficient to justify a large output. In the making of a pair of shoes in a modern factory, for instance, there are nearly 100 distinct operations. For each of these specialised tools are used, thereby reducing the costs of production. Later, in Chapter 18, we show how important such capital equipment is to increasing output and therefore to improving the standard of living.

Finally, from the employer's point of view, output can be measured and estimated better. In the Ford factory it is known exactly how many cars and tractors will be built in a day. Moreover, time-and-motion studies enable an employer to improve methods of production because he is able to estimate exactly where, in the productive process, reorganisation is required.

We see then that the division of labour brings a great increase in material welfare. But it is a system which requires the keeping of good faith between one worker and another. 'Co-operation' is the essence of any system which depends on teamwork, and in this respect the whole economic system can be regarded as one big team working together in order to produce the goods it needs. The same principle that 'I will do this for you, if you do that for me' is continually operating in our economic life between individuals, between localities within the same country, and between the various countries of the world.

2. LIMITATIONS TO THE DIVISION OF LABOUR

People will specialise only if they can exchange the products they make for the goods made by other people. In short, to divide in production we have to unite in exchange. The division of labour is thus dependent on exchange facilities, chiefly money and good transport.

Secondly, it is also dependent on the extent of the demand for the product. A job cannot be divided up into several processes using special labour and machinery if the total demand is small, or if demand does not increase a great deal as price falls following the introduction of methods of mass-production. The crucial question is whether demand is large enough to standardise production. While Burton's, to a large extent, have managed to grade suits into a few standard sizes, the Savile Row tailors cannot do so. Hence there are very many separate operations, each undertaken by a different worker, in the production of a Burton suit, but with the Savile Row suit they are much fewer. In the same way we cannot have much division of labour in the production of model gowns and model hats for ladies, or top hats for men. Demand must be sufficient to keep all men and machines fully occupied and so, because with a large market, output is large, there is greater specialisation. In this connection it should be noted that the development of transport, by increasing the size of the market, has led to increased division of labour.

Thirdly, on the supply side, the nature of the product itself may limit the extent of the division of labour. Sometimes, in the production of a good, the technical processes do not permit the job to be broken down into a number of processes. For instance, the writing of a book, particularly a novel, is usually the work of one person. A still better illustration is provided by contrasting production in a factory with that on a farm. In the factory, all operations of production proceed simultaneously. Thus all the stages in the making of a motor car are going on at the same moment. On the farm, however, this is not so, for the processes are dependent on Nature, and hence ploughing, harrowing, sowing, weeding and reaping all take place at different times. Men cannot, therefore, spend all their time on one operation such as ploughing, for they have to switch from one job to another as the seasons come along, and the result is, instead of having specialised ploughmen, specialised hay-makers, and so on, we have a 'general agricultural labourer'. This limitation to the division of labour applies particularly to the rendering of personal services. The same barber, even in a large shop, shaves and trims, shampoos and singes the hair once he commences to attend to a customer. In teaching, too, where a knowledge of the individual boy is particularly desirable (as in his early school career), we have general form-masters teaching many subjects rather than specialists.

Lastly, the division of labour may be limited by the number of labourers available. Robinson Crusoe, for instance, had to do everything for himself until, with the arrival of Man Friday, he was able to delegate a few jobs. In the same way, under-populated countries, such as Australia, have in the past been restricted in the extent to which they could adopt division of labour.

3. The Disadvantages of the Division of Labour

To be complete, we must view the division of labour in its proper perspective by drawing attention to some of its major disadvantages. First, it may result in monotony of work. No longer is it possible for a craftsman to take the same interest in his job as when he was responsible for the whole task of shaping the raw material into a finished article. Instead he is engaged in doing the same minor task hundreds of times a day, day after day, week after week. A girl in a super-market may pass her working life sticking on price labels, while a man in a dairy may spend his whole time putting the covers on milk bottles. It is doubtful, however, whether this monotony is as real or serious as is often imagined. For example, one girl when asked if she were not bored in spending her time in wrapping toffees replied: 'Not at all; in the first place, I do not have to think about what I am doing, and, secondly, I can talk to the girl next to me whilst I am working.' Above all, it must be pointed out that, largely through the division of labour itself, the standard of living has improved immensely. One aspect of such an improved living standard is the increased leisure we enjoy. Compare this situation with that of the 'jack-of-all-trades' medieval peasant, who had to work from dawn to dusk to produce the bare essentials of life. Today the worker has free time in which to pursue his hobbies, enjoy holidays and entertainments, and engage in cultural interests. Hence, though there may be some monotony of work, he can enjoy a much more varied life as a whole.

Secondly, production by division of labour results in stan-dardisation of products (e.g. cars, furniture, typewriters), because specialised labour and machinery can only be used profitably if output is on a large scale. But before we condemn standardisation, we must draw attention to two points. In the first place, standardisation is not objectionable so long as we believe in allowing the individual to decide how to spend his income, for then he can decide whether to buy the standardised product at the low price or pay much more in order to obtain a variation which meets his individual requirements (see page 64, 'the predominance of the small firm'). Secondly, with standardisation, it is often easier to obtain replacements, e.g. in machinery, motor cars and electrical equipment. In-deed, in this type of industry, the trend is towards greater standardisation, achieved largely by the amalgamation of firms.

Thirdly, the division of labour has increased the complexity of the economic structure and this has led to greater instability of employment. The worker is dependent on those before him in the process of production. A power strike may stop work in the factories, while a shortage of a component may lead to redundancy among workers making cars. Similarly, the development of unemployment abroad may lead to a drop in the demand for our exports. Or, when methods of production change, a worker may not be able to adapt himself to the new techniques, particularly if he is old. For example, some tram drivers could not switch over to driving buses. We discuss this more fully when dealing with the problem of the general immobility of labour (Chapter 24).

Fourthly, our earlier warning that division of labour entails co-operation tends to be ignored. People forget they are working as a team and regard themselves primarily as railway-men, steel-workers, electricians, printers, artists and so on, separated socially, and very often, as in the case of coal-miners, geographically. One frequent result, for instance, is that particular occupations strike to benefit themselves, although their action, because of the inflationary effect, is really at the expense of the rest of the community.

Lastly, certain diseases are associated with certain jobs. A man who spends all his working life in the mines is prone to catch pneumoconiosis; a painter or a man making lead paint may catch dermatitis.

II. INTERNAL ECONOMIES

The advantages of large-scale production which a business-man can plan to achieve directly by increasing the size of his output are known in economics as 'internal economies'. This is to distinguish them from certain other economies which arise *indirectly* from the growth, not in the size of the *firm*, but in the size of the *industry*. These latter are known as 'external economies' and they will be discussed later.

Following Professor E. A. G. Robinson, internal economies can be conveniently classified under five headings: technical, managerial, commercial, financial and risk-bearing.

1. TECHNICAL ECONOMIES

In the actual making of the good, as distinct from its distri-bution, economies result when production is on a large scale.

In the first place, the process of production can be broken down into a number of different jobs and different men can be employed on each. At once all the advantages of the division of labour are achieved. In the production of the lower-priced men's suits, for instance, the multiple tailor employs in his factory a 'flow' method of production. One specialises in the actual cutting of the cloth, another tacks the various parts together. Later in the process a girl might concentrate on the making of the buttonholes, while another sews the buttons on. All this is similar to Adam Smith's example of pin-making and it takes place in the production of most goods today. The larger the scale of production, so the further can the degree of specialisation usually be carried, especially when, as with the motor car, the product largely consists of a multitude of tiny parts.

The large producer is also able to employ specialised machinery because he can keep it fully occupied. For instance, Ford at Dagenham have sufficient output to keep their own blast furnace at work whereas a firm producing only a few cars a week could not do this. Similarly, a large bootmaking factory has special machinery with which to cut out in one movement the soles, heels, uppers, tongues, etc., but the small bootmaker has to cut out the same parts laboriously by hand, for machinery would stand idle for most of the day. In the same way, it is only the large firm which can afford to carry out research or to provide canteen and welfare facilities for its employees.

Thirdly, the initial outlay may be lower, and operating costs may be saved by using a large machine even when two or more machines could do the same work. For instance, a double-decker bus can carry twice as many passengers, but the initial cost is not twice as much nor are the running costs doubled, because one driver and one conductor only are still required. It may even be that there is a mechanical advantage in working on a large scale. In farming, for instance, the tendency with modern machinery is for fields to become larger, for less time is wasted in turning the bulkier machines. Professor Cairncross compares the mechanical advantage involved in employing one large ship instead of two smaller ones each of half the carrying capacity of the large ship. 'The carrying capacity of a ship increases in proportion to the cube of its dimensions; the resistance to its motion increases, roughly speaking, in proportion to the square of its dimensions. The power required to drive a given weight through the water is less, therefore, in a large than in a small ship.'

Lastly, economies are achieved through linking processes. Fuel and power are saved wherever processes can be carried on in conjunction with one another in order to conserve heat. For instance, in steel-making the large mills are able to roll the steel ingots into steel sheets before they are allowed to cool, thus obviating the necessity of re-heating them. Similarly, one of the arguments for the nationalisation of road transport was that the lorries, having delivered a load, had to return empty whereas with the larger organisation clearing arrangements could be made for the lorry to pick up a return load.

Generally technical economies fix the size of the unit actually producing, rather than the size of the firm, which may consist of many units. Where technical economies of scale are great, the size of the typical unit will tend to be correspondingly great, as, for example, in motor-car manufacture, steel-strip making and the production of gas and electricity. Where, however, larger production merely means duplicating and reduplicating machines, then the tendency will be for the unit to remain small. For instance, in farming at the moment at least one combine harvester is necessary for about 160 hectares. Thus the size of the individual farm tends to remain small, for as yet there are no great technical economies to be derived from large machines. Where few technical economies can be enjoyed and yet the firm is large, consisting, as with chain stores, of many operating units, its size has usually been increased to achieve other types of economy, as follows.

2. MANAGERIAL ECONOMIES

On the managerial side economies may result when output increases because specialists can be fully employed. In other words, the division of labour can be introduced into the task of management. For instance, in a shop owned and run by one man, the owner, whilst he has the ability to order supplies, manage his books, and sell the goods, has yet to do the trivial jobs of sweeping the shop floor, weighing up articles and packing parcels, jobs which could be done by a boy who had just left school. The volume of his sales may not warrant, however, the employment of a boy. The large business overcomes this difficulty. A brilliant organiser can devote himself wholly to the work of organising, while the routine jobs can be left to a lower-paid worker.

The function of management can itself be divided up. Expert

administrators can be put in charge of production, of sales, of transport, and of personnel departments. The departments themselves might even be subdivided, the sales department, for instance, being divided into sections for advertisement, for exports, and for the study of customers' welfare.

3. COMMERCIAL ECONOMIES

Economies are achieved by the large firm both in the buying of raw materials and in the selling of the finished product, though, as we showed earlier, we must examine these advantages to see that they are not secured by 'monopoly' methods. On the buying side, for instance, because the large firm takes a high proportion of the total supply of the particular materials put on the market, it may be able to obtain them more cheaply simply by pushing home its bargaining advantage. Thus, while it enjoys lower costs in the purchase of materials, the saving is achieved only at the expense of other purchasers. Nor is the community likely to benefit from a lower price of the finished product, for it is far more likely to lead to an increase in the profit margin accruing to the large firm.

On the other hand, the favourable terms may be granted to the large firm placing a large order for materials because such an order is more valuable to the firm engaged in the production of those materials. It may mean, for instance, that the plant of the latter firm can be worked to capacity, or that the large order to one specification can be turned out without frequent delays due to adjustments of machines and tools. This principle of special charges for a bulk order applies in various stages of production. The price of photographs advertising a product, for instance, would be quoted by the photographic firm according to the size of the order, while, for the transport of the finished goods, special rates would probably be obtained by the large firm because costs of transport, especially rail transport, do not increase in the same proportion as the volume of the goods to be transported.

Economies can be achieved, too, in the selling of the product. Very often the sales staff are not being worked to capacity and hence a far greater quantity of goods can be sold at little extra cost. In any case much less work is involved proportionately in packaging and invoicing a large order than when a similar amount of goods is split up into many orders. Moreover, the large firm often manufactures many products and then one commodity acts as an advertisement for another. Thus Wall's ice-cream is also an advertisement for their pork pies and sausages, while Hoover's vacuum cleaners help to sell their refrigerators and washing-machines. In addition, a large firm may be able to sell its by-products although to a small firm this might be unprofitable. Indeed, one large cinema group has claimed that its box-office takings fail to cover expenses, the overall profit only being due to its ice-cream sales!

Finally, when the scale of business is sufficiently large, the principle of the division of labour can be introduced on the commercial side, expert buyers and sellers being employed.

4. Financial Economies

In raising finance for expansion, the large firm has nearly all the advantages. It can, for instance, offer better security to bankers and, because it is large and well-known, will be able to raise money in shares and debentures more easily than a small firm. There are two reasons for this. First, investors have more confidence in the large, well-known firm. Secondly, they prefer shares which are regularly dealt in and quoted on the Stock Exchange, for then it is comparatively easy and quick, when it is so desired, to dispose of the shares in exchange for money.

5. Risk-bearing Economies

Here we can distinguish three sorts of risk. First, there are risks which can be insured against. With these, the small firm is not at so great a disadvantage, for the principle of an insurance company is to enable such firms to secure the advantages of pooling risks on a large scale. The larger the size of this company, the more likely are losses to be spread according to the law of averages. Nevertheless, some undertakings, such as London Transport, are large enough to carry their own risks and can thus save the profits made by the insurance company.

Secondly, certain businesses usually bear some risk themselves in order to increase profits. Here the large firm is at a definite advantage. In banking, for instance, when a run on a bank occurs in a particular locality, a large bank can call in resources from other branches and thus, by meeting all demands, restore the confidence of the public. Similarly, it is rarely the large 'bookie' who has to run for the early train when the favourite wins!

The third kind of risk is one that cannot easily be insured against—risk arising from changes in the demand for the product or in the supply of raw materials. A large firm may guard against such risks in a variety of ways. To meet variations in demand it can produce more than one product and so, by diversification of output, avoid 'putting all its eggs in one basket'. This was one of the reasons behind the development of mixed farming in England, and we can see a similar motive at work with T. Wall & Sons, Ltd. (who produce not only ice-creams but also pork pies and sausages), and with the ice-cream seller (who sells hamburgers in winter). Or, secondly, the firm can develop different markets for its product. Water heaters, thermostats and electric light bulbs are supplied to industrial as well as private users. On the supply side, materials used may be obtained from many different sources, thereby guarding against a crippling loss of vital supplies due to an increased demand by other users, crop failures, political upheavals or simply the raising of prices by a single supplier. Lastly, risks may also be avoided by varying the processes of production. For instance, in a wet season, the large farmer who has the implements to make silage has an advantage over a smaller farmer who has only a mower and confines himself to making hay.

'Horizontal' and 'Vertical' Integration

It is convenient to define here two kinds of combination by which large-scale production may come about (although they may be prompted by monopoly motives). *Horizontal integration* occurs where firms producing the same product combine together under the same management. Thus, in the production of ice-cream, Wall combined with Cremier, while with motor cars, we have had mergers between Rolls and Bentley, Morris and Riley, and BMC and Leyland. *Vertical integration* consists of the amalgamation of firms engaged in the different stages of

the production of a good. Thus the Co-operative Wholesale
Society runs its own tea plantations, Cadbury owns cocoa
plantations in Malaya, Reed International is engaged both in
the production of paper and in publishing, while Ford
manufactures its own pig-iron, engine castings and car
bodies.

III. THE PREDOMINACE OF
THE SMALL FIRM

The above discussion has emphasised the fact that certain
advantages are possessed by the large firm. Yet when we
examine the actual size of firms operating in the United
Kingdom, it is remarkable how the small firm predominates.
This applies not only to agriculture and retail distribution
where, as we shall see, there are basic reasons for the existence
of the small firm, but even in manufacturing where, one would
imagine, technical economies of scale would be all-important.
Table 11 illustrates this fact.

TABLE 11.—*Size of Manufacturing Establishments
in Great Britain, June 1968*

Employees	Number of firms	Percentage of total firms	Number of employees (ooo's)	Percentage of total employed
1–10	31,627	38	158	2
11–99	37,761	45	1,318	17
100–999	12,797	15	3,538	46
Over 1,000	1,198	2	2,702	35
TOTAL	83,383	100	7,716	100

Table 11 shows the size of the technical unit, the factory or
workshop, in *manufacturing* only. It should be noted that a
firm can consist of more than one establishment.

If we ignore this qualification, however, the Table reveals
two very important features: (i) the small establishment is
typical of manufacturing in Great Britain, over four-fifths
employing less than 100 persons; (ii) these small firms employ
only one-fifth of the labour force.

Such figures as are available indicate that there is little difference in other lines of production. Some 62 per cent of retailing firms consist of only one shop, while three-quarters of all construction firms have less than 8 employees. In farming, we find that two-thirds of the total holdings are less than 20 hectares in size.

REASONS FOR THE PREDOMINANCE OF THE SMALL FIRM

Any explanation of this predominance of the small firm has to cover two essential facts. These are: (i) variations in the size of firms exist even within the same industry; (ii) small firms are especially important in particular industries, such as agriculture, retail distribution and personal and professional services. Broadly speaking, the first point is explained in the early part of the discussion which follows, while the second is covered chiefly in the latter part, which deals with the obstacles which arise, particularly on the managerial side, as a firm expands beyond a certain point.

First, it must be emphasised that many of the small firms in manufacturing are in an early stage of growth, and to that extent represent big firms in the making. Such firms may remain fairly small for a considerable period as they often find it difficult to pass a certain point when expanding. Further growth, for instance, might entail the construction of a new factory or the moving of the business to other premises, too large for their present needs but nevertheless necessary in order to allow for expected future expansion. Many firms hesitate to incur this increase in their overhead costs, fearing that their capital resources are inadequate, and for this reason carry on a vastly increased business in the original but overcrowded premises. Or it may be that there are certain physical obstacles to expansion. Small firms, for instance, may find it difficult to raise the necessary capital. In certain cases, too, as in farming where capital transfer tax makes it difficult to maintain a large estate intact, institutional factors limit growth.

Secondly, when we examine the demand for the product, we often find that the market is a small one. This means that the extent to which the size of the firm can be increased in order to achieve technical and other economies is limited. This point was emphasised earlier when discussing the limitations to

the division of labour. The demand may be of a local nature—
and so the village store remains small. Or it may be impossible
to standardise the product simply because variations in design
are essential. Thus machines, which may themselves produce
many thousands of goods, often have to be designed and produced separately for the job in hand. For the same reason iron-
foundries tend to remain small. A slightly different reason
occurs when a firm deliberately endeavours to break up the
market, in order to secure a limited part for itself, by what is
known as 'product differentiation'. Largely through a process
of suggestion by costly advertising campaigns, people are induced to prefer one particular brand of good to another,
although basically there may be little difference between the
goods produced by different firms. Thus we have many
varieties of toothpaste, and people generally stick to one particular brand often because they prefer its special flavour,
though dentists say that, in efficiency, there is little to choose
between any of them. In the motor-car industry, too, a variety
of models are produced by different firms who thereby in
practice split up the market for motor cars. This is the opposite
process to standardisation. The result is that the full advantages
of large-scale production are often not achieved. For this
reason the government has recently encouraged companies
to combine in order to concentrate their resources on fewer
models.

But the chief reason for a small market is that transport costs
and difficulties limit it geographically. These are discussed in
detail in Chapter 10. Where the consumer requires the personal
services of such persons as doctors, dentists, solicitors, dress-
makers and tailors, both time and costs of transport limit the
extent to which either the consumer will journey to the producer or the producer will travel to the consumer. Similarly
some goods cannot be transported long distances either because
they are perishable or because their bulk renders costs of
transport prohibitive. Trade barriers also split up markets. In all
these cases the market remains small, and production is carried
on by a number of firms each supplying a separate region.

Even where demand is extensive, limitations in the size of
the firm may arise on the supply side. The technical process
itself may have been broken down so that each firm is per-

forming only a small part. Such vertical disintegration exists, for instance, in car and cycle manufacturing where different firms supply certain parts, such as electrical equipment, steering wheels, reflectors and pedals to larger firms who assemble the finished article. More important, economies of large-scale production may eventually become negative and change into dis-economies, thereby putting a brake on further growth. While the large firm can achieve economies in purchasing its raw materials up to a point, it may eventually find suppliers in the market ranged against it. The small firm, on the other hand, may do better by being able to 'shop around the market' for small quantities at low prices. It is for this reason that large firms sometimes split up their demand, employing representatives to buy for them without revealing for whom the purchases are being made. From the point of view of risk, too, the advantages do not lie entirely with the large firm. While technical economies are gained by using highly specialised machinery, lack of adaptability to fluctuations in demand may also have resulted. Demand may fluctuate owing to changes in fashion, variation of the seasons and, above all, to a general trade depression. For this reason firms often sacrifice technical economies of scale in order to achieve greater adaptability. For instance, two small furnaces may be employed for heating instead of one large one because, when demand is halved, only one need be fired.

But it is in management that, on the supply side, the main obstacles to the growth of the firm arise. First, the manager of a large firm needs to be a superman, and such supermen are in short supply. Secondly, while the large firm can achieve economies by subdividing management, if the process is carried on indefinitely dis-economies may result. Personal rivalries may spring up between managers or it may become difficult to co-ordinate the work of each specialist. Above all, quick decisions and adaptability may be impossible because, before such decisions can be arrived at, a meeting of managers has to be called to agree on policy. A labour dispute could soon develop into a costly strike for this reason. But the problem is particularly serious where personal decisions are frequently required. This occurs where: (a) demand is inclined to change rapidly, as with fashion goods; (b) frequent variations in the weather call for a quick response, as in farming; (c) attention to the requirements of individual customers is called for, as with retailing and personal services; (d) attention to detail is all-important, as with agriculture, particularly with regard to such jobs as sowing and the tending of cattle.

One other reason for the survival of the small firm, but of a slightly different nature, exists on the managerial side. A proprietor who places value on his own independence may be willing to work longer hours or to take a smaller return for his labour. Small farmers, especially in dairy farming, often survive because they are willing to perform themselves the Sunday and holiday work involved, while the small shopkeeper and café-proprietor compete with the larger firms by remaining open longer.

IV. EXTERNAL ECONOMIES

So far we have considered only 'internal economies', that is, economies which result from an increase in the size of the individual firm. They can be estimated in advance and a firm can, as we have seen, set out to secure them by a deliberate policy. It is convenient at this stage to digress slightly in order to discuss 'external economies', that is, economies of production which result from an increase in the size of the industry as a whole. These do not depend on the size of the individual firm, and while the firm can hope that they will arise as the industry expands, it cannot plan to achieve them by a deliberate policy of increasing its output.

External economies can be grouped together into three classes.

1. ECONOMIES OF CONCENTRATION

As the industry grows, so improvements in the supply of the factors of production, particularly labour, result. Workers in the area may become skilled in that particular kind of work —as, for example, are the workers in the small engineering and light metal industry of the West Midlands. A firm in the area, therefore, finds it easier to replace or to expand its labour force. Moreover, through close association with the particular industry from childhood, people in the district unconsciously accept working conditions which an outsider would find distasteful—the humidity of a cotton-mill, the dirt of a coal-mine, the restrictions of an office, etc.

Common services, too, come to be provided when an industry grows in size, especially when the industry is confined to one district. The expansion may be of such a size as to justify the building of a new road. Thus the M4 motorway was routed close to the growing manufacturing town of Swindon. Banking and insurance services also develop and, as raw-material requirements increase, so grading is often instituted, thereby facilitating the supply of the raw material. Thus Lancashire has her own grading of raw cotton, a grading which is followed by the rest of the world.

Closely connected with the common services are the specialised institutions which develop. Training schools may be set up by the industry, specialist courses particularly suited to the needs of the workers in the district may be provided by local technical schools and evening classes, and a chair may even be endowed at the nearest university to train scientific personnel and to carry out research. Manchester University, for example, has connections with the cotton industry, and Leeds University with the woollen industry.

Marketing organisations, which specialise in the requirements of the particular industry, also come into being. Examples of these are the Liverpool Cotton Exchange and the Manchester merchandising organisation for the marketing of piece goods. Through the Liverpool Cotton Exchange a manufacturer can safeguard himself against rises in the cost of his raw materials (see page 124).

Sometimes other firms come to the area to produce goods especially required in that area. Textile machinery is now manufactured chiefly in the Manchester area. Besides helping the industry to obtain the machines it wants quickly and without large transport costs, it means, above all, that the spinning and weaving firms are freed from the worry of making their own machines—they can leave it to a few firms who will make the machines for the whole industry and by so doing achieve for themselves the advantages of large-scale production.

Finally, where an industry comes to be concentrated in a particular area, a local reputation may be built up for the quality of the goods produced. Thus the reputation of Sheffield cutlery and Staffordshire pottery is established all over the world.

We must not forget, however, the dis-economies which sometimes result from concentration. These include congestion on the roads and the evils of large towns, such as lack of open spaces, overcrowded houses and smoke-filled air. These will be considered more fully when we deal with the disadvantages of the localisation of industry.

While external economies do not influence the businessman when planning the size of the firm, he must (when deciding where to situate it) take into consideration those economies of concentration which may be gained by going to a certain district, for all such economies help him to keep down the cost of the final product.

2. ECONOMIES OF INFORMATION

As an industry grows in size, so the workers doing the same sort of job or making the same kind of product group themselves together in unions, associations and societies. These groups often issue periodicals and publications by which improved methods of work are disseminated. Firms in the same industry also form associations to speak for the industry as a whole in negotiations with the government (e.g. the National Farmers' Union, the Federation of Master Cotton Spinners' Associations) and to carry out a common research programme.

The provision of information and research services often applies, not only to the expansion of one particular industry, but to the expansion of industry as a whole. In this case the services are often provided by the government, examples being the special weather reports for shipping and the research work of the Department of Trade, whose results are made available to all firms.

3. ECONOMIES OF DISINTEGRATION

When a firm first commences production it may have to make every part of the good itself. As other firms start producing, however, and the industry thereby grows, it may pay one firm to specialise on the production of one particular part and to supply it to the whole of the industry. This firm thus secures the economies of large-scale production for that part alone. Such a process of 'vertical disintegration' has happened frequently with the motor industry. Smiths, for example, now produce most of the clocks and instruments, Lucas supply most of the electrical equipment, while a few firms are engaged in the production of the tyres, batteries, sparking-plugs, etc.

In the same way, while it will not pay a single firm to go to the trouble of selling small amounts of its waste and by-products, when the industry grows large enough a special firm will arise to deal with a particular by-product for all the firms. Thus in London there are a number of waste merchants collecting waste paper from printers there.

These external economies are important, particularly in the later history of the industry. As we shall see, the original reason why an industry concentrates in a particular area may die out, but the industry continues to be located in that area largely because of the external economies which have been built up.

CHAPTER 5

THE ORGANISATION OF A FIRM UNDER PRIVATE ENTERPRISE WITH SPECIAL REFERENCE TO THE PROVISION OF CAPITAL

So far we have spoken only in a very general way of a 'businessman', the person who is making decisions regarding his firm. The firm itself consists of a number of factors of production—land, buildings, machinery, raw materials, workers and so on—assembled together for the production of a certain good or goods. It may be that the firm is under the direction and control of one man who has himself provided the capital required and therefore makes all the decisions regarding the policy of the firm. On the other hand, especially if the firm is a large one, it is more likely that it will be a joint-stock company with its capital provided by a considerable number of persons each of whom have bought 'shares' in it. These shareholders will then have the ultimate control over the company's policy. Economists generally refer to the person or group of persons who control the policy of a firm as the *entrepreneur*. In a later section we shall examine the meaning of this term in a little more detail, but for the present we shall accept the above definition without further comment. Our task now is to examine the various legal ways in which 'entrepreneurship' may be organised and, since the form of entrepreneurship is closely related to the size of the firm, we shall discuss it in connection with the problem of raising the capital which the firm requires. It should be pointed out here, however, that our problem is largely one of raising long-term capital and it is chiefly this type of capital which we have in mind in the following discussion. For 'working' or 'short-term' capital a firm can find help in a variety of ways, most usually through the commercial banks, but also by hiring buildings and sometimes machinery, buying factors on the hire-purchase system, obtaining the customary trade credit terms of one to three months, and taking deposits in advance from customers.

I. SOLE PROPRIETOR

The sole proprietor or 'one-man' firm is the oldest form of entrepreneurial organisation. Even today, from the point of view of numbers, small firms predominate, but in their total productive capacity they are far less important than joint-stock companies (see Table 11). Such one-man firms range from the 'rag and bone' man, chimney-sweep and window-cleaner working on his own account to the farmer, shopkeeper and small factory-owner who employ other workers and may even own many separate units. Nevertheless these businesses all have the same characteristic of being owned and controlled by a single person. It is this person's task to make all decisions regarding the policy of the firm and it is he alone who takes the profits and bears the brunt of any losses which are made. This makes for energy, efficiency, a careful attention to detail and a close relationship between employer and employee.

The sole proprietor, however, suffers from two main disadvantages. First, the development of such a firm must proceed slowly because the sources of capital are limited. The success of the venture, especially in its early stages, depends very largely on the person in charge, and nobody is likely to provide capital for the business unless he has that confidence in the proprietor which comes from personal contact. Hence the main source of capital for this type of business is the personal savings of the owner himself, together with such additional sums as he may be able to borrow from relatives or close friends. In time, development and expansion of the business may take place by 'ploughing back' profits, but this will probably be an extremely slow process and such firms generally remain comparatively small.

The second disadvantage is that, in the event of failure, not only the assets of the business, but also the private assets and property of the proprietor can be claimed against by creditors. In short, there is no limited liability.

Because of these disadvantages, the sole-proprietor form of

organisation is, in the main, confined either to those businesses which are just starting up, or to certain industries, such as agriculture and retailing, where requirements of management make the small technical unit desirable.

II. PARTNERSHIP

A larger amount of capital is available when persons combine together in a 'partnership', though not more than twenty (ten in the case of a banking concern), may so join. Each partner provides a part of the capital required and shares the profits on an agreed basis. Yet the amount of capital which can be raised in this way is still inadequate for modern large-scale organisations. The result is that partnerships remain relatively small, being particularly suitable to that type of business, such as retailing and the professions (doctors, dentists, consulting engineers and lawyers), where the capital provided is not so much in the form of money as in professional skill and experience, each partner probably specialising in a particular branch.

Moreover, in securing capital through partners, disadvantages are incurred. The risk inherent in unlimited liability is increased because all partners are liable for the firm's debts irrespective of the amount of capital which each has individually invested, and private fortunes may be called upon to meet the demands of creditors. Only if a partner takes no share in the management of the firm and there is at least one ordinary partner can the privilege of limited liability be enjoyed. Secondly, any action taken by one partner is legally binding on all the other partners. From this it follows that not only must each partner have complete confidence in the others, but that, as the number of partners increases, so does the risk inherent in unlimited liability. Finally, by giving notice to the others, one partner may terminate the partnership at any time, while it is automatically dissolved upon the death or bankruptcy of any one partner. This means that surviving partners have either to buy his share or find a purchaser who is acceptable to everyone. In such circumstances, therefore, the continuation of the business often involves great trouble and expense.

III. JOINT-STOCK COMPANY

Because of the disadvantages of sole proprietorship and partnerships, it was necessary to devise some other form of entrepreneurial organisation. This form is known as the joint-stock company. The joint-stock company first developed in Tudor times when foreign trade began to expand. The government, wishing to foster such trade, often granted the promoters a charter, which enabled them to form a company and to carry on trade in various parts of the world, usually free from outside competition. Two of the most famous of these companies were the East India Company (1603–1857), and the Hudson's Bay Company (formed in 1670 and still in existence today).

Nevertheless, until the middle of the nineteenth century, people were reluctant to join joint-stock companies. The reason for this was that they enjoyed no limited liability. By purchasing only one share a person risked, not merely the loss of the money invested but, should the company be forced into liquidation, the whole of his private fortune. Moreover, unlimited liability made it virtually impossible for an individual to adopt the technique of spreading risks by investing his capital outlay in a number of different companies. The Industrial Revolution, with the introduction of machines and large-scale organisation, made it essential that more capital should be available to industry. Hence, in order to induce small savers to invest, the privilege of limited liability was granted by an Act of Parliament in 1855. This is the meaning of the letters 'Ltd.' which are now seen after the name of companies.

Today, therefore, the joint-stock company is the most important form of business organisation. The advantages it enjoys over the partnership are chiefly that there is limited liability, a larger amount of capital can be raised, since investors can spread their risks and sell their shares easily, and, should the need arise, expansion is much easier. Indeed, some kinds of businesses could not be conducted on a small scale. Such businesses, therefore, have to start from the beginning as joint-stock companies, either being sponsored by important interests, or else developed as subsidiaries of existing large firms.

Against these advantages, however, certain disadvantages, which could add to costs, have to be considered. The chief of these arises under corporation tax, to which a small firm becomes liable by trading as a company instead of as a sole trader or partnership. The company's corporation tax could be more than the income tax which would have been paid had the business remained as a sole trader or partnership. Furthermore, any assets of the company which have been built up over the years will increase the value of the original shares (usually owned by the family). When the time comes to wind up the company, e.g. owing to retirement, any increase in the value of the shares will be subject to capital gains tax.

1. FINANCE OF A COMPANY

The finance of a company is obtained in two ways: (a) by selling 'shares' in the company; (b) by borrowing.

1. Shares

A 'share' is exactly what the name implies—a participation in the provision of the capital of a company. Shares may be issued in various units, usually from 10p upwards, and a person can vary the degree to which he participates by the number of units he purchases. The investment of money in a company does involve certain risks, of which two are paramount. The first is that the return on the capital invested may be less than expected because profits are disappointing. The second is that share prices in general may have fallen at the moment when the owner wishes to sell his holding. To minimise these risks, investors usually spread their investments over a variety of concerns and vary the magnitude of the risks undertaken by having a portfolio of shares of different types, debentures, corporation stock and government bonds.

(a) Ordinary shares. The dividend paid to the ordinary share-holder depends entirely on the proportion of such shares he owns and on the prosperity of the company. If profits are high, the dividend is usually correspondingly high; if there are no profits, then there is usually no dividend. Moreover, the payment of a dividend to an ordinary shareholder ranks last in the order of priority, while if the company should be forced into liquidation, the ordinary shareholder is repaid only after other creditors have been paid in full. Thus the 'ordinary share' is termed 'risk capital', for its holder bears the risks of the business venture. In return, each ordinary shareholder has a say in the running of the company, voting according to the number of shares held. At the general meeting, directors can be appointed or removed, changes made in the company's method of raising capital and conducting business, and auditors appointed. Thus the ordinary shareholders, because they take the major risks and decisions regarding the policy of the company, are the real 'entrepreneurs'. In practice, however, their rights are rarely exercised. Providing the company appears to be doing reasonably well, few shareholders take the trouble to attend the general meetings. Moreover, unless the company is very large, the directors are often in a strong position in that they will probably hold or control a large proportion, or even a majority of the ordinary shares. Indeed, such control may be deliberately secured by issuing only ' A ' shares (carrying no voting rights) when more capital is required.

(b) *Preference shares.* If the investor prefers a slightly reduced risk, he can buy a preference share. Such a shareholder has a claim on the profits for dividend payment before the ordinary shareholder, but offsetting this advantage, the dividend is a fixed per cent no matter how high the profits of the company are. In addition, only in exceptional circumstances, such as when it is proposed to alter their rights or to wind up the company, or when their dividends are in arrears, are these shareholders allowed to vote at ordinary meetings. Should, however, the company be forced into liquidation it is usual for the preference shareholder to rank above the ordinary shareholder in the redemption of capital.

Today preference shares are no longer issued. The main reason is that dividends, although a fixed per cent, do not count as a charge against the profits of a company in calculating corporation tax. It is better, therefore, to raise money through debentures.

Preference shares may also be 'cumulative'. This means that if the company cannot pay a dividend one year, arrears may be made up in succeeding years before the ordinary share-holders receive any dividend.

2. *Borrowing*

The long-term loans of a company are usually obtained by issuing 'debentures'. These bear a fixed rate of interest (about 14 per cent), irrespective of the profit made by the company. This interest payment is a first charge on the income of the company and so the risk to the investor of there being no return at all is not so high. Moreover, should the company fail, debenture-holders are paid out first. In fact, 'mortgage debentures' are secured on a definite asset of the company. One other advantage of debentures is that they are redeemable after a specified period. Should the company be unable to meet its interest charges or to redeem the loan when due, the debenture-holders can force it into liquidation.

Unlike the ordinary shareholder whose investment is bound up with the fortunes of the company, the purchaser of a debenture has eliminated as far as possible the risks attached to the possible failure of the company. In essence, he is merely lending the company money. Hence he enjoys no ownership rights of voting on management and policy. It is obvious, however, that a company whose profits are subject to frequent and violent fluctuations is not in a satisfactory position for raising much of its capital by issuing debentures. Such a method is really suitable only to a company making a fairly stable profit (sufficiently adequate to cover the interest payments), and possessing assets (such as land and buildings), the value of which would not have depreciated a great deal were the company to go into liquidation.

2. KINDS OF JOINT-STOCK COMPANIES

Joint-stock companies are of two main kinds, private and public.

1. *The private company*

The organisation of a business as a private company, while

conferring the advantage of limited liability, allows it to be privately owned and managed. Moreover, the formalities involved in its formation are few. Under the Companies Act, 1948, it has to fulfil the following conditions: (a) neither shareholders nor debenture-holders exceed 50 in number; (b) shares are not offered for sale by public issue; (c) directors have the power to disapprove any proposed transfer of shares; (d) none of its shares are held by another company, unless the aggregate shareholding of the two companies does not exceed 50; (e) no corporate body acts as a director; (f) nobody other than the registered holder has any interest in the company's shares; (g) no person or body outside the company is in a position to control its policy.

Hence the private company is particularly suitable for either a medium-sized commercial or industrial organisation not requiring finance from the public or for a speculative venture where a small group of people wish to try out an idea and are prepared to back it up financially to a definite limit before floating a public company. While private companies are considerably more numerous than public companies, they are much smaller.

The reason why they remain small is often because of the difficulties encountered when they wish to expand. In the past, the chief source of additional capital was the profits which were 'ploughed back' into the business, but today government taxation of profits reduces the funds available for such expansion. Alternatively, where the company owns its own property, a mortgage can be arranged. If neither of these methods realises sufficient capital, the only alternative is to look round for additional investors. It is at this point that the private company is at a disadvantage. Neither its shares nor debentures can be offered for sale to the public, while any transfer has to be approved by the directors. In short, the shares of a private company tend to be somewhat illiquid. Thus, in order to find the additional investors, it is usually necessary to convert the business into a public company with its shares 'quoted', that is, dealt in on the Stock Exchange.

The formation of such a company, however, is not an easy or simple step. The main obstacle arises from the fact that the costs of a public issue are so high that it is not usually economic to raise less than £150,000. Thus before embarking on such an issue, the company must already have attained a fairly substantial size. The difficult stage in its expansion occurs, therefore, when its capital is in the region of £50,000, for then it is still too small to make a public issue. The gap can be bridged in three main ways. First, it may be possible for a stockbroker to arrange for a life-insurance company or an investment trust to purchase shares or debentures. (Such companies are usually in a position to ignore the disadvantages of holding securities of private companies.) Secondly, help might be obtained from the new-issue market, which has developed considerably over the past thirty years from two main directions. On the one hand, there have come into being a number of Issuing Houses who specialise in this kind of work. On the other, the merchant bankers, forced to find other outlets for their services when lending abroad was reduced in volume, have devoted their attention to issuing securities for firms at home which require relatively small amounts of capital. Both Issuing Houses and merchant bankers may themselves provide long- or medium-term capital to bridge the gap prior to making a public issue, though it should be noted that their main work is connected with public issues. Thirdly, there are a number of specialised finance corporations. Thus, for agriculture there is the Agricultural Mortgage Corporation, which will lend on the security of land and buildings. For small firms, the Charterhouse Industrial Development Company and Credit for Industry Ltd are among those who will help with long-term finance. The most important source, however, for such capital is the Industrial and Commercial Finance Corporation, a body backed by the government although mainly financed by the joint-stock banks. Its object is to provide the necessary capital for businesses, not necessarily companies, too small to make a public issue. But in order to obtain a loan, the firm has first to pass a searching investigation regarding its present financial position and business prospects.

2. *The public company*

Where a large amount of capital is required, for instance

above £150,000, it is usually raised by forming a public company (having a minimum of seven shareholders), with its shares quoted on the Stock Exchange. This is achieved by sending a letter asking for permission to have the shares 'quoted', that is dealt in on the Stock Exchange, and this letter will be examined by the Council. If permission is granted the affairs of the company have to be advertised very fully in at least two leading London newspapers, while if no new issue is being made, a supply of shares has to be made available by existing shareholders sufficient to make dealing and the price fixed realistic.

Once the introduction has been completed, the capital required can be raised either by a Stock Exchange 'placing', an 'offer for sale', or by a 'public issue by prospectus'. The first is the usual method when only about £150,000 is required, for the costs of underwriting and administration are less. An issuing house, stock broker or investment company agrees to sell blocks of the shares privately to persons who it knows are likely to be interested in them.

For larger amounts up to £300,000, an offer for sale is a likely method. The shares are sold *en bloc* to an issuing house, which then offers them for sale to the public by advertisement similar to a public issue.

When more than £300,000 is required, a public issue by prospectus is the method usually employed. Here the company's object is to obtain from the public in a single day the additional capital it requires. Hence it must advertise well and price its shares a little on the cheap side. The advertisement is in the form of a prospectus which sets out the business, history and prospects of the company together with its financial standing and the security offered. It must be issued at least 3 days before the allotment of the securities so that the prospectus can be adequately examined and reviewed in the financial papers. Attached to the prospectus there is usually an application form which the would-be subscriber completes and sends with his application money (which may be required in full or in part).

In practice, the sale is usually conducted through an Issuing House which advises on the terms of the issue. It will also arrange to have the issue underwritten; that is, it will find a number of institutions, such as merchant bankers, who, in return for a small commission, will take at an agreed price whatever part of the issue is left unsold. Nevertheless such underwriters do not have to rely entirely on permanent investors to buy the securities on the day of issue, for speculators, known as 'stags', are usually operating and they buy the shares hoping to re-sell them quickly at a small profit. In addition, in recent years, there has been an increasing tendency to give existing shareholders the first option on the purchase of new shares. This is done through a ' rights issue ' which offers the right to buy new shares up to a given proportion of shares already held, usually at a favourable price.

IV. HOLDING COMPANIES

It might well be that the optimum technical unit of a business is much smaller than the optimum financial unit. In this case the financial economies of scale can be achieved by organising the financial side of a group of firms through a single ' holding company ', leaving the individual subsidiaries to continue working in their own name as separate technical units and retaining a great deal of independence of action.

However, while there may be this theoretical justification for the formation of a holding company, in practice such companies have been formed in order to obtain controlling interests, often for monopoly purposes. Moreover, through the method of its formation, control of the whole group of companies may be concentrated in the hands of a few men, owning comparatively little capital. Suppose, for instance, that this capital is £100,000. This can be used to control the affairs of a company which has a total capital of £400,000 if only half of this is in the form of ordinary shares. Similarly this capital can be used to hold half the ordinary shares of a company whose capital, half in shares and half in debentures, is in the region of £1,600,000. So the process can be continued. In practice, the persons in control see the whole group of companies as one firm and their policy will be such as will benefit the group as a whole. The result is that the interests of the minority shareholders, who are not members of the controlling group, may suffer considerably if the subsidiary company in which they have their money invested has to be sacrificed, as it were, to the interests of the group as a whole. Until the Companies Act, 1948, it was difficult to obtain information as to the control exercised by holding companies over subsidiaries and the public often invested in such subsidiaries unaware of the controlling power of a holding company. The 1948 Act, however, endeavoured to remedy this state of affairs by requiring holding companies to publish either separate accounts for all companies in their group or a consolidated account for the whole group together.

V. CO-OPERATIVE SOCIETIES

Although there were many co-operative societies in operation before the Rochdale Pioneers, 1844, it is they who started the modern co-operative movement. The Rochdale Pioneers consisted of a group of 28 artisans, mostly cotton weavers, who, by subscribing a few pence per week, managed to obtain an initial capital of £28 with which they rented a small store in Toad Lane, Rochdale, and started trading with small stocks of flour, oatmeal, sugar, butter and candles. Profits were distributed to members in proportion to their purchases. Today the number of retail co-operative societies in Great Britain and Northern Ireland is 244 with an aggregate membership of 10½ million. Capital amounts to £378 million, while the value of trade is about £1,300 million, accounting for nearly 8 per cent of Britain's retail trade. In addition, these retail societies largely provide the capital and control the operation of the Co-operative Wholesale Society.

The minimum shareholding in a retail co-operative society is usually £1. Only if a full share is held does a member enjoy voting rights, but not more than one vote per member is allowed irrespective of the number of shares held. Until fairly recently, the traditional way of paying the Co-op 'divi' was to distribute profits in proportion to the member's purchases over the period. Societies charged the current market price for their goods. Today, however, most societies return the dividend to members through the National Dividend Stamp scheme operated by the Co-operative Wholesale

Society. Stamps are given to customers in proportion to their purchases, and a book of stamps can be redeemed for 40p cash or 50p in goods or for 50p deposit in a share account, in which case a bonus of an extra 10p is usually added. Not only has this system allowed the Co-operative shops to compete with the supermarkets and other stores, but it is much cheaper to operate than the old 'divi' method. Nor does the member have to wait at least six months before receiving the dividend, while the national stamp can be gummed in the book irrespective of the source, e.g. petrol stations.

Co-operative Societies described above are organised directly by consumers and are therefore called 'Consumers' Co-operative Societies'. Producers also associate together in 'Producers' Co-operative Societies' for the purpose of marketing the produce of their members and sharing the proceeds between them. They are chiefly important in the marketing of agricultural produce, particularly where production is carried on by many small farmers, as in Denmark, New Zealand and Spain. Nevertheless, they have not been developed to any great extent in the United Kingdom. Instead, when marketing difficulties have arisen in agriculture in this country, the government has exercised control through Marketing Boards.

CHAPTER 6

STATE ENTERPRISE

WE ended Chapter 2 by considering the various reasons why the State should interfere in the operation of a Capitalist economy. Such intervention takes various forms. Sometimes it merely involves making regulations which modify the complete operation of the price system, as when subsidies are granted, import duties imposed or prices controlled. At other times, however, the State supervises, or actually undertakes, the production of goods and services. This could occur because:

(1) certain goods and services, such as defence, the maintenance of law and order, provision against sickness, unemployment and old age, cannot be safely left for private enterprise to provide;

(2) at times, private firms do not consider the full social cost or benefit of their operation;

(3) greater efficiency is achieved in production by means of the resources of the State;

(4) full employment is more easily secured.

It has usually been considered that it is the duty of the State to provide for defence, the maintenance of law and order, and certain social benefits. On the other hand, interference for the last three reasons is much more a matter of opinion, not so much because the objectives are disputed, but rather over the actual degree of State interference which is entailed. Principally for the third reason, efficiency, it is considered by some people that the State should own industries formerly organised under private enterprise and itself produce the goods and services required. This is obviously a radical step, though it should be noted that it falls short of the extreme form of Collectivism described in Chapter 2 in that it does not entail direction of labour. But the object of service to the community replaces the object of making a profit, although most of the nationalised industries are expected to cover costs by receipts over a given period of time. In this chapter we consider the particular economic advantages and disadvantages which are likely to result from 'nationalisation' and then conclude with a brief discussion of the various methods of organising State enterprise.

I. THE POLICY OF NATIONALISATION

It must be noted at the outset that nationalising certain industries in the United Kingdom in order to improve the operation of the Capitalist system is a policy vastly different from one that advocates nationalisation as a general principle to be applied to all production. The latter is simply Collectivism as we have defined it. Roughly speaking, what has happened in the United Kingdom is that industries selected for possible nationalisation have each been considered on their merits, and the decision whether to nationalise or not has been taken on this individual assessment. Since, however, with all industries there are arguments for and against State ownership, the decision finally arrived at is, as we have already indicated, a subjective one. It depends upon the relative emphasis which is placed upon the advantages of State ownership, as compared with the disadvantages. Consequently, while the economist can point out the pros and cons of the situation, it is the politicians who make the final decision. In practice the Labour Party lays stress on the reasons for nationalisation, while the Conservative Party puts more emphasis on its disadvantages. Here we take no sides in the *political* controversy which rages round the question of nationalisation. Instead we merely point out the various economic arguments for and against nationalisation. The reader, like the politicians, will be left to form his own view as to the desirability or otherwise of each particular policy.

In recent years, chiefly since the war, the government of the United Kingdom has nationalised the Bank of England, cable and wireless services, civil aviation, gas and electricity undertakings, the coal-mines, transport (road, canal and rail), atomic energy and the iron and steel industry. In all, the nationalised industries account for approximately one-eighth of the economic activity of the United Kingdom.

Nationalisation does not mean that the property of the industries is confiscated. Instead the existing shareholders are given compensation by exchanging their shares for stocks of the nationalised industries. In this way the government buys out the shareholders of the relative undertakings which then come under State control. The yield received from the converted stock is usually smaller than the yield from the shares, though there is some justice in this owing to the fact that less risk is involved in government stock than in shares. If owners do not wish to retain such safe, fixed-interest-bearing securities then they can sell them on the Stock Exchange and purchase the type of security which they prefer. In addition, it should be pointed out that the method of organising the industry upon nationalisation has varied, the more recent tendency being towards greater decentralisation; we shall return to this later.

II. REASONS FOR NATIONALISATION

Since industries differ in such matters as their importance, size and type of product, problems concerning their ownership and organisation similarly vary. Hence not all the economic arguments for and against nationalisation apply equally to each industry. Nevertheless, in what follows, an attempt has been made to generalise on the economic advantages and disadvantages of State ownership, thereby providing a theoretical structure on which the suitability of an industry for nationalisation can be tested from the economic aspect. We shall commence with the advantages.

In the first place, complete ownership of all the firms in an industry may make it easier to achieve the full advantages of large-scale production. Particularly where the industry consists of a few large firms, competition between them may force each firm to work at a size less than the optimum, owing, for example, to the uncertainty involved in guessing at the plans of one's competitors. While the firm may be confident that its own proposed expansion is justified, it might consider that, should rival firms adopt a similar policy, the market would not absorb the increased production, and hence the firm would sustain heavy losses. Since all the firms in the industry may think along these lines, the result may be that, through playing for safety, they all remain smaller than the optimum rather than involve themselves in the cost of expansion, especially where this involves building much specialised and durable plant. A nationalised industry, where the State owned all the firms producing, could, through the elimination of such uncertainty, co-ordinate the production of the various units.

Perhaps more important are the large-scale economies which could be directly achieved through reorganisation when all the firms in an industry come under a single owner. Such a policy is usually referred to as 'rationalisation'. Even before 1939 it was found desirable in the cotton, iron and steel and ship-building industries to have an overall controlling authority to supervise production and rationalisation schemes, and, though it did not amount to nationalisation, the controlling authorities, nevertheless, enjoyed the blessing of the government of the day. While there is probably more scope for achieving economies of the technical, commercial and financial kinds, managerial and risk-spreading economies may also be possible. On the technical side, the number of different models produced by the industry can be reduced, greater standardisation effected, and production can be concentrated on the more efficient units. Thus, to quote but one example of standardisation, the Coal Board has developed a standard pattern of miner's safety helmets. Advocates of complete State control of the motor-car industry base their arguments largely on the need for rationalisation. They point out that, in the United States, production of the three leading models accounts for over a half of total production and that the number of each model produced is larger than the total production of cars in the United Kingdom. Thus, it is claimed, nationalisation could achieve further technical economies for, instead of there being a situation where,

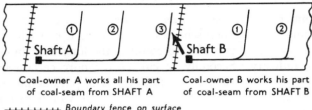

Coal-owner A works all his part   Coal-owner B works his part
of coal-seam from SHAFT A   of coal-seam from SHAFT B

++++++++ *Boundary fence on surface*

FIG. 5.—An advantage of common ownership in coal-mining. Before nationalisation separate owners meant separate workings and long haulages when workings had reached 3. Under nationalisation, this sector of coal-mine A can be more economically worked from SHAFT B, in the direction of the arrow

for example, at least 6 large producers each turned out approximately 4 models (amounting to 24 in all), production could be organised so that 6 times the number of 4 models only would be produced. A further example of how common ownership may produce more efficient working is illustrated in Fig. 5. It shows how coal-seams which, under different private ownership, have had to be worked from two separate shafts with much wasteful underground haulage may, under nationalisation, be worked from the most suitable shaft.

Similarly, nationalisation secures commercial and financial economies. Thus competitive advertising costs between firms are eliminated, while, in borrowing, a State-owned industry can usually obtain better terms than a private firm.

Secondly, particularly in the heavy industries, nationalisation may be necessary because owners of firms have not the resources for, or else are unwilling to commit themselves to long-term capital projects. Modern methods of production often involve such a vast amount of initial capital outlay that only the government can provide the necessary resources. Thus the development of atomic energy has been undertaken by the State, both for security and technical reasons, while, on the railways, a costly modernisation programme has been undertaken. On the other hand, under private ownership, investment occurs on the basis of expectation of profit. During periods of depression in industry, such expectations are at a low level, and thus capital projects are not undertaken simply because they do not seem profitable. Such a situation did in fact prevail in the coal and the iron and steel industries between the wars. For various reasons, however, the government is less likely to be deterred by a trade depression from undertaking such schemes. First, since it can withstand temporary losses, it is able to consider the long-term interests of the industry. Secondly, it can even ignore certain losses because it estimates that the industry is of paramount value to the nation in time of war. Thirdly, it would probably recognise that such investment in the industry in a slump has a reviving effect on the whole of the economy. In fact, many people, while not advocating complete Socialism in order to achieve full employment, would yet recommend the nationalisation of some important industries since, because it owns them, the State can help to steady cyclical fluctuations by continuing to work and invest in those industries even though they may be running at a loss. Left to private ownership, they would merely be caught up in the general pessimistic outlook.

Thirdly, it must be recognised that, no matter how much we disapprove of it in principle, some industries must inevitably be organised as monopolies, since such monopolistic power is often derived from legal powers conferred directly by the State. The grant of legal monopolies applies particularly to the public utilities, such as electricity, gas, railways, telephones, water, where, if there were more than one firm in operation, chaos might result. Nevertheless it must be recognised that the monopolies established may yet abuse their position in order to make large profits for themselves rather than to serve the public. Hence, it is argued, the simplest way of controlling a monopoly is for the State to own it. There is then an assurance that it will work in the public interest and not merely operate to make high profits.

Closely connected with this is a fourth argument in favour of nationalisation. Some industries are basic industries inasmuch as either in peacetime they are the key industries on which all other production depends, or, in times of war, their efficiency is vital to defence. Such industries, which include the coal and iron and steel industries and possibly the motor and aircraft industries, should not, it is argued, be regarded merely as a source of private profit (to be increased in periods of tension or shortages) but should be run by the State in the general interest of the nation. In the same way that the provision of men for the fighting services is not left to private enterprise, neither should be the arms which they require.

Lastly, it is claimed that the workers will work better under nationalisation. Not only will they enjoy better working conditions, but the fact that the State is the employer, and not a company striving for its own profit, will have a psychological result reflected in increased output. Experience of nationalisation has so far lent little support to this view. Nationalisation of the railways was probably essential for their reorganisation, but even so there has still been friction between workers and management, numerous demands for wage increases and no startling increase in the enthusiasm of the average railwayman.

III. DISADVANTAGES OF NATIONALISATION

The arguments upon which the opposition to nationalisation are based stem largely from the fact that State ownership results in the creation of monopolies. In the first place, it is argued that a State monopoly has weaker incentives than privately-owned firms to adopt an enterprising policy. Under private enterprise, a firm goes all out to make profits. Competition forces it to adopt new techniques and to follow a progressive policy, for failure to do so results in losses and eventual bankruptcy. Since most of the nationalised industries, however, are free from competition, they would still manage to survive in spite of the fact that the policy being followed was devoid of initiative. But the argument goes farther than this. The fact that nationalisation creates publicly-owned monopolies means that the industry must, in some way or other, be made accountable to the public for its operations. Unfortunately, however, this may have the effect of producing timid and cautious decisions. Policies have in the end to be justified in Parliament. Therefore, when considering such matters as future plans, new methods of production, new products or alternative sources of supply, the argument might proceed as follows: 'If we pursue a bold policy (which nevertheless involves some risk of failure), it is unlikely, even if it succeeds, that we shall receive full credit in Parliament. On the other hand, if the policy proves to be a failure, then much political capital will be made out of it both in Parliament and in the Press. Let us, therefore, not lay ourselves open to such a risk, but rather follow a safer, if a less imaginative, policy.' As we shall show later, in adopting the organisation of the public corporation or Board, rather than a government department, for their newly nationalised industries, the government did recognise, and aim at removing, the cramping effect of continual Parliamentary criticism on the day-to-day running of these industries.

Secondly, while it is not suggested that the public would be exploited in the deliberate manner which has occurred in the past with privately-owned monopolies, it is nevertheless argued that, since they are the sole producers of the good, less obvious defects might result. Thus there may be some loss of 'consumer's sovereignty', a 'take-it-or-leave-it' attitude existing in its place. Again, prices will have to be fixed so that costs can be covered over the long period. But it is asked, since prices are fixed on a cost basis, what guarantees do the public have that the costs are being kept to a minimum by efficient running? With competition, we can compare the running costs of various firms to arrive at a criterion of efficiency, but this is impossible with a State monopoly. These fears have been somewhat awakened in recent years, and rises in transport charges and in the prices of coal, gas and electricity have led to frequent demands for inquiries into their efficiency.

A third criticism which is levied against nationalisation is that, in setting up one controlling body for the whole of the industry, it creates a unit which is too large for efficient management. In other words, managerial dis-economies arise. Decisions tend to be made according to precedent and set rules and, whenever possible, even simple problems are passed on to a superior for a decision. In short, there may be a persistence of 'red tape'. While there may be something in this argument, it must be pointed out that this is a criticism which applies not only to nationalised industries. Giant concerns and holding companies exist under private enterprise and these have to face the same problems of management. There appears to be no basic reason why the State industry should be relatively inferior in this respect.

Fourthly, it is argued that, on many occasions, a State-owned industry will force the government of the day to intervene in its management for *political* reasons. Experience since nationalisation has shown these fears to have some justification. Thus the Labour Party, which set up the industries, has been forced into the position where it feels that it has to act as a defender of them on almost every occasion, whether or not it agrees with the criticisms being made. Even so, the problem of strikes in these vital, basic industries has not been solved. Workers feel secure in their employment when deficits are continually covered by government assistance, and demands for wage increases have been frequent.

IV. THE METHODS OF ORGANISING STATE ENTERPRISE

Even after it has been agreed that the State should either supervise or undertake the production of goods and services, it still remains to be decided how the management shall be organised. Nationalisation of many of Britain's basic industries has brought this problem to the fore, since when the State is the entrepreneur, two fundamental principles, each pulling in opposite directions, need due consideration.

The first principle arises because British democracy requires that where the State is granted powers, it shall be answerable, in some form or another, for the way in which these powers are exercised. This is known as the principle of 'public accountability'. Our past history has shown that it is not sufficient to assume that the State can always be relied upon to act in the 'public interest'. Often the 'State' consists of a collection of government departments, run by officials who, either misguidedly or wilfully, translate the 'public interest' into policies which suit their own ends. Thus, in the political field, it has been necessary to protect the individual by such devices as trial by jury and habeas corpus. Similarly, the individual needs safeguards when the State is acting in the economic field, a view for which the classic example is provided by the Crichel Down case, 1954. He wishes to be satisfied that the powers granted to enable the State to produce goods are not being abused by authoritarianism, inefficiency or monopolistic exploitation. The method by which the individual obtains such satisfaction is by requiring that the bodies owning these powers shall be made answerable for the way in which they are exercised.

The most efficient form of accountability is achieved when a government department produces the goods or services. The department usually has a Minister at its head who accepts full responsibility for the work of his department. This Minister is subject to examination in Parliament and it is his task to explain general policy in debate and to answer questions on even minor details of administration. Any individual, therefore, who has been aggrieved in his dealings with a government official can take the case to his M.P., who will, if he considers the complaint is justified, take the matter up with the authority concerned and even put down a question to be answered in Parliament. In the financial field, too, there is also a strict control, for the Treasury is careful to see that money is spent economically and within the limit which Parliament has previously authorised.

This method of a government department's providing goods and services was the one generally used before World War I. (The chief exception was where they were basically of a local nature and they were then provided through a local authority, a method which will be discussed in more detail in Chapter 22). Thus government departments organised defence, made arrangements for the provision of law and order and either provided or supervised certain social services, such as poor relief, health, education, old-age pensions, and health insurance. Sometimes, departments were responsible for providing goods and services which might have been left to private enterprise. Thus postal services were supplied by the Post Office, munitions by the Ministry of Munitions, and public houses and hotels in Carlisle by the Home Office.

Nevertheless, the government department method of organisation or control cannot be used in all cases. In the first place, owing to the growth of the State's economic activities in the present century, Parliament would simply not have the time to exercise a detailed control over those activities. Hence, we must reserve the department method for special cases and invent other methods for the remainder. Secondly, it may well be that, although the service has national implications, basically it is still a local one. In such cases, it would be undesirable to give full control to a central government department. Consequently, for the administration of the ports and docks of London and Liverpool, we have had created the Port of London Authority and the Mersey Docks and Harbour Board respectively, over which the Minister for the Transport Industries exerts a remote authority by appointing a small proportion of the Board's members. Thirdly, the nature of the service may be judicial rather than administrative. This was one of the basic considerations behind the creation of the Civil Service Commission. Fourthly, it may be vital to ensure that there is complete political neutrality in the administration of the service, a requirement virtually impossible to achieve if the service is directly controlled by a Ministry and subject to continual attack from the Opposition in Parliament. Hence we have the establishment of the Civil Service Commission, the British Broadcasting Corporation, the Supplementary Benefits Board and the University Grants Committee.

Above all, the government department, while ensuring the maximum public accountability, has certain weaknesses in providing economic goods and services, weaknesses which become more apparent where it has been or is possible to organise the production through private enterprise. Apart from inherent deficiencies in the Civil Service organisation (such as lack of initiative, addiction to red tape and the rigid methods of Treasury control of finance and accounting), the principle of public accountability itself entails some conflict with our second principle, that of 'economic efficiency'.

This principle was discussed in Chapter 2, and it was shown how private enterprise was very effective in solving the two main aspects of efficiency, the estimate of consumers' demand and efficiency in supply. Individuals decide what and how to produce in order to make a profit. If their decisions are correct, a profit is their reward; if they are wrong, and production is misdirected, then they, and only they, are the losers. Persons who take the risk of producing, therefore, are primarily answerable only to themselves.

But what happens when the department is the producer and its civil servants are accountable to Parliament for day-to-day details of administration? The result is the 'play-for-safety' attitude already commented on. Moreover, this form of accountability through Parliament has certain additional defects. First, it might lead to difficulties in pursuing long-term industrial and commercial objectives because the Minister in charge is being changed frequently through either reorganisation of the Government or a swing of the political pendulum. Secondly, it is likely that much of the Parliamentary questioning on day-to-day matters would either be irrelevant and ill-informed, because it dealt with a technical matter beyond the understanding of the average Member of Parliament, or even positively harmful, in that it was used solely as an instrument of political opposition.

The result of this conflict between the two principles of public accountability and economic efficiency has been the development of a variety of special governmental (sometimes called 'quasi-government') bodies, variously termed Commissions, Boards, Authorities and Corporations, but all having at least one thing in common in that they are subject to some form of public control. This control may be exceptionally slight, as in the case of the Church Commissioners who submit an annual report to Parliament. On the other hand, as with the nationalised industries, the Minister may appoint the whole of the Board and give directions as to general policy. Moreover, for such industries, additional forms of control have been devised which will be described in more detail later.

Although we can trace the use of such quasi-government bodies even in Tudor times, it was not until the twentieth century that they were developed extensively. Until then, new services were generally made the function of a particular government department, but it is obvious that, as the State began to interfere more and more in the economic field, so it had to resort increasingly to the use of the quasi-government body. Today these bodies number over 200, though they vary in the nature and importance of the functions performed

as well as in the degree of independence enjoyed. Fig. 6 gives
an indication of the nature of their functions.

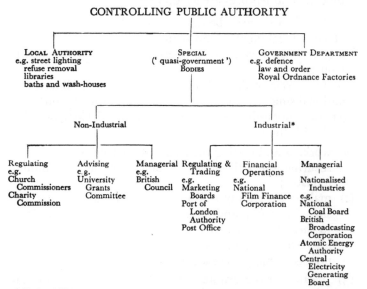

CONTROLLING PUBLIC AUTHORITY

LOCAL AUTHORITY
e.g. street lighting
refuse removal
libraries
baths and wash-houses

SPECIAL
(' quasi-government ')
BODIES

GOVERNMENT DEPARTMENT
e.g. defence
law and order
Royal Ordnance Factories

Non-Industrial

Industrial*

Regulating
e.g.
Church
Commissioners
Charity
Commission

Advising
e.g.
University
Grants
Committee

Managerial
e.g.
British
Council

Regulating &
Trading
e.g.
Marketing
Boards
Port of
London
Authority
Post Office

Financial
Operations
e.g.
National
Film Finance
Corporation

Managerial
Nationalised
Industries
e.g.
National
Coal Board
British
Broadcasting
Corporation
Atomic Energy
Authority
Central
Electricity
Generating
Board

* ' Industrial ' in this context means the bodies are connected with a particular industry or serve
industry in general.

FIG. 6.—Forms of public organisation for the supervision or provision of
goods and services

V. THE ORGANISATION OF THE NATIONALISED INDUSTRIES

So far we have given only a general picture of the various
methods of organising State control of goods and services. In
this chapter, however, we are primarily concerned with the
nationalised industries and for this reason alone we must give
more detailed attention to their organisation. But there are
additional reasons. In the first place, they are basic industries,
far exceeding in importance the earlier subjects of quasi-
government control. Secondly, the great majority of them were
previously organised under a private-enterprise system. And
lastly, they represent the latest attempt in this type of government control and their common features, although subject to
slight modifications, demonstrate the fact that they have been

organised on carefully thought-out principles, crystallised usually from the results of the earlier experiments.

These general features are as follows:

(1) The Boards are 'bodies corporate'. This means that they have a legal identity and therefore, like a company, have a life of their own, can own property, and sue and be sued in the Courts.

(2) The assets of the industry are vested in the Board and the nationalising Act usually gives the Board instructions as to its general responsibilities. Thus the National Coal Board is charged with the duties of:

(a) working and getting the coal in Great Britain;
(b) securing the efficient development of the coal-mining industry;
(c) making supplies of coal available, of such qualities and sizes, in such quantities and at such prices, as may seem to them best calculated to further the public interest in all respects, including the avoidance of any undue or unreasonable preference or advantage.

(3) A Minister is given an overall control of the Board. He exercises, as it were, the shareholders' rights in a company, the 'shareholders' with a Board being the public. It is the Minister, therefore, who appoints the Board's members, although the nationalising Act usually specifies their general qualifications. In addition, the Minister may give the Board directions of a general character as to how they shall exercise and perform their functions with regard to matters which appear to him to affect the national interest. This usually includes authorising capital development, supervising borrowing and appointing auditors. In general, with the post-war Boards the Minister can exercise a far greater degree of control than with the earlier ones. The aim, therefore, is to give the Board freedom in its day-to-day administration with the possibility of some subordination in its general policy. Boards are not subject to Parliamentary questioning on detailed matters of administration, but they are required to submit Annual Reports to Parliament, for which the government usually sets aside a day to debate.

(4) In financial and staffing matters, the Boards are free

from control by the Treasury and the Civil Service Department. They are required to pay their way, taking one year with another. They engage their own staff, arranging directly through employees' trade unions or associations, pay and conditions of service.

(5) In order to obviate the necessity of Parliamentary questioning on matters of detail and to ensure a degree of direct representation by consumers, Consumers' Councils have been established for the coal, electricity, gas and transport industries. They consist of twenty to thirty unpaid members, appointed, except in the case of Air Transport, by the Minister. Nominations for membership are put forward by bodies whom the Minister selects as being representative of consumers, e.g. local authorities, women's organisations, professional associations, trade unions, and trade associations. The coal industry has two National Councils, one for industrial and one for domestic users, but the 'Consultative Councils' of the other industries are organised on a regional basis. The functions of these Councils are:

(a) to deal with complaints and suggestions from consumers, although they are also expected to act on their own initiative in such matters;

(b) to advise both the Boards and the Minister of the general views of consumers.

Unfortunately so far, either through ignorance, the remoteness of the offices, or general lack of confidence, little use has been made by the consumers of these Councils.

In short, therefore, the new public corporations try, as it were, to get the best of both worlds: on the one hand, the world of energetic industrial enterprise found in the Capitalist system; on the other, the world of accountability to the public, to whom it belongs and whom it serves.

The detailed internal organisation of the Corporations has varied. Two illustrations will serve to illustrate this point. The Coal Industry Nationalisation Act, 1946, set up a *National* Board consisting of a Chairman and seven full-time and four part-time members, with the responsibilities already mentioned. But the rest of the organisation of the coal industry was such as this Board should determine. In practice, it created eight Divisional Boards to control districts corresponding roughly to the main coal-bearing regions. In 1969 these Divisions were abolished and replaced by 17 Areas, each under an Area Director. He is directly and personally responsible to the Board for supervising and co-ordinating the work of the collieries within the Area. The day-to-day work of running the collieries is under the direction of colliery managers.

It seems, however, that originally the problem of size was under-estimated, for subsequent nationalising Acts brought an increasing tendency to decentralisation. Thus the Electricity Council and the Gas Council, which were established in 1948, were really only central representative bodies for the industry as a whole, and were composed mainly of the chairmen of the twelve Area Boards, with an independent Chairman or Vice-Chairman appointed by the Minister. In both cases, the nationalising Acts established the twelve Area Boards, and the assets of the industry were vested in them. The Area Boards were also given the *statutory* responsibility for the distribution of electricity and the supply of gas. Each Board adopted its own pattern of organisation and arrangements for fulfilling its statutory obligations.

Circumstances, however, may mean that a new organisation is desirable. Thus the discovery of natural gas meant that its distribution had to be organised centrally. Hence in 1973 the original organisation of the gas industry was scrapped, and the supply of gas was brought under the British Gas Corporation, which took over the assets of the Area Gas Boards.

The nationalisation of certain industries led to economic problems, many of which were discussed earlier under the disadvantages of nationalisation—how to give consumer sovereignty, how and when to award wage increases to staff, how to ensure efficiency and so on. Many of these problems are still far from solved. As regards efficiency, for instance, the practice seems to have developed of setting up periodically independent Committees of Inquiry to consider the industry. But the method of organisation through the public corporation has also involved problems of a constitutional nature. One, the form of its internal organisation, has already been commented on. Others are even more important—how far the Minister is responsible to Parliament for the operations of the Board;

whether Parliament has sufficient powers and time available to make the Boards adequately accountable; how far Parliament, which is primarily a political institution, is a satisfactory body to examine objectively the operations of a large industrial and commercial unit, especially, for instance, when the Annual Report is being debated. Since the answers to these and many other problems are still being worked out, we must expect further developments in the organisation of the nationalised industries as additional experience is gained in operating them.

CHAPTER 7

THE DISTRIBUTION OF GOODS
TO THE CONSUMER

I. WHAT DO WE MEAN BY 'PRODUCTION'?

So far we have spoken about 'production' in a rather loose way, and if we are to understand the part played by persons in the various stages of distributing the goods to the final consumer our first task must be to explain exactly what economists today mean by the term.

Early economists, such as the French Physiocrats of the eighteenth century, considered that only work in the extractive industries (agriculture, mining, and fishing) was productive. Adam Smith, however, went one stage further, for he included manufacturing in the term 'productive labour', though he was careful to deny that persons who merely rendered services were productive. In a much-quoted passage he states: 'The labour of the menial servant does not fix or realise itself in any particular subject or vendible commodity. His services generally perish in the very instant of their performance. . . . Like the declamation of the actor, the harangue of the orator, or the tune of the musician, the work of all of them perishes in the very instant of its production.' Nevertheless, the inadequacy of this definition can be realised at once for, according to it, the persons who make the dresses for the actresses and the scenery for the stage are productive, while the actors and actresses themselves are not, and the farmer who grows food is productive while the cook is not!

To arrive at a more satisfactory definition we have to ask: 'Why do people work? What is the reason for production?' The answer is simple—to satisfy wants. Sometimes a person does this directly, as, for example, when he services his own car. Usually, however, the wants are satisfied indirectly, the car for example, being serviced by a garage. As we have seen, this indirect satisfaction of wants arises because production is organised so as to take advantage of specialisation. We can now see that persons who render services must be regarded as being productive. The actor, the soldier, the valet and the shoe-black are all satisfying wants. While the latter two satisfy the wants of only one person at a time, the actor and the soldier satisfy the wants of many people at the same time. But the principle is the same. Similarly in a factory, the clerk who calculates the wages and the boy who sweeps the floor are just as productive as the man who makes the nuts and bolts. The difference in occupation merely arises because the manufacturer obtains the numerous advantages of specialisation by organising production in that way. For example, he sees that having a wages clerk saves the factory hands from leaving their work benches to calculate their weekly wages, income tax and so on.

Production, therefore, covers all activity directed to satisfying wants, and it is essential to recognise this fact. Unfortunately such a definition is too wide for practical purposes. Today attempts are made to measure production (see Chapter 18). The simplest way of doing this would be to total the value of all goods and services produced. But the big drawback is that this would necessitate giving a value to what people do for themselves. The cabbage grown in the allotment, the washing done by the housewife, the labour of oiling his cricket bat by the schoolboy, would all have to be included. Once this was commenced there would be no end to the process, and such jobs as shaving, washing-up, blacking one's boots and making the beds would all have to be valued.

Thus the term 'productive labour' is limited to labour done to satisfy the wants of *other people through exchange.* In other words, only if the labour, or the produce of labour, is sold is there considered to be production. The merit of this definition is that it is serviceable; the drawback is that it is not completely accurate and the exclusion of labour not paid for renders somewhat artificial results. For instance, the housewife who cleans her own windows or does her own washing would not be included as being ' productive ', whereas if she pays somebody else for this same work then they are 'productive'. Similarly, the work of an honorary secretary is not productive, but identical work performed by a paid secretary is!

What we must do, then, is to recognise the essential nature of production—work directed to the satisfaction of wants—and then admit that, for practical reasons, it has to be limited to work which is paid for either directly, as with a service, or indirectly by being included in the price paid for the good.

II. THE STAGES IN PRODUCTION: WHOLESALERS AND RETAILERS

Since the aim of economic activity is to satisfy the wants of people, the production of a good is not complete until the good is in the hands of the actual consumer. Hence anybody who takes a part in this complete process, whether he be, for example, the farmer who milked the cow, the lorry driver who

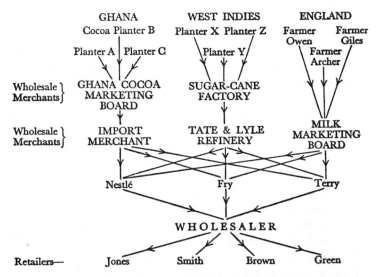

FIG. 7.—The part played by the wholesaler and retailer in the 'production' of chocolate

drove the milk-float to the town, or the roundsman who delivered the bottle on the doorstep, are all producers in the sense outlined above. In other words, in an exchange economy, even after the good has been 'made', the further stage of getting the good to the actual consumer is necessary before production is complete.

Sometimes the 'manufacturer' sells to the consumer directly. Farmers, for instance, sell eggs at the door and many brewers own their own public houses. The majority of goods, however, especially foodstuffs, clothing and goods used in the home, are distributed in two main stages, performed by first the wholesaler, who buys in bulk from manufacturers, and secondly, the retailer, who buys from the wholesaler and sells to the actual consumer (Fig. 7). These wholesalers and retailers are the final links in the chain of production and we must now examine in detail the part they play.

III. THE WHOLESALER

The work of the wholesaler consists in buying goods in bulk from the manufacturer and selling them in small quantities to retailers according to their requirements. The respective parts played by the wholesaler and retailer in the chain of production are well illustrated in the French equivalents for them, *commerçant en gros* and *commerçant en détail*.

In carrying out this main task the wholesaler performs many valuable functions which justify his existence as a specialist in the chain of distribution. These functions can be stated as follows:

1. HE ECONOMISES IN DISTRIBUTION

Since many shops, especially shops which stock a large variety of goods, can order their supplies only in small quantities, it is not economical for each producer to sell directly to the shop. Such a practice would mean employing many salesmen and representatives, packing many separate parcels and making numerous transport journeys in visiting each shop in turn. This fact is illustrated by Fig. 8, which shows that 16 contacts

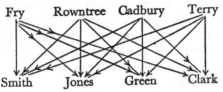

Fig. 8.—How the wholesaler economises in production—distribution without wholesaler

and van journeys are necessary when 4 chocolate firms deliver directly to 4 retailers.

Fig. 9, on the other hand, shows that when the goods are delivered in bulk by each to a wholesaler, the number of contacts and journeys is reduced to eight.

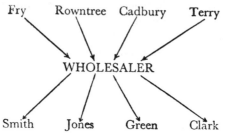

FIG. 9.—How the wholesaler economises in production—distribution through wholesaler

In agriculture particularly, where the goods are perishable, it simplifies matters considerably if the farmer, instead of trying to contact retailers himself, can deliver his produce to a wholesaler or commission salesman, for example at Covent Garden, and leave the actual selling to him.

2. HE KEEPS STOCKS

Customers like the convenience of being able to go to a shop and obtaining a good just when they require it. But such ready service entails the holding of stocks. Often, however, the retailer has neither the facilities nor the financial reserves to hold large stocks. So he leaves this to the wholesaler, knowing that, should there be a sudden run on a good, he can obtain supplies from him within a few hours.

In addition, the holding of stocks often performs a service to the producer. A farmer, for instance, could not afford refrigerators to store the meat which would accumulate at the end of each year through his heavy autumn killings, and so he is glad to leave this task to such persons as the Smithfield wholesalers. Similarly, a wholesaler, who orders in advance goods having a seasonal demand, ensures an even flow of work throughout the year.

In other ways, too, the costs of storage are removed from the producer or retailer. While loss through fire, flood or rats can be insured against, no insurance can be taken out to cover a loss through a fall in demand. Thus a wholesaler, who holds stocks of a good which is liable to go out of fashion, relieves the manufacturers and the retailers of that risk.

The holding of stocks is, in itself, a valuable economic function. Stocks help to even out fluctuations in price resulting from sudden but temporary fluctuations in demand and supply. Thus coal stocks in the hands of merchants are replenished during the summer and run down during the winter.

3. He Arranges Imports from Abroad

Manufacturers abroad could rarely be bothered to ship small parcels to individual retailers or undertake the foreign currency transactions involved. These tasks are left to a wholesaler, the import merchant, who is known and trusted. Often the import merchant goes abroad to establish and develop trade connections.

4. He Carries out Many Specialised Functions

In order to make selling easier, the wholesaler often carries out many special functions. Thus milk is pasteurised, hams are cooked and sugar is refined, while certain commodities, such as cotton, wheat and wool tops, are graded. In the case of tea, different varieties are blended in order to give choice combinations.

5. He Gives Information and Advice

The wholesaler often advises the manufacturer, particularly as regards advertising and marketing the product. In fact, the wholesaler himself will often advertise, especially if the good is being imported from abroad.

Moreover, he acts as a channel of information to and from retailers. Suggestions which customers make to the retailer are passed on to the wholesaler, and the latter, especially when he sees that such suggestions are representative of a wide area, passes them on to the manufacturer. Thus the manufacturer discovers how his product could be improved or how he can anticipate fashion changes.

6. HE ASSISTS IN THE DAY-TO-DAY MAINTENANCE OF THE GOOD

With many products, particularly vehicles and machinery, the manufacturers insists that the wholesaler provides an efficient maintenance service for the convenience of customers. Such a service includes minor repairs, periodic overhauls, and the stocking of an adequate range of spare parts. In this way both the manufacturer and the customer benefit. The former can guarantee quality of service and thereby preserve the reputation of his product, while the latter knows that his machines can be repaired quickly and efficiently by a local agent.

IV. THE RETAILER

The retailer performs the last stage of the productive process, for it is he who puts the goods in the hands of the actual consumer. His work has been summarised as 'having the right goods in the right place at the right time', and his functions, as set out below, are chiefly an enlargement of this. It must be appreciated, however, that, in actual practice, there is not always a clear distinction between the wholesaler and the retailer, and thus it will be found that, in some cases, their functions appear to overlap.

1. HE STOCKS SMALL QUANTITIES OF A VARIETY OF GOODS

What is the 'right good' depends on the customer, for different people have different tastes, and what suits one may be undesirable to another. Thus having the 'right good' depends largely on keeping a stock of the different varieties of the good so that each customer can make his or her individual choice, pay for it, and take delivery there and then. In part, his shop consists of a showroom wherein the customers can examine and compare the different goods one with the other and make their own selection. This is particularly helpful to customers when choosing goods which are only bought infrequently.

The size of the stocks the retailer carries will depend on many factors. Some manufacturers even stipulate that a certain minimum stock shall be carried before they will allow a retailer to sell their goods. Usually, however, it is left to the retailer himself. He will consider the popularity of the product, the possibility of obtaining further supplies quickly, the perishability of the good or the likelihood of its going out of fashion, the season (especially if it is approaching Christmas or if there is a seasonal demand for the good) and the possibility of a future change in its price. Above all, he must allow for the cost, in the form of interest rates on bank advances, of carrying stocks.

2. HE TAKES THE GOODS TO WHERE IT IS MOST CONVENIENT FOR THE CUSTOMER

Taking the goods to where it is most convenient for the customer may merely mean that the retailer sets up his shop within easy reach of the customer. It is for this reason that we see retailers congregated together in the centre of most towns, though, with goods such as groceries, which are in everyday use, small shops are often dotted around residential districts. Where customers are very dispersed, however, as in country districts, it is quite likely that the retailer will own a 'travelling shop' of some form or another.

While, with the majority of goods, customers take their purchases with them, the retailer may arrange delivery. This occurs with certain goods, such as coal and furniture, where transport is essential, but it also applies where the customer requires the extra convenience of having his goods delivered, as, for example, with milk, the early morning newspaper, laundry, and groceries supplied by high-class stores. The cost of such transport is often contained in the price of the good, though, in some cases, as with the delivery of newspapers, an extra charge is made.

3. HE GRANTS SPECIAL SERVICES TO CUSTOMERS

In the course of his main business, the retailer performs many services for the convenience of his customers, all of which help to build up goodwill. The customer is made to feel that he is getting individual attention. Where the good is not in stock, he will order it, and, in other matters where contact with the manufacturer is necessary, the retailer will often act for the customer. Thus goods are returned to the manufacturer for repair, though it should be noted that often, in the interests of speed, he himself maintains a repair service, e.g. cycle shops, radio and television retailers.

With many goods, too, such as fishing tackle, photographic equipment, musical instruments, machinery, and sports gear, special or technical knowledge is required. Here the customer, often a layman, is at a disadvantage when making his purchase. The retailer, however, is usually in a position to give advice and, in fact, some manufacturers insist on some technical competence in their retailers before allowing them to sell the product and may even go so far as to run a course at the works in order to provide them with the necessary knowledge.

Finally, for the greater convenience of customers, goods may be sent on approval or credit facilities granted. The latter may be done by opening accounts against which purchases are debited, by granting credit for a week or a month, by organising clubs into which so much is paid each week for spending at a future date, or by granting hire-purchase terms, though the latter is now usually arranged through a separate company, with the retailer collecting the repayments.

4. He Advises the Wholesaler and Manufacturer

A retailer maintains close contact with his customers. From them he discovers, either through a chance remark in the course of conversation or by direct suggestion, how a good could be improved or what type of good there is a large demand for. This information finds its way to the manufacturer, who will probably act upon it, and eventually the modification or the new good will be produced.

V. TYPES OF RETAIL OUTLET

Retailing might be widely defined to include all shops, mail-order firms, garages, bus companies, launderettes, betting shops or indeed any organisation which sells products or services to the consumer. It is usual, however, to take a narrower view and to confine retailing to shops and mail-order outlets. These can be classified as follows.

1. *Independents*

These are mainly small shops with no other branches, and they account for just under half of the total sales through shops. Yet, in spite of their advantages of individual attention to customers, 'handy' locations for quick shopping trips, and the willingness of owners to accept a lower return for the benefits of being one's own boss, these independents are steadily losing ground to the larger stores.

A major bid to avert the decline has come through the voluntary chains, such as Spar, Mace and Wavy Line, of which over 32 per cent of independents are members. While retaining their independence, members buy in bulk from the wholesaler (often at times and at minimum quantities dictated by him) and use common advertising and display techniques.

2. *Multiples*

These can be defined arbitrarily as organisations of ten or more shops. Some, such as Mothercare and Dorothy Perkins, sell a particular type of good. Others, such as Littlewood, Woolworth, Boots, and Marks and Spencer, have a fairly extensive range of products. Together they comprise over 35 per cent of the market.

Their chief advantages are that they can obtain the economies of bulk buying and centralised control, eliminate the wholesaler, invite instant recognition through their standardised shop fronts, and establish a reputation through brand names.

3. *Supermarkets*

These may be defined as self-service shops with a minimum selling area of 200 sq. metres. While organisationally they would count as multiples, their share of the food trade warrants separate attention. In 1974 they accounted for half the grocery trade and nearly a third of total retail food sales.

The field is led by the four major retail grocery chains: Tesco, Sainsbury, Allied Suppliers and Fine Fare. They thus secure the benefits of economies of scale, low labour costs, a clear and attractive display of merchandise and bulk buying to the extent of their own labelling (e.g. Sainsbury's cornflakes,

Tesco coffee). As a result they have gained ground rapidly through highly competitive prices.

Indeed, many of these self-service organisations have extended their activities beyond groceries, to clothing and hardware for example, where profit margins are usually higher.

4. *Hypermarkets*

Urban congestion, lack of adequate parking space and rising land prices or rents have made the High Street an increasingly expensive place from which to sell goods. The American and, to an increasing extent, the European answer to these problems has been the very large (2,000–4,000 sq. metres), 'out-of-town' shopping centre or 'hypermarket' to cater for the car-borne weekly shopper.

In the United Kingdom, however, the development has been slow. This is mainly because planning permission for such schemes is not readily forthcoming. The Department of the Environment continues to keep a watchful eye on the expansion of these space-consuming establishments, largely with the problems of 'down-town decay' and spoiling of the countryside in mind.

5. *Department stores*

Competition from multiples has forced department stores to alter somewhat the traditional picture of separate departments under the control of a buyer enjoying some degree of autonomy (which led to the epithet 'many stores under one roof'). Instead, a more streamlined approach with an increasing degree of bulk-buying by central office, more self-service, and extended credit facilities have allowed them to retain about 5 per cent of the market.

The main groups are Debenhams, House of Fraser, John Lewis Partnership, Great Universal Stores, and Sears Holdings.

6. *Co-operatives* (*see* pp. 83–4)

7. *Mail order*

While retail sales in general rose by about 27 per cent between 1966 and 1971, mail-order business increased by 32 per cent. By 1975 mail-order houses accounted for 6 per cent of the market.

The five major companies—Great Universal Stores, Littlewood's Mail Order, Grattan Warehouses, Freeman's and Empire Stores—sell by agency and illustrated catalogues, purchases usually being arranged through weekly interest-free payments. Over one-half of all sales are accounted for by women's clothing and household goods.

Factors affecting the type of retail outlet

Over the last twenty years, the pattern of retailing has moved away from the small, independent shop towards the larger organisation, notably the multiples, supermarket chains and mail order firms. This trend reflects a greater emphasis on competition through lower price rather than by better service.

The larger firms are in a strong position to cut prices. Not only do they obtain the advantages of large-scale production (particularly those of selling a whole range of goods and of buying in bulk), but they can use their bargaining strength to secure further price discounts from manufacturers. Indeed, the largest may force the manufacturer to supply goods under the retailer's 'own-brand' label at a price below that at which other retailers can buy the manufacturer's national brand. Moreover, since the large retailers cater for a whole range of shopping, e.g. food, they can attract customers into stores by 'loss-leaders'.

Economic factors influencing this trend have been:

(1) *Increased income*, which has led to a swing in expenditure towards the more expensive processed foods and towards consumer durable goods.

(2) *An increase in car ownership*, which has enabled people to move from the city centre to the outer suburbs. Shops have followed, not only to be near their customers, but also to obtain larger sites with parking facilities. In doing so, they avoid the high rents and congestion of city centre sites.

The car has also made customers more mobile, enabling them to travel to good shopping centres where they can purchase all their requirements at a single stop.

(3) *An increase in the number of married women going to work*, which has promoted the demand for convenience foods and labour-saving devices. It has also led to the reduction of the number of shopping expeditions which can be made, and this trend has been helped by the wider ownership of refrigerators and deep-freezers.

These factors are likely to remain important in the future. It seems probable, therefore, that new supermarkets will take the form of discount stores or hypermarkets selling a wider range of products whose profit margins are larger than those on groceries. Moreover, if planning permission is forthcoming, these new stores will develop outside the town. Cash-and-carry warehouses may also be open to those consumers who can buy in bulk and transport their goods.

Such changes are likely to be at the expense of the medium-sized business, for the retail trade will largely consist of small local retailers offering convenience services and the large out-of-town shopping centre.

VI. IS THE 'MIDDLEMAN' NECESSARY?

The people who come between the actual manufacturer and the consumer, the wholesalers and retailers, are often referred to as 'middlemen', though more usually the term is applied only to the wholesaler. Criticism of 'middlemen', however, is often heard. Indeed some critics even go so far as to say that middlemen are unnecessary, while all are at least of the opinion that for what they do they take too large a share of the selling price of the good. It is argued, for instance, that car distributors who receive $17\frac{1}{2}$ per cent of the selling price for acting as wholesalers and retailers between the consumer and the manufacturer (or approximately 5 to 10 per cent when they leave the retailing to agents), are receiving too much, and that the price of the car would be reduced were they eliminated by establishing direct contact between the manufacturer and the consumer.

But we have seen that wholesalers and retailers do perform

useful functions. Farmers, for instance, although they complain bitterly about the system, have great need of them. In the first place, since farmers produce many different products for many different kinds of consumer, the marketing services of the middleman are essential. Secondly, farm products are often bulky relative to their value, and transport facilities, which the farmers themselves do not possess, are necessary to get them to the consumer. Thirdly, some goods are highly perishable and need to be sold quickly, while others are of varying quality and therefore require grading. Above all, production, instead of being continuous throughout the year, occurs irregularly, while from year to year it is subject to gluts and shortages. Indeed, this last factor makes farmers so weak in marketing such commodities as milk and potatoes that the government now effects a general control through its Marketing Boards.

The suggestion that wholesalers and retailers could be eliminated altogether is, therefore, ridiculous and reveals ignorance of their respective functions. Through them, as we have seen, the farmer obtains the advantages of the division of labour and large-scale production in the specialised functions of marketing his products. We can illustrate this further by returning to our example of the distribution of cars. In the same way as it pays a manufacturer to let other firms make the tyres, sparking-plugs, electrical equipment, etc., so it is advantageous to him to leave the actual selling of the car to the customer to a separate firm. In fact, the distribution of a good by the wholesaler and retailer can best be regarded as just another instance of the division of labour in production or, put more precisely, of vertical dis-integration. Any producer who thought he could sell more cheaply by by-passing the middleman would do so; but the isolated attempts of farmers to do this in Great Britain have not been happy.

However, this general case for middlemen does not mean that all criticism of them is unjustified. Sometimes their profit margins are too high. This may occur through the perpetuation of antiquated methods or by the playing-off by a single middleman of one small producer, such as a farmer, against another (hence the formation of producers' co-operatives).

In recent years, there has been a tendency for the wholesaler to be eliminated. This has been due to: (i) the growth of large shops, such as the co-operative society, multiple store and supermarket, which can order in bulk; (ii) the development of road transport, which reduces the necessity of holding large stocks; (iii) the desire of manufacturers to retain some control over retailing outlets in order to ensure that their products are pushed or that a high standard of service, freshness, etc., is maintained; (iv) the practice of branding many products, which eliminates many specialised functions. In other cases, however, the elimination of the wholesaler has been confined to those goods which are of high value, such as furniture and television sets; to circumstances where the producer and retailer are close together, as with the market gardener who supplies the local shop; and cases where the manufacturer does his own retailing.

On the other hand, the wholesaler has, as we have seen, responded to this challenge by developing in two main directions: (a) the cash-and-carry warehouse, sometimes called 'the retailers' supermarket'; (b) becoming the organiser of a voluntary chain of retailers, who are supplied, and to some extent controlled, by him.

Selling direct to consumers by the manufacturer occurs chiefly where: (a) he wishes to push his product (e.g. beer and footwear), or ensure a standard of advice and service (e.g. sewing machines); (b) the personal service element is important (e.g. made-to-measure clothing); (c) he is a small-scale producer–retailer, often selling a perishable good (e.g. cakes and pastries), or serving a local area (e.g. printing); (d) so wide a range of goods is produced that a whole chain of shops can be fully stocked (e.g. Lyons, Unigate); (e) the good is highly technical or made to individual specifications (e.g. machinery).

VII. MARKETS

In the above discussion we have emphasised the useful nature of the functions performed by persons, not only in the manufacture of the goods, but also in the various stages of distribution to the final consumer. The full process of production as defined above, however, necessitates a multitude of exchanges.

Almost every person engaged in production acts as both a buyer and a seller. The manufacturer buys raw materials and sells his finished product; the wholesaler buys the finished product in bulk and sells it in small quantities; the retailer buys in small quantities and sells to the final consumer. There must be a means, therefore, by which buyers and sellers can be brought together in order that they may effect exchanges. The requirement is met by what is known as the 'market'. Thus we have many different markets—organised produce markets for basic foodstuffs and raw materials (such as the Rubber Exchange and Liverpool Cotton Exchange); markets for money and capital (such as exist in the City of London); markets for labour (such as the government Employment Exchanges and private secretarial and domestic servants employment agencies); wholesale markets (such as the Smithfield meat market); and retail markets which exist in each town and may be organised by a large departmental store, a barrow-boy or the government. In the market, a price is arrived at by which the amount demanded is brought into line with the supplies coming on to the market over a given period of time. How this price is arrived at will be described in detail in the next chapter. Here we shall examine a little more closely what economists mean by the term 'market'.

Generally speaking, the term 'market' calls to mind the place where goods are bought and sold, for example Covent Garden (the wholesale market for fruit, flowers and vegetables), the Baltic Exchange (the chief market in grain), the Stock Exchange (the market for securities). This idea of a market, however, is a relic from the Middle Ages when, because of transport difficulties, trading was localised in one particular spot. Many towns had, and still have, their weekly markets for local produce.

With the development of transport and communications, the area of the market has been extended. For example, the market for wheat, cotton and wool is now a world market. Alongside these developments there has been a revolution in the methods of buying and selling some commodities, for instead of inspecting on the spot the quantities which are to be bought, the commodity is 'graded' or a sample is delivered. Hence a dealer in raw cotton is able to order a certain grade knowing full well what its quality—length of fibre, texture, tensile property—will be.

Therefore, we can no longer speak of a market as being that particular place where the goods are bought and sold, for the whole business might be conducted by telephone. The organisation by which buyers and sellers are brought together may be formal or informal. Moreover the economist is chiefly interested in the market from the point of view of its function— the fixing of the price of the particular commodity—and the actual organisation is studied chiefly from this aspect. Thus a 'market' is defined as an area over which buyers and sellers are in such close and regular contact with one another that the price obtained for a commodity in one part of that area affects the price paid for it in other parts. The result is that the same price, allowing for costs of transport, tends to be established for the same commodity within the area.

In connection with this definition, however, it is necessary to emphasise that it refers to the same commodity only, that is, the goods are similar in all respects or, in other words, they are perfect substitutes for each other. Thus, a difference in the time of delivery between two goods means that they are really different commodities. Purchasers of ships, computers and machines usually ask for a date of delivery. If that date is too far ahead, the order may not be placed because, as far as they are concerned, the machine which can be delivered out of stock is a different commodity to one for which they have to wait twelve months. Where goods, such as wheat, cotton and wool tops, are physically capable of being graded, all units within the same grade are homogeneous and are the 'same commodity' as defined above.

Today modern transport is so extensive and so rapid that many commodities have a 'world' market; that is, a change in the price of the commodity in one part of the world affects the price in the rest of the world. Such commodities are wheat, frozen meat, oils, fats and the basic raw materials such as wool, cotton, mineral oil, rubber, tin, lead, zinc and uranium. What are the necessary requirements for a commodity to have such a wide market?

In the first place, there must be a wide demand. The basic necessities of life (e.g. wheat, frozen meat, wool, cotton) answer this requirement. Goods, however, which have only a local demand, such as national costumes, books translated into little-used languages, souvenirs, postcards of local views and foods which satisfy local tastes, do not have a wide demand.

Secondly, commodities must be physically capable of being transported. Land and buildings are almost impossible to transport. Some goods, such as beer, do not travel well. A customer may require a personal service from the producer, but the distance he can travel is usually limited. Labour, too, is particularly immobile, workers being reluctant, in spite of the attraction of a higher wage, to move to a different country or even to a different locality (see Chapter 24). Closely connected with this is the action of governments who, by a tariff policy or import quotas, may effectively debar certain commodities from entering the country. Today, the movement of capital out of the United Kingdom is restricted by the government.

Thirdly, the costs of transport must not be prohibitive—they must be small in relation to the value of the commodity. Suppose, for instance, that it costs £2 to transport 16 km 1,000 bricks worth £12 at the kiln, and that the cost of transport rises proportionately to mileage. As soon as the distance reaches 96 km, therefore, the cost of transport equals the total value of the bricks and any greater distance would almost certainly be prohibitive. With diamonds, however, the cost of transporting them even many thousands of miles is a negligible fraction of their value. Hence the market for bricks is small, whilst that for diamonds is world-wide. Similarly, wheat and oil are cheap to transport compared with coal because they are more easily loaded and unloaded, though as sea transport is the cheapest form of transport, coal mined near the coast in Northumberland, Durham and South Wales can be, and is, sent long distances.

Lastly, the commodity must be durable. Goods which perish quickly, such as milk, bread, fresh cream and strawberries, cannot be sent long distances. Nevertheless, modern developments, such as the refrigeration and canning of goods and the development of air freight transport, are extending the area of the market.

Perfect and Imperfect Markets

In any one market, the price of a commodity ruling in any part of it affects the price paid for the same commodity in another part. Hence the same price (allowing for costs of transport) tends to be established for the same commodity, provided that all units are homogeneous as defined above. Where in any one market, price differences for the same commodity tend to be eliminated quickly and easily, we say that the market is a 'perfect market'.

For a market to be perfect, certain conditions have to be fulfilled. In the first place, it is necessary that both buyers and sellers have exact knowledge of the prices which are being paid elsewhere in the market. The development of communications, particularly the telephone, has facilitated this. Secondly, both buyers and sellers must base their actions solely on price. This means that neither buyers nor sellers have a preference to purchase from or to sell to one particular person because of loyalty or mere unreasonableness. If, for instance, one seller suddenly puts up the price of his good, then his customers immediately go to one of the other sellers in the market who are cheaper. Similarly, if he were to lower his price, customers would so flock to him that he would sell out quickly unless he raised his price to that asked elsewhere.

Examples of perfect markets are the precious-stones market of Hatton Garden and, above all, the organised produce markets and the Stock Exchange, both of which will be described later. In these markets the two essential conditions are fulfilled. The buyers and sellers are usually professional dealers who make their income by watching prices carefully and buying accordingly. It is essential, therefore, for them to be acquainted with any fluctuations in price in any part of the market and the result of their operations is that variations in price are quickly eliminated.

But these conditions are not usually met with in other markets. Neither is there perfect knowledge amongst buyers and sellers, nor do they act solely on the basis of price. The ordinary housewife, for instance, cannot always afford the time to 'shop around the market' by going from one shop to another comparing the prices of her everyday purchases, though it is noticeable that she is usually much more careful when spending on the more expensive goods bought at infrequent intervals. In the same way, shopkeepers do not always have the means to know what other shopkeepers are charging for similar goods. In fact, one of the advantages to the shopkeeper of selling branded goods at a fixed minimum price is that he does not have to worry about the price-fixing policy of his competitors. Moreover, purchasers are influenced by considerations other than price when deciding from whom to buy. Thus they may continue to deal with one particular trader even though he is charging a slightly higher price simply because they are loyal to someone who has given them good service in the past. It is this personal relationship which is the basis of the 'goodwill' built up by a business. Moreover, although two goods may be virtually the same physically, in the mind of the purchaser they may be entirely different. This process of making the good slightly different from other producers' is known as 'product differentiation', and over one-half of present-day advertising is directed to convincing people of the superiority of these individual brands of goods. Such advertising, therefore, renders the market less perfect and should be contrasted with the other type of advertising where the aim is to inform the public. This latter type tends to widen the market and to render it more perfect.

The result is that only where the market is composed of many professional dealers is it likely to be fully perfect. In other markets, price differences persist and such markets are said to be 'imperfect'. Imperfect markets are often found in retailing.

VIII. ORGANISED MARKETS

As we have shown above, the market for certain commodities is a very wide one, largely because they have a high value relative to their cost of transport and are non-perishable over a long time. Moreover many of these commodities are in general and constant demand, either because they form a basic raw material for the manufacture of a widely-used finished good or because they constitute one of the main foodstuffs or beverages for a large section of the world's people. Such commodities, therefore, figure prominently in international trade and it is these with which we are concerned in the following discussion.

England's foreign trade commenced with the export of raw wool in the thirteenth century and it was extended by the subsequent development of the Chartered Companies. These were based on London and it was here that merchants gathered to buy and sell the produce which the Companies' ships brought from abroad. This commerce conducted by London not only grew larger as trade extended but became more continuous as supplies of commodities came forward at different times of the year from different parts of the world. It was natural, therefore, that in London the same buyers and sellers would meet regularly to conduct business and to exchange information. Their first regular meeting-places were the coffee-houses of the City. Thus the 'Jerusalem', founded in Bishopsgate in 1625, became the centre for those merchants trading with the Mediterranean and the Levant, while 'Garraways', which popularised the drinking of tea in England from 1657 onwards, was patronised by dealers in tea and wool and provided the site for the first fur sales of the Hudson's Bay Company.

From these regular meetings of merchants in the coffee-houses of London, organised markets developed. The big change, however, came about with the expansion of the United Kingdom's international trade following the Industrial Revolution. During the nineteenth century, the United Kingdom became the greatest importing and exporting nation of the world. London, her chief port and commercial city, not only imported the goods which were required for the people of her own country but, assisted by the fact that British ships were the great carriers of the world's trade, built up an important entrepôt business, acting as a 'go-between' in the distribution of such commodities as tea, sugar, hides, skins and wool, to many other countries, particularly those of Western Europe.

Hence during this period the formal 'organised markets' developed. These markets are distinguished from other sorts of market in that buying and selling takes place in a recognised building, business is governed by agreed rules and conventions, and often only a limited number of recognised persons are allowed to engage in transactions. Generally the public are excluded, even from watching. They are thus a very highly developed form of market and today London has Exchanges or Auction Centres for the buying and selling of such commodities as rubber, wool, tea, coffee, furs, metals (tin, copper, lead and zinc), grain and shipping freights (the Baltic Exchange). It must not be thought, however, that such organised produce markets exist only in London. Because of the development of its trade with the New World, Liverpool has Exchanges for cotton and grain which are as important as London's Exchanges, while most of the large trading countries such as the United States (wheat, maize, and cotton) and Australia and New Zealand (wool) have their own Exchanges. In fact, with the development of shipping services by other countries from the end of the nineteenth century, the tendency has been for trade which formerly passed through London to be sent direct from the producing countries to markets nearer the consuming populations. Nevertheless, in addition to the goods which are re-exported, a considerable amount of buying and selling in certain commodities, such as sugar, metals and grain, is still conducted in London although the goods go directly to other countries and never actually pass through the port. Payment is received by the merchants, however, for the business they transact, and this forms a part of the 'invisible exports' which Britain receives for services rendered to other countries.

Broadly speaking, organised markets fulfil three main functions. In the first place, they enable manufacturers and wholesalers to obtain supplies of raw materials and commodities easily, quickly and at the competitive market prices. Markets provide a centre where expert buyers and sellers, each having very complete knowledge concerning the particular commodity in which he deals, can meet in close contact for the purpose of dealing. In them, price is very sensitive to any change in demand and supply and, as already indicated, they are then 'perfect markets'.

Secondly, for those commodities which can be graded very accurately, these markets provide a means whereby persons who would be adversely affected by a change in the prices of these commodities can protect themselves from heavy loss. Thus the producers of rubber or tin would prefer to know what price they will receive for their output before it is actually delivered to and sold on the market, and so they have to guard themselves against a fall in the price in the meantime. On the other hand, a cotton spinner has to protect himself from a rise in the price of raw materials between the time of quoting a price for his yarn and the time of manufacture. This is achieved through what is known as 'hedging' on the 'futures' market.

Where a good is bought today for delivery today, the deal is known as a 'spot' transaction and the price agreed upon is the 'spot price'. With many goods, however, it is possible to buy today for delivery sometime in the future. The good may not actually be in stock, but the seller contracts to obtain and deliver the good at the agreed time. Such a deal is known as a 'futures' transaction, and the price agreed upon as the 'future' or 'forward' price. For a commodity to be dealt in on a 'futures' market, certain conditions must be fulfilled. These are: (a) that the commodity is durable, thereby enabling stocks to be carried; (b) that the commodity can be easily graded and its quality determined by tests which yield almost identical results without the aid of samples when applied by different experts; (c) that dealings are sufficiently frequent to occupy professional dealers; (d) that the commodity is one which is subject to price fluctuations.

Where 'future' dealings take place the market is usually divided between brokers and dealers. The broker merely carries out the wishes of his client, whereas the dealer is the person who uses his expert knowledge to make a profit on what he considers will be the future price of the commodity. If he thinks that the price is likely to rise, he is known as a 'bull', and he will buy and accumulate stocks now in order to sell at a profit later. On the other hand, if he thinks the price is going to fall, he is known as a 'bear' and he will sell stocks, even if he does not have them, hoping to buy at a lower price when delivery is due. At any time, a dealer will quote a price (according to the view he takes of the future movement of prices) at which he is prepared to buy or sell at some future date the particular good in which he specialises. Thus a cotton grower can cover himself against the risk of a fall in price by selling his produce forward at a price which will cover his cost of production and yield a reasonable profit, while a cotton spinner can quote a weaver a price for yarn and guard himself against loss by buying the raw cotton forward. Thus both are covered against adverse price changes, the risk being accepted by the dealer.

In doing this, the dealer usually performs the third main function of organised markets—the evening-out of price fluctuations due to changes in demand and supply. At a time when an increase in supply would cause the price to fall considerably, he adds his demand to the normal demand in order to build up his stocks and therefore keeps the price up. On the other hand, when the good is in short supply, he releases his stocks of the commodity and so prevents a violent rise in price. In this respect the dealer performs a parallel function to the wholesaler. The difficulty is that speculation on the future price may dominate the real forces which influence it and then prices are subject to violent fluctuations in response to waves of optimism and pessimism.

PART III

WHAT TO PRODUCE

CHAPTER 8

PRICE IN THE FREE MARKET:
ITS FORMATION AND FUNCTIONS

I. VALUE AND PRICE

As soon as we wish to know what to produce, there immediately arises the question: 'How can people indicate what they want?' A mere statement of want is meaningless, for as we showed in Chapter 1, people are rarely satisfied and thus always *want* something. A want is significant in economics only when a person is prepared to give up something in order to satisfy it. As the strength of the different wants varies, so will the amounts which people are willing to give up in order to satisfy them. We can say, in other words, that people are willing to give up different amounts for different goods because these goods have a different *value* to them. For example, if Miss 'A' is willing to work 5 hours for the money which will buy a hat, we say that the value of the hat to her is greater than the value of the 5 hours' leisure forgone. Value therefore means the rate at which a particular good or service will exchange for other goods. It is important to note, however, that while a good to have value must be capable of satisfying a want, a good which satisfies a want need not necessarily have value. For example, air satisfies a want; but, in normal circumstances, the supply of it is so great that nobody will give anything in exchange for it. Because it has no power to command other goods in exchange, it has, in economics, no value. We call such goods 'free goods'. All other goods are 'scarce goods' implying, in economics, no more than that their supply is not unlimited.

In modern economic systems we rarely exchange goods directly against other goods. We make use of a 'go-between', or, as it is usually said, a medium of exchange. This medium of exchange is money and the values of goods are expressed in terms of money. In other words, we *price* the goods and services. Price can be defined, therefore, as the value of a commodity or service measured in terms of the standard monetary unit. By comparing prices, we can compare the *rates* at which different goods can be exchanged.

It should be noted that *price* is not the same as value. For instance, if *all* prices rose or fell, the values of the goods would not have changed; it would simply mean that the value of money had fallen or risen.

PRELIMINARY ASSUMPTIONS

The price of an article depends upon two distinct sets of forces operating in a market, namely demand and supply. We shall examine each of these in turn. In order to simplify our analysis, we must assume three conditions:

(1) A perfect market.
(2) *Perfect competition;* this means that there is an absence of 'monopoly' on both the demand and supply side—no one buyer being able, by his own action, to influence the price by the fact that his demand is so large, or any one seller being able to do likewise by deliberately withholding supplies. This implies that there must be a large number of buyers and sellers.
(3) The government does not interfere with the market, e.g. by price control. (It can enforce contracts, test product quality and ensure fair dealing.)

II. DEMAND

Demand in economics is the desire to possess something and the willingness and the ability to pay a certain price in order to possess it. In other words, it is not merely a wish or a desire but an effective demand, that is, demand backed by money. Thus a person's demand for tomatoes is what he is able and willing to buy at a given price, *not* what he would like to buy *if* he could afford them. Furthermore, it must be a demand at a price over a certain unit of time. This can be a year, week or day, but since most workers are paid by the week and, therefore, most housewives plan their expenditure on a weekly basis, it is usual to take the week as the unit of time. Summing up, the demand for anything at a price is the amount of it which will be bought per unit of time at that price. It can be expressed as an individual or community demand.

What determines the extent of the demand for a good? In answering this question it is necessary to distinguish two separate factors. These are:

1. Price.   2. The Conditions of Demand.

1. PRICE, WHERE THE CONDITIONS OF DEMAND (TO BE EXAMINED LATER) REMAIN UNCHANGED

Generally, we should expect more of a good to be demanded the lower the price. For example, suppose a housewife estimates that she has £1.20 to spend each week on the main breakfast item for a family of four. We shall imagine, too, that one pound of tomatoes will provide a breakfast for the whole family. Now when tomatoes are 24 pence per lb., one-fifth of her weekly breakfast allowance has to be given up in order to buy enough tomatoes for the family's breakfast. Our housewife therefore decides that she can afford one pound of tomatoes per week but only for a salad. For breakfast, she buys eggs which, say at 4p each, she considers are better value for her money.

But what happens when the price of tomatoes falls to 20p per lb.? Now only one-sixth of her breakfast allowance has to be given up in order to buy a tomato breakfast. This tempts her, for she thinks that tomatoes would be a nice change from other dishes such as eggs, which she still needs nearly one-eighth of her allowance to buy. In short, the terms on which she can obtain tomatoes have improved relative to eggs. Hence the fall in their price induces her to buy an extra pound of tomatoes and four fewer eggs. Indeed, if the price of tomatoes falls low enough, they may represent such 'good value' to her that she will devote some of her weekly housekeeping allowance to buying them for bottling. It can be noted here that this example illustrates an important point—that *all prices are relative.*

Similarly, we should expect the housewife to buy fewer tomatoes as the price rises. In both cases, however, it must be emphasised that changes in conditions of demand have been excluded. For instance, to isolate the effect of a, fall in price on the demand for tomatoes we must assume that the price change does not coincide with a sudden cold spell causing people to eat fewer salads, and therefore fewer tomatoes. Thus the weather is assumed unchanged.

For each individual housewife, we can draw up a schedule showing the quantity of tomatoes she would buy at each particular price. Not every housewife's *demand schedule* will be identical, but if we total the demand schedules of all the housewives shopping in the same market we get a demand schedule, i.e. a table setting out the quantities of tomatoes that would be bought at various prices per unit of time in that market. A purely imaginary demand schedule for Nonsuch Market might be as follows:

Price of tomatoes (pence per lb.)	Quantity demanded (lbs.)
24	500
20	1,800
16	3,000
12	4,000
8	5,000
4	7,000

This information can be shown graphically as follows:

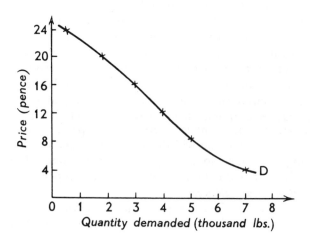

The above is the normal shape of the demand curve given the conditions of demand. It is a single curve sloping downwards from left to right, showing that, as price falls, demand expands, and, conversely, as price rises, demand contracts.

2. THE CONDITIONS OF DEMAND, PRICE ASSUMED TO BE GIVEN

The demand for a good may alter although there has been no change in price. This is because what are termed 'the conditions of demand' have altered. These conditions of demand may alter for the following reasons:

1. *A change in the prices of other goods and services*

Because our incomes are limited, nearly all goods, in that they compete for our limited income, are to some extent substitutes for one another. When the prices of other goods fall, the particular good under discussion becomes *relatively dearer*, and therefore less of it is demanded. When the prices of other goods rise, the particular good under discussion becomes relatively cheaper, and therefore more of it is demanded.

But the effect on the demand for the particular good is, as we have already shown, likely to be more pronounced where the good whose price has changed is a close substitute. Thus when the price of apples falls, people will buy more apples, thereby causing a falling off in the demand for pears. Secondly, where goods are 'jointly demanded' a change in the price of one good has a pronounced effect on the demand for the other. For example, a fall in the price of cars results in more cars being purchased, and eventually this leads to an increase in the demand for tyres and petrol.

2. *Changes in tastes and preferences*

Tastes and preferences may change for various reasons. Seventy-five per cent more bottles of squash are sold in summer than in winter; a new fashion, such as denims, brings an increase in the demand for certain materials; a successful advertising campaign, e.g. for washing powders, will cause people to demand one type of good in preference to another; new inventions, such as colour television and pocket calculators, induce people to spend their incomes differently.

3. *Changes in real income*

Real income increases by roughly 1 to 3 per cent each year. As incomes increase, the tendency is to spend a smaller proportion on foodstuffs and necessities, and a greater proportion on luxuries. Thus, compared with ten years ago, more is now being spent on motoring, cine-cameras and hairdressing, and less on bicycles and cinemas.

4. *Changes in the state of trade*

When trade is good, entrepreneurs are keen to buy new machines, expand factories and so on. At such times, too, income is high and so consumers' demand generally increases.

5. *Changes in the distribution of wealth*

Since the war the incomes of wage-earners have increased relatively to other incomes, while persons with fixed incomes have in comparison lost. There has also been an approach, through heavy income tax and death duties, to more equality in incomes. The result is a fall in the demand for the very expensive luxury goods (e.g. large houses and estates with high upkeep costs), and a rise in the demand for the cheaper luxuries which now come within the range of many people who could not afford them before (e.g. holidays abroad).

6. *Changes in the size and composition of the population*

A population which is growing rapidly, either through an increase in the birth rate or by immigration, will need to be provided with new schools, new houses, new gas and water services, and so on, to satisfy the ever-increasing demand. A population which is stationary or declining, however, need only improve its existing schools, etc., and does not need to worry about increasing them. Thus a larger proportion of its labour and material resources can be devoted to the production of goods for immediate consumption. Moreover, as we have already seen, a falling birth rate will eventually bring about an ageing population. This changes the demand for various goods.

A large inflow of immigrants, who bring their own particular customs with them, may also change demand. Thus the Jews who came to England before and during the war, owing to persecution in Germany, increased the demand for kosher meat wherever they settled. Indeed it is the effect on demand of a change in religion which is referred to when, in *The Merchant of Venice*, Jessica says: 'In converting Jews to Christians, you raise the price of pork.' (Act III, Scene 5).

7. *Expectations regarding future price changes*

If people think that the price of a good is likely to rise, they will buy as soon as possible, and vice versa. Thus pre-Budget expectation of an increase in purchase tax will increase the demand for a good, but there is little business after the tax has risen.

8. *Government policy*

The government affects the demand for a good in many ways. Directly, it is itself today a large spender, varying its demand for strategic materials, defence equipment, etc., according to its estimate of the prevailing international situation. Indirectly, it affects consumers' demand by adjusting taxation, regulating hire-purchase terms, and so on.

What effect will a change in the conditions of demand have on the demand curve? Suppose there has been an increase in the demand for tomatoes because a sudden spell of hot weather has led to more salads being demanded. Now more tomatoes will be demanded at the old price, or, looking at it in a slightly different way, the same amount of tomatoes will be demanded even if the price is higher. We therefore have a new demand schedule, which is as follows:

Price of tomatoes (pence per lb.)	Quantity demanded (lbs.)
24	2,400
20	4,000
16	5,000
12	6,000
8	7,400
4	9,800

At a price of 12p per lb., 4,000 lbs. were originally demanded. Now owing to the heat-wave, 6,000 are demanded at this same price. Or, looking at it in a slightly different way, if the price

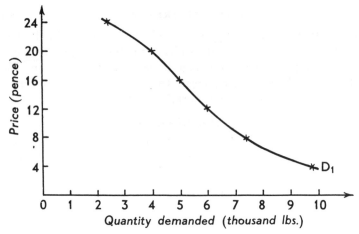

rose to 20p per lb., 4,000 lbs. would still be demanded. We can see that the new demand curve, D_1, is to the right of the old one, D. Similarly, with a fall in demand, the demand curve would shift to the left of the old one. The important point to note is that, whereas the effect of *price* on demand is to fix the *slope* of the demand curve, the effect of the *conditions of demand* is to fix its *position*.

III. SUPPLY

In the same way as we gave demand an exact meaning, so we must be careful to define supply. We say that the supply of anything at a given price is the amount of it which will be offered for sale per unit of time at that price.

What determines the extent of the supply of a good? Once again we have to distinguish two separate factors:

   1. Price.   2. The Conditions of Supply.

1. PRICE, WHERE THE CONDITIONS OF SUPPLY (TO BE EXAMINED LATER) REMAIN UNCHANGED

The motive of supply is to make a profit. Generally, therefore, we should expect more of the good to be supplied the higher the price. For example, we can imagine a market gardener who produces a small quantity of tomatoes per week. As the price increases, so he sends more to market and keeps fewer for his own use. In the same way, a manufacturer, who has to keep a watch on his costs of production, can afford to pay increased wages and increased prices for raw materials (in order to attract labour and materials from other uses), as the price of his product rises. We must emphasise, however, that changes in the conditions of supply have been excluded. For instance, to isolate the effect of a rise in price on the supply of tomatoes we must assume that the rise does not coincide with an abnormal frost which kills off the tomato plants and spoils those tomatoes that are already ripe.

For each market we can draw up a schedule showing the quantity of a good which will be offered for sale at each particular price. The supply schedule for tomatoes may be as follows:

Price of tomatoes (pence per lb.)	Quantity supplied (lbs.)
24	8,000
20	6,300
16	5,000
12	4,000
8	2,500
4	1,400

This information can be shown graphically as follows:

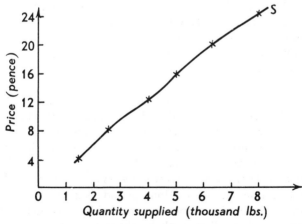

The above is the normal shape of the supply curve, given the conditions of supply. It is a single curve sloping upwards from left to right, showing that, as price rises, supply expands, and, conversely, as price falls, supply contracts.

We can now state the *first law of price*. Usually a larger quantity of a commodity will be demanded at a lower price than at a higher price, and a larger quantity will be offered for sale at a higher price than at a lower price.

There is, however, an important difference between demand and supply curves. Demand responds much more easily and quickly to a change in price than supply. For instance if the price of tomatoes falls, people can adjust their demand for tomatoes right away. But producers do not find it so easy to vary the supply of tomatoes. They can withhold some from the market, building up their stocks instead; but since tomatoes perish quickly, stocks cannot be held indefinitely. It takes time for the producer to vary his supply in the sense of the amount that is produced.

Economists, therefore, often find it desirable to divide the period of supply into two stages.

(1) *The short period*, that is the period during which supply is altered, not by making any adjustment to fixed capital (buildings, plant, machinery, etc.) but by altering the output of such fixed capital as already exists by adjusting the hours it is worked, the amount of raw materials used, and so on. For example, suppose there is a temporary increase in the demand for motor cars. As we shall see later, the result in a free market is that the price of cars rises. It now pays manufacturers to offer increased prices for sheet steel, to take on more labour and to pay overtime rates, or even to work double-shifts. Where the increase in demand is short-lived, nothing further will be done.

(2) *The long period*. If the increase in demand (and, therefore, of price), is expected to be permanent, it will probably pay to invest fresh capital in production, so that the total capacity to produce, that is the fixed capital, is increased. More machines will be bought, the factory extended, additional skilled workers trained, extra offices built, and so on. But this will take time, and so the 'long period' is defined as the period of time sufficient for output to be varied by making adjustments to fixed capital. Thus with a rubber tree, which needs seven years to mature, the 'long period' is very long indeed. But

when the new capacity comes into production, supply will increase and price fall (see page 165).

2. The Conditions of Supply, Price Assumed to be Given

The supply of a good may alter although there has been no change in price. This is because the conditions of supply have altered, and this may occur for the following reasons:

1. Changes in the cost of production

The cost of producing a commodity depends upon the prices of the various factors used. A fall in the price of any of these factors (e.g. a reduction in the wages of workers or in the cost of raw materials) will reduce production costs. Conversely, a rise in the price of any of these factors will increase production costs. In both cases there has been a change in the conditions of supply. When production costs fall, it costs less to supply the same quantity, or, looking at it in a different way, more can be offered for sale at the old price. The result is that we have to draw a new supply curve to the right of the old one. When costs rise, the new supply curve is to the left of the old one.

2. Technical improvements

New inventions and improved methods of production enable a given amount of a commodity to be produced at a lower cost.

3. Changes outside the control of man

The weather, storms, floods and droughts affect particularly the production of agricultural goods. Fire and war may destroy capital equipment (e.g. a steelworks), and affect supply.

4. Taxation and subsidies

Taxation on output, or on the possession or use of a factor of production (e.g. an employer's higher contribution to the insurance stamps of his employees) will raise costs of production. A subsidy on production has the opposite effect.

5. The discovery of new, or the exhaustion of old, supplies of raw materials and power

Let us summarise the effect of a change in the conditions of supply on the position of the supply curve. If, as a result of the change in conditions, costs of production are reduced, the same amount can be supplied at a lower price, or, which is the same thing, more can be supplied at the old price. On the other hand, if costs of production rise, the same amount can be supplied only at a higher price. Suppose, for example, that there is a fall in the wages of gardeners and in the price of fertilisers. This means that it costs less to grow tomatoes and hence we have a new supply schedule, as follows:

Price of tomatoes (pence per lb.)	Quantity of tomatoes supplied (lbs.)
24	10,000
20	8,600
16	7,200
12	6,000
8	5,000
4	3,800

The new schedule shows that, whereas before only 5,000 lbs. would be supplied at 16p per lb., 7,200 lbs. would now be supplied at that price. Or, looking at it the other way, whereas before 5,000 lbs. were supplied at 16p per lb., these can now be supplied at 8p per lb. The new supply curve, S_1, is to the right of the old one.

Similarly, with a rise in the costs of production, the curve

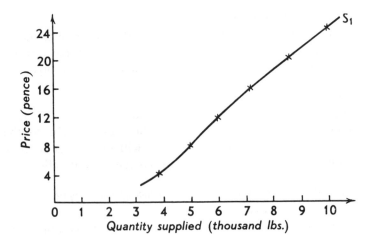

would shift to the left of the old one. Once again, the effect of price on supply is to fix the slope of the curve; the conditions of supply fix its position.

IV. DEMAND, SUPPLY AND PRICE

So far we have plotted demand and supply curves on separate graphs. By measuring both demand and supply along the x-axis, however, it is possible to plot the curve on the same graph. Since the curves usually slope in opposite directions, they will cut each other.

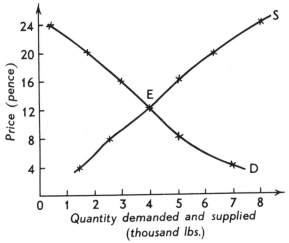

It can be seen from the above diagram that at the point where they cut, E, with price 12p per lb., the same quantity, 4,000 lbs., is both demanded and supplied. Therefore, we say that at the price of 12p, demand and supply are in equilibrium and that, therefore, 12p per lb., is the 'equilibrium price'.

If the demand and supply curves drawn above represent at a particular moment the conditions of demand for and supply of tomatoes, then, provided there is no change in those conditions, the price of tomatoes tends, in a free market, to settle at the equilibrium price. We can illustrate this statement by seeing what happens when price is above or below the equilibrium price. Suppose the price is 16p per lb. At this price 3,000 lbs. are demanded, but 5,000 lbs. are supplied. There is thus an excess of supply over demand of 2,000 lbs. This means that this excess supply cannot be sold at 16p per lb. In order to sell it, price must fall and, as this happens, so demand will expand while the amount offered for sale contracts. This continues until the fall in price is no longer necessary, that is at 12p per lb., where demand and supply are equal. If, on the other hand, the price is 8p, we have an excess of demand over supply of 2,500 lbs. In this case there are queues in the shops and shop-keepers soon sell out of tomatoes entirely, many people being unable to buy. The shopkeeper, therefore, raises his price which contracts demand and brings forth more supplies, and this price rise continues until the price of 12p per lb. is reached, when demand and supply are once again equal. The function of price is thus to 'ration' out scarce goods.

We can now state the *second law of price*: price tends to make equal the amount which buyers wish to buy and the amount which sellers are prepared to offer for sale.

V. THE EFFECT OF CHANGES IN THE CONDITIONS OF DEMAND AND SUPPLY ON PRICE

1. THE EFFECT OF A CHANGE IN THE CONDITIONS OF DEMAND ON THE EQUILIBRIUM PRICE

Suppose that there is an increase in the demand for tomatoes because a sudden warm spell causes people to eat more salads. The demand curve now shifts (as we have already seen) from D to D_1.

The new demand curve (D_1) now cuts the supply curve at E_1, thus giving a new equilibrium price of 16p per lb.—higher than the old one. Supply has expanded from 4,000 to 5,000 lbs.

Similarly, if the demand for tomatoes decreased (because, for instance, a fall in the price of eggs caused people to eat more eggs for breakfast in place of fried tomatoes), the new demand curve would be to the left of the old one and would cut the supply curve so as to give a lower equilibrium price. Thus another function of price is to indicate to suppliers whether more or less of the good is required.

From the above we derive the *third law of price*: an increase

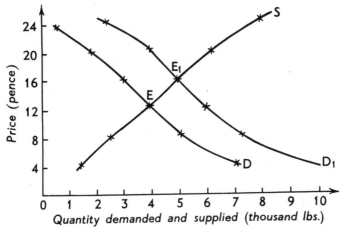

in demand tends to raise the price and to expand the supply (conditions of supply remaining unchanged). A decrease in demand tends to lower the price and to contract the supply.

2. THE EFFECT OF A CHANGE IN THE CONDITIONS OF SUPPLY ON THE EQUILIBRIUM PRICE

Suppose that there is an increase in the supply of tomatoes because of weather exceptionally favourable to their growth. The supply curve now shifts (as we have already seen) to the right, from S to S_1.

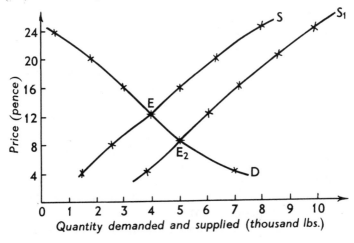

The new supply curve now cuts the demand curve at E_2, thus giving a new equilibrium price of 8p per lb.—lower than the old one. Demand has expanded from 4,000 to 5,000 lbs.

Similarly, if the supply of tomatoes decreased (because, for instance, of a sudden frost), the new supply curve would be to the left of the old one and would cut the demand curve so as to give a higher equilibrium price.

From the above we derive the *fourth law of price*: an increase in supply tends to lower the price and to expand the demand (conditions of demand remaining unchanged). A decrease in supply tends to raise the price and to contract demand.

So far we have assumed, in order to make our explanation easier, that changes in the conditions of demand and supply do not take place at the same time. Of course, in reality this is not always so. It may be that at the very time when supply decreases, demand also increases. For example, the wages of the gardeners growing tomatoes may go up at the same time as people decide to eat more tomatoes. In this case we can say what will happen to price—it will rise. Suppose, however, that at the very moment when supply decreases, demand also decreases. Here the change in supply would raise price but for the fact that the decrease in demand tends to lower it, and we cannot say definitely whether the final price will be higher or lower, for it depends on the relative strengths of the supply and demand changes.

VI. EXERCISES IN DEMAND AND SUPPLY ANALYSIS

Let us take two examples in order to show how we can use this demand and supply analysis to answer specific problems.

(i) *What will be the likely effect on the price of 2-year-old cars if tests for road-worthiness are extended to them?* Our first task is to establish an imaginary existing price. This is done by drawing imaginary demand and supply curves, as in Fig. 10. (Here we use the generally accepted form of diagram, measuring demand and supply in general terms by means of letters, as in geometry.) This price is OP, demand and supply being in equilibrium at quantity OM.

Now the price of a commodity will, as we have seen, alter

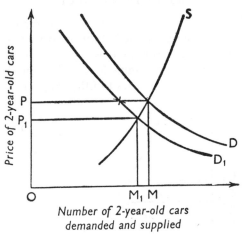

FIG. 10.—The effect of government tests on the price of 2-year-old cars

whenever there is a change in the conditions of demand or supply. Hence our next task is to ask whether either the conditions of demand or supply have changed, being careful to distinguish on which side the change has occurred. In our example, it is obvious that tests will affect the demand for two-year-old cars owing to the additional trouble and expense which will be involved with them. Finally, we have to decide whether it is an increase or decrease in demand or supply by asking the question: 'Will more or less be demanded or supplied at a given price?' According to our answer we put a cross somewhere to the left or right of the original amount and then draw a curve through this cross. In our example, demand will decrease and the new demand curve D_1 will be to the left of the old one. Now we can read off the effect on price, which is lower at OP_1.

It is obvious that a similar reasoning could be applied to analyse like problems, such as the effect on the price of large cars of a substantial rise in the price of petrol. (The reader can test himself by demonstrating why the result would be the same.)

(ii) *What will be the likely immediate effect on the price of mutton of a rise in the price of wool?* We start as before by establishing an existing price OP. But now we have a change in the conditions of supply, for sheep-farmers will be less willing to kill off their

145

lambs and sheep as they can obtain more money for wool. Thus less mutton will be supplied at the old price than formerly, and our cross, and therefore the new supply curve, S_1, is to the left of the old one. The immediate effect on the price of mutton, therefore, is that it rises to OP_1 (Fig. 11).

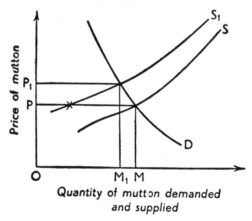

FIG. 11.—The effect on the price of mutton of a rise in the price of wool

Summing up, then, we can say that whenever we wish to see the effect on the price of a good of given events, we have to proceed by an analysis of fluctuations in the *conditions* of demand or supply.

VII. THE FUNCTIONS OF PRICE IN THE FREE MARKET

Our analysis of the formation of price under perfect competition enables us to see more clearly the part played by price in the solution of the 'economic problem'. We can summarise it as follows:

1. PRICE 'RATIONS' OUT THE SCARCE GOODS AND SERVICES AVAILABLE IN THE MARKET AT A PARTICULAR MOMENT

Any good or service having to be produced by some of the limited factors of production is not superabundant and is, therefore, termed 'scarce'. The quantity of a good can be increased by diverting to its production some of the factors used in the production of another good. But this usually takes time and so, at any particular moment, the supply of all goods on the market is relatively fixed. How is this supply to be apportioned amongst all the people who want some of it?

The answer to this question under the price system depends upon the fact that demand responds to a change in price. Generally, if price rises, demand contracts; if price falls, demand expands. Hence a price can be found where demand just equals the available supply—the 'equilibrium' price. Thus, the price system has been introduced to help solve the traffic problem in Central London. Through the device of parking meters, people are made to pay for what was once free parking space.

What happens when the price of a good is controlled, as with certain unfurnished flats at the present time?

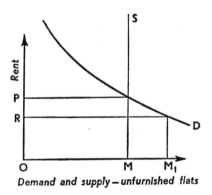

Demand and supply – unfurnished flats

Let us assume that the number of these flats is fixed at OM. The maximum rent that can be charged is controlled at OR. This is below the equilibrium market rent, OP, for otherwise there would be no point in controlling the price.

At rent OR, the demand for these flats is OM_1, but supply is OM. Thus there is an unsatisfied demand equal to MM_1, and only the sitting tenants are lucky. The rest are forced to buy their own houses. These can be obtained (but at high prices) because the price is fixed by demand and supply.

2. Price Indicates Changes in 'Wants'

People's wants are not constant. They vary sometimes from day to day, but more conspicuously from week to week, season to season, and year to year. We have shown that such changes in wants are not the *result* of price changes, but are due to what we describe as a change in the *conditions* of demand. When such a change was depicted by demand curves, a decrease in demand meant that a new curve had to be drawn to the left of the old one, while an increase in demand meant that the new curve had to be drawn to the right of the old one. The decrease in demand produced a fall in price, and the increase produced a rise. Thus, if the conditions under which a good is supplied remain unchanged, a rise in price indicates that people want more of the good relative to other goods, while a fall in price indicates that they want less.

3. Price brings about Variations in Supply in Accordance with these Changes in Wants

The supply of a good on the market at a particular moment is fixed and an equilibrium price is arrived at which will just dispose of that supply. In time, however, the producer can vary the amount of the good he supplies, usually more of the good being supplied at a higher price then at a lower price. Thus if the price obtained in the market does not cover his costs of producing the good, he will contract his supply of it. On the other hand, if the price amply covers his cost of production, then the supply will be expanded. In this way, if there were no changes in the conditions of demand or of supply, equilibrium prices would eventually be established for the whole range of goods and services.

But in Chapter 1 of this book we showed how, at any particular moment, income is limited because the factors of production themselves are also limited. In short, total demand and total supply, when all the factors are employed, can be taken as fixed. The fact that income is limited means that an increase in consumers' demand for one good can be achieved only by a decrease in the demand for another good. Thus as the price of one good rises, so the price of some other good falls. But more of a good can be supplied at a higher price because higher rewards can now be bid for labour and raw materials to attract them from other uses. From which uses can this labour and these materials come? (It is evident that, if overall supply is fixed because factors are fully employed, the supply of one good can be increased only by moving factors away from the production of another good.) Obviously they must come from the production of that good where price has fallen, because here supply must contract as only lower wages and prices for materials can now be offered. Thus, moved by the profit motive, the seller of hot-dogs in winter becomes the ice-cream vendor in summer, although the change is usually not so simple or direct as this. It might take a long time to work out and may have to proceed as a series of reshuffles of labour from one occupation and industry to another (see page 143). The fact that, through the price system and the profit motive, variations in supply take place in response to changes in wants is often summed up in the phrase 'the consumer is king'.

One final point which follows from the above analysis is worth noting. Let us suppose that the price of agricultural machinery is rising while the price of motor cars is falling. This will lead to relatively higher wages being paid in the agricultural machinery industry than in the car industry and, ignoring questions of immobility of labour, will move workers from the car industry to the agricultural machinery industry. What we wish to draw particular attention to here, however, follows from the reason for the higher wages in the production of agricultural machinery. The employer has raised them chiefly because the good his workers produce is fetching a higher price (see Chapter 17). To a large extent, therefore, the reward paid to factors of production is dependent on the price of the good they make. Indeed, if there were no changes in the conditions of demand or supply (total factors, techniques, etc.), we would have a whole range of prices covering not only finished goods and services but also all factors of production, with all these prices dovetailing into one another. In short, there would be complete equilibrium in the economic system! Of course, this is only a very simplified, abstract and theoretical picture. In the real world, many considerations, such as constant changes in the conditions of demand and supply, immobility of the factors of production, the time element involved in production and so on, prevent any fixed equilibrium of this nature.

VIII. FIXED AND FLUCTUATING PRICES

In practice we find that the prices of the majority of goods do not vary from day to day but remain fairly stable over weeks or even months. What are the reasons for this?

In the first place, we can see from our demand and supply analysis that where the conditions of demand and supply for a product are comparatively stable, that product will have a price which is relatively fixed. Such relatively fixed prices apply generally to manufactured goods, e.g. fountain pens, bicycle tyres, processed foods (such as jams, pickles, potato crisps, and ice-creams), cutlery and so on, where the demand is not subject to violent fluctuations and the supply is not affected by the weather and seasons. But there are certain types of goods, the most important of which are goods subject to changes in fashion, where changes in demand occur frequently. A particular style of ladies' clothes and shoes may be outstandingly popular one moment and out of fashion the next, with the result that they have to be sold off at greatly reduced prices. By comparison we can note that such 'sales' are not held so frequently for goods such as flat-heeled leather walking-shoes or mackintoshes, which are less subject to changes in fashion. Similarly, there are goods where conditions of supply change frequently. In the case of natural-food products from the farm and agricultural raw materials (such as cotton, rubber, wool), not only is demand changeable, but supply is greatly affected by the weather. Where these goods can be stored against shortages, then price fluctuations are less violent, but where they are perishable, as with most foodstuffs, supplies come on the market in greatly varying quantities throughout the year and even from year to year. Thus we get seasonal price variations (the good being cheaper when it is in season) and also yearly price variations (the good being cheaper if there is a glut in the supply). In fact, the main reason for the setting-up of the various Marketing Boards is to regulate the supply of the product in order to eliminate wide price variations.

A second reason for stability of price, particularly in the case of manufactured goods and processed foodstuffs, is that for the sake of convenience to the manufacturer, wholesaler, retailer and consumer, prices are not altered to correspond with minor variations in conditions of demand and supply. For instance, it is probable that more jellies and ice-creams are eaten in the summer—yet prices are maintained constant throughout the year. This is possible because manufacturers try not to vary the prices which they charge retailers for their goods, and since each manufacturer expects his rivals to observe a tacit agreement to act in the same way, he feels reasonably safe in following this policy. It does not necessarily mean that the consumer pays more; it merely means that when prices could be raised for a short time, they are not, and when they could be lowered, they are not. Instead an average price is fixed for a long period.

On a somewhat different plane is the case of the big monopolist who has come into being, either because he is the sole producer of a good, or because he has joined a 'ring' which comprises all the producers (see Chapter 9). He is careful to release just that quantity which will sell at that price where his profit yield will be the greatest possible. Since he has no competitors, it is relatively easy for the monopolist to fix a price and he usually finds it to his advantage to maintain that price, once the public has got used to paying it, over long periods.

The fourth reason why stable prices exist is that some maximum prices are fixed by law or need a special procedure to alter. Thus the rent of certain unfurnished rooms is controlled by Rent Acts, while bus fares have to be submitted to a Transport Tribunal.

IX. ELASTICITY OF DEMAND

As we have seen, normally more of a commodity is demanded the lower the price. As price falls, so demand tends to expand; as price rises, so demand tends to contract. But the extent to which the quantity demanded changes in response to a price change varies. Sometimes a small fall in price will call forth a large expansion in the amount demanded. In other cases, demand may hardly change at all as the result of a price change.

From this we get the concept of elasticity of demand, the extent to which demand stretches out in response to a fall in price or contracts in response to a rise in price.

1. THE MEASUREMENT OF ELASTICITY OF DEMAND

The above, however, is merely a rough and ready first approach. We require a more accurate definition of elasticity of demand. In order to obtain this we relate the *rate* at which demand expands to the *rate* at which price falls. If the former is greater than the latter, we say that demand is elastic; if it is smaller, we say that demand is inelastic. When they are equal, elasticity of demand is said to be equal to unity. Using this definition, elasticity of demand can be measured in two ways. One is direct, showing the degree of elasticity; the other is indirect, merely indicating whether the demand for the good is elastic or inelastic.

1. *A direct comparison of the rate at which demand changes with the rate at which price changes*

When we wish to compare *rates* of change, we have to work in terms of proportionate (or percentage) changes. We can therefore define elasticity of demand as the proportionate change in the amount demanded in response to a small change in price divided by the proportionate change in price. Let us consider the demand schedule for tomatoes on page 126. When price falls from 20p to 16p, demand expands from 1,800 to 3,000 lbs. Therefore elasticity of demand equals

$$\frac{\dfrac{1,200}{1,800}}{\dfrac{4}{20}} = \frac{\frac{2}{3}}{\frac{1}{5}} = 3\tfrac{1}{3}$$

Similarly, for a rise in price from 16p to 20p, elasticity of demand equals

$$\frac{\dfrac{1,200}{3,000}}{\dfrac{4}{16}} = \frac{\frac{2}{5}}{\frac{1}{4}} = 1\tfrac{3}{8}$$

The difference in the two results arises from the fact that we are measuring elasticity from two different points, in the first case where the price is 20p, in the second where it is 16p. The change in price of 4p is a relatively large one. As the change becomes smaller, so the two points converge and, when the price change becomes infinitely small, measurement takes place from the same point, at which there is only one elasticity of demand.

Thus, given an accurate demand schedule, we can obtain an accurate measurement of the elasticity of demand for a good at any particular point. In practice, however, it is more usual to simplify matters by simply referring to the demand for a good as being either elastic or inelastic. If this is all that is required, method 2 is adequate.

2. *A comparison of total outlay as price changes*

We can say that the total amount of money which would be spent upon a commodity at a given price is the 'total outlay' on the commodity at that price. Now it is obvious that if the rate at which demand is expanding as price falls is greater than the rate at which price is falling, then the total outlay on the good must be increasing. Similarly, if the rate at which demand is expanding as price falls is less than the rate at which price is falling, then the total outlay on the good must be decreasing. (The careful reader will note that this may not apply exactly as elasticity approaches unity. This discrepancy results from the fact mentioned above, that we are measuring elasticity between two points and not at a single point on the demand curve.) Thus, if total outlay increases as price falls, demand is elastic; if total outlay decreases as price falls, demand is inelastic. The relationship between price, total outlay and elasticity of demand is shown in the following table:

Price of tomatoes (*pence per lb.*)	Quantity demanded (*lbs.*)	Total outlay (*£*)	
24	500	120	
20	1,800	360	Elastic demand
16	3,000	480	Elasticity of demand
12	4,000	480	equals unity
8	5,000	400	Inelastic demand
4	7,000	280	

Regarding elasticity of demand, certain specific points should be noted.

(1) Whilst we have emphasised the concept of elasticity of demand with regard to a small fall in price, it can be applied equally to a small rise in price. If, for instance, a small fall in price brings about a comparatively large increase in total outlay, a small rise in price will choke off demand and bring about a comparatively large decrease in the total expenditure. In other words, demand is elastic. Similarly, if demand is inelastic, there is little action consumers can take in response to a rise in price. In this case, total expenditure increases as price rises. Thus we see that it is only a matter of a different approach to the demand schedule—whether we read it for a fall in price (downwards), or for a rise in price (upwards).

(2) Elasticity of demand is usually different in different parts of the demand schedule. This can be seen at a glance if, for example, we plot total outlay against price (Fig. 12). Where total outlay increases as price falls (that is, from 24p to 16p), the curve slopes downwards to the right and demand

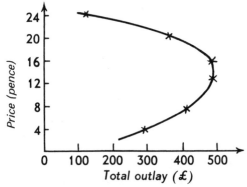

Fig. 12.—Elasticity of demand at different prices

is elastic; where the curve moves downwards to the left, demand is inelastic; where the curve is vertical, elasticity of demand equals unity.

Three important exceptions are:

(a) *Demand absolutely inelastic*, people buying exactly the same amount of a commodity whatever its price.

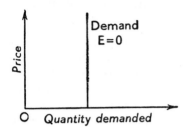

(b) Demand perfectly elastic, people ceasing to buy the commodity at all if its price rises slightly. This is the demand curve for his good which faces an individual seller under conditions of perfect competition.

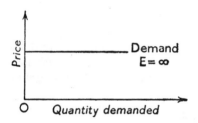

(c) Elasticity of demand equal to unity, where total outlay is constant at all prices. The curve here is known as a rectangular hyperbola and all rectangles representing outlay (price × quantity demanded) are equal. For example, rectangle OABC equals rectangle OPQR.

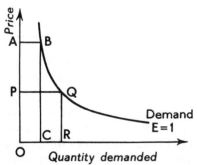

Even if demand is represented by a straight line, not vertical or horizontal, elasticity of demand varies at different prices.

155

Although a straight sloping line means that demand changes by a constant amount for a given price change, the *rate* at which price itself is falling depends on the price from which we start. This rate will therefore be higher for a given price change the lower the price under consideration.

(3) Usually we cannot compare the elasticities of demand of different goods by comparing the slopes of the respective demand curves. The slope of the demand curve depends, not only upon elasticity of demand, but also on the vertical and horizontal scales chosen. Furthermore, even if the same scales are chosen for different commodities, we cannot safely say that, where the demand curve for one commodity slopes more steeply than another, the demand for the first commodity is less elastic. This is because, as shown in (3) above, elasticity of demand varies at different points of the curve. Compare, for example, parallel demand curves D_A and D_B in Fig. 13. At the same price OP, elasticity of demand for commodity A is equal to 2, while for commodity B it is equal to 1.

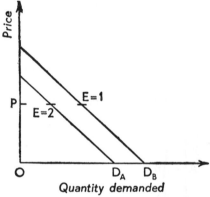

Fig. 13.—Comparison of elasticities of demand

The reason for the difference is that, although we have taken the same price, we have started measuring proportionate changes in quantity demanded from different quantities. Only at the position where two demand curves with different slopes cut, can we be *certain* that the difference in their slopes will reflect a difference in the elasticity of demand.

2. Factors Determining Elasticity of Demand

1. *The possibility of substitution*

As the price of a commodity falls, so the terms on which it can be obtained have, in comparison with other commodities, become more favourable. The tendency, therefore, is to substitute this commodity for the others. The extent to which this is done depends on a number of factors.

In the first place, it depends on the physical characteristics of goods and how far slight differences in them can be ignored by consumers. Goods within a particular class are easily substituted for one another. Beef is a substitute for mutton, bloaters are a substitute for kippers, and so on. Thus if the price of beef falls, people will buy more beef and less mutton. Between one class and another, however, substitution is more difficult. If the price of meat in general falls, there will be a slight tendency to buy more meat and less fish, but this tendency will be very limited because meat is not nearly so perfect a substitute for fish as beef is for mutton.

Secondly, substitutability depends on the proportion of one's income which is spent on the good. If the expenditure is only a fraction of one's income, a rise in price will not lead to a frantic search for substitutes. Thus a rise in the price of mustard will not stop many consumers from buying mustard, nor will a moderate rise in the price of chromium mean that car manufacturers cease to chrome bumpers and radiator grills, for the cost of such chromium is only a fraction of the total cost of the car. This consideration helps to explain two other facts: (i) generally speaking, especially with the cheaper commodities, rich people have a less elastic demand for goods than poor persons, for whereas the poor man has continually to be considering how he can spend his income to the best advantage and is therefore sensitive to changes in price, the rich man, faced with a rise in price, may not bother to look for a substitute; (ii) demand tends to be more elastic at high prices than at low prices.

Thirdly, in practice, the time factor must be taken into account when discussing substitutability. Price changes may occur so frequently that people are unable to adjust their pattern of spending accordingly, especially when habit plays a large part in deciding their purchases.

2. *The possibility of new purchasers*

In discussing the possibility of substitution above, we have looked at elasticity of demand from the point of view of the individual consumer. But when we are considering the market demand curve, we must allow for the fact that as price falls, new consumers will be induced to buy the good. In fact, with many goods, such as cars, television sets, washing machines, etc., of which people require only one, it is the fall in price bringing the good within the range of the demand of new consumers which leads to the increase in demand. Hence a fall in price which induces people in a numerous income-group to buy will result in a considerable elasticity of demand. A fall in price which affects only the higher and smaller income-groups, however, will not produce many new customers and hence the market demand schedule tends to be inelastic in this price range.

3. Practical Uses of the Concept of Elasticity of Demand

The concept of elasticity of demand may at first sight seem somewhat artificial. It may be questioned, for instance, whether it is possible in practice to obtain an accurate demand schedule from which elasticity of demand can be calculated. Admittedly complete accuracy is impossible, but market-research organisations do exist in order to obtain information which is invaluable to a number of people who are interested in the elasticity of demand of certain goods.

In the first place, a monopolist is not faced with a horizontal, that is a perfectly elastic, demand curve when selling his product, for the price of the good is affected by the quantity of it which he puts on the market (see Chapter 9). Therefore, he looks at the demand schedule for his good and fixes the amount, and thus the price, at which he makes the highest profit. By way of illustration let us imagine a football club which is staging a very important Cup tie. Let us further imagine that there is no comparable attraction within fifty

miles and that the price of admission, instead of being regulated
by the Football Association, is fixed by the club, which pursues
the policy of making as big a profit as possible. Expenses of the
club will be roughly the same whether few or many watch the
game. The relevant portion of the demand schedule is as
follows:

Price of admission (p)	Number of spectators willing to pay that price	Total outlay by spectators (£)
25	60,000	15,000
50	56,000	28,000
75	50,000	37,500
100	32,000	32,000

The club, therefore, fixes the price of admission at 75p, and
the total number of spectators at the game is 50,000.

Similarly, a manufacturer, who intends to mass-produce
large quantities of a particular commodity in order to produce
at a lower price, must have an idea of the size of the demand
for his good at the lower price. Lord Nuffield, for instance,
who in 1922 reduced the price of his two-seater Morris Cowley
from £299 to £225, was correct in his belief that the
demand was sufficiently elastic to justify the move. Likewise
the 'cut-price' supermarket expects demand to be highly
elastic.

Secondly, the Chancellor of the Exchequer must always
consider the elasticity of demand when imposing a special
(selective) tax on a good. The demand may be so elastic that
the increase in price might cause such a falling-off in the
demand for the good that the total tax received was less than
formerly. Suppose, for instance, the demand schedule for a
commodity is as follows:

Price (p)	Quantity demanded
20	1,000
30	600
40	200

Assume also that supply is perfectly elastic and that the market
price is 20p, at which 1,000 units are being sold. The Chancellor
of the Exchequer now decides to tax the good, imposing a tax
of 10p on each unit. The result is that only 600 are now sold

and his total tax receipts amount to £60. Later he goes further, increasing the tax to 20p per unit. This raises the total price of the good from 30p to 40p. Between these two prices, demand is very elastic. Only 200 are now sold at 40p, and the Chancellor's tax receipts are reduced to £40. It should be noted, however, that when the Chancellor of the Exchequer puts on a selective tax in order to choke off demand for a certain good, then the best goods to tax are those which have an elastic demand. Usually, however, with indirect taxation the Chancellor wishes to raise revenue and then he looks for a good to tax which has an inelastic demand. This is one reason why the selective taxes on tobacco and alcohol are so liked by him. After a while people consume almost as much tobacco and drinks as they did at the lower price and, since they are regarded as luxuries, the higher price is not considered to be too serious a burden on the consumer.

Lastly, the elasticity of demand for a good has great practical significance when we are considering changes in the conditions of supply. We can best illustrate this by discussing practical examples.

1. *The effect of improvements in the conditions of supply on the size of the industry*

An improvement in the conditions of supply—through better techniques, new inventions or lower cost of the factors of

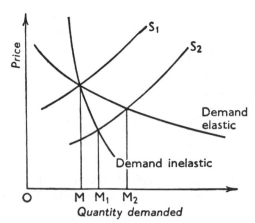

FIG. 14.—The relationship of elasticity of demand and changes in output

production used—causes the supply curve to move to the right. Output will now expand according to the elasticity of demand for the good. This can be seen from Fig. 14. Where demand is elastic, the effect of an improvement in supply $(S_1$ to $S_2)$ is to bring about a much larger increase in output than when demand is inelastic. In the former case, output increases from OM to OM_2, while in the latter it increases only from OM to OM_1.

2. *The effect of subsidies and taxes on production*

The effect of a subsidy to producers is to lower costs of production and therefore to move the supply curve to the right. Therefore it can be seen that, if the government wishes to increase employment by means of a subsidy, it is much more likely to provide a greater volume of employment if the subsidy is given to an industry, the demand for whose good is elastic. Conversely, the effect of a tax on the good is felt much more by an industry the demand for whose good is elastic.

3. *The possibility of raising wages*

A rise in wages causes the supply curve to move to the left. Hence, where demand is elastic, this will have the effect of considerably contracting output and therefore of bringing about unemployment in the industry. This is likely to deter the demand for higher wages. On the other hand, a demand for higher wages is likely to be much more successful where the demand for the good the workers make is inelastic. Since the demand for our exports tends to be elastic, because importing countries have other countries as sources of supply, it means that it is much more difficult for workers in the export industries to obtain a rise in wages than in industries which cater almost entirely for home demand.

4. *The marketing of agricultural produce*

Generally speaking, the demand for foodstuffs and raw materials is inelastic. Consequently, when there is a bumper harvest and price falls, the total expenditure is less. This total expenditure, however, can be assumed as roughly representing the income of the farming community. The result is that, to prevent violent fluctuations in the income of farmers, many governments have intervened by setting up Marketing Boards or by holding stocks, the main function of both being to

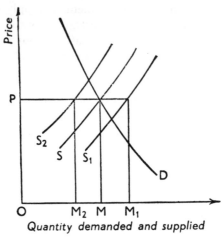

FIG. 15.—The use of government stocks to prevent fluctuations in prices and incomes

regulate supply in order to even out income fluctuations.

Alternatively the government can concentrate on preventing price fluctuations. In Fig. 15, when supply increases from S to S_1, the government itself stockpiles an amount equal to MM_1. The effect is to maintain price at OP. Similarly, if the next year supply falls to S_2, the government releases from its stockpile a supply equivalent to MM_2. In this way, the government, by making its own demand for the good positive, when it buys stocks, or negative, when it sells, adjusts the total demand for the product so that its price remains stable.

X. ELASTICITY OF SUPPLY

We have seen that the quantity of any good which a manufacturer is willing to produce generally varies directly with the price. Normally more will be supplied the higher the price. This relationship is a consequence of production usually taking place under conditions of increasing cost. A higher price means that existing firms can expand their output and sub-marginal firms can now compete, the increase in price covering the increased costs incurred by the industry as a whole in attracting factors of production from other uses.

This relationship of price to the quantity supplied can be carried one stage further by defining and measuring elasticity of supply. Elasticity of supply at any price or at any output is the proportional change in the amount supplied, in response to a small change in price, divided by the proportionate change in price. If, for instance, as a result of a rise in the price of fountain pens from 80p to 84p the number offered for sale by the manufacturers increased from 10,000 to 11,000, we should say that the elasticity of supply at 80p equals 2. It must be noted, however, that elasticity of supply cannot be calculated by the method of comparing the total sums of money involved when price is multiplied by the amount supplied because, under conditions of increasing cost, this sum would always increase as price increased.

FACTORS INFLUENCING THE ELASTICITY OF SUPPLY

1. *The extent to which the time element is thwarted by expectations*

Earlier in this chapter, attention was drawn to a major difficulty when discussing supply, namely that adjustments to supply take time. Additional supplies of a good can be obtained almost immediately only where:

(a) *Stocks are carried.* On the organised markets, stocks are carried by wholesalers and dealers. Such institutional factors have a great influence on elasticity of supply in the exceptionally short period. Nevertheless, while a producer or dealer can always continue accumulating stocks so long as the good is not perishable and he has the financial resources to do so, there is a limit to which stocks can be depleted. In short, supply to the market may be more elastic in contraction than in expansion.

(b) *Production has been planned in advance or surplus capacity retained.* Most production takes place for an estimated demand and we shall return to this later when discussing profit. Somewhat different, however, is the case of a monopolist who may have been working his plant under capacity and therefore finds it comparatively easy to expand output as price rises.

(*c*) A firm makes different products and switches factors from making one to the other according to price changes.

2. *The elasticity of supply of factors of production*

Apart from the methods outlined above, supply can only be varied by varying the quantities of the factors of production already possessed. Thus we are interested in the elasticity of supply of the factors of production and this is affected by:

(*a*) *The period of time under consideration.* As we have already indicated, variation of supply in the sense of the amount actually produced can usually only be achieved after a period of time. Thus 'time' is the main influence on the elasticity of supply. Indeed, when discussing the formation of price, we showed how, in order to overcome this difficulty, the device of referring to the 'short period' and the 'long period' was adopted. For a time, certain factors are immobile or 'specific', meaning that during this given period (the 'short period') they are 'fixed' factors since they cannot be transferred to any other use. Highly specialised machinery (such as blast furnaces and motor-body presses) and many factors employed in agricultural processes (such as land already sown, beef cattle and rubber trees), are examples of relative specificity. Other factors, such as labour (especially piece-rate) and raw materials are 'variable' because they can be adjusted proportionately to output.

In the short period, supply can be varied only by adjusting the 'variable' factors. For example, the number of men on a machine can be increased and additional raw materials bought. Normally, however, this entails a decrease in efficiency and therefore extra cost, because the factors are not being combined in the best proportions. The result is that a considerable rise in price is often necessary for a comparatively small increase in output. In short, especially where production is carried on with a high proportion of fixed to variable factors, supply is more inelastic in the short period than in the long period. In the long period, when factors can be combined in the best proportions, the effect of price changes on supply is influenced only by the cost of attracting factors from other uses (which influence, of course, also applies to the short period).

(*b*) *The cost of attracting factors from other uses.* Unless there are factors unemployed, increased production of a good necessitates offering a higher price to factors in order to attract them from their other uses. In short, the price of the factor, *in all its uses*, rises. This has two effects. In the first place, producers of the 'alternative goods' will try to substitute other factors for it. If there is a high degree of such substitutability it will release much of the factor for its new use and hence its supply will be fairly elastic. Secondly, the price of the 'alternative goods' will rise according to the proportion of total costs borne by the factor whose price has risen. Thus the amount of the factor released depends upon the elasticity of demand for the 'alternative goods'. If the cost of the factor forms a large proportion of total costs and elasticity of demand is high, then much of the factor will be released for its new use.

In conclusion, it is instructive to draw attention to an interesting difference between the short-period and the long-period curves due to the adoption of a change in techniques. Over the long period an entrepreneur may adopt a different technique of production. He may continue for some time to produce by his old methods but his long-term position may be on entirely different lines. He may, for instance, switch over to the flow method of mass-production. The result may be that the new long-period supply curve shows an increased output at a lower cost and, therefore, the final price of the good may be lower than the original one.

ELASTICITY OF SUPPLY OVER TIME AND THE PRICE OF THE GOOD

We are now in a position to show how the difference between the short and the long periods affects price. Let us consider the question: 'How will an increase in the demand for eggs affect their price?'

Suppose the original demand curve is D, and the price is OP. Demand increases to D_1. In the short period, supply can be expanded only by giving the hens more food, light and heat. We therefore have a fairly inelastic supply curve, S_1, because a small increase in output by such methods is comparatively expensive. Price rises to OP_1.

In the long period, however, supply can be increased by

adding to the number of hens. This is a more efficient method of increasing the supply of eggs, and the supply curve is more elastic, S_2. This gives a lower price, OP_2.

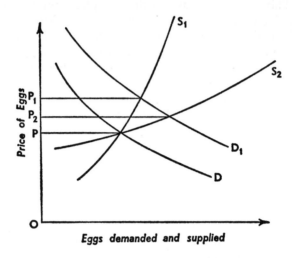

Eggs demanded and supplied

CHAPTER 9

MONOPOLY

I. WHAT DO WE MEAN BY 'MONOPOLY'?

TRANSLATED in a strictly literal way, the word 'monopolist' means 'one seller'. Yet, for the purposes of economic analysis and as a guide to practical policy, such a definition does not take us very far. Because our income is limited, all goods, except for a few absolute necessities such as salt and water, compete one with the other for a part of that limited income to be spent on them. In this sense, therefore, all goods are to some extent substitutes for each other and consequently only a person who sold all the goods and services in the community would be an absolute monopolist.

Yet, while all goods can be regarded in this way as having substitution properties, the degree of such substitution varies. Thus, whilst there is considerable substitution between beef and mutton, there is less substitution between meat and fish, and still less between meat and vegetables. Consequently, although we can speak of a chain of substitution linking all goods and services, we must recognise that in this chain there may be weak links or even gaps. Sometimes one good, or a very small group of goods, may be separated by such gaps, and over the supply of this good or group of goods one person may have secured a dominant or controlling position. The question as to what constitutes a 'dominant or controlling position' is one, however, which is not easily answered. Probably the simplest and most practical method is to find out what proportion of the total output of a good is produced by the dominant firm. This is the method which was adopted by the British Government in 1948 when it set up the Monopolies Commission.

We can throw further light on this concept of 'monopoly' by looking at the problem from the point of view of the monopolist himself—the man who has secured control over the output of a group of very close substitutes. We begin by recalling two essential features of perfect competition as set out in Chapter 8.

(*a*) *Sellers have no control over the price of a good by the amount of it which they place on the market*

In short, they have to accept market price as given. This means that they, and all the other sellers in the market, see the demand curve for their good as one that is parallel to the horizontal axis (measuring 'quantity demanded'). When the demand curve is so shaped it means that a very tiny reduction in the price by any one seller would bring him no advantage by increased sales since his total output could have been sold just the same at the higher price, while a slight rise in his price would cause all his customers to forsake him for his competitors. On the other hand, where a seller can influence the price of a good by the amount of it he offers for sale, then the demand curve for his good slopes downwards to the right. A slight rise in his price will not cause all his customers to go elsewhere although he will lose some, the number depending on the availability of substitutes and the willingness of people to change to them. Such a seller is to some degree a mono-polist.

It should be noted, however, that the monopolist cannot fix both the price and the amount to be sold at one and the same time. He can decide either the amount of the good he puts on the market, in which case he must leave it to the market to fix the price, or, as usually happens with monopolies, he can fix the price of the good, thereby leaving it to the market to decide how much is sold.

(i) Under perfect competition   (ii) Under some degree of monopoly

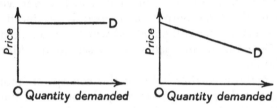

Fig. 16.—The demand curve for his good as seen by a single seller

(*b*) *Purchasers, in deciding from which seller to buy their goods, base their actions solely on the price charged and buy from the cheapest seller*

This does not occur where buyers form an 'attachment' to one particular seller, either through habit or simply because the product is made to appear to be different by advertising. Where there is such an 'attachment', buyers ignore price fluctuations. Instead, the seller has succeeded in establishing some control over them by creating or widening, more often psychologically than physically, a gap in the chain of substitution. He is, therefore, to some degree, a monopolist.

To sum up, then, whilst there is no absolute or complete monopolist, there exists some degree of monopoly in any market which is not perfectly competitive, that is, where any one producer sees a downward-sloping demand curve for his good. It is in this sense that henceforth we shall use the term 'monopoly', for while the degree of imperfection in the market varies, all imperfect markets have this in common that the producers have to watch and regulate either the price of the good or the quantity they supply in order to maximise their profits.

II. THE CAUSES OF MONOPOLY

The origin of a monopoly lies in the two facts, outlined above, which must both be taken in conjunction with one another: (*a*) there is a break in the chain of substitution; (*b*) a producer can secure some control over the output of a group of goods so separated by excluding competitors. Hence, an analysis of the causes of monopoly really consists of a more detailed examination of these two points, emphasising how, in practice, a break may come about and how competitors are excluded.

1. HISTORICAL CAUSES

Quite often it happens that firms first in the field develop strength which makes it hard for newcomers to compete on equal terms. In the first place, the industry may be one where production on a very large scale is essential in order to achieve the economies which result. Now while the original firm or firms may have been able to build up their size gradually, new firms entering the industry, in order to compete in costs, have to start on that scale of production already reached by the well-established firms. This necessitates the raising of large sums of capital, a task which may prove difficult to new firms.

Secondly, in the course of development the manager of a firm learns certain 'tricks of the trade', or 'know-how' as it is more usually termed, connected with his business. Since this 'know-how' can often be gained only by experience, the long-established firm is in a favourable position from the point of view of excluding competitors. This applies although the process may be a small one, such as mosaic-laying, provided that it is very technical, requiring a high degree of craftsmanship.

Thirdly, we must draw attention to the 'goodwill' which frequently exists with an old-established firm. Such goodwill may have been built up throughout the lifetime of the firm in a variety of ways, though mainly it is achieved by paying attention to the individual needs of every customer. The result is that it may be a long time before persons forsake a regular dealer even though another firm offers the product at a slightly lower price. Retail markets are often imperfect for this reason. Thus grocers who charge the full price for their goods are able to exist alongside cut-price shops. Moreover, closely connected with this goodwill, though in a somewhat negative form, is the inertia of many customers when it comes to changing from one good to another. Many are inclined to insist on a dearer good or to go to the nearest shop chiefly through force of habit. We shall have more to say about this later when we discuss product differentiation and the psychological effect of advertising.

2. TECHNICAL CONDITIONS OF SUPPLY

It may well be that a source of monopoly power exists in the technical conditions of supply or manufacture of a commodity. This applies particularly with regard to the production of certain minerals and precious stones. Thus the diamonds mined at Kimberley at one time formed so large a proportion of the total world supply that their price could be kept artificially high by restricting output.

Where technical conditions on the supply side bring about a limitation of the market we have a somewhat similar result. Such a limitation occurs chiefly either where transport costs are high relative to the value of the product or where the product is perishable. The effect is to split up an area into a number of relatively small markets over each of which there is a supplier who exercises some monopolistic control. In contrast to such markets, we have some which are world-wide, and here the good is generally supplied by many sellers in competition with each other. For this reason the prices of such goods as gilt-edged securities, gold, wheat, tea, wool and minerals are highly competitive.

Above all, we must emphasise the source of monopoly power resulting from the fact that the minimum technical unit of production is large relative to the market. This means that a considerable capital outlay is necessary for the supply of such services as gas, water, electricity and telephones to cover a small locality. Here competition between firms is eliminated. In the first place, we could not have many separate companies for each service, all digging up the roads and laying their own pipe-lines and cables. Secondly, were two companies each to make the necessary capital outlay in order to compete with one another, the relative smallness of the market would mean that neither could make a profit, with the result that one or both would eventually be forced into bankruptcy. The latter was one of the major considerations in granting monopolies to the railway companies during the nineteenth century. Nevertheless it should be noted that, with most of these services, it is still possible to promote some competition. Thus electricity has to compete with gas, while the railways have to compete with road transport. Moreover, in the long run, different Area Boards selling gas or electricity do compete with one another in that entrepreneurs tend to site their businesses in those districts where their factors of production are cheapest.

3. A Legal Conferment

A large number of monopolies derive their favourable position, directly or indirectly, from the policy of the government. James I in particular granted monopolies as a means of raising revenue. But today the State does so from higher motives, and at the same time endeavours to provide safeguards which will as far as possible protect the public from exploitation.

First, under the present-day Patent Acts, a person who discloses and registers his invention at the Patents Office is given a monopoly of working it for a period of sixteen years. The government considers that the grant of such a patent is, in a private-enterprise system, the best method of promoting invention and the development of new ideas. Where, however, the patent is for producing food and medicine, or is not being fully worked, the right to manufacture may be granted to other persons by the Controller of Patents.

Secondly, monopolies are granted to 'public utility' companies. The services they provide are not only important to the community as a whole but, for technical reasons, are unsuitable for operating in open competition. Hence, for the supply of water and the regulation of docks and harbours special legal powers have been granted to certain individual companies which operate subject to some form of control by the government. Most of the other public utilities have, however, been nationalised. This carries the process one stage further, for the monopoly then comes under the direct control of the State. In Chapter 6 we studied the organisation of and reasons for nationalising these industries. Such reasons vary with the different industries, but most of them have two points in common: (a) the technical scale of operations is so large that, from an economic point of view, they can operate efficiently only if they work on a very large scale; (b) they are of essential public importance, either because they produce necessities or because they are vital to economic stability. As a result of (a), the monopolistic element looms large, and so, in view of (b), it is felt that the State should own and operate them as the best method of ensuring that the monopoly powers are not abused. Nevertheless the fact that these nationalised industries are also monopolies must not be overlooked. The corporations running them are all charged with the responsibility of providing an efficient service. This means that, on the demand side, they must make an accurate estimate of the demand schedule while, on the supply side, they must produce whatever quantity they decide on at the minimum possible cost. Over the long period they must balance total costs and total income. However, this must be achieved, not by using their monopoly powers to fix high prices, but by making sure that there is the maximum efficiency in supply and that inefficiencies are not ignored or even covered up.

Thirdly, monopoly power may result from controls which are exercised by the government. Thus, in order to eliminate violent fluctuations in farming incomes, Marketing Boards have been set up where a majority of the producers of a commodity are in agreement. These Boards, which now cover milk, potatoes, wool and hops, became compulsory on all producers and they control the production and sale of the various commodities, limiting supplies to the market where prices would otherwise drop too low. Although they contain representatives of consumer interests, in practice the producer's wishes are dominant. Similarly, a minor source of monopoly power results from certain controls imposed by the government to regulate international trade. Where quotas exist for the import of goods from abroad, the firms fortunate enough to obtain a share of the quota can, unless the price of the finished good is also controlled by the government, make abnormal profits.

4. DELIBERATE POLICY BY THE PRODUCERS TO EXCLUDE COMPETITION

The existence of high profits in an industry serves, under perfect competition, to attract new entrants. (We shall examine this term 'profits' more thoroughly in Chapter 16.) The result is an increased output which, by reducing the price of the good, eventually leads to the disappearance of the high profits. On the other hand, where a producer can exclude competitors, he can continue to make high profits. Hence a monopolist's power is ultimately based on the difficulty or impossibility of entry into an industry.

This restriction of competition falls into two main groups. On the one hand we have the sources of monopoly power described so far. These have, as it were, resulted indirectly from a particular policy conceived outside the firm and not from any deliberate action by producers. In fact, such monopolies can almost be described as 'spontaneous'. We must contrast these 'spontaneous' monopolies with the second kind—those which are artificially created with the deliberate object of making abnormal profits by restricting supplies.

It is essential to recognise the distinction between the two groups when it comes to formulating policy. While the 'spontaneous' monopolies may still abuse their fortunate position in order to make high profits, there is some element of inevitability about them and the general policy towards them must be one of control rather than destruction. On the other hand, monopolies which have arisen with the specific object of following restrictive practices detrimental to the consumer should, where possible, be broken up. In practice, however, as we shall see later, it is often difficult to draw a distinct line between the two different kinds of monopoly. A firm may increase the scale of its production, or firms may combine, with both of two objects in view—increased economies of scale and the forcing out of competitors to achieve greater control of total supply.

The devices employed to deliberately create a monopoly can be divided into two main groups, each group broadly representing a different method of approach to the problem of achieving some control over the price of a good in a particular market. The first is to take both the market and the good to be sold as they stand and to control the supply or price of the good in that market as much as possible by combined action with the other suppliers. This method corresponds to the formation of combinations and associations. The second is to divide up the market for the particular good by so varying the product that it represents, in the minds of purchasers, a slightly superior good to the others with which it competes. This is achieved by what is known as 'product differentiation'. We will now examine these two main groups in more detail.

1. *Combinations and associations*

Methods used to bring about monopolies by combinations are not only numerous but differ in character. They range from those where combination brings, in addition to the monopoly power, the advantages of large-scale production to those which, by a more offensive policy, sometimes obnoxious in character, drive out competitors or force them into joining the combination or association. As we saw in Chapter 4, in

general, combinations may be divided into 'horizontal' or
'vertical', though here it must again be emphasised that very
often such combinations are formed, not with the restriction
of competition as the driving motive, but to integrate production in order to secure the economies which result from
working on a large scale. When the latter is the main object,
it is more usual to emphasise the fact by speaking of 'integration' rather than of 'combination'. Moreover, apart from
seeking to achieve the economies of linked processes, a vertical
combination may be defensive in origin, arising from the wish
to ensure regular supplies of materials which otherwise may
themselves fall under the control of a monopolist.

Both types of combination vary in the degree to which they
are integrated. Some firms are linked together by an agreement the purpose of which is merely the adoption of a common
policy in the marketing of their products. Such combinations,
horizontal in character, are more correctly referred to as
'associations'. Their methods of controlling the market vary.
As in the case of South African producers of diamonds and
certain coal cartels in Germany before the war, all the output
may be turned over to a common selling agent which distributes
the profit it makes among the producers. The more common
method, however, especially among those industries investigated by the Monopolies Commission in the United Kingdom,
is to fix a minimum selling price for the good. Output may
also be regulated on a quota basis among the members of the
association. Such associations exist even in certain industries
where work is normally tendered for, the association deciding
who shall be allotted the work, the other members either not
submitting estimates or tendering ones which are higher.
Associations may have to take offensive action to drive out
competitors. Thus they may use their financial resources
in a temporary price-slashing campaign or, where they
represent a major customer for the material they use, they may
bring pressure to bear to cut off supplies to their competitors.

In contrast to the marketing associations, we have the more
comprehensive form of combination, both horizontal and
vertical in character, represented by the holding company.
This holds a majority of the shares of each of the separate
companies and is therefore able to control general policy in the

interests of the whole group. On the other hand it has the advantage that the individual companies still retain some freedom of action together with the privilege of limited liability. In the United Kingdom, both Unilever, Ltd. and Great Universal Stores, Ltd. are organised as holding companies. Eventually looser combinations may develop into a complete merger, though more often mergers come about without preliminary association. The businesses then lose their separate existence and become a single undertaking. This is what has happened with such firms as the British Leyland Motor Corporation, (BMC and Leyland), Tate and Lyle, and the General Electric Company (GEC and English Electric).

So far, in discussing associations, we have stressed their importance in the sphere of the production and sale of goods. We must not, however, neglect their vital character in the sale of labour and services. Trade unions are primarily combinations of workers formed with the object of obtaining higher wages and improved conditions of work (see Chapter 17). Moreover certain professions, such as medicine, the law, accountancy and engineering, although they vary in power one from the other, also have their associations which regulate qualifications, methods of entry, professional conduct and often the scale of fees to be charged. Inasmuch as they can regulate the supply of these services by limiting entrants or can control the fees charged, so they must be regarded as a form of monopoly.

2. *Product differentiation*

The object of the monopolies described above is the exclusion of competition among the producers engaged in the manufacture and sale of the same commodity. Product differentiation, on the other hand, emphasises the fact that a good may meet competition from substitutes. Hence it is an attempt by producers to lessen the degree of substitutability by giving their good some particular characteristic which makes it slightly different from other goods in the same class. This characteristic may be merely a physical one. A distinctive wrapping, shape or special direction for using or serving may appeal to certain people, while gift tokens may be distributed with the product as an extra inducement to prefer the good. Far more important, however, are the efforts of producers to make people think that the good is slightly better or to lead consumers to ask for a certain good out of mere habit. This is the motive of the greater part of present-day advertising. While some advertisements still seek to inform the public on genuine properties of a product or the advent of a new product, most attempt to have a psychological effect on potential consumers and start from the assumption that if you tell the people something often enough, eventually they will believe it and act upon that belief either directly or else subconsciously. If this type of advertisement can, however vaguely, hint that the good leads to increased sex-appeal or has a scientific basis, then it has multiplied its chances of success. Thus descriptions of cosmetics, soaps, toothpaste, hair-styles and clothes all emphasise the sex-appeal aspect, while processed food advertisements stress the vitamin and energy-producing virtues of their respective products.

III. THE RESULTS OF MONOPOLY

In the minds of most people, the term 'monopoly' is associated with restriction of supplies and exorbitant prices. To some extent this is true. All monopolies, whether 'spontaneous' or 'deliberate' will, if operating under the private-enterprise motive of maximising profit, restrict supplies to less than they would be under perfect competition and the price of the product will be correspondingly higher. The extent to which, in practice, each monopoly tries to maximise profit by this means varies. It is obvious that those formed deliberately are likely to pursue the aim further than those which arise spontaneously where other reasons are largely responsible for the existence of the monopoly.

On the other hand, people often give little thought to the fact that public benefits may result from an industry's being organised as a monopoly. Our analysis of the 'spontaneous' monopolies revealed how monopolies arose because of the desire to secure large-scale economies, the wish to encourage and develop inventions, the necessity of making either one firm or the State responsible for the operation of public utilities, and so on. The public benefits arising from such monopolies are obvious. But, even with monopolies that have been deliberately fostered, certain public advantages may be secured. While such benefits vary from one monopoly to another, it is vital to recognise their existence when formulating policy. Therefore, before passing to the uneconomic and even evil results of monopoly, we must examine in more detail these advantages. We shall term them 'social benefits' to distinguish them from 'private benefits', the increased profits which accrue to the individual producer.

THE POSSIBLE SOCIAL BENEFITS ARISING FROM MONOPOLY

1. *Economies of co-ordination*

Monopoly, as we have seen, may be necessary in order to secure the maximum advantages of large-scale production. This is particularly true when it comes to working out a co-ordinated policy for the industry as a whole and is one of the main arguments for the nationalisation of certain industries. In the first place, it becomes possible to supply the commodity or service according to an overall scheme which makes the best possible use of the plant or equipment available. Thus the Central Electricity Board was set up in 1926 to co-ordinate the national production and interchangeability of the supply of electricity in order to utilise to the full the available plant and to avoid surplus capacity. As a result the proportion of reserve plant held for periods of peak supply fell from over 40 to 15 per cent. Similarly, when studying the reasons for the nationalisation of industry we saw how the National Coal Board could economise in the working of different pits, and that one argument in favour of the nationalisation of road haulage was that more efficient use could be made of lorries by having a central office for the collection of orders.

Secondly, the creation of a monopoly may enable common services to be developed which, under competition, would not have been undertaken by any one producer since, quite naturally, he would refuse to bear the cost of something from which his rivals derived equal benefit. Such services include research, grants to universities, export sales promotion, training schemes for employees and improved marketing arrangements. A monopoly or an association of producers can agree to provide these services out of a common fund to which they all subscribe. In a similar way, trade unions, and particularly professional associations, disseminate new ideas and improved methods and techniques among their members.

Thirdly, the formation of a monopoly may enable a co-ordinated investment programme to be worked out. Small firms competing with one another are often afraid or cannot afford to commit themselves to large-scale capital development, while such capital projects as they do undertake are frequently wastefully duplicated by many firms. It is essential, therefore, that in such industries as coal, iron and steel, civil aviation and the production of atomic energy, all of which need capital outlay on a very large scale, a co-ordinated plan be drawn up in order to make resources go as far as possible.

2. *The saving of some competitive costs*

A slightly different form of co-ordination is the saving of certain competitive costs by the establishment of a monopoly. Thus much competitive advertising between separate firms can be eliminated, though we must note that, especially with product differentiation, the opposite may be true and the setting up and maintenance of the monopoly may be achieved only by heavy expenditure on advertising. More important, however, is the fact that a monopoly enjoys greater security than an individual producer working in competition with many others. Since he does not have to guess at the policy of his rivals, the monopolist can take a long-term view, especially with regard to capital development. Thus, as we have already shown, competition has virtually been eliminated from all the public utility industries which usually require large capital expenditure for efficient operation. Similarly, Marketing Boards have been established to control the production of certain agricultural products which, without any long-term policy, are subject to wide short-term variations in price. Such price variations increase the risk when farmers engage in capital improvements, and therefore discourage it.

3. *The elimination of existing excess capacity may be facilitated*

A firm will continue to produce in times of depression so long as its immediate costs (e.g. on labour and raw materials) are being covered. However, unless conditions eventually improve, it will be unable to replace machinery as it wears out, and it therefore goes out of business. But this process of elimination may take a very long time. Continued production by outdated firms delays the concentration of supply on the more efficient plants, perhaps preventing such plants from working to capacity. It may be possible, however, to pool the interests of the different firms and thereby hasten the long-run position by artificially eliminating the inefficient excess capacity of the industry. This happened in both the cotton and shipbuilding industries during the 1930's, when the government gave active support to the schemes. The respective associations—the Lancashire Cotton Corporation and the Shipbuilders' Security Company Ltd.—imposed a levy on all its members which provided a fund out of which inefficient units could be bought up and taken out of production.

4. *Prescribed minimum standards of work*

Where the monopoly takes the form of an association of producers or of a trade union, it often lays down standards regarding the qualifications, professional conduct and work of its members. Both professional associations and trade unions may require qualifications and experience before accepting persons to membership. Since, in many cases, such acceptance is necessary before a person is allowed to follow the profession or trade, it serves as a means of guaranteeing a minimum standard of work. Many associations deal themselves with breaches of professional conduct and draw up a scale of fees, while some, such as the traders' guilds which insist on standards of cleanliness for foodstuffs, take measures whenever possible to improve the quality of their product.

ECONOMIC AND SOCIAL DISADVANTAGES WHICH MAY RESULT FROM MONOPOLY

1. *Restriction of output*

The power of the monopolist to make high profits rests on the fact that he does not have to fear competition from other producers. He can, therefore, restrict supplies in order to force up the price he receives for his good, and the more inelastic the demand for his good, the greater is his power. In short, it means that to some extent consumers are held to ransom. Such restriction of supply may take various forms. If possible the monopolist will limit his capacity to that output at which his profits will be a maximum but, where demand fluctuates, he is more likely to adjust output by varying the productive resources he leaves idle. On the other hand, where nature plays a dominant role in production, it may have to be the actual amount of the good coming on to the market which is restricted. In the past this has led to the destruction of commodities, e.g. coffee, fish. In practice, restriction of supplies is the most widespread and serious abuse of monopoly power and it results in the inefficient functioning of the free price system.

2. *Lack of enterprise*

Normally competition forces firms to adopt the new methods of production or to manufacture the improved products which are developed. If they failed to do so, the more go-ahead firms would force them out of business. However, a monopoly is, at least in theory, under no such compulsion. Indeed it can buy up inventions and then patent them itself in order to prevent competitors manufacturing its commodity at a cheaper rate. How far, in practice, monopolies do check technical improvements is difficult to judge. We have all probably had experience of the old-fashioned shop or firm which, secure in goodwill, seems to maintain its position regardless of the changes going on around it. Yet it is probable that, especially in the case of the larger monopolies with their great resources, research is not less than it would be under conditions of competition and may be even better co-ordinated and therefore more effective. Indeed the patent laws, which limit competition, are considered to be an effective means of stimulating research and invention, e.g. in the pharmaceutical industry.

3. *A waste of resources through artificial division of the market*

When discussing the division of labour, it was pointed out that the extent to which it could be applied was limited by the size of the market. In the same way it is not possible to produce on a large scale when the market is too small to take the output contemplated. The result of monopoly power secured by such methods as product differentiation is often to divide up artificially the potential market into a number of small parts. Consequently the full advantages of large-scale production are not achieved, for each firm, by producing its own particular brand of product, has to remain fairly small.

Moreover, agreements are often reached among producers not to reduce their prices below a certain level. The result is that competition, instead of resulting in progressive price reductions, takes the form of excessive advertising, gift coupon schemes, fancy wrappings and so on. The consumer has to take these instead of lower prices. Thus he loses some freedom of choice in spending his income.

4. *The exertion of political influence*

The larger monopolies often represent a vast concentration of economic power. In the past, therefore, it has been possible for monopolies to put pressure on governments to act in their interests at the expense of the consumers who are comparatively unorganised. Today, however, particularly in the United Kingdom, such political pressure by producer interests is more difficult and would probably be engaged in only at the risk of nationalisation. There is far more danger that demands of this nature would be made by the more powerfully organised trade unions who, in periods of full employment, find themselves in a particularly strong position, both economically and politically.

IV. THE CONTROL OF MONOPOLY

As a result of our analysis of the causes of monopoly it was found possible to divide monopolies into two groups; (a) those which were 'spontaneous', that is, to some degree inevitable; (b) those which were 'deliberate', in that they were fostered with the principal object of eliminating competition.

With the 'spontaneous' monopolies obvious benefits result. They may arise because it is necessary to work on a very large scale. If production were to be split up among a number of small competing firms, the price to the consumer, as a pre-war committee discovered when investigating the manufacture of sewing cotton by J. & P. Coats, would probably be higher. Or such monopolies may even have been fostered by Government policy under the Patent Acts, by nationalisation, or simply to meet a particular need of the time. The formation of the Bank of England in 1694 and of the Marketing Boards during the depression of the 1930's are all examples of monopolies created by the government in special circumstances. Indeed, in 1967 an Industrial Reorganisation Corporation (since abolished) was set up to promote the merging of firms in order to secure the advantages of larger producing units. Such mergers were secured in the motor, computer and heavy electrical industries. We can do nothing but accept 'spontaneous' monopolies. At the same time we must be careful to recognise the fact that, since they may use their power to the detriment of the consumer, some government control is called for.

With the second group, the ' deliberate ' type of monopolies, a more positive action, even aiming at their disintegration, may be necessary. How far such a policy should be carried depends chiefly on the public benefits which may accrue through the existence of the particular monopoly. If the advantages are great, so that the public harm resulting from its destruction exceeds the gain resulting from the restoration of competition, then obviously regulation, and not disintegration, would again be the correct policy. On the other hand, where the monopoly results in little but restriction of supply and higher prices to the consumers with no attendant benefits, then government policy must aim at its destruction.

In practice, the decision regarding policy is complicated. An exact assessment of the public benefits and disadvantages resulting from a monopoly is difficult. Very often, too, the decision as to whether a monopoly is useful or unsocial in character depends on circumstances and therefore varies from one period to another (note the fostering of monopolies in the 1930's). Moreover, if legislation is proposed, the term 'unfair competition' has to be closely defined by lawyers, though, for the purposes of control, it really requires an elastic interpretation based on economic issues. Lastly, government policy in another field may influence the problem of monopoly. Thus tariff protection, by restricting competition from abroad, enhances the possibility of establishing monopolies in the home market.

We will now examine briefly the various lines of government action.

1. State Ownership

When it is important not to destroy the advantages of monopoly, the problem may best be solved by the state taking it over completely; the public then appears to be effectively protected. Freed from the incentive of the profit motive, there should be no tendency for the state-owned monopolies to make high profits. But if such profits were made they would eventually be passed on to the public in lower future prices, or in relief of taxation.

In practice, however, profits may be masked by inefficiency in operation or by the payment of wages to employees above the current economic level. Consequently, provision must be made for the examination of the prices charged by an independent council and for efficiency checks by independent experts.

2. Legislation and Administrative Machinery to Regulate Monopolies

This method is usually employed when it is desired to retain monopolies because of the benefits they bring but leave them fairly free to operate under private ownership. It was the policy consistently followed in Germany before the war, but not until 1948 did the United Kingdom set up machinery for investigating monopolies.

The Monopolies and Restrictive Practices Act, 1948, set up a Monopolies Commission, the members of which were appointed by the President of the Board of Trade. Under the terms of the Act, the Board of Trade could, whenever it appeared to the Board that in the supply, processing or export of goods not less than one-third was in the hands of one concern or group acting to restrict competition, refer the matter to the Commission. The Commission could be told either to ascertain facts only or to go further and assess the effect of the monopoly on the public interest and recommend appropriate action. Upon the Commission's report, the Minister could issue an Order declaring certain arrangements or practices illegal. No criminal proceedings, however, could be brought under the Order, but the Crown could seek an injunction. Subjects investigated include: supply of electric lamps, household detergents, colour film, flat glass, chemical fertilisers and wallpaper; tendering practices by builders in the Greater London Area; collective discrimination; restrictive practices in the professions.

The Act was subject to two main criticisms. First, it specifically excluded investigation of the nationalised industries and trade unions. Secondly, it did not possess any 'teeth', only civil action following the breach of a Ministerial Order. Nevertheless, publicity, rather than direct action following an adverse report, usually influenced firms to mend their ways.

3. Breaking up or Prohibition of the Monopoly

Where the monopoly is on balance detrimental to consumers, policy can take the form of breaking it up or prohibiting it by legislation. Thus the state can reduce the period for which patents are granted or make their renewal more difficult. Similarly, it may pass Company Acts requiring firms to publish profit statements, so that other firms can ascertain quickly if super-normal profits are being made.

Alternatively, the state can outlaw attempts to eliminate competition, whether by unfair practices, the formation of cartels or restrictive agreements. Total prohibition was the policy at one time followed by the U.S.A. The Sherman Act, 1890, made every contract or combination in restraint of trade illegal and any attempt to monopolise trade a misdemeanour. Yet difficulties arose which made it hard to enforce. Some administrations acted vigorously, while others were passive. Again, the purposes of the Act were often frustrated because of the difficulty experienced by lawyers in assessing economic conditions and terms. Above all, after a monopoly had been successfully prosecuted, it often found alternative means of circumventing the law, such as by substituting 'gentlemen's agreements' in place of written contracts. In practice, while the Act may have deterred the creation of new monopolies, it did not succeed in breaking up those which already existed.

In the United Kingdom, largely through the publicity resulting from an investigation by the Monopolies Commission into certain restrictive practices, a Restrictive Trade Practices Act was passed in 1956.

This Act: (a) allowed manufacturers and traders to enforce *individual* resale price maintenance through the ordinary civil courts; (b) banned the *collective* enforcement of resale price maintenance through such practices as private courts, stop lists and boycotts; (c) required other restrictive pacts, such as common price and level tendering, to be registered with a new Registrar of Restrictive Trading Agreements, appointed by the Crown; (d) appointed a new Restrictive Trade Practices Court. The Court sits as three-member tribunals consisting of at least one judge and two lay members, and for a practice to be allowed it must be justified as being 'in the public interest' according to any of seven closely defined 'gateways'. The tribunal's decision is made on a majority basis.

But the 1956 Act still permitted individual suppliers to enforce resale price maintenance for their own products. This was amended by the Resale Prices Act, 1964, which made minimum resale price maintenance illegal, except for goods approved by the Court. To be approved, the resulting benefits to consumers must outweigh any detriments.

The Monopolies and Mergers Act, 1965, strengthened and extended the legislation on monopolies. It permitted the Board of Trade to refer a merger or proposed merger to the Monopolies Commission where the merger would lead to a monopoly (at least one-third of the market) or would increase the power of an existing monopoly. The Act also increased the government's powers to enforce the findings of the Commission (for example, by giving it powers to prohibit mergers or to dissolve an undesirable monopoly).

The Fair Trading Act, 1973, introduced a new concept with regard to monopoly and consumer protection. Unlike the earlier Monopolies Acts, whose primary concern with monopolies was whether they might be harmful to economic efficiency and thus not in the 'public interest', the object of this new Act has been stated to be to 'strengthen the machinery of *promoting competition*'. The Act:

(1) creates an office of Director-General of Fair Trading. Not only does the Director take over the functions of the Registrar of Restrictive Trading Agreements, but also those of the Department of Trade with regard to discovering probable monopoly situations or uncompetitive practices. Thus the Fair Trading Office will become a new central source of information and advice for Ministers on consumer protection, monopoly, mergers, and restrictive practices.

(2) empowers the re-named Monopolies and Mergers Commission to investigate local as well as national monopolies, and extends their powers of inquiry to the activities of nationalised industries, and even to investigate restrictive labour practices (though with limited follow-up powers).

(3) reduces the criterion for a monopoly situation to a one-quarter (minimum) market share.

PART IV

WHERE TO PRODUCE

CHAPTER 10

DISPERSED INDUSTRIES

I. DISPERSAL AND CONCENTRATION

So far we have seen how variations in the prices of goods reflect changes in consumers' demand, thereby indicating *what* to produce. Moreover, we have noted how, under Capitalism, production takes place with the object of making a profit. A producer will, therefore, go on increasing his output so long as it adds to his profit. Thus profit is an indication of *how much* of the good should be produced.

We now turn to a consideration of the problem: '*Where* shall the production of the good take place?' Under Capitalism, this is, as we shall see, largely decided by the producer, who chooses a particular place for his factory because his costs of production are lower there than elsewhere. Our aim is to discover general principles which make for such lower costs, and we begin by analysing the factors which have influenced the situation of the various firms of the more important industries of the United Kingdom.

First, however, it is necessary to give a word of explanation as to the selection of industries. The basis upon which the relative importance of each industry has been decided is the number it employs as shown by the classification of the Department of Employment. What defines one industry and separates it from another is that the firms within each industry produce a similar type of product and perform a similar service (both defined fairly broadly), while their product or service is distinct from that of any other industry.

Now, when we consider the geographical location of these industries, we are immediately aware of an important fact— some of the industries are highly concentrated in one or a small number of localities (the usual term for concentration being 'localisation of industry'). On the other hand, others show no tendency to concentrate, but are dispersed throughout the whole of the country, often serving a market in their immediate neighbourhood. Table 12 shows the importance of the major industries of the United Kingdom in terms of the number of insured employees, and also groups them according to whether they are concentrated or dispersed.

TABLE 12.—*Dispersed and Concentrated Industries, United Kingdom, 1973*

Group A—Dispersed Number of insured employees (thousands)		Group B—Concentrated Number of insured employees (thousands)	
Distributive trades	2,744	Coal-mining	315
Construction	1,380	Iron and steel	389
Food, drink and tobacco manufacturing	754	Motor vehicles and cycles . . .	555
Professional and scientific services .	3,250	Aerospace manufacturing and repairing	202
Insurance, banking and finance . .	1,058	Shipbuilding and marine engineering .	187
Catering and hotels	794	Cotton and man-made fibres (spinning	
Motor repairing, garages, etc. . .	465	and weaving)	168
Public administration . . .	1,583	Woollen and worsted . . .	108
Miscellaneous services . . .	894		
Clothing, hosiery and footwear . .	574		
Road transport	472		
Postal services	445		
Railways	224		
Printing and publishing . . .	354		
Gas and electricity	300		
Bricks, pottery, glass and cement .	305		
Timber and furniture . . .	292		

Engineering (including agricultural and textile machinery, ordnance and small arms)	1,128
Other metal goods	567
Agriculture and forestry	423
Electrical	808
Chemical and allied industries	427
Paper and board	220

Most industries shown as dispersed have high concentrations in the Greater London area (*see also* pages 244–7).

The six industries at the foot of the Table do not fall easily within either group. Each of them is dispersed, yet within each there are sections which are concentrated in particular localities.

The engineering industry as a whole is dispersed. Unlike the industries producing iron and steel, the raw materials used in engineering do not lose weight. Moreover, the industry makes greater use of electricity. Thus it is not tied to its sources of raw materials or to the coalfields to anything like the same extent. Firms can afford to go nearer consumers. With agricultural machinery, in particular, this serves a double purpose, for wage-rates are relatively lower in the smaller country towns.

Yet, while the industry as a whole is dispersed, certain sections of it concentrate in certain areas. The production of textile machinery is highly concentrated in the textile areas. In Lancashire it is found particularly in Manchester and the large spinning and weaving towns such as Oldham, Bolton, Rochdale, Accrington and Blackburn, while other areas of production are Leeds, Nottingham, Leicester and Dundee. Agricultural engineering takes place in many of the county and large market towns, e.g. Ipswich, Lincoln and Stamford, for machinery is produced to suit local differences of soil, size of fields and physical relief of the land. But there are larger centres such as Leeds, Derby and Birmingham, the latter, for instance, producing most of the lawn mowers. Locomotive engineering is concentrated in Crewe, Derby, Doncaster, and Eastleigh, while marine engineering is found chiefly in the great shipbuilding districts of Newcastle and the Clyde. These industries provide examples of how industry, when not tied to its raw materials, moves to the consumption centre, where it can also keep in close contact with the users.

In addition to engineering goods, many metal products, e.g. tools, bolts, cutlery and wire are made by firms of various sizes scattered throughout the country. Again, however, there are concentrations, e.g. in Birmingham and Sheffield.

Agriculture, while dispersed as a group, has similarly various areas of specialisation, of which Evesham (fruit), Kent (hops), East Anglia (corn), are but examples.

As regards the electrical industry, the wide range of products ensures its dispersal, though at present one-third of the production is concentrated in the Greater London area.

The chemical industry embraces many products, e.g. chemicals, dyes, explosives, paint, printing ink, plastics, man-made fibres, fertilisers. Again there are concentrations of production, e.g. Tees-side, the Humber, Manchester, Cheshire, Merseyside and oil refinery towns on the coast (Fawley, Avonmouth, Thames Haven).

The raw materials of paper and board are wood pulp and waste paper. Thus large, integrated plants are found where wood pulp is imported (e.g. the Thames Estuary, Ellesmere Port) or local wood is available (e.g. Fort William in the Scottish Highlands).

II. REASONS FOR THE DISPERSAL OF CERTAIN INDUSTRIES

It is convenient to commence our study by asking: 'What are the causes of the dispersed nature of the industries within Group A?' Certain general reasons can be suggested.

In the first place, it is essential, for the productive capacity of an industry to be spread all over the country, that there is a nation-wide demand for the good or service produced. If the demand is a purely local one, as it is for haggis or local newspapers, then those goods will probably be produced only in particular localities. But the converse is not true—that goods with a nation-wide demand are produced only by dispersed industries. In fact, the products of all the concentrated industries have a nation-wide demand. Thus, while an extensive demand is a prerequisite of dispersal, there are more vital reasons.

An examination of the industries will reveal a feature common to many of them—that they render a direct personal service to the consumer. In retail distribution, for instance, the service consists either of taking the goods to the consumer or of letting him see the goods before a purchase is made, especially where the good sold is not of a uniform or ' branded ' type. Similarly with catering and hotels, the personal service which they give necessitates their being located wherever the consumer is found. The same applies to such personal services as are rendered by doctors and dentists, or supplied by a dressmaker or tailor, who make an article which requires a number of personal fittings. Such industries are scattered simply because the consumers are scattered and cannot be separated from the production of the actual goods. When stated in this way, it can be seen that rail and road transport of passengers and also the construction industry, particularly decorators and repairers, must be dispersed for the same reason. Of course, where we find a heavy concentration of population, as in the London area, then there is more concentration of these personal service industries, so much so, in fact, that certain localities have become noted for them, e.g. Harley Street for doctors, Savile Row for tailors, and Bloomsbury for hotels.

But the main reason for dispersal cannot be seen until we have discussed briefly the problem of transport costs. A producer chooses a situation which keeps his costs of production to a minimum. Here transport costs are important (though as we shall see later, the location of an industry in a particular region may reduce costs for reasons other than economies in transport). Usually transport costs have to be incurred both in assembling the raw materials before production is commenced and in the distribution of the finished good to the consumer. It is possible, however, to reduce transport costs in assembling raw materials by building the factory where those raw materials are found. Similarly, distribution costs of the finished good can be largely avoided by transporting the raw materials to a factory located in or near the market for the good. The actual course adopted will depend on the nature of the industry. With some industries, materials lose weight in the course of manufacture, while with others, the product gains weight. Two examples will make this clearer.

For the production of one ton of pig-iron, four tons of raw materials are necessary. Hence, in the process of manufacture, three tons of raw materials are lost (Fig. 17). Thus

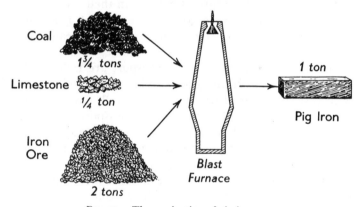

Coal
1¾ tons
Limestone
¼ ton
Iron Ore
2 tons
Blast Furnace
1 ton
Pig Iron

FIG. 17.—The production of pig-iron

it is far cheaper to transport the finished product to the consumption centre than it is to transport the raw materials. Such 'weight-losing' industries, therefore, are concentrated where the raw materials are found, which, as we shall see, has lead to a heavy concentration on the coalfield areas.

In contrast to the iron industry, however, we can select brewing, where weight is gained in the process of production because water is added to the malted barley and hops. Here, in order to keep transport costs to a minimum, the centres of production should be as near the consumer as possible, and thus it is that the production of beer is for a relatively local area, and breweries are dispersed throughout the country. Indeed, the basic difference is well illustrated in the production of mineral waters and cordials. Mineral waters contain large quantities of water which would be costly to send over the countryside, and are therefore manufactured locally, usually within 30 miles of the consumer. Cordials, on the other hand, are concentrated juices which can more easily bear transport costs and are therefore manufactured by national producers, found mostly in south-east England. Building, which uses bulky materials most of which can be produced locally, likewise tends to be dispersed.

A similar position arises where the transport costs of the finished product are higher than the costs of transporting the raw materials because the finished product is bulkier, e.g. potato crisps and furniture. Once again then, the tendency is for firms producing these goods to be situated near the consumer, and, therefore, since consumers are spread, so is the industry.

Generally, the difficulties of transport are reflected in the costs of transport. If the goods can be loaded and transported with ease, the costs of transport are usually low. If they are heavy, bulky or fragile, the costs of transporting are higher. With some goods, however, obstacles in transportation are more fundamental, again making for dispersal in their production. We have already noted such difficulties in transporting personal services. Physical difficulties also impose limitations to the area of production. The production of water and gas by a single large firm, for instance, tends to be limited by the costs of piping them over great distances. Even so, such obstacles decrease in importance when the cost of producing at a particular centre is very low, e.g. North Sea gas. Finally, where a good is perishable, as with bread, ice-cream and fresh garden produce, production must be near the consumer. Hence, bakeries, ice-cream factories and market gardens are spread all over the country, generally very near the large consumption centres.

CHAPTER II

THE CONCENTRATED INDUSTRIES

I. THE FUEL AND POWER INDUSTRIES

TABLE 13 shows that, while coal was easily the major source of power in 1950, it has been rapidly supplanted by oil and natural gas. Indeed, over the period, manpower in the coal industry has decreased from 700,000 to 250,000. Changes in relative prices is the main reason, for over this period oil and natural gas were cheap in comparison with coal. It is doubtful whether the quadrupling of oil prices in 1973 will check the trend for long. High wage settlements for miners and, above all, the development of Britain's North Sea oil deposits by 1980, will tend to erode the price advantage which coal at present enjoys.

TABLE 13.—*Primary sources of power of the United Kingdom* (million tons coal equivalent)

	1950	*1960*	*1973*
Coal (net) . . .	201·1	195·5	131·3
Oil	22·2	65·5	159·4
Nuclear energy . .	—	0·9	9·9
Natural gas . . .	—	0·1	43·5
Hydro-power . . .	0·9	1·7	2·0
TOTAL . . .	224·2	263·7	346·1

Source: United Kingdom Energy Statistics

Industry, however, still tends to be located on the coalfields. It came there originally because, in the days of steam-power, coal represented a raw material which was used up in the course of production. It stays there because of acquired advantages (page 192). Thus we must begin any study of concentration by looking at the coalfields.

8 WHERE TO PRODUCE

1. Coal-mining

With coal-mining, the main factor governing its location is obviously the natural occurrence of the coal measures; 200 years ago, however, two other conditions were necessary. The first was that the seams should be relatively near the surface, as machinery necessary to sink deep shafts and to cope with the flooding and gas accumulations which occur in deep pits had not been developed. The second was that the measure should be relatively near navigable water, for until the construction of canals and railways, the cost of inland transport was prohibitive. Thus the first coalfield to be worked on a large scale was that in Northumberland and, during the Tudor and Stuart periods, there were frequent protests in London against the increasing use of Newcastle 'sea-coles' which were said to smell abominably and to pollute the air with soot!

The construction of canals from 1760 and the development of the railways after 1830 allowed a rapid development of the inland coalfields. Today the major coalfields are shown in Fig. 18 and Map 1.

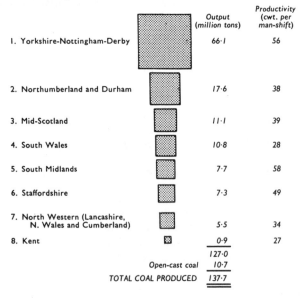

	Output (million tons)	Productivity (cwt. per man-shift)
1. Yorkshire-Nottingham-Derby	66·1	56
2. Northumberland and Durham	17·6	38
3. Mid-Scotland	11·1	39
4. South Wales	10·8	28
5. South Midlands	7·7	58
6. Staffordshire	7·3	49
7. North Western (Lancashire, N. Wales and Cumberland)	5·5	34
8. Kent	0·9	27
	127·0	
Open-cast coal	10·7	
TOTAL COAL PRODUCED	137·7	

FIG. 18.—Coal output of the major regions of the United Kingdom 1972/3

Four major coalfields provide 83 per cent of the total output and, of the total, the Yorkshire-Nottingham-Derbyshire coalfield produces one-half.

If coal is to remain a competitive fuel, production costs must be held down. In 1972–3 coal cost an average of £7·66 per ton, and over half of this was due to wages. Hence the importance of productivity, measured in 'cwt per manshift'. Productivity has risen steadily in recent years, chiefly through increased mechanisation in cutting and moving the coal and by closing down the more inefficient pits.

As the figures in Fig. 18 show, there are wide differences in productivity in different areas. Some collieries, notably the Yorks-Notts-Derby, have regular and little-faulted seams which have made possible straightforward planning, the use of machinery and large size of colliery (1,000 to 1,500 men).

Others, particularly South Wales and Scotland, have thin, faulted and steeply-inclined seams. Further hazards include roof-falls, the presence of explosive gases, and excessive water making constant pumping necessary. In some cases, however, such areas produce especially valuable types of coal, such as the anthracite of South Wales and the coking varieties of Durham and Kent which are vital for the iron and steel industry.

Nevertheless, future expansion is likely to be confined to the better coalfields, e.g. at Selby in Yorkshire where the N.C.B. intends to develop new collieries to work the broad coal seams lately discovered there. In all, the development plan for Britain's coal industry involves expenditure of £600 million in the years 1974–84.

Of course, in discussing the future of the coalmining industry, the importance of political factors must be borne in mind. On the one hand, unprofitable pits may continue to be worked for social reasons. On the other, despite the high price of oil, the electricity generating industry remains anxious about over-dependence on coal especially when strikes disrupt supplies. In recent years, the government has intervened to discourage the construction of oil-fuelled power stations in favour of coal. But it may be reluctant to do this when large quantities of North Sea oil become available.

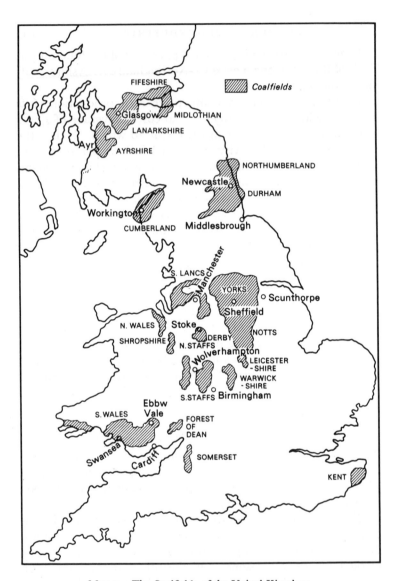

Map 1.—The Coalfields of the United Kingdom

2. ELECTRICITY

At first it might seem that electricity generation is a highly-dispersed industry. Indeed in 1918 this was so, for there were over 500 electricity undertakings throughout Great Britain, and even quite small towns had their own power stations. Not until 1926, when the Central Electricity Board was set up, did a national system begin to develop, and from then on a more definite locational pattern gradually emerged. The first task of the C.E.B. was to provide a national network of transmission lines (a 'grid'), and by 1933 the main power stations were all linked with the chief areas of consumption. The new system made it possible to switch-in power from other parts of the country (and even from France) in order to cope with any emergency or sudden increase in demand. The result was both greater reliability of supply and a saving in generating plant.

Size and efficiency. To appreciate the changes of the past half-century, one must understand something of the technology and basic cost structures of electricity generation.

Electricity is produced when a generator is turned at high speed. Except in the cases of hydro-electric power and of a few small gas-turbine stations, this rotation is achieved by a steam turbine. So power station designs vary only in the way the steam is produced: it may be by boilers fired by coal, natural gas or oil, or the steam may be supplied by the heat from nuclear reactors. The problem is that the steam used to power the turbine generator must be *high* pressure steam. Having been through the turbine once, the steam has still a lot of heat and energy left but is no longer suitable for electricity generation. Therefore it is condensed so that the resulting pure water may again be used in the boilers, but the heat is wasted. (The Battersea Power Station in London uses this low pressure steam to provide cheap heating for the Pimlico housing estate on the other side of the Thames.)

As a general principle, large generators and boilers are more efficient than smaller ones, and concentrations of generating equipment on one site more efficient than a scatter of smaller plant. Thus the large stations achieve thermal efficiencies of 35 per cent (that is, about a third of the heat produced by the furnaces is converted into useful electricity). By contrast, the smaller (and older) stations barely reach a thermal efficiency of 10 per cent.

Total capacity of the electricity supply industry must be fitted into the pattern of demand, which is variable (Fig. 19), and to the supply condition that electricity cannot be stored. Fortunately, the existence of the National Grid means that the more efficient generators can supply the constant 'baseload' of the power required, so that they are working near to full capacity most of the time, while the least efficient need only be called upon during the brief periods of peak demand.

The pricing system is also used to even out demand. Off-peak electricity (e.g. storage heaters and battery-operated milk-carts which are re-charged at night) is charged at a lower rate.

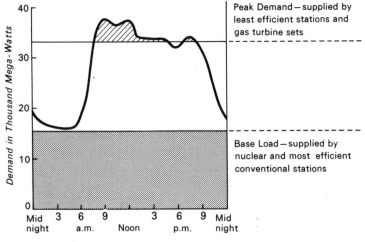

FIG. 19.—Typical 24-hour period demand for electricity

Location of 'conventional' power stations. A large power station must be located to keep its costs to a minimum. The availability of large supplies of water is a principal consideration; also important is the cost of transporting coal or oil. Thus oil-burning stations are on the coast near refineries (e.g.

Fawley and the Isle of Grain). Coal-burning stations obtain 20 per cent of their coal from Yorkshire and 30 per cent from the Midlands. There may be rail-links for special coal trains, but water transport is important. Thus there has been a build-up of generating capacity along the Aire and Calder Navigation and associated waterways in Yorkshire, and also along the Trent in Nottinghamshire. The navigable reaches of the Thames are another favoured location for coal-fuelled power stations. Not only are they accessible for the fleets of collier ships, but they are close to London, an area of great demand for electricity.

Nuclear power. Nuclear power stations do not need large intakes of fuel. One tonne of uranium can produce as much electricity as 10,000 tonnes of coal. Nuclear power stations are not therefore tied to bulk transport routes.

Yet, like other power stations, they require large supplies of water. Thus all are actually at points along the coast-line of Britain, with the exception of Trawsfynydd, which is by a Snowdonian lake.

But a major problem of nuclear power is the fear that an explosion might damage the reactor-housing and release dangerous atomic radiation into the atmosphere. The reactors are therefore contained in immensely strong 'pressure vessels' with massive concrete shielding. As an additional precaution, nuclear power stations are usually sited in areas of low population, like Sizewell on the Suffolk coast and Wylfa on Anglesey. This remoteness adds significantly to their cost. The local road system has to be improved to carry the heavy construction traffic, and long linkages with the national grid cost about £50,000 a mile.

Once built, however, the operating costs per unit of output of a nuclear station are less than half those of a conventional coal or oil station. If used to capacity, therefore, the nuclear station may save enough on operating costs to offset its higher construction costs. The best solution would seem to be nuclear stations (assuming they were fully efficient and reliable) to deal with the 'base load', and conventional stations to handle the less constant load, supplemented by highly flexible gas-turbine equipment for the short, peak-demand periods.

Hydro-electricity. Hydro-electricity contributes only a small proportion of the total national output. Construction costs are high, and it is confined to the wet highland districts of Scotland and Wales. However, in certain of its 'pump-storage' schemes, hydro-electricity provides an example of an attempt to harmonise fluctuating demand with supply. During periods of high demand electricity is fed into the national grid in the normal way. But when demand is slack, the power house reverses its function, drawing power from the grid to pump water from a lower reservoir to replenish the level of the upper reservoir from which it derives its power. Thus more power is available to feed back into the grid at times of heavy demand.

3. Natural Gas

In 1959 a huge natural gas field was discovered in the North Sea off the Dutch coast. This intensified exploration off Yorkshire where similar geological conditions occurred. At that time, a country's territorial rights over the sea-bed extended only as far as the three-mile limit, but in 1964 an international agreement divided up the shallow waters of the Continental Shelf among the bordering nations. Thus the United Kingdom obtained mineral rights over the whole of the western half of the North Sea, and large parts of the Irish (or 'Celtic') Sea.

In 1965 British Petroleum discovered gas in the West Sole field, 40 miles off the Yorkshire coast. Conditions were difficult and drilling had to reach a depth of 10,000 feet, but the quality of the gas was high. The first gas was brought ashore in 1967.

The largest gasfields were discovered on the Leman Bank off the Norfolk coast. The gas is piped to Bacton, from where land pipe-lines radiate to London, the Midlands and the West, and link up with the main trunk route running northwards to Leeds, later extending to Glasgow. By the mid-1970s the demand for gas had trebled, and natural gas was increasingly substituted for coal and oil, not only for industrial processes and domestic heating, but also in the few power stations which the government, anxious for the coal industry, had allowed the generating authorities to adapt for gas-firing.

4. OIL

Crude oil consists of various hydro-carbons—light petrols, heavier fuel-oils and tar, together with impurities such as sulphur. These products are separated out and treated in refineries.

Since the 1920s oil has become of increasing importance in the British economy. Almost all transport now depends upon it; power stations and gas-works have been turning towards it as an alternative to coal; industrial heating and processes use it; and the petro-chemical industries produce a wide range of substances (including plastics) based on oil.

Until the late 1970s, most of Britain's oil requirements will continue to be imported. Before 1939, most oil imports were in the form of refined products, especially petrol. However, because of the post-war growth of the petro-chemical industries, it has been cheaper overall to import crude oil.

It is more economical to bring the crude oil to Britain in 'super-tankers' of over 100,000 tonnes than in a greater number of small ships, especially following the closure of the Suez route from the Middle East in 1967. Thus exceptionally deep water is required for berths. This means that refineries are usually located by deep-water harbours, if possible near major industrial centres, e.g. Thames-side and Tees-side (Map 2). Indeed, a refinery can itself act as the nucleus of an industrial complex. There is usually an adjacent petro-chemical works, and often a plastics or synthetic rubber factory nearby, as well as an oil-fired power station—all using the products of the refinery.

Where necessary, pipelines are used by the oil and petro-chemical industries to reduce transport costs between coastal installations and major consumers. Thus although Milford Haven is an excellent deep-water harbour it is remote from the main industrial areas of South Wales. Consequently, much of the crude oil landed there is taken by pipeline to another refinery at Llandarcy, near Swansea. Similarly, a pipeline carries aviation spirit from Fawley to London Airport, while another connects I.C.I.'s Tees-side refinery with the company's other works to the south of Manchester.

Britain's North Sea oil. The geological formation which suggested the presence of natural gas also indicated the likelihood of there being oil nearby. But the search for oil in the wild seas 160 kilometres off Aberdeen proved to be an even greater challenge. More advanced technology (usually imported) and massive amounts of capital were required. Thus even the large oil companies often thought it advisable to form consortia to pool their resources.

In 1970 British Petroleum made the first major discovery, in the 'Forties' field, east of Aberdeen. This was followed by further strikes by Shell-Esso, first in the 'Auk' field, and later, to the east of the Shetlands in 'Brent'. The success rate was high, one strike being made for every seven 'dry' drills. By 1974 activity had extended to the north of the Shetlands, and even to the 'Celtic' sea.

To date, some 300 wells have been drilled, but the estimates of Britain's oil reserves have still not been accurately determined. For quality, North Sea oil compares favourably with Arab oil. It gives a rich yield of petrols and has a fairly low sulphur content. But the cost of extracting it is some thirty times that of Middle East oil, and it is mainly the greatly increased price of the latter and the strain imposed on the U.K.'s balance of payments, which has accelerated the development of North Sea oil.

Pipelines are being constructed to connect the oil fields with terminals in the Orkneys, Shetlands and the mainland. However, a few oil fields are to be served directly by tanker. In fact, the first North Sea oil landed in Britain came from Norway's 'Ekofisk' field. Owing to a fault in the sea-bed between Ekofisk and the Norwegian coast, it was decided to lay the pipeline westwards to supply the refineries and petrochemical industries of Tees-side.

It is estimated that by 1980 Britain should be self-sufficient in oil, and perhaps a net exporter, but the rate of development could be held back by unforeseen technical difficulties,

MAP 2.—Britain's Oil and Natural Gas Industries

inclement weather and vague government plans for 'public participation' and higher taxation which serve to make the oil companies doubtful as to whether the return on capital will be sufficient to compensate for the risks involved.

II. THE IRON AND STEEL INDUSTRY

Most of the United Kingdom's iron and steel production is now undertaken by the nationalised British Steel Corporation. However, there are several 'independent' producers: some are small, specialist companies, others are associates of general engineering combines.

The iron and steel industry produces many different products but, in studying the reasons for its location, we shall simplify matters by dividing it into its two main sections, the production of pig-iron and the production of steel. It should be noted, however, that the production of steel and finished products is increasingly being integrated with the pig-iron process.

1. THE PRODUCTION OF PIG-IRON

In nature, iron occurs as an ore (haematite), in which an oxide of iron is mixed with many chemical impurities and much earthy material such as sand and clay. To produce iron, it is necessary to remove these impurities, but especially to liberate iron from its bondage to oxygen in the oxide. This is done by heating the iron ore in a blast furnace together with a form of carbon (originally charcoal, more recently coke), whereupon the oxygen combines with the carbon, leaving iron. At the same time the chemical impurities combine with limestone, which is added as a 'flux', and are drawn off in the form of molten slag.

If the iron produced by a blast furnace is poured into standard-sized moulds (traditionally called 'pigs'), the metal is known as 'pig-iron'. Alternatively, the iron may move straight on from the blast furnace to the steel-making stage in molten form, when it is termed 'hot metal'.

All that remains to be done in order to produce steel is. to re-process the iron in another furnace to burn off remaining impurities and to change the chemical structure by adding a small proportion of carbon and small amounts of other substances (such as chrome or manganese). Finally, the 'crude' steel is put through various mills to produce more useful forms of the metal than mere 'ingots', such as beams or strips.

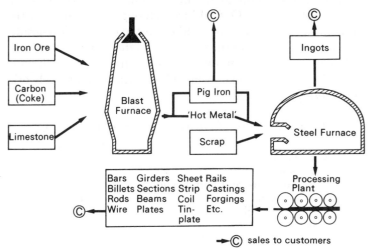

FIG. 20.—Iron and steel production

Over the last 250 years the location of the industry has been affected by changes and improvements in processes. Before the Industrial Revolution, when charcoal was used for smelting, the centres of pig-iron production were the Weald, the Severn Valley and the West Midlands, areas where timber and iron ore were found close together. In the 1730s, however, Abraham Darby of Coalbrookdale discovered an efficient method of turning coal into coke for smelting iron ore. But when coke was first used, consumption was heavy, at least 8 tons of coal being required to smelt 1 ton of pig-iron. Production thus tended to centre on the coalfields. Hence until the middle of the nineteenth century, when technical improvements began to reduce the proportion of coal used, the West Midlands and South Wales were the two leading centres of production.

This, however, is not the whole of the story. As the better ores became worked out, so the proportion of iron ore required per ton of pig-iron rose. In addition, fuel-saving developments reduced the coal required. The industry has tended, therefore, to move to two main types of centre.

The first was the belt of lower-grade ironstones which stretches from Frodlingham in Lincolnshire south through Northamptonshire to Oxfordshire. Here production is centred on Scunthorpe and Corby. Although the ores are low-grade, they are relatively near the surface (and thus open-cast mined) and, being mostly calcareous, require no limestone for fluxing. From the start, the coke ovens, blast furnaces and steelworks were closely integrated.

Table 14.—*Production of Pig-iron in the United Kingdom, 1973*

		(*million tons*)
1.	Wales	6·0
2.	North	3·8
3.	Yorkshire and Humberside	3·2
4.	Scotland	1·8
5.	East Midlands	1·2
6.	Others	0·9
	TOTAL	16·9

The second is where high-grade iron ore is imported, chiefly from Sweden, North Africa, Spain and even Newfoundland, South America and Australia. Coking coal is also imported. Deep water and large docks are required with special handling facilities. Usually these ore terminals have been established near the traditional steel-making areas since skilled labour is locally available, e.g. South Wales, Clydeside and Tees-side (Map 3). Furthermore, in order to save fuel and transport costs, the blast furnace is integrated with the steel plant and rolling processes to produce a finished product such as beams, sections and girders for structural engineering; plates for ship-building, sheet steel and coil for the motor industry; tin-plate for food canning; and pipes and tubes.

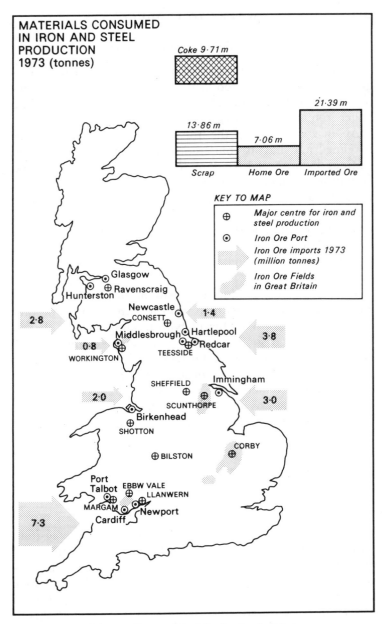

MAP 3.—Iron and Steel Production in Britain

2. THE PRODUCTION OF STEEL

Pig-iron can be best regarded as a raw material for subsequent processes as it is too brittle and contains too many impurities to be used unprocessed. It has to be converted into either iron castings, wrought iron, or steel.

About 20 per cent of the iron made is foundry iron. This is refined and has its composition adjusted for making iron castings in a special kind of furnace known as a cupola. Foundries are more widespread than blast furnaces or steelworks because they are nearer the market. Moreover, since they often produce castings to individual specifications of which no great quantity is required, firms tend to remain small. Cast iron is used in making such articles as motor vehicle components, kitchen stoves, manhole covers and drain-pipes.

Wrought iron is produced by hammering molten pig-iron and by puddling. In its final form it is malleable, and thus easily worked and capable of withstanding sudden shocks. Hence it is used for fancy gates, railway couplings, ships' anchor cables, horseshoes and marine engines. Because quality in the product is important, firms tend to remain small. The chief areas of production are those where the process of using coke for smelting was first adopted—the West Midlands, West Scotland, York-Notts-Derby, Lancashire and the North-east Coast.

Today, steel, owing to its wide use, is the most important product. In fact, more steel is produced in the United Kingdom than pig-iron, the difference being made up by adding scrap collected internally and by importing pig-iron and scrap. There are three main processes.

(1) The *Open Hearth* method is so called because pig-iron, scrap and limestone are charged into a shallow 'hearth' and exposed to the heat of the furnace flames. The high temperatures cause impurities to oxidise and combine with limestone to form a slag, and this process is assisted by the injection of oxygen through water-cooled lances. As it takes ten hours to produce 350 tonnes of steel, great control over the quality of the product is possible, but the heavy fuel consumption and

the time involved has meant that today only 30 per cent of steel production is by the Open Hearth process.

(2) The *Electric-Arc* furnace uses scrap entirely. The circular furnace has a movable roof through which three carbon electrodes can be raised and lowered. First the roof is opened and the electrodes withdrawn so that the furnace can be charged with scrap. Then the roof and electrodes are replaced and a powerful electric current melts the scrap. A large furnace can produce 150 tonnes in four hours. Originally the electric-arc furnace produced only special steels, e.g. for stainless steel and gas turbine engines, but it is now in more general use, and accounts for 20 per cent of production. The furnaces are fairly widespread, but many are found in the Sheffield area producing fine steel.

(3) The *Basic Oxygen Steel-making* process (B.O.S.) is the main rival to the old Open Hearth process because, being integrated with the blast furnace, it makes more use of hot metal. The furnace is charged, first with scrap and then with hot metal in the proportions of 30:70. An oxygen lance is lowered into the furnace, and during this 'blow' the oxygen combines with impurities, and lime is added to work as a flux. At the end of this process, the whole furnace is tilted to pour off first the steel and then the slag. In this way 350 tonnes can be produced in 40 minutes, and the process now accounts for 48 per cent of steel production. This advance has been achieved largely over the last 15 years, despite the relative stagnation of total crude steel output in Britain.

TABLE 15.—*Production of Steel in the United Kingdom, 1973*

		(*million tons*)
1.	Wales	8·4
2.	Yorkshire and Humberside	6·6
3.	Northern	4·5
4.	Scotland	3·2
5.	West Midlands	2·0
6.	East Midlands	1·2
7.	Others	0·7
	TOTAL	26·6

As already mentioned, the integration of the hot metal and steel production means that the B.O.S. process is confined mostly to the ore-receiving locations.

Nowadays only about half Britain's steel is produced from pig-iron, the rest coming from scrap. However, this use of scrap is not spread evenly throughout the industry, but is concentrated in the Sheffield area and those areas where large quantities of scrap are generated, e.g. the engineering industries of the Midlands and Clydeside. Here it is mainly used in the 120 remaining open hearth furnaces.

The future of the British steel-making industry. Location of steel production has been chiefly, but not always, based on production cost considerations. For instance, the Ebbw Vale works, 40 km inland from Newport, was developed in the 1930s to reduce local unemployment. Similarly, although physically suited, the Thames estuary has not been developed because of the high level of employment already in the Southeast.

But the British Steel Corporation is increasingly having to recognise that it must be cost-conscious if it is to compete with Japan, Germany and the U.S.A. It therefore has in hand a ten-year development programme for the modernisation and expansion of its activities. Expansion is to take place at five existing sites—Llanwern and Port Talbot (Wales), Ravenscraig (Scotland), Redcar (Tees-side) and Scunthorpe (Lincolnshire). The latter is not on the coast but it has local iron orefields and the oil terminal of Immingham is not too distant.

The plan, however, will involve the closure of works which are small, old or in unfavourable locations, and the discontinuance of some steel-making at other plants. This includes Ebbw Vale, which will be confined to tin-plate, and Shotton (North Wales), which will specialise in 'coated steels'.

Britain's membership of the European Coal and Steel Community through the E.E.C. may also effect changes. Until now, the B.S.C. has had a system of uniform pricing whereby transport costs were averaged out so that customers paid the same prices however distant from the steel works. By contrast, the E.C.S.C. insists on separate charges for transport. This system, particularly with rising transport costs, will tend to influence the locational pattern of steel producers and steel users.

III. THE MOTOR VEHICLE INDUSTRY

Although attention is usually concentrated on the assemblers of passenger cars, the motor industry covers all kinds of road vehicle. Moreover, the industry contains many specialist component makers, some of whom, such as Lucas, Dunlop, and Guest, Keen, Nettlefold, rival for size British Leyland and the U.K. operations of General Motors (Vauxhall), Ford and Chrysler.

TABLE 16.—*Production of Motor Vehicles in the United Kingdom (private and commercial)*

Year	1913	1923	1938	1949	1955	1962	1968	1973
Production (thousands)	34	95	447	628	1237	1765	2225	2154

Although the importance of the British motor industry dates from the 1920s, its origins were much earlier. At first it was largely an offshoot of other industries, particularly of the cycle firms (like Rover) which were anxious to diversify their production, first because of the seasonal nature of the demand for their goods and, second, because of the falling-off of demand in the 1890s. Cycle and motor cycle production was concentrated in the West Midlands, and thus it was that Coventry, Birmingham and Wolverhampton became the main centres for the new motor industry.

But the region had other characteristics which made it suitable for the production of motor vehicles in workshops, characteristics which were just as essential when the industry adopted mass-production in the 1920s. First, because the area had specialised in the production of minor metal goods, there existed a number of independent firms possessing machinery capable of turning out the multitude of small parts needed in the construction of a motor car. Secondly, there was a reserve of skilled and semi-skilled labour; and, third, the region had easy access to all parts of Great Britain, including the major ports.

There were similar reasons for the growth of the motor industry in Oxford. Morris (Lord Nuffield) was originally a maker and repairer of cycles at Oxford. He then turned his attention to the production first of motor-cycles and then of motor-cars. Just when he wanted to expand, his old school at Cowley came up for sale, and it was in its grounds that the new assembly workshops were established.

Thus to some extent the actual location at Cowley was a matter of chance. But the Oxford area did have certain advantages. It had speedy access to the Midlands for supplies of components. Skilled labour could also be recruited from the West Midlands though, as division of labour resulted from the breaking-down of the production process into a large number of simple, repetitive operations, fewer skilled workers were required. Historical factors also played their part. During World War I, production switched to war materials and, to increase output, the government provided capital to build new sheds. These premises were useful for normal motor production when it resumed in 1918. Lastly, like its rivals in the Midlands, the Morris company was well placed for distribution of its vehicles to the major markets within Great Britain; for exports, the ports of London and Southampton were not far away.

The other long-established centres of production are South Essex (especially Dagenham) and Bedfordshire (Luton-Dunstable). These are areas where the emphasis has been on large-scale production from the beginning, and the resulting economies are all-important. Nevertheless, certain special advantages are gained by the choice of these sites.

Ford's operations in Britain began in 1911 when an assembly plant was opened at Trafford Park, Manchester. The company also acquired a foundry at Cork in Ireland. By the early 1920s, Fords were looking for a site on which to build their European headquarters, and in 1924 they bought 300 acres of Thames-side marshland. The land was cheap and flat, thus facilitating the 'flow' method of production, but it required special preparation for building.

To a great extent the factory would be self-sufficient, having its own ironworks, foundry and power-station. A wharf was constructed on the Thames to bring in iron ore and coal, and to export completed vehicles. Although certain key personnel were transferred from Manchester and Cork, most of the large labour force was recruited locally, especially from the Becontree housing estate which the London County Council constructed between 1922 and 1938.

Although the Ford plant was highly integrated, the company still bought many components. Attracted by large orders from Ford, several manufacturers set up factories adjacent to the Dagenham site, notably Briggs Bodies and the Kelsey-Hayes wheel company.

Since 1945 the company has expanded. Briggs and Kelsey-Hayes were among those companies bought up and integrated into the Dagenham plant which now covers over 600 acres. Nor is this the end of the impact of Ford on the economy of South Essex. All along Thames-side are scores of satellite establishments: component factories, research centres, parts depots, the tractor plant at Basildon and a huge office complex at Brentwood. Here, indeed, is a modern example of industrial concentration.

The government and the motor industry

The government exercises a great influence over the motor industry. First, its taxation decisions can have a marked effect on sales, and thus profitability. Second, its employment policy affects location of new plant. Third, although no definite nationalisation proposals have been made, it may take a major interest in return for providing finance.

During the early 1960s, the proposed large-scale expansion projects of the motor industry were viewed by the government as a possible solution to the unemployment problems of Merseyside and central Scotland. Motor factories were seen as 'location leaders', acting as focal points for new industrial centres to which a wide range of component suppliers would be attracted. Accordingly BMC (Austin-Morris) and Hillman (Chrysler) were encouraged by large grants and loans to set up new factories near Glasgow. About the same time, Vauxhall and Ford built new plants on Merseyside.

Ford showed some reluctance, preferring to expand nearer

Dagenham, and the government did eventually allow development in South Essex. Ford had hinted that, unless government pressure on the company's location decisions was relaxed, further expansion might be diverted to the Continent. As it turned out, the transport problems of linking the main Ford plant at Dagenham with the Halewood factory at Liverpool were tackled by direct rail services, three special goods trains running daily in each direction. Labour relations on Merseyside, however, proved to be no better than at Dagenham (where they were notoriously bad), workers demanding for one thing 'pay parity' with Dagenham.

Although this influx of car factories into the North-west represented a definite change in the locational pattern of car production, the region, notably Leyland and Foden, had built commercial vehicles for a long time. This traditional strength was later reinforced by the setting up of a large modern bus factory (the result of co-operation between Leyland and the National Bus Company) in the depressed area of Cumberland.

The government exercised further influence over the motor industry in 1968 when it induced the B.M.C. group (Austin-Morris-Jaguar) to join Leyland-Triumph-Rover, thus forming the British Leyland Motor Corporation. However, the group took a long time to rationalise its production of car models and this, together with labour disputes which caused production loss, led to lack of finance for future development. As a result, further financial assistance from the government was sought in 1975.

Generally, during the early 1970s, the progress of the motor industry has been fairly modest, although exports contribute annually about £1,000 million to the balance of payments. Even this, however, was not fully up to expectations and, in addition, foreign imports from Japan, Germany, France, Italy and Sweden made serious inroads into the home market. Particularly since Britain's membership of the Common Market, continental truckmakers also gained ground in British markets.

Despite this foreign challenge, the internal difficulties of British motor firms continued. These included problems of organisation and insufficient modern equipment. However, the major concern was the disruption caused by strikes. Negotiations in most factories were complicated by the large number of unions, some 17 in the U.K. compared with one in both the U.S.A. and Germany. In addition, even when the immediate causes of disputes are removed, the basic attitudes usually associated with repetitive jobs on an assembly line remain.

As distinct from the actual production of motor vehicles, the repairing industry, as might be expected, is more widespread. It has a large concentration, however, in the Greater London area.

IV. THE AIRCRAFT AND AEROSPACE INDUSTRY

The aircraft industry, with its aerospace developments, has many of the characteristics of the motor industry, with which it is closely associated. It employs varied, light materials; many components are prefabricated elsewhere; labour requirements are similar. Nevertheless, the demand for aircraft is not sufficient for them to be manufactured by the flow method. Moreover, this method is difficult to organise because work on each part takes longer. Hence only parts of the aircraft are made on an assembly line, being brought together later for final assembly.

Before World War II much of the aircraft industry was to be found in southern Britain. On the fringes of London, Vickers' Supermarine factory at Weybridge (Surrey) and De Havilland's at Hatfield (Herts) were particularly famous. Further west were Gloster Aeroplane and the Bristol company.

Many aircraft factories (like Vickers) were set up by engineering companies diversifying. Thus Rolls, an early aviator, persuaded Royce to produce aero engines, following his success with cars. The Bristol company had curious origins, growing out of the city's tramway repair shops. Short Brothers, the Rochester barge-builders, turned to making flying-boats.

After 1936, when war seemed more likely, military aircraft

production expanded greatly. New factories were opened, especially in the North-west which was felt to be safer from enemy attack. New materials and techniques were devised so that companies, never before associated with aircraft, could contribute their machinery and labour forces. At the end of the war, there were a million aircraft workers.

In 1945 the industry had to contract, often painfully. Some military aircraft were still required but, even with the growing demand for passenger aircraft, the total market was only a fraction of wartime productive capacity.

Although the British industry developed several successful aircraft, it found difficulty in meeting the costs of more advanced types, especially in competition with the American giants, Boeing and Douglas. Even when the government supplied funds to develop new military planes and aerospace weapons, contracts were frequently cancelled as costs rose and economies had to be made in public expenditure.

These mounting difficulties enabled the government in 1959 to persuade the aircraft frame manufacturers to re-group. Hawker-Siddeley led one group (including Blackburn and De Havilland), while most of the other companies, especially Bristol, English Electric and Vickers, took shares in the new British Aircraft Company (B.A.C.). Only Westland (the helicopter and hovercraft specialists), Short Brothers and Harland (now based in Northern Ireland) and the fiercely independent Handley-Page stayed outside this organisation. By now employment in the industry had fallen to about 200,000.

Despite this restructuring and rationalisation, government financial assistance was still essential for new technological development. In order to spread research and development costs, companies co-operated internationally. When a supersonic airliner was suggested, B.A.C. formed a joint project (later known as 'Concorde') with the French company Sud-Aviation (Aérospatial). Even so, massive backing from both the British and French governments was still necessary.

In Belfast, the Short Brothers Company was kept going only by considerable government assistance, mainly on account of the high level of unemployment there. Even the most famous companies experienced grave difficulties. In 1972 Rolls-Royce incurred such high costs, accelerated by inflation and technical problems, in developing the RB 211 engine, that the company had to be rescued by nationalisation.

In 1975, the Secretary of State for Industry announced the Labour government's plans to nationalise the remainder of the aircraft industry, principally Hawker-Siddeley and B.A.C. Although likely to arouse political controversy, this represents only the final phase of long government involvement in the industry.

V. SHIPBUILDING

Before the Industrial Revolution ships were built wherever there was deep water, timber and skilled labour. Shipbuilding, therefore, could be found round most of the coast of Britain. There were, however, certain more important centres, such as estuaries where the rivers passed through woods or where there was a port which could receive timber easily from abroad. The Thames is an example of the first type of estuary, for the tributaries on the right bank passed through the wooded Weald. Millwall and Deptford, for example, had important shipbuilding yards. The Mersey is an example of the second type, for much of the trade of the Port of Liverpool was concerned with the import of planks and spars from North America.

The coming, first of the iron ship and, later, the steel ship brought about a great change. Heavy metal plates, joists, girders and beams were now required, and so the industry moved to those areas where the iron and steel industries were within easy reach of the coast. Thus the principal centres became the Clyde (Glasgow and Greenock), and the North-eastern rivers of the Tyne, Wear and Tees. Today these two areas produce two-thirds of the U.K.'s total tonnage, but at the beginning of the century they built a similar fraction of *world* tonnage.

There are other important centres. At Belfast, Harland and Wolff has yards capable of building the largest super-tankers. The Vickers yard at Barrow specialises in nuclear-powered submarines. On the Solent, Vosper-Thorneycroft build fast missile warships, fibre-glass minesweepers and support vessels for the North Sea oil-rigs.

As regards the precise location of shipbuilding, it should be noted that construction takes place on estuaries at some distance from the actual ports. Prior to the nineteenth century the ports themselves carried on the building of ships, but from that date they decayed, for with the increase in trade, the great ports, such as London and Liverpool, required most of their waterside space for docks and quays and the shipbuilding industry could not, therefore, be accommodated. Only the Cammel Laird yard still survives on the Mersey.

During the 1930s depression, demand for shipping fell and unemployment was severe in British shipyards. World War II reversed the situation.

After 1950, however, the British industry again came under severe pressure, this time from the competition of modern yards in Japan, Scandinavia, Germany and Spain. Patterns of demand also altered, super-tankers, container ships and large ore-carriers being required rather than passenger liners and general cargo ships. For meeting this new demand, British yards were often found to be badly-sited or outdated, lacking large pre-fabrication sheds, modern cutting tools and giant construction cranes. Furthermore, trade union 'demarcation' disputes caused delays and high labour costs. Thus companies found themselves squeezed by inflationary pressures and caught in the trap of fixed price contracts, with penalty clauses for late delivery.

In 1966 the Geddes Committee of Enquiry reported to the government. It urged substantial financial assistance and mergers to strengthen the industry. The choice lay between building a modern industry with a slimmer, efficient labour force, or continuing with outworn methods which gave no safeguard against financial failure, yard closures and redundancy. The government accepted the report, and the amalgamations which followed resulted in seven major groups being responsible for nine-tenths of the annual output. In 1973 this was one million tons, about the same as France, Norway, Denmark, Holland and the U.S.A., but well behind Japan, which launched over 15 million tons.

VI. THE COTTON INDUSTRY

The cotton industry is the most localised industry in the United Kingdom, nearly 97 per cent of its total production being concentrated in the East Lancashire and North Cheshire area. Moreover within this area the two main processes of spinning the thread and weaving the cloth each show a high degree of concentration. The spinning towns, chiefly Bolton, Oldham, Rochdale and Bury, are in the south-east; the weaving towns, chiefly Blackburn, Preston and Accrington, are in the north-east.

Although in the seventeenth century some Flemish refugees had started making cotton cloth around Manchester, the early use of cotton in the area was chiefly in combination with a linen warp to produce a cloth known as 'fustian'. This was mainly a cottage industry, carried on to supplement agriculture. The linen was imported through Liverpool, chiefly from Ireland, but also from north-eastern Europe. Raw cotton was imported via London chiefly from the Mediterranean, Turkey and Cyprus. Yet throughout the eighteenth century woollen cloth easily remained the leading textile industry of the United Kingdom.

The rise of the cotton industry and its concentration in Lancashire is associated with the Industrial Revolution, and early on it became a machine and factory industry. It was helped by influences on both the supply and demand sides. On the supply side the new machines, e.g. Hargreave's spinning-jenny, 1770, Arkwright's water-frame, 1775, and Crompton's 'mule', 1778, were supplied with a much cheaper cotton fibre from the United States by Whitney's invention of the 'cotton gin' in 1792. Hence fustians were displaced by all-cotton goods. Moreover, the industry developed at a time when possible rivals on the Continent were engaged in revolution and war. On the demand side, an increasing home demand for the new cotton cloths was swollen by an overseas demand which largely originated from Britain's overseas possessions and the U.S.A. Thus from the beginning the industry developed a large foreign trade and by 1815 its exports were far greater in value than those of the woollen industry.

But until the nineteenth century the industry was dispersed, mostly over those parts of western Britain where water power was to be found. Centres outside the Lancashire area included Nottingham, Bakewell (Derbyshire), Kendal, Carlisle, Belfast, North Wales and the lower Clyde Valley. All had the advantage of a humid atmosphere, but only Lancashire and Western Scotland were near coalfields. Thus, when by the eighteenth century the superiority of steam power had resulted in its almost complete displacement of water power, the other districts were at a disadvantage. Western Scotland declined for different reasons. In the first place her fine cloths were not suitable for the Far Eastern market and, secondly, she had greater relative superiority over other districts for the production of iron and steel. It was the latter industry to which she devoted her productive resources. Hence the cotton industry concentrated on Lancashire.

Lancashire thus had historical and relative advantages over other areas. Her natural advantages are of three kinds— geological, geographical and climatic. The principal surface rock of the Pennines is millstone grit. Being non-porous it meant, first, that there was plenty of surface water producing fast-flowing streams to provide the water power used in the early days, and secondly, that being surface water, it was also soft water, which facilitated washing, bleaching, dyeing and printing the materials. Moreover, because the soil was poor agriculturally, the farmers were enforced to supplement their income by textile spinning and weaving. Again, the coal measures of South Lancashire meant that coal was available when, from 1790 onwards, steam power was used to drive the machines. Lastly, the salt deposits south of the Mersey around Northwich (Cheshire) were important in the bleaching process.

The area had geographical advantages both in the import of raw material and in the distribution of the finished goods. The import of flax from Ireland early on gave Liverpool experience in handling textile raw materials. When the source of the raw material became the West Indies and the United States at the end of the eighteenth century, Liverpool, besides being very favourably situated for trade with the New World, had already developed considerable connections with those areas, largely through trade in slaves and sugar. For the export of the finished goods, which went mainly to the Far East, Liverpool was again well situated, while the flatness of the South Lancashire plain and the immediate gaps in the Pennines facilitated the construction of railways by which the goods could be distributed throughout England.

The humid atmosphere, which is a characteristic of the climate of the area, is essential to both spinning and weaving in order to prevent frequent breakages in the thread.

These natural factors all played their part when the industry was located originally, but today they are of little importance. Electricity has replaced steam as power; soft water and a humid atmosphere can be produced artificially; and Manchester competes with Liverpool as a cotton port. However, in the course of the development of the area, other advantages have been acquired which, by helping to reduce costs of production, maintain Lancashire's supremacy. The area attracted firms which specialised in the production of textile machinery. Through the Liverpool Cotton Association an organisation was set up to facilitate buying, storing and dealing in raw cotton, while the Manchester merchants organised the sale of the manufactured product. Moreover, trained labour was always available in the area and even the new entrants were familiar with and accepted the conditions of labour in the textile mills. Lastly the construction of the Manchester Ship Canal in 1894, which enabled raw cotton to be sent direct to Manchester, reduced costs still further.

Throughout most of the nineteenth century, the cotton industry was our main export industry. Since then, however, it has suffered a decline owing to: (a) increased production by countries which formerly bought their requirements from Lancashire; (b) competition from Japan, India and other countries; (c) the demand for substitutes such as rayon, nylon, terylene and acrylics. Recently the government has subsidised the removal of surplus capacity, the modernisation of equipment and the introduction of new techniques. In addition, the structure has changed from the small firms of the nineteenth century towards large vertically-integrated companies such as Coats-Paton, Courtauld and Carrington-Viyella.

Synthetic fibres. Especially since World War II, synthetic fibres have been increasingly used to supplement the natural varieties, each contributing its own special characteristic. Although these synthetics are often regarded as a very modern development, a process of making threads from nitro-cellulose was patented in 1884, and by 1892 rayon yarn was being produced by Courtauld in Coventry.

Today there are four main types of synthetic fibre:

(a) *Rayon*, which is derived from cellulose (wood pulp), and is used for garments, tyre-cord and carpets. The main centres of production are in N. Wales, Merseyside, and Humberside.

(b) *Nylon*, a coal- or oil-based fibre, discovered in America in 1937. It is produced as a raw fibre by I.C.I. on Tees-side, but there are nylon spinning plants at Pontypool, Doncaster and Gloucester. It is also produced in Northern Ireland, chiefly by 'British Enkalon', a subsidiary of a Dutch firm.

Nylon is very durable and forms the material for women's stockings, socks and shirts.

(*c*) *Terylene*, a British discovery, is the I.C.I. brand name of an oil-based polyester fibre. It blends well with wool, and production is centred on Tees-side and Northern Ireland.

(d) *Acrylics* are particularly suitable for jerseys and blankets, being soft but durable. Courtauld produces 'Courtelle' at Coventry and Grimsby, and in Northern Ireland there are factories producing 'Acrilan' for Monsanto Chemicals and 'Orlon' for the U.S. Du Pont company.

VII. WOOL-TEXTILE INDUSTRY

The products of the wool-textile industry are worsted 'tops' and both woollen and worsted yarns and cloths, but for our purposes it is possible to group them together and to refer to the wool-textile industry as a whole. The difference between woollen and worsted goods lies in the difference in the yarns from which they are woven. In spinning a worsted yarn, long fibres ('tops') are used. They pass through a process known as combing which rakes the fibres parallel to one another and produces a fairly fine yarn. For the spinning of woollen yarn, however, shorter fibres, together with 'shoddy', that is waste and wool recovered from rags, are used. The fibres are not combed, but carded, that is mixed up together in order to get an even texture, producing a less closely spun yarn and one that is not so strong as worsted. Thus, when the cloth is woven from the two types of yarn, the worsted cloth is smoother and finer than the woollen cloth and hence it is used mostly for suitings and outer garments. Woollen cloth, however, is softer and can be produced in many varieties, simply by varying the composition of the yarn. It is, therefore, chiefly used for feltings, blankets, rugs and underclothing.

Before the Industrial Revolution, the industry was mainly a cottage industry, the workers combining spinning and weaving with agriculture. Its location was determined by the production of the raw wool and hence the main centres were: the West Country (Wiltshire, Gloucestershire, Oxfordshire, Somerset and Devon), whose high-quality and renowned broadcloths were exported both to Europe and to America; East Anglia, which was the centre of the worsted industry; and the West Riding of Yorkshire, which produced cheaper quality cloths and exported to Scandinavia and Russia.

With the introduction of water power, the industry of the West Riding was at an advantage and factories sprang up along the banks of the streams from the Pennine slopes. When steam power replaced water power, Yorkshire's importance increased, for coal was produced in the area. Thus the West and East of England production declined and today the West Riding of Yorkshire area (centred around the towns of Bradford, Huddersfield, Halifax, Leeds, Wakefield and Dewsbury) produces nearly four-fifths of the total production of the United Kingdom. Lancashire's production is small and is really an offshoot of this area. The Tweed Valley in Scotland and the West of England are minor producing areas.

Two reasons have been indicated so far for the concentration of the woollen-textile industry in the West Riding. The initial reason was the local production of raw wool; the later one was the presence of water power and then coal. In the process of producing a given amount of cloth, the weight of the fuel used is approximately four times that of the raw wool. Hence the main pull in location is towards the coalfields and away from the wool-producing regions, though as home supplies eventually proved inadequate, the fact that the West Riding could obtain supplies of raw wool through the ports of London, Liverpool and Hull is not without significance.

The other advantages possessed by South-east Lancashire for the production of cotton goods were also shared by the West Riding for the production of woollen goods. For instance, soft water is even more important for the processes in the woollen industry than in the cotton industry; and, as the surface rock of the Pennines in the West Riding is similarly millstone grit, so there were supplies of soft water. Again, the humidity of the atmosphere facilitated the spinning of the wool yarn, though humidity is not quite so important in the woollen industry as it is in the cotton industry.

CHAPTER 12

THE LOCALISATION OF INDUSTRY

1. GENERAL FACTORS GOVERNING THE LOCALISATION OF INDUSTRY

Our examination of certain concentrated industries can be used as a basis for suggesting general reasons for the localisation of industry. But we must not forget that, in the last resort, government policy may decide where firms locate their factories (see page 471).

The advantages possessed by certain areas are broadly of three kinds—natural, acquired and relative.

1. NATURAL ADVANTAGES

Natural advantages are important chiefly in locating the industry initially. Even so, outside the heavy industries such as the iron and steel industry, it must not be assumed that they are decisive. The Barlow Report on the Distribution of the Industrial Population, 1939, while recognising the natural advantages of Lancashire for the cotton industry, quotes a Board of Trade statement which emphasises the important part which even historical accident may play. This statement even goes as far as to assert that the cotton industry first 'settled in Lancashire for no particular reason, except perhaps that the woollen industry was already there, the foreigners were kindly received and that Manchester had no corporation' (thereby being free from restrictive practices).

We can distinguish the following main natural advantages:

1. *Nearness to raw materials*

Especially when communications were poor, industries developed around the source of their raw materials. For example, the rearing of sheep on the Yorkshire Wold originally decided one of the areas for the production of woollen cloth. Similarly the nearness of the iron ore, coke and limestone led to the concentration of the iron and steel industry in the North-east Coast areas. Where raw materials had to be imported, however, a site within easy reach of a suitable port was advantageous. As an example of this we can point to the cotton industry, where the position of Liverpool was of vital importance.

2. *Nearness to power*

The dominant influence of nearness to power on the localisation of industry came about with the Industrial Revolution. The introduction of steam power meant that industries were pulled towards the coalfields, since coal is a bulky material entirely consumed in the process of manufacture. In the woollen industry, for instance, West Yorkshire had an advantage over the West and East England centres as soon as water power replaced hand power, and, with the introduction of steam power, the woollen industry concentrated almost entirely in the West Riding. But the development of electricity as a source of power has had the opposite effect. Its costs of distribution are low, and so firms adopting it as their source of power are freed from the desirability of being near the coalfields in order to save on costs of transport. Industry can therefore afford to be nearer the consumption centres, with the result that it tends to be more dispersed, especially in the case of the light industries. On the other hand, so large is the London market that, since World War I, there has been a heavy concentration of such industries in the Greater London area (see Chapter 13).

3. *Nearness to markets*

An industry should be so situated as to keep transport costs to a minimum, other things being equal. As we have seen, the general rule is: if weight is lost in the course of manufacture the industry will tend to be near the source of its raw materials; if weight or bulk is gained the industry will tend to be near its market. Where nearness to markets is paramount, then the industry tends to be scattered, except for concentrations around densely populated areas; where nearness to raw materials has been the main consideration, the industry tends to be concentrated.

4. *Suitability of climate*

Climate is one of the main reasons why certain branches of agriculture concentrate in particular areas. In the United Kingdom, for example, we have the corn-producing region of East Anglia and the fruit-growing region of the Vale of Evesham. We have seen, too, how the humidity of the atmosphere assisted in the spinning and weaving processes in the production of cotton and woollen cloths during the early stages of the industry.

2. ACQUIRED ADVANTAGES

Improved methods of production, the development of transport, the provision of alternative sources of power and new inventions may change the importance of the natural factors. In the case of the pig-iron industry, we have seen that as the supply of the better iron ores became exhausted and improved techniques reduced the consumption of coal, the tendency has been for the industry to shift to the iron-ore fields of the East Midlands. Similarly improved transport may upset the relative pulls. By transporting coal and iron ore to Dagenham, the Ford motor company is able to produce pig-iron on a *consumption* centre, while, though construction was described as a dispersed industry, we must not forget that today bricks tend to be made at fewer but larger brickworks, and prefabricated houses are being made in factories and transported over a wide area. Similarly, the expansion of industry in the Greater London area has come about with the development of motor transport and electricity. Finally new inventions, such as 'humidifiers' for producing a damp atmosphere and water-softeners, all help to relieve an industry from dependence on the natural factors of a particular locality.

Yet we must not overstress the importance of the above changes. Even when natural factors have entirely disappeared, an industry often continues to be located in the same region. Thus the steel industry persists in most of its older centres and cotton production still concentrates in Lancashire. Indeed, it has been said that the ability of a locality to hold an industry greatly exceeds its original ability to attract it. This is because of the acquired or 'man-made' advantages which arise as the industry expands. Such advantages were largely considered in Chapter 4 when we studied the external economies of concentration. They include a skilled labour force, communications, marketing and commercial organisations, nearby ancillary industries (either to achieve further economies of scale or to market by-products), training schools, etc., in the locality, and a widespread reputation for the products of the region. All help to lower the costs of production, thereby making the locality attractive to new firms which are considering where to produce a particular good.

3. RELATIVE ADVANTAGES

When discussing the advantages of the division of labour, we saw that a man specialised, not in that occupation wherein he had the greatest absolute advantage, but in the one where he had the greatest relative advantage. He was attracted into the latter industry by the wage differential. The same applies to specialisation of localities—an industry will go to the locality where the relative advantages are the greatest. In the early development of the cotton industry, it seemed at one time that the Clyde might be a rival centre to Lancashire. It had all the latter's natural advantages—port connections, a humid atmosphere, a coalfield and plenty of soft water. But the Clyde also had advantages for the building of ships, and in this her superiority was more marked. Thus, many of the factors which could have been advantageous for the production of cotton goods were turned to the production of ships, and the cotton industry was left to concentrate elsewhere. Similar processes are continually taking place today. Thus in London's Oxford Street, shops, particularly dress shops, have ousted other businesses, while in Mayfair, houses have been converted into offices.

In short, because industries have to compete with each other for land and labour, natural and acquired advantages do not give a complete explanation of the reasons for localisation. If the particular advantages of an area are relatively greater for one type of industry, a firm in that industry will be able to offer higher prices for the land and so force the other industries elsewhere. An industry, for instance, whose outlay on unskilled labour forms a high proportion of its total costs will, other things being equal, be able to bid more for land in an area where there is plenty of cheap unskilled labour than an industry where the cost of such labour is a comparatively minor item.

4. GOVERNMENT POLICY

A firm, left to its own decisions, is concerned with the costs it will itself incur ('private costs') in one locality compared with another. But there are also 'social costs'—traffic congestion, polluted air, etc.—to be considered. For this reason, the government may influence the siting of a factory either by offering financial inducements or by exercising its planning powers. We now consider these 'social costs' in more detail.

II. DISADVANTAGES OF THE LOCALISATION OF INDUSTRY

The advantages of the concentration of industry or industries within a particular area are partly offset by certain disadvantages which result. These disadvantages can be stated as follows:

1. LARGE CONCENTRATED URBAN AREAS

During the nineteenth century, population tended to concentrate in two types of area. The first type was the shipping and commercial centres such as London and Liverpool; the second was the industrial centres based on the coalfields. The result is that the population of Great Britain is largely an urban population. Moreover, within these urban areas, there are many concentrations of population well over the million mark. These are Greater London, Greater Birmingham, Greater Manchester, Merseyside, Glasgow and West Yorkshire (see page 249).

Now, with the increase in the size of a particular town or city through the localisation there of more industries, certain general advantages, or 'social gains', might occur in addition to those which benefit only the industry. For example, better shops and entertainments, more specialised and improved hospitals, libraries and educational facilities can be provided. Yet, while bearing these in mind, we must be careful to draw attention to the disadvantages of such large concentrations of the population. 'The concentration of population in the great towns, especially since the Industrial Revolution of more than a century ago, has been marked by a disastrous harvest of slums, sickness, stunted population and human misery from which the nation suffered in mid-Victorian years, and continues, though fortunately to a much lesser extent, to suffer today' (Barlow Report, 1939). Such great areas are largely overcrowded. The countryside has been so encroached upon that those in the centre find it becoming increasingly remote to them while, within the area, an inadequacy of parks and open spaces persists. The houses, too, were often erected in a hurry and, because of the long hours of work and the fact that transport developments had not proceeded to the stage where workers could be taken to work quickly, they had to be built near the factories. The result is that today many people live in poor houses, which have no gardens, are subject to noise from nearby industry and suffer, with their inhabitants, from the effects of air polluted by soot from adjacent factory chimneys. The result was pointed out by a Joint Medical Committee to the Barlow Commission: 'Despite the enormous improvement in the health conditions of large industrial towns over the last half or three-quarters of a century, the health of rural districts remains today better than that of urban districts.'

Often the industrial towns have expanded, without discrimination, at the expense of excellent agricultural land in the immediate vicinity. In any case, competition from industry and commerce forces up land values in the centre of the town. This has two effects: (a) residential areas are pushed ever further away from the centre and thus the workers are involved in increasing cost, time and fatigue in travelling to and from work; (b) a local authority, wishing to carry out an improvement scheme, is involved in high costs of compensation.

Finally, the movement of materials to and from the industrial centres of the town leads to traffic congestion, while the movement of workers, particularly during rush hours, throws a heavy burden on the public transport system.

2. DEPRESSED AREAS

Long-term changes in demand and improvements in the techniques of production both necessitate adjustments in the industries concerned. Some have to contract, while others expand. The adjustment is made easier if the factors of production, capital and labour, are mobile. Often, however, difficulties arise in transferring the factors of production. Sometimes machinery can be transferred to other uses, as, for example, certain cotton-spinning machines which can be adapted to rayon spinning. On the other hand, much machinery is limited to one particular task only—a blast furnace, for instance, can be used only for smelting iron ore, and, if there is no demand for pig-iron, it has to stand idle.

Labour, too, is comparatively immobile. In fact it has been said that 'of all baggage, human baggage is the most difficult to transport'. Workers are often reluctant to be trained for new jobs, especially the older workers who have spent most of their lives in learning a particular skill. When, however, they also have to uproot their homes and leave the associations of a lifetime in order to find the new jobs, the problem is even more difficult. And it is this latter problem which arises through the localisation of industry. When the local industry decays and no new industries take its place, there is little other work in the district to which the workers can turn. Since workers are reluctant to move, a high level of unemployment persists in those districts.

Such a situation occurred in its most hideous form in the 1930's. Economic activity in general was at a low level and in most of our concentrated industries the depression was particularly serious. Many of them, such as the iron and steel, shipbuilding and engineering industries, are constructional industries in which fluctuations are most marked. Others, such as the coal and cotton industries, were hit by increased foreign competition and by the invention of substitutes. Moreover, the new and expanding light metal industries did not come to the districts concerned, but concentrated instead in the Midlands and south of England. The net result can be seen in such towns as Jarrow (Durham) and Merthyr Tydfil (South Wales) where in 1932 unemployment rose to between 70 and 80 per cent of the total insured population, remaining above 40 per cent even in 1937, by which year improvements in trade and some migration had taken place.

But the fact that so many people were unemployed in the predominant industry had certain effects which aggravated the problem. In the first place, it meant that they had little money to spend and so persons dependent on them, e.g. retail traders and the service industries, were similarly hard hit. Secondly, those people who migrated to the relatively more prosperous areas of the Midlands and South-east England were just the persons that the depressed area could least afford to lose, for they were usually the young persons, those with the most energy and initiative. This, together with the increased rates which had to be levied owing to the poverty of the districts, made them still more unattractive to expanding firms. The general result was that, not only the capital equipment of the particular industry became useless, but such 'social capital' as schools, roads, railways, cinemas and theatres, went to waste as the people moved out.

3. LACK OF INDUSTRIAL BALANCE

Apart from the problem of the depressed areas, the lack of industrial balance resulting from the predominance of one industry in a locality has other disadvantages. The industry may offer employment chiefly to one particular type of labour, while other types of labour are hardly required. A coal-mining district, for instance, requires mostly strong manual labour. But what of those persons who are incapable of this, particularly women? The problem has become more acute with a higher proportion of women wishing to work.

Moreover, many people may not wish to work in the local industry. Many of the best boys from South Wales, for example, after proceeding to the university, do not return to their home district to work but look elsewhere because they consider that the local industries, such as coal and steel, offer insufficient scope. The result is a loss to the South Wales locality, for such men could make a valuable contribution to the municipal and cultural life of the district.

III. STATE POLICY WITH REGARD TO THE LOCALISATION OF INDUSTRY

State control of the localisation of industry is not a simple problem. We have seen that industries become localised in particular areas because, within those areas, certain advantages are possessed which enable the firms engaged in the industry to produce the goods at the lowest possible cost. Thus large-scale interference with this location would lead to some loss of these economic advantages and therefore to a decrease in economic efficiency. On the other hand, it is necessary that the State take some part in offsetting the disadvantages which result from localisation. As we shall see, the difficulty is partly overcome by varying the methods of intervention and by suiting them to the particular problems of each separate region. We discuss State action by dealing in turn with the main disadvantages of localisation as already listed.

1. LARGE CONCENTRATED URBAN AREAS

Our present large urban areas were largely the product of two periods. The first was the early nineteenth century when the rapid industrial development brought with it the unplanned and unrestricted growth of the towns, particularly in the coal-field areas. Not until well into the twentieth century was it recognised that such growth should be controlled, by which time, largely through the development of road transport and electrical power, further damage had been caused by 'the twentieth-century sprawl', an unchecked and hideous industrial and residential expansion around the large towns, particularly in the Midlands and the South of England, and more especially in the Greater London area.

Since then government policy has been mainly along two lines. The first is to improve the existing layout of towns wherever possible. A commencement was made in this direction before the war. Slums were cleared and spacious buildings erected in their place, while streets were widened and improved. However, the necessity of turning over all available resources to the war effort and the need to restrict capital development after the war slowed down progress on these schemes.

The second line of action has been to ensure that all future development is regulated and planned in advance. For instance, such planning is aimed at seeing that good agricultural land is not built on while poorer land could be used equally well; that factories and residential areas are not mixed up indiscriminately; that building does not sprawl out haphazardly into the country, often hugging the main roads almost exclusively; that the development of industry and the design of factory buildings is in keeping, wherever it is possible, with the preservation of the beauty and amenities of the country- side; that towns are laid out with some unity of design with regard to residential areas, shopping centres, civic administra- tion, educational and cultural facilities and centres of amuse- ment.

The major step was taken by the Town and Country Planning Act, 1947, which recognised that much planning must be done on a national basis. The responsible local authorities have to survey existing conditions and propose development plans for the future. Such plans have to be submitted for the approval of the Secretary of State for the Environment and are required to be revised every five years. Moreover, the Act laid down that persons wishing to develop land have first to submit plans and obtain the approval of the planning autho- rity. The authority examines such plans and assures itself on two points: first, that the proposed type of development con- forms with its own scheme for the particular piece of land (which would mean, for instance, that the building of a factory would not be permitted on land reserved for residential pur- poses); secondly, that the design of the building itself is in keeping and good taste with the other buildings in the vicinity.

Greater London, on account of its size, represents a special problem, yet an outline of its recent development indicates the pattern of progress in other large concentrations of popu- lation. First, open spaces within the area have been preserved and added to wherever possible in order to ensure that, as far as possible, each district has an adequate share. Secondly, the outward growth of Greater London has been halted by the establishment of a 'green belt' within which no further development will be permitted (Map 4). Thirdly, a reduction in the population of the County of London and controlled future development of the region has been achieved under the terms of the New Towns Act, 1946, and the Town Develop- ment Act, 1952. The first provided for the building of eight 'satellite' towns (Harlow, Hemel Hempstead, Stevenage,

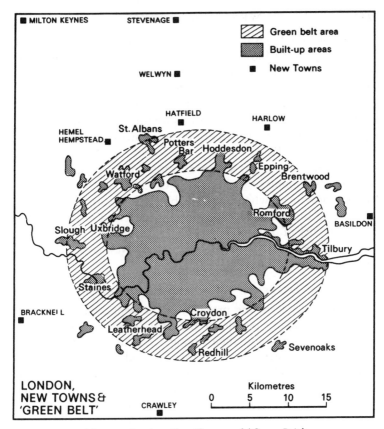

MAP 4.—London, New Towns and 'Green Belt'

Bracknell, Basildon, Crawley, Hatfield and Welwyn), all of which lie outside the 'green belt', and a further one, Milton Keynes, has now been started upon. The second augmented this plan by giving towns which would like to expand, such as Swindon, Bletchley, Ashford, and Basingstoke, financial assistance (chiefly through the transfer of the house-building subsidy), if they take surplus population and industry from London. Fourthly, these new towns have been planned from the beginning with regard to roads, shops, educational and recreational facilities, housing, and industry. They are new communities, with a life and personality of their own. The industrial area, served by railways and arterial roads, is, as far

239

as possible, confined to the northern parts of the town so that prevailing winds blow the smoke away from the residential districts. Residential districts are developed as self-contained 'neighbourhoods', only central services such as local government, technical colleges and main shops being found in the centre of the town. The layout provides for plenty of open spaces everywhere. By 1973, 33 new towns had been designated in the U.K.

The government has set an example in decentralisation by its policy of taking branches of the Civil Service from London to the provinces whenever possible. For example, certain sections of the Admiralty have been transferred to Bath, parts of the Board of Inland Revenue to Liverpool, the Department of Health and Social Security to Newcastle, and the National Giro to Bootle.

2. and 3. DEPRESSED AREAS AND ILL-BALANCED INDUSTRY

As we have seen, the problem of the depressed areas arose because too many people in the district were dependent on a single industry for their living. Expanding and newly-developed industries, such as the car industry, were almost entirely absent from the districts and the result was that when the main industry failed, a high proportion of persons became unemployed. The problem would have been less acute had the surplus labourers moved to the relatively better-off areas. Such a move, however, involves a change of district and possibly of occupation and at once we are up against the broad problem of the general immobility of labour. It is this difficulty which must be overcome in dealing with the depressed areas. The solution lies along two main lines of action: the movement of workers out of the area and into new industries must be facilitated; the basis of production must be broadened by introducing new industries into the area. Both these aspects of government policy are discussed in detail in Chapter 24, to which the reader should refer.

CHAPTER 13

THE GEOGRAPHICAL DISTRIBUTION OF THE POPULATION

THE geographical distribution of the population of Great Britain is dominated by two features. The first is that, instead of the population being evenly distributed, it is concentrated in a few main districts. The second is that this concentration is in urban and not rural areas. Each of these features will now be examined in more detail.

I. THE CONCENTRATED NATURE OF THE POPULATION

Before the Industrial Revolution, Great Britain was predominantly an agricultural country and hence her population tended to be dispersed. Nevertheless at least two-thirds of the people lived south-east of a line joining the Humber and the Bristol Channel. This pattern of distribution was changed by the application of steam power to industry. Apart from London, the south-eastern area declined in importance as industry migrated to and developed on the coalfields which were located in the Midlands and north of England. Largely because of her natural advantages, Great Britain became a manufacturing and mining country, and this was accompanied by a corresponding decline in her agriculture. Today, in spite of the fact that by using electricity as a source of power, factories are freed from being located on the coalfields, the coalfield areas are still the centres of the basic industries of Great Britain and a high proportion of the population still finds employment directly in them. Moreover, many persons in the professions, entertainments, commerce (including distribution), building and contracting, public administration and transport and communications all find employment in serving the wants

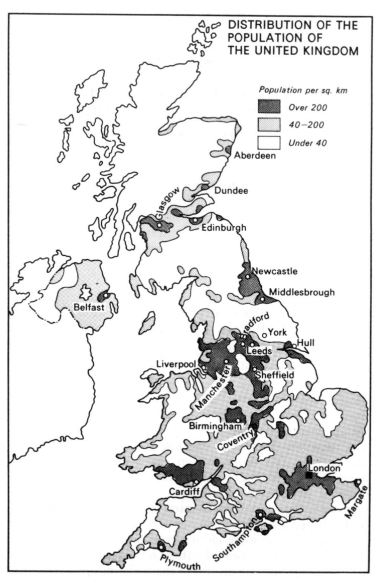

MAP 5.—Distribution of the Population of the United Kingdom

of those persons directly engaged in manufacturing and mining. Thus the connection between the distribution of industry and the geographical distribution of the population is obvious. Even today, 45 per cent of the population is concentrated in the coalfield areas, the only other concentration of population which is comparable being around London. This relationship between the coalfield areas and the distribution of population can be seen by comparing maps 1 and 2. The development of the concentration is best studied in three separate periods, 1801–1921, 1921–1937, 1937–1971.

TABLE 17.—*Distribution of the Population of Great Britain*

Area	*1801*	*1861*	*1921*	*1937*	*1971*
			Proportionate population (%)		
1. (a) London and the Home Counties	18·0	20·1	23·5	25·7	27·3
(b) Greater London .	10·6(i)	—	17·5(i)	18·8(i)	13·8(ii)
2. Lancashire . .	6·4	10·5	11·6	10·9	9·5
3. West Riding, Notts. and Derby . .	8·5	9·4	10·9	10·8	10·4
4. Staffs., Warwick, Worcs., Leics. and Northants. . .	8·1	9·0	9·5	9·7	10·9
5. Northumberland and Durham . .	3·0	3·7	5·2	4·8	4·1
6. Mid-Scotland . .	3·7	5·1	6·2	6·0	7·9
7. Glamorgan and Monmouth . .	1·1	2·1	4·0	3·4	3·2
8. Rest of Great Britain					
(a) . . .	51·2	40·1	29·1	28·7	26·7
(b) . . .	58·6	—	35·1	35·6	40·2
	100	100	100	100	100

Definitions: (a) Home Counties = Bedfordshire, Buckinghamshire, Essex, Hertfordshire, Kent and Surrey.
(b) (i) Greater London = City of London and Metropolitan Police District; (ii) Greater London Council area.

Sources: Barlow Report. Preliminary Report on Census 1971.

1801–1921

The early movement of the population to the coalfields was brought about by the introduction of steam power. Nevertheless it might, at first sight, seem remarkable that this movement should continue almost at the same rate until 1921. However, it must be remembered that throughout the nineteenth century the extent to which Great Britain was specialising in manufacturing increased. Furthermore, towards the end of the century, the acquired advantages of the localisation of industry were reinforcing the natural advantages (see Chapter 12). Thus new firms were still attracted to the coalfield areas in spite of the development of electricity. In fact the acquired advantages exerted a pull even on the new industries. Thus the bicycle and car industries concentrated in the Midland coalfield region largely in order to take advantage of local technical skill and machinery.

London was the only concentration of population not situated on a coalfield. To explain her growth other reasons must be found. Even at the beginning of the Middle Ages, London was a relatively high-populated area and during that period her importance increased enormously. From the reign of William I onwards, London was the permanent capital of England. In addition, through the river Thames and its tributaries, she had an outlet to the sea and inland water connections, so that she became a centre for the import and export of goods for a large area. Thus, early in the development of England's wool trade, London was an important centre for exporting wool to Flanders and Northern Italy, and both the Merchant Adventurers and the Hansards set up their headquarters there. Evidence of the wealth of London can be seen in the prosperity of her Merchant Guilds and Livery Companies.

Because of her trade, London also became a financial and commercial centre. Moreover, in addition to the merchants and bankers, courtiers, civil servants, judges, and lawyers were drawn to the Court and administrative centre. All had to be fed, clothed, housed and waited upon. So the size of the population was swollen by persons who provided for those needs. Hence certain industries, even from early times, came to London, not because, as in the north of England later, they wished to be near their sources of power and raw materials, but primarily owing to the fact that London represented a great consumption centre. Thus, apart from wholesale and retail distribution, London has flour-milling, brewing, clothing, furniture and instrument-making industries. Others such as insurance, banking, financial activities and marine engineering result from her commerce. In short, the growth of London was of a 'snowball' nature and it continued throughout the nineteenth century. By 1921 the Greater London area contained nearly one-fifth of the total population of Great Britain. In the next section we shall see how the movement of industry to the Greater London area gained momentum during the period between the wars.

<h3 style="text-align:center">1921–1937</h3>

This period is marked by: (a) the cessation of the movement of population to the coalfield areas; (b) the continued growth of the Greater London area, especially when we include the Home Counties; (c) a fall in the population of the Inner London area; (d) a persistent loss of population in certain rural areas.

The relative decline which occurred in the coalfield areas, except the Midlands, was due to the fact that these areas were associated with the old-established and basic industries of Great Britain, all of which were in the throes of a trade depression (see Chapter 11). Moreover, any change in the basic industries of an area influences those engaged in the secondary and service industries, thereby giving momentum to the initial population movement. The net result, therefore, was that people tended to migrate to the Midlands and the south of England, where the new industries, such as the motor, light metal and rayon cloth industries, continued to expand even during the depression.

These new industries contributed to the continued growth of the Greater London area and the Home Counties. They include a large part of the motor industry, together with accessories and the provision of spares and service; luxury household goods, such as hair-cream, cosmetics, and scented soaps; processed foodstuffs; light metal goods; radio and electrical apparatus; paper-making and printing works; office equipment; and goods for sports and hobbies. It will be noticed that such industries produce mostly semi-luxury goods and they grew up after 1921 largely because of the rise in real income of the community. Moreover, they were attracted to the Greater London area because London represented, not only a great consumption centre but a comparatively *wealthy* consumption centre, though similar industries have often grown up on a smaller scale on the outskirts of other large cities. Thus the pull of the market has been the dominating influence in the concentration of industry around London. In the industries established, very little raw material is lost in the course of manufacture, the adoption of electricity as a source of power has removed the necessity for the industry to be located on the coalfields, while it is often more difficult to transport the finished product than the raw materials because of its fragility or bulk. Finally, the development of the internal combustion engine and road transport freed the factories from dependence on the railways and they could now be located on the outskirts of London, where land was cheaper. This was important for the 'flow' method of production (which is more extravagant of land as all processes take place on the same level) and for the provision of playing-fields for employees.

Within the Greater London area itself, changes were taking place in the distribution of population, for the people were moving from the centre to the periphery. This is characteristic of the growth of all towns, for as retailing and commerce expand, so they compete for the more central sites and the consequent rise in land values pushes the residential population outwards. This movement was assisted by the gradual increase in real income, for as Londoners became richer, so they could afford better homes in the suburbs. Improvements in transport, particularly the development of the underground railway, facilitated this. The result of this outward movement of the population was a fall in the population of the Inner London area, though it should be noted that this decline had commenced, admittedly on a small scale, at the beginning of the century. Between 1921 and the outbreak of World War II, however, the Inner London area lost nearly half a million of its inhabitants.

During this period there was also widespread rural depopulation, the Highlands of Scotland, Wales, the North Pennines, parts of the North Yorkshire moors, North-east Suffolk, parts of

Wiltshire and Devonshire being particularly affected. For this there were two main reasons. First, the low prices for farm products led to the development of those branches of agriculture which required less labour, while low agricultural wages prompted farm workers to seek the better employment possibilities of the towns. Secondly, people were lured from rural areas to the towns by better living conditions and social amenities. Usually it is the younger people who leave for these reasons, and this makes depopulation worse through the low rate of natural increase which results.

1937–1971

Here we find a reversal of many of the trends of the preceding period. Changes in the distribution of the population during this period are: (a) stability in the coalfield areas; (b) the recovery of certain rural areas; (c) the rapid development of certain new districts.

Table 17 shows that, from 1937 onwards, the population in most of the coalfield areas tended to be a little more stable. Government measures, such as the promotion of new industries in the 'assisted areas', have brought them greater prosperity. Nevertheless, except for the Midlands and Mid-Scotland, the relative loss of population in the coalfield areas has continued although on a reduced scale. Many of their basic industries, especially shipbuilding and cotton, have found difficulty in retaining markets in face of foreign competition.

Since 1937 certain rural areas, particularly Suffolk and Wiltshire, which during the 1921–37 period were losing population, have recovered. This has largely been due to the revival of agriculture. But there are other reasons which will be discussed in the next section. On the other hand, rural depopulation still continues in a number of districts, notably the remote high regions of Scotland, Central Wales, the North Pennines and Exmoor, all of which have failed to attract outsiders or occupations alternative to agriculture.

However, the relative loss of the coalfield areas has been accompanied *pari passu* with a relative gain in the rest of Great Britain. The gain from migration has been most marked in the West Midlands, North Midlands, South and South-east

England (with the exception of Central London) and parts of South-western England. It should be noted, however, that most of the conurbations are now losing population.

Migration to the West Midlands has been due to the further development of her light engineering industries, while the North Midlands' gain is attributable almost entirely to the rapid growth of the iron and steel industry in Northampton-shire and Lincolnshire. South-western England (particularly the counties of Wiltshire, Somerset and Gloucestershire) benefited from the revival of agriculture, though a part of their recovery is attributable to the development of light industries, notably aircraft and agricultural machinery, chiefly around Gloucester and Bristol but also in some of the smaller market towns. Parts of the coasts of Devon and Cornwall have also registered gains from migration. This is a phenomenon which is characteristic also of the south and south-east coasts of England. It is chiefly due to residential attractions, especially for retired persons, though to some extent it might be a reflection of the increased prosperity of holiday resorts with the general rise in the standard of living. Thus we see that such places as Felixstowe, Clacton, Herne Bay, Whitstable, Broadstairs, Eastbourne, Bexhill, Seaford, Portslade, Littlehampton, Shoreham, Worthing, Bognor, Poole, Weymouth, Newquay and Weston-super-Mare have all registered gains more than double that of the national average.

Much of the growth of southern and south-eastern England has resulted from the overflow of London's population into the surrounding counties. This movement of population has been artificially stimulated by the development of the New Towns. But population has also been attracted by the expansion of the new light industries, particularly in the Home Counties. It is expected that the population of South-east England will grow by $2\frac{1}{2}$ million over the next decade, partly by migration from other parts of the country.

Summing up, we can see that changes in the distribution are affected by two main factors: (a) the opportunity of employment, which affects the distribution of the population of the country as a whole and accounted for the concentration on the coalfields during the nineteenth century and for the decline in those areas after 1921; (b) the density of population which produces local changes, people moving to the suburbs as towns become too crowded or as the standard of living improves, or as residential buildings are converted into offices.

II. THE URBAN NATURE OF THE POPULATION

When industry concentrated on the coalfields, long working hours and the lack of local transport meant that people had to live relatively near to their work. Hence towns sprang up in the industrial areas and workers migrated from rural districts to these towns. Thus the concentration of population is an *urban* concentration, not a rural one as occurs in some agricultural regions of the world, such as the Nile and Ganges deltas where the land is farmed intensively.

Urban areas can be defined according to the designation of the local authorities. We include within the term 'urban' all the county boroughs, municipal boroughs and urban districts and the County of London. Using this definition, the relative size of the urban and rural population is shown in Table 18.

TABLE 18.—*Percentage Distribution of the Urban and Rural Population, England and Wales*

	1901	1911	1921	1931	1939	1951	1961	1971
Urban -	77·0	78·1	79·3	80·0	82·4	80·7	80·0	78·3
Rural -	23·0	21·9	20·7	20·0	17·6	19·3	20·0	21·7

Source: Preliminary Report on 1961 Census of England and Wales and Annual Abstract of Statistics.

We can see that throughout the twentieth century roughly 8 out of every 10 people in England and Wales have lived in an urban area. In fact, between 1901 and 1939 the proportion of town-dwellers was slowly rising, continuing the trend which commenced with the Industrial Revolution. Since 1939, however, there has been an increase in the proportion of the total population in the rural section, reversing the trend towards town life of the previous 150 years. It seems that there are long-term factors moving people back to rural areas—the mobility afforded by the motor car, the improvement in utility and social services, and a greater appreciation of rural life.

Of the total urban areas included in the above definition, 154 in 1971 had a population of over 50,000 and as such could be called 'large towns'. In 1971 these 'large towns' contained some 24 million people or about 50 per cent of the total population of England and Wales.

The seven largest towns of the United Kingdom in order of importance are London, Birmingham, Glasgow, Liverpool, Manchester, Sheffield and Leeds, but only the first three have a population of over a million. This, however, does not give a true reflection of the size of these exceptionally large urban areas, for the towns mentioned above are merely the central portion of 'conurbations' of population where urban areas are contiguous. The main conurbations are as follows:

	Population 1971 (Thousands)
Greater London	7,452
S.E. Lancashire (Manchester)	2,393
West Midlands (Birmingham)	2,372
Central Clydeside (Glasgow)	1,728
West Yorkshire (Leeds and Bradford)	1,730
Merseyside (Liverpool)	1,267
Tyneside (Newcastle)	805

It will be seen that these seven conurbations contain nearly one-third of the population of Great Britain.

CHAPTER 14

INTERNATIONAL TRADE

I. INTRODUCTION

T H E subject of international trade has been introduced at this stage because it is really but a further example of the principle of specialisation and is thus closely akin to the division of labour and the localisation of industry. As we saw in the last chapter, factors of production are not distributed evenly within a country and hence certain industries concentrate in particular areas according to the factors of production they use. Similarly, factors of production are unevenly spread between one nation and another. In fact, uneven distribution of the factors between nations tends to persist longer than between one locality and another within the same country. As we have seen, even within the U.K. there is some immobility of labour when it comes to moving from a low-paid to a higher-paid area. When, however, their movement involves a transfer from one country to another, factors prove even more immobile. Investors are chary about investing capital abroad, often because they are ignorant and suspicious of the economic and political conditions of that country, while today capital movements out of the U.K. are restricted by the government. Above all, labour is exceptionally reluctant to move to a foreign country, particularly where there are differences in language, religion and customs. In addition, the cost of the journey and immigration restrictions may make such movement impossible. The net result is that some countries possess advantages for the production of a particular good. They may have ample land, mineral resources or plentiful supplies of cheap labour. What happens, therefore, is that they specialise in the production of that good and exchange a part of the total production for goods produced by other countries. Thus international trade results.

If international trade is thus but another example of specialisation, why do we need to devote a separate chapter to it?

The reason arises largely from the fact that, however desirable
it might be, the world is not yet composed of a 'family of
nations'. Governments still act nationally. Their foremost aim
is not the service of the interests of the world's peoples generally,
but the securing of the best advantage for their own nationals.
Often this does entail co-operation with other countries and
the formulation of international rules to regulate relationships.
But, generally speaking, nations will not enter into such
agreements unless they think that no disadvantage to them is
likely to result.

The result is that, unlike internal trade where the free
operation of the price system moves goods, trade between
persons of different countries is frequently regulated by the
governments concerned. The reasons for such regulation will
be studied later. It may be noted here, however, that two facts
make such regulation simple. The first is that nations are
bounded by frontiers, watched closely by troops and customs
officials. There are thus ready-made physical barriers to the
movement of goods. The second is that since most countries
have their own monetary systems, international trade necessitates the changing of currencies. A government can, therefore, not only control the process of exchange, but fix the rate
to the advantage of its own nation, and then regulate trade in
order to bolster and maintain that rate.

Our discussion of international trade will commence with a
brief review of the advantages to be derived from it and a
survey of the reasons why governments should need to interfere
to limit such advantages. This will be followed by a consideration of how these advantages regulate the pattern of the
international trade of the United Kingdom and of how the
United Kingdom pays for her imports at the present time. It
will conclude with a brief discussion of the methods open to the
United Kingdom to rectify a deficit in her balance of payments.

II. THE ADVANTAGES OF
INTERNATIONAL TRADE

The advantages of international trade correspond in nature
to the advantages of the division of labour and can be briefly
stated as follows:

1. INTERNATIONAL TRADE PERMITS COUNTRIES TO OBTAIN THE ADVANTAGES OF SPECIALISATION

The world's resources of the factors of production, such as land, climate, minerals, capital, skilled and unskilled labour, are not evenly distributed throughout the world. Taking countries as a whole, each must possess an abundance of some factors and a shortage of others. Thus, in the same way that different persons have ability in different directions and to a different degree, so countries vary in their ability to produce different goods. The result is that, like individuals who specialise in particular occupations, so countries tend to specialise in those commodities which depend for their production on the factors which the country has in relative abundance. Thus Iran produces oil because the wells are located in the country, Australia produces wool and mutton because she has the land and a suitable climate, while Egypt produces cotton, for in addition to a suitable climate, she has the necessary cheap labour. However, we must note that, as in the case of the localisation of industries, it is the *relative* advantages which really decide which industries predominate within a country. Thus Great Britain imports much cheap cotton cloth from India although she could produce it herself. But it pays her to do this because her skilled labour is better employed in making the finer cloths for the Irish and South African markets. Nor, in concentrating on the supply side, must we lose sight of the influence of demand on international trade. It is the difference in relative prices which moves goods between countries. Hence, although a country may be favourably placed to produce certain goods, a large home demand and thus a relatively high price may mean that it is a net importer of that good (as the United Kingdom is of coal and the U.S.A. of oil).

Certain advantages result from this international division of labour and the trade between countries which follows. In the first place, it enables a greater variety of products to be obtained. If there were no international trade, many countries would have to go without some products. This applies literally to certain minerals which are not found within the country. Thus, without trade, Malta and Iceland would have no coal,

Spain no gold, and Egypt no diamonds. Since, however, most commodities can now be produced in any chosen place provided a sufficient outlay of capital is made to secure the right conditions, it is in a relative rather than a literal sense that a greater variety of products can be obtained. For instance, the United Kingdom could produce rubber and petroleum synthetically, while bananas and oranges could also be grown by her provided suitable soil were transported and greenhouses erected to afford the necessary conditions. But, because such use of the factors of production would be at the expense of the production of other goods, it would prove so wasteful relatively that the cost of the goods produced artificially would be so exorbitant that the vast majority of the people of the United Kingdom would have to go without them.

Secondly, and much more important, specialisation leads to an increase in total production. We can show this best by means of a hypothetical arithmetical example which is on parallel lines to the one we gave when discussing the advantages of the division of labour. Let us suppose that two countries, A and B, each using X units of the factors of production, land and labour, in the production of wheat and tea, differ, nevertheless, in their respective climates. As a result we will assume that country A is more suitable for the production of wheat and country B for the production of tea. Suppose that, in the course of a year and with these factors, A can produce 1,000 units of wheat *or* 200 units of tea, whereas B can produce 200 units of wheat *or* 1,000 units of tea. Now if neither specialise, but divide their factors equally between the production of wheat and tea so as to produce some of each, A will produce 500 units of wheat *and* 100 units of tea, while B produces 100 units of wheat *and* 500 units of tea. Thus together they have produced 600 units of wheat and 600 units of tea. By specialising in production, however, A concentrating in growing wheat and B in growing tea, 1,000 units of each can be produced. A, we will now imagine, can exchange 500 units of wheat for 300 units of tea. Thus A has 500 units of wheat and 300 units of tea, while B has 500 units of wheat plus 700 units of tea. Clearly both have gained through specialisation and, while in our example A has an absolute advantage in producing wheat and B in producing tea, the same principle would apply even though A has an advantage in both lines of production, for both would still gain provided A specialised in producing the commodity in which her relative advantage is greater.

2. It Permits an Industry to Take Full Advantage of the Economies of Large-Scale Production

If certain goods were produced only for the home market, it would be impossible to achieve the fullest advantages of large-scale production. Indeed, attention was drawn to this point when it was shown that the extent to which the division of labour could be carried was limited by the size of the market. Selling a good abroad as well as at home extends the market and production can therefore be on a larger scale. This results in economies, particularly in the case of those goods, such as steel, motor vehicles, ships, electrical goods and chemicals, where the optimum size of the firm is large for technical reasons. Once again all countries gain by the better use of the factors of production through specialisation, for both the producing country and those countries to which it exports are able to obtain the goods more cheaply.

3. It is Often a Safeguard Against the Development of Monopolies

Without international competition, the home market would be so limited that it would be comparatively easy for combinations of firms in many industries, e.g. motors, paper, and electrical apparatus, to exercise some control over it.

4. International Trade Leads to Links with Other Countries

Cobden, one of the leaders of the free-trade movement in the first half of the nineteenth century, stressed the fact that commercial relations would lead to an interchange of knowledge, ideas and culture between countries. He argued that this would produce a better understanding of those countries and, therefore, reduce the possibility of war. Such an argument today, however, appears rather naïve, for history provides us with many examples of where international trade has not led to improved relations between countries. In fact, commercial rivalries resulting from trade have sometimes been among the major causes of war.

As regards the United Kingdom, however, the argument is of some real significance. Much of the trade of the United Kingdom is conducted with the countries of the Commonwealth, and this trade is important in maintaining and strengthening its bonds. Moreover, there is an exchange of advantage in both directions, for, as we shall see later, the forces which draw the Commonwealth together also foster trade within the Commonwealth. To some extent, too, one of the motives for the European Economic Community (the Common Market) is to bring the nations of Western Europe together politically.

III. GOVERNMENT CONTROL OF INTERNATIONAL TRADE

The advantages of specialisation in production can be achieved in full only if there is complete freedom of exchange. Generally speaking, there is such complete freedom for persons living within the same country. Thus the man who specialises in making suits sells those suits in a free market to anybody who is willing to pay the price he asks. With the money so obtained, he purchases his requirements from anybody he chooses. On the other hand, when the persons exchanging goods live in different countries, that is, the trade is international, we find that transactions are subject to considerable regulation by the governments of the respective countries with the object of controlling the volume and direction of trade. Thus imports may be limited by import duties, quotas, and exchange control. On the other hand, exports may be expanded by the government, not only by indirect encouragement, but also directly by granting export bounties. Subsidies on home-produced goods similarly affect the volume of imports and exports. In other words, instead of allowing the free operation of the price system to move goods, trade is distorted according to the policies of the governments of different nations. But restrictions on trade result in a limitation of the advantages of specialisation, and in effect, therefore, people are poorer. Thus what a government has to decide is whether, by its policy of regulation, other advantages are secured which more than offset the loss to its people through the reduction in specialisation. Let us now consider what these other advantages are likely to be.

REASONS FOR GOVERNMENT CONTROL OF INTERNATIONAL TRADE

1. *The maintenance at home of a high level of employment*

A trading country, such as the United Kingdom, must reckon with additional forces, compared with a non-trading country, in securing conditions of full employment. A country, which is more or less self-sufficient, can by its own measures control its economy. A trading country, on the other hand, is influenced by economic conditions, chiefly the level of income, in the countries to which it exports. Thus, if in the economies of its customer countries there has been a hitch in the efficient operation of the price system (such as occurs when insufficient investment brings about unemployment and a falling income), then those countries will be unable to buy imports. The result will be depression, unemployment and a smaller income in the export industries of the selling country, possibly spreading to its other industries. Her own imports must, therefore, be reduced, and so the depression spreads internationally. In fact this was one of the causes of the world-wide depression of 1928–34, when the agricultural countries could not sell their produce and so were unable to buy the products of the manufacturing countries.

On the other hand, the falling-off in demand may be due to a long-term change in the conditions of demand, perhaps because a cheaper and more efficient substitute has been invented or because a rival country is producing the good cheaper. Thus, before the war, the Lancashire cotton industry suffered from Japanese competition, while in the early 1960s our shipbuilding industry found it difficult to obtain the orders necessary to keep its manpower fully employed. Whatever the cause of the fall in demand, 'depressed areas' may result because, as was pointed out when discussing the localisation of industry, factors of production are immobile. Above all, the fall in demand is particularly serious when a country is very dependent on the production and export of a particular good, as for example, Iran (oil), Malaya (tin), South Africa (gold), Australia (wool).

The governments of all trading countries, therefore, are apprehensive lest demand for exports fall. Thus the United Kingdom watches carefully for any signs of a trade recession in the U.S.A. and desires an international agreement that countries should take measures to maintain full employment as soon as adverse symptoms appear (see p. 484). On the other hand, countries do not, as a rule, take general measures to limit trade solely because of their vulnerability in a world depression. Instead each country usually leaves protection until the depression actually occurs. Then by the imposition of import duties and quotas, it reserves the home market for the home industry, and by a series of barter (bilateral) agreements endeavours to secure markets for its own exports in exchange for the particular products of other countries.

2. *The raising of revenue*

In the same way that indirect taxes are levied on goods produced at home in order to raise revenue, so most governments put import duties on many articles, such as wines, cigarettes, and all goods subject to purchase tax. If such goods bear the same rate of tax as those produced at home or if the importing country does not produce the goods, then the real purpose of the duty is to raise revenue.

All duties, however, upset relative prices and therefore interfere with the pattern of international trade, but the distortion is not so great when the primary aim is to raise revenue, for the demand for the goods taxed is usually inelastic.

3. *The improving of the terms of trade*

Where a country is the dominant world buyer of a good, it may be able, by imposing an import duty on it, to restrict its demand so that the price falls in the world market. This is particularly effective if the supply of the good is inelastic. It means that the terms of trade have been improved, the foreigner being made in effect to pay part of the import duty (see page 361).

4. *The avoidance of dependence on foreign countries for a good which is essential in time of war*

The supply of certain goods is vital to the waging of a war. Germany, in the 1930's, realised that rubber was such a good, and therefore developed her synthetic rubber production by restricting the import of natural rubber. The United Kingdom, for the same reason, has fostered artificially her home production of foodstuffs. The difficulty is that so many goods can be included in the category of 'essentials' that, if care is not taken, claims for protection for this reason are made by all producers, each wishing to secure an advantage.

5. *The protection of an 'infant industry'*

Sometimes it is considered that an important industry could be developed if it were given some government help in its early stages. This is necessary if it is to withstand competition from similar industries of other countries, industries which have overcome their technical difficulties, are achieving large-scale economies and have established a reputation. A young industry has teething troubles to overcome and has to obtain customers. Governments, therefore, often protect the home market from foreign competition or give their 'infant industries' subsidies. It was for this reason that many of the United States' import duties on foreign manufactured goods were imposed, while in 1924 the United Kingdom gave her sugar-beet industry a subsidy of nearly £1 a cwt. The difficulty is that, once the government assistance is given, the industry comes to rely on it, and it becomes difficult to remove. Thus United States' manufactured goods still enjoy a large degree of protection, while the United Kingdom's subsidy to the sugar-beet industry, granted at first for ten years, is given today in larger measure than ever.

6. *The strengthening of political links*

Between 1932 and 1973 (when Britain joined the E.E.C.), tariff agreements gave preferential treatment to trade between Britain and the Commonwealth. Such trade helped to strengthen Commonwealth ties.

Similarly, while the immediate objects of the Common

Market external tariff are economic, a wider aim is to develop stronger political links between Western European countries (see Chapter 15).

7. *The correction of an adverse payments deficit*

It is convenient if a consideration of this reason be reserved until after the actual international trade of the United Kingdom has been examined in more detail (see page 274).

IV. THE UNITED KINGDOM'S TRADE WITH OTHER COUNTRIES

From a study of the reasons for international trade, we can proceed a long way in deducing what the pattern of the United Kingdom's trade is likely to be. Since, in the first place, trade arises because factors of production are unequally distributed, we have to ask: (*a*) what are the factors of production of which the United Kingdom can be said to have a relatively plentiful supply; and (*b*) what are the factors of production in which she is deficient?

In answer to (*a*), we can point to the United Kingdom's coal reserves, her skilled working population, and the stock of machinery and factories which she has built up in the past through the thrift of her people. In addition she has a high proportion of very skilled and highly educated administrators, engineers and technicians, and commercial and financial experts. All these men can render services to other countries, particularly to those countries less advanced in development. Thus administrators go abroad to start businesses, technicians plan and construct railways and bridges, while commercial and financial experts and institutions perform services for countries other than the United Kingdom. In addition, her strategic island position in the North Atlantic has, besides helping in the development of her own trade, enabled the United Kingdom to build up a large merchant navy carrying goods for other countries.

As regards (*b*), however, the United Kingdom lacks land (chiefly for agriculture because of the size of her population); plentiful supplies of very cheap, unskilled labour; certain minerals (such as nickel, zinc, aluminium and copper), petroleum reserves; certain chemicals (such as sulphur and nitrates); and the climate which is necessary, both as regards warmth and rainfall, for the production of many foodstuffs (such as cane sugar, vegetable oils and tropical fruit), beverages (such as tea, coffee and cocoa), and raw materials (such as cotton, rubber and tobacco).

Thus, analysing the problem simply from the aspect of the distribution of resources, we are able to say something in a general way, first, about the nature of the goods in which the United Kingdom deals with the rest of the world, and, secondly, about the countries with which she deals.

1. The Commodities of the United Kingdom's International Trade

The above consideration of the relative supply of the United Kingdom's factors of production suggests that the United Kingdom will export mostly manufactured goods and also, by using her highly trained men and by carrying goods in her merchant ships, render services to other countries. In return, she will import raw materials and foodstuffs (which she is unable to grow herself, either through shortage of land or of the necessary climate), together with petroleum, minerals and chemicals (which are not found in sufficient quantities within her own borders).

While the nature of the services which are rendered by the United Kingdom must be left for later consideration, the broad divisions of the goods exported and imported by her in 1973 are given in Table 19 below and they show that our surmise regarding the nature of them was correct: 44 per cent of the value of her total imports consists of food, drink, tobacco, basic materials, and mineral fuels, while 84 per cent of the value of her total exports are manufactured goods.

2. The Countries with Which the United Kingdom Trades

Referring once again to the analysis of the distribution of the United Kingdom's resources as compared with those of other

TABLE 19.—*The United Kingdom's Imports and Exports 1973*
(by value)

	Imports		Exports	
	£mln.	%	£mln.	%
Food, beverages and tobacco .	3,098	20	876	7
Basic materials . . .	1,965	12	433	3
Mineral fuels and lubricants .	1,727	11	370	3
Manufactured goods . .	8,914	56	10,456	84
Miscellaneous (postal packages; live animals not for food) .	150	1	320	3
TOTAL	15,854	100	12,455	100

countries, it seems likely that the United Kingdom will import goods from countries having relatively much agricultural land, from countries enjoying a tropical or semi-tropical climate, and from countries possessing the petroleum, minerals and chemicals which she herself lacks. Where these countries need the United Kingdom's manufactured goods, as in the case of Australia, imports from them can be paid for directly by the

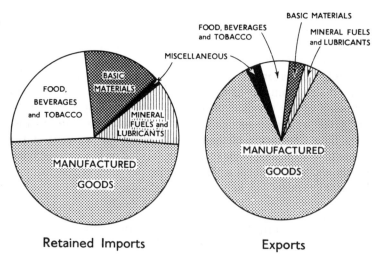

FIG. 21.—Percentage distribution of the United Kingdom's imports and exports 1973

export of manufactured goods. But where the country, such as the U.S.A., does not require these manufactured goods, then imports have to be paid for indirectly. This is achieved through triangular or multilateral trade. Thus Malaya and South Africa export tin and gold respectively to the U.S.A., but the latter sends comparatively little to them directly in exchange. Instead she exports such goods as wheat, cotton, tobacco and machinery to the United Kingdom, who, in return, pays off the debt of the U.S.A. to Malaya and South Africa by sending them manufactured goods.

V. THE UNITED KINGDOM'S TRADE WITH THE COMMONWEALTH

Table 21 shows that, in value, nearly one-quarter of the United Kingdom's trade is with the Commonwealth. How can we account for this very significant fact?

TABLE 20.—*Percentage Distribution of the United Kingdom's Foreign Trade, 1938–73, between Commonwealth Countries and the Rest of the World*

	Imports %		Exports %	
	1938	*1973*	*1938*	*1973*
Commonwealth countries .	38·9	25·6	44·6	21·0
Foreign countries . . .	61·1	74·4	55·4	79·0
TOTAL . . .	100	100	100	100

The main reason has already been given—it arises because Commonwealth countries have factors of production which are complementary to those of the United Kingdom. This does not give, however, a complete picture, for as we suggested earlier in this chapter, there are special reasons why the United Kingdom's trade with the Commonwealth should predominate.

In the first place there exist certain ties which can be summed up in the phrase 'a feeling of brotherhood'. The development of the Commonwealth has been pioneered by British emigrants. These took with them a common language, common trading methods and a common loyalty to the Crown, while many

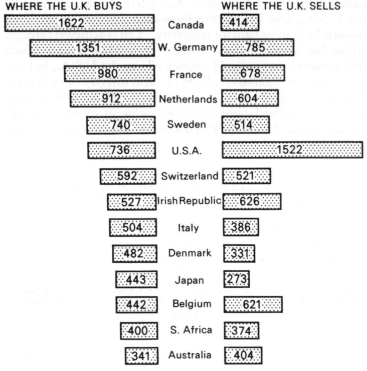

WHERE THE U.K. BUYS   WHERE THE U.K. SELLS

1622	Canada	414
1351	W. Germany	785
980	France	678
912	Netherlands	604
740	Sweden	514
736	U.S.A.	1522
592	Switzerland	521
527	Irish Republic	626
504	Italy	386
482	Denmark	331
443	Japan	273
442	Belgium	621
400	S. Africa	374
341	Australia	404

Fig. 22.—The principal exporters to and importers from the United Kingdom 1973 (by value, £ mln.)

settlers still possess, through their families, links with the United Kingdom. Because of these various connections it is only natural that these countries should turn to the United Kingdom both for a market for their own goods and for their supplies of the goods they need.

Again, the fact that British capital was invested in the Commonwealth meant that the repayment of the interest and capital had to take place by their exporting goods to the United Kingdom.

Finally, until recently, two important arrangements fostered Commonwealth trade. The first was a result of the Ottawa Conference, 1932, where it was agreed that direct encouragement should be given to trade between the Empire countries by preferential tariff rates. The second brought together all the Commonwealth countries, except Canada, into the 'Sterling Area'. Within the Sterling Area, currencies were freely convertible, when, during and after the war, dollar transactions were limited. This facilitated trade between countries within the area.

When Britain joined the E.E.C. in 1973, preferential tariffs for Commonwealth goods were virtually ended. As regards convertibility, there is now little difference between sterling and other currencies.

VI. THE UNITED KINGDOM'S TRADE WITH THE EUROPEAN ECONOMIC COMMUNITY (E.E.C.)

Table 21 shows that, in value, almost one-third of the U.K.'s trade is with Common Market countries.

TABLE 21.—*Percentage Distribution of the United Kingdom's Trade between the E.E.C. and the Rest of the World*

	Imports %		Exports %	
	1964	*1973*	*1964*	*1973*
E.E.C.	23·0	31·6	27·6	30·2
Rest of the World . .	77·0	68·4	72·4	69·8
TOTAL . . .	100	100	100	100

Two points should be noted. Much of this increase in trade took place even before the U.K. joined the Common Market in 1973, and it is likely to increase as the common external tariff is applied (see Chapter 15). Second, the trade is mostly in manufactured goods, particularly chemicals, machinery and cars.

The reason is that specialisation is now no longer confined to manufacturing as opposed to agriculture. Specialisation has been carried further so that, within manufacturing itself, different countries concentrate on producing particular goods. Thus in cars, the German Volkswagon 'beetle' appeals to certain people in the U.K., while the Rolls-Royce and Jaguar may be wanted in Germany. Such specialisation can give rise to considerable trade between countries which have reached the same stage of industrial development (see also Fig. 22).

VII. HOW ARE IMPORTS PAID FOR?

We can best answer this question by first considering the purchases made by an individual, say a housewife, Mrs. Jones. Each week she buys a variety of goods for the house. No shop-keeper will *give* her these goods. They have to be paid for. What is important for our purposes, however, is that there are at least seven sources from which she can obtain the money to effect the payment.

The first and most usual source is the week's earnings. Her husband probably makes her an allowance from his wages each week and Mrs. Jones pays the shopkeeper on the spot for her goods with this money. It must be noted, however, that what in fact Mrs. Jones is really doing is exchanging the goods which Mr. Jones has specialised in producing for all the other goods which are needed. Thus, if Mr. Jones is a tailor, the suits he makes are sold, and it is from the money thus obtained that Mrs. Jones buys the goods she needs. Money, as we shall see later, only comes into the transaction in order to facilitate the process of exchange. We must also draw attention to the fact that very often money is earned, not by making goods, but by performing a service. Thus Mrs. Jones herself may earn wages by working a day each week for the shopkeeper, sending out his accounts and answering his correspondence. Lastly, a small amount of current income might be obtained by means of interest from savings. Provided that all the weekly expenses are met out of this combined weekly income, we should say that the Jones family was 'paying its way'.

It might happen, however, that Mrs. Jones's expenditure was not covered by the current weekly income. This might occur, for instance, because she bought a costly good, such as a washing machine or an armchair, which was not a regular item of weekly expenditure. In such circumstances, Mrs.

Jones would have to raise the money from other sources. In the first place, she could draw money from her National Savings in the Post Office or from some other 'nest-egg'. Secondly, she could sell some good from her household stock, such as the piano or the television set, for which she had a less urgent need. Thirdly, she might be able to borrow the money from a friend or, what amounts to the same thing, ask the shopkeeper to forgo payment for the time being. Finally if she were extremely fortunate, she might be able to obtain a gift of money, say from a doting father. Such methods of effecting payment would be fairly satisfactory for a good which is in use over a very long period, provided that her National Savings were gradually replenished from week to week or the assets sold were replaced by other assets of equal value, or that the loan was repaid during the lifetime of the good. Where, however, such replenishment of savings and assets or repayment of the loan are not made, either because insufficient savings are put by out of weekly income or because the over-expenditure is a weekly or frequent occurrence, then we would say that Mrs. Jones is 'not paying her way'. In time her savings would run out, her home would be sold up, and she would be unable to obtain any more loans or credit from the shopkeeper.

1. Payments for Imports by 'Exports'

Broadly speaking, a nation trading with other nations is in exactly the same position as Mrs. Jones. The same alternatives are open to it for the payment of goods imported from other nations. These goods are paid for chiefly by the money which is received from the sale of current exports. Fig. 22 shows the principles on which the payment is arranged and also the main outlines of the procedure through which an export earns foreign currency. In normal times, importing and exporting is done by private individuals and firms, and payments are arranged through banks, who exchange the currency of one country for the currency of another *provided that they have the necessary reserves of that currency.* Such reserves are earned by customers who export to foreign countries.

Assume: (a) rate of exchange is 2.40 dollars to the £ sterling;
       (b) no currency restrictions;
       (c) 'A' is U.S. exporter of wheat; 'X' is U.K. importer of wheat;
       (d) 'B' is U.S. importer of cars; 'Y' is U.K. exporter of cars.

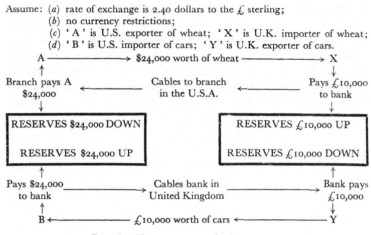

Fig. 23.—How exports pay for imports

The actual process is as follows. 'A' exports $24,000 worth of wheat to 'X', who, in order to settle the debt, pays £10,000 into his bank in London. 'A', however, wants payment in dollars and so the bank cables to its branch in New York, authorising it to make this equivalent dollar payment. It can only do this if it has these dollars in reserve.

These reserves have been secured by the payment into the bank of $24,000 by 'B', who has imported British cars to that value. 'Y' is paid from the £10,000 which 'X' deposited for the wheat. Thus the two transactions cancel out and the reserves remain the same.

2. INVISIBLE IMPORTS AND EXPORTS

The term 'exports', however, is a very wide one. In the same way that Mrs. Jones received payment for the service of sending out the shopkeeper's accounts, so a nation may receive payment, not only for the goods it exports, but also for services rendered to other countries. Goods exported are termed 'visible exports', because they can be seen and recorded as they cross the political boundaries between countries. Services performed for people of other countries, however, are called 'invisible exports', because they cannot be seen and recorded as they cross frontiers. Nevertheless, since both goods and services involve payment by persons of the importing or receiving countries to persons in the exporting country, they are both 'exports' in this wider sense.

The goods imported and exported by the United Kingdom

have already been described. Here we may glance at the main sources of her invisible earnings and payments.

1. *Government transactions*

The United Kingdom government spends money abroad in a variety of ways. Thus it has to maintain Armed Forces in such places as Germany and Gibraltar, paying the troops in the currency of the respective country, hiring local labour, and buying supplies of fresh food. Similarly, money is also spent on diplomatic services and on grants to colonies. On balance, the United Kingdom paid £790 million under this heading in 1973.

2. *Shipping services*

When a foreigner is a passenger in a British-owned ship, such as the *Queen Elizabeth 2*, or goods are transported by a British-owned ship for a foreign firm (as often happens because such ships frequently make the return trip with imports for the United Kingdom), it means that the British owners of the ships are rendering services to nationals of foreign countries. Such services have to be paid for in the same way as imports from the United Kingdom. Thus an exporter in the United States pays dollars into his bank in the United States in settlement of the debt he owes to the British shipping company, and the bank then instructs its branch in London to credit the shipping company's account to the value of the amount in £ sterling. Similarly, an American travelling to England in the *Queen Elizabeth 2* has either to change his dollars into pounds at his bank before leaving or pay the Cunard Line for his passage in dollars. Irrespective of which procedure is adopted, dollars, which can be used to purchase imports, are earned by the United Kingdom.

The Balance of Payments Account shows that in 1973 the United Kingdom paid a net sum of £75 million for shipping services.

3. *Civil Aviation*

This covers in a similar way the overseas transactions of British Airways and the British independent airlines, and net payments to overseas airlines by United Kingdom residents.

4. *Travel*

An overseas resident coming to the United Kingdom, either on business or on holiday, needs British money to spend on hotels, entertainment, travelling, and so on. This means that he must change his own currency into pounds sterling. Hence the United Kingdom earns foreign currency. On the other hand, a British person going abroad on holiday to such places as France or Switzerland needs French and Swiss francs, and thus the United Kingdom spends foreign currency.

It can be clearly seen that, with such countries as Switzerland, one of the biggest exports is an 'invisible'—the rendering of holiday services to people who come from abroad. Indeed, the promotion of tourism in the United Kingdom produced a net receipt of £6 million in 1973.

5. *Other services*

Before 1914, when Britain was the chief commercial nation of the world, other countries, because they had faith in the stability and integrity of Britain's banks and insurance companies, did much of their business with them. For instance, discount houses and banks discounted their bills of exchange, while insurance companies insured their goods and ships. To some extent this still happens today, and thus the charges the discount houses and banks make for their services, and the profits the insurance companies make on their transactions with foreigners, represent an earning to the United Kingdom of foreign currency.

Under this heading are also included the royalties which are received in respect of books and records and the net remittances for films.

The net gain in 1973 from the various services included under this heading was £982 million.

6. *Interest, profits and dividends*

Before 1913, the international economic position of the United Kingdom was so strong that the value of her total exports was greater than the value of her total imports and she was able to lend money abroad. People in the United Kingdom bought stock issued by foreign governments and also purchased debentures and shares in foreign companies. From these investments, interest and dividends are received, and this means that once again the United Kingdom earns foreign currency.

In 1973 the United Kingdom had a net gain of £1,095 million from this source, though pre-war this figure was comparatively larger. During the war, the United Kingdom was unable to make and export goods to pay for her imports. In other words, she was not 'paying her way'. It was necessary, therefore, to draw out some capital assets (as Mrs. Jones did when she drew on her National Savings) and to sell some of her possessions (as Mrs. Jones did when she sold the piano). As regards the latter, what the United Kingdom government did was to purchase foreign capital holdings from their owners in the United Kingdom. These assets were then sold, chiefly to the U.S.A., and, with the foreign currency so realised, the United Kingdom paid for her imports.

The 'take-over' of a British firm, e.g. Rootes, by an American (or foreign) firm, e.g. Chrysler, has a similar effect.

7. *Private transfers*

People who emigrate to a foreign country often send money back to their homeland, either because they expect to return and therefore want the money as a reserve, or else because they wish to assist their parents or other dependants. The Italians in the U.S.A., for example, send much money home in this way. Similarly, if a person or charity abroad (such as the Carnegie and Rockefeller Trusts) makes a gift or leaves an estate to somebody in another country, money has to be transmitted to the beneficiary. In all these cases, currencies have to be changed and thus the country of the person receiving the money earns foreign currency. In 1973, the United Kingdom lost on balance £114 million under this heading.

VIII. THE BALANCE OF PAYMENTS

We are now in a position to set out the 'balance of payments' of the United Kingdom for the year 1973. This is merely a statement of the United Kingdom's monetary transactions with other countries *during* the year. Such transactions occur when sterling is used to buy foreign currencies or when foreign currencies are used to buy sterling for any of the reasons previously mentioned. The nationality of the person buying or selling sterling is immaterial.

The balance of payments statement is set out in two accounts: (i) the current or 'income and expenditure' account; (ii) the capital or 'investment and financing' account.

1. THE CURRENT ACCOUNT

The current account consists of the 'visible' items (the 'balance of trade' account) plus the 'invisible' items (receipts and expenditure regarding services). It will be noted that imports and exports are valued 'f.o.b.' ('free on board'), representing their value when they leave the country from which they are sent. They could also be quoted 'c.i.f.' ('cost, insurance, freight'), their value on arrival. Valuing goods f.o.b. enables the cost of the shipping and insurance services to be included in the 'invisible' items, as a debit if imports are being brought by a foreign ship, and as a credit if exports are carried by a British ship.

It will be seen that in 1973 income from exports did not cover expenditure on imports (taking visible and invisible together). Yet this expenditure must have been met from some source. Obviously the deficit had to be covered by drawing on capital. It is in this sense that we can say that 'the balance of payments always balances'. We will now examine this in a little more detail.

2. THE CAPITAL ACCOUNT

Let us return to our illustration of Mrs. Jones and her weekly expenditure.

In 1973, the United Kingdom was in exactly the same position as the Jones family would have been in if their weekly expenditure could not have been met out of the joint earnings of Mr. Jones (who was making suits) and of Mrs. Jones (who was rendering a service to the shopkeeper). The United

TABLE 22.—*The Balance of Payments of the United Kingdom, 1973*
Current Account

Debits	£mln.	Credits	£mln.
IMPORTS (f.o.b.) . . .	13,810	EXPORTS AND RE-EXPORTS	
		(f.o.b.)	11,435
INVISIBLES:		INVISIBLES:	
Government . . .	933	Government . . .	143
Shipping . . .	2,185	Shipping . . .	2,110
Civil aviation . . .	420	Civil aviation . . .	481
Travel	674	Travel	680
Other services . .	726	Other services . .	1,708
Interest, profits and		Interest, profits and	
dividends . . .	1,457	dividends . . .	2,552
Private transfers . .	409	Private transfers . .	295
TOTAL DEBITS . . .	20,614	TOTAL CREDITS . .	19,404
		Balance of current trans-	
		actions	+ 1,210
			20,614

Capital Account

	£mln.
Long-term borrowing (net)	+ 59
Short-term borrowing (net)	+ 1,361
Increase in reserves of gold and foreign currencies	− 210
(− = increase)	
	+ 1,210

(Note: In order to simplify, a balancing item of £408 million has been included with short-term borrowing.)

Kingdom, similarly, could not meet her yearly expenditure out of the joint earnings from the sale of her goods and from the sale of her services.

However, as we saw, Mrs. Jones would have been able to overcome such a difficulty in any one of four ways or by a combination of each—by selling certain of the family assets, by drawing from the family savings, by borrowing from a friend or the shopkeeper, or by having the good fortune to receive a gift of the money. And these same alternatives are open to a nation in meeting a deficit in its income. It can sell assets to a foreign country; it can draw from its gold and foreign currency reserves; it can borrow from another country or from the International Monetary Fund; and it may obtain foreign aid. In 1973, the United Kingdom's deficit of £1,210 million on current transactions was covered by net long-term investment of £59 million in the U.K. by foreign countries, but mostly by short-term borrowing. Indeed since the latter amounted to £1,361 million, the gold and foreign currency reserves increased by £210 million.

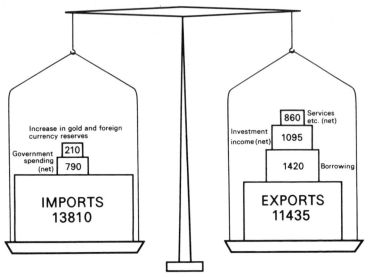

FIG. 24.—The Balance of Payments 1973

IX. THE CORRECTION OF A BALANCE OF PAYMENTS DEFICIT

It may be that a country has a deficit in a certain year because, for instance, it has spent heavily on imported stocks of raw materials. The year following, however, it is probable that, as those raw materials are made into manufactured goods which are exported, so the deficit is turned into a favourable balance, thus cancelling out the previous year's deficit. There is little need to worry about such a deficit.

On the other hand, a far different situation occurs where the tendency is for a deficit to occur year after year. Returning to the United Kingdom's position in 1973, for instance, it is obvious that countries will not continue to hold their balances in the United Kingdom or even to lend on a long-term basis unless they can see some prospect of receiving their money back, in the form of exports from the United Kingdom, in the near future. In other words, if they are to continue lending, they must foresee that the United Kingdom will become solvent once more. In such a situation, therefore, some definite action must be taken to prevent the persistent recurrence of the deficit.

Emphasis has been laid on the problem of a deficit because it is this which, over the last quarter of a century, has faced the United Kingdom.

In 1913, because her invisible earnings were so large, the United Kingdom had a current account surplus of over £200 million, and this surplus was mostly invested abroad. During and after World War I, however, a different situation arose. Exports, both visible and invisible, shrank so much that, by 1939, the surplus had been converted into an average annual deficit of about £50 million. The situation was made worse by the sale of foreign assets during World War II, for this led to a drop in investment income from abroad.

As a result, Britain, in order to pay for her current imports, has, in recent years, had to make an all-out effort to increase her exports.

But the situation has been aggravated by her desire to lend to the poorer members of the Commonwealth for their economic development. In the long run, such lending can only come out of a current surplus, though for a time it may be covered by drawing on the reserves or by borrowing elsewhere.

The result of both over-spending and over-lending is that, from time to time, there have been alarming runs on Britain's gold and foreign currency reserves. Corrective measures have had to be taken. These will now be discussed against the background of the different methods which can be used, or have been in the past.

1. DEFLATION: THE GOLD STANDARD

Throughout the nineteenth century, and until 1914, the correction of a deficit was achieved automatically through the operation of what was known as the 'gold standard'. All countries whose currency could purchase gold at a fixed rate and without restriction were said to be 'on the gold standard'. This made gold a common medium of exchange and, by comparing how much of each country's currency was required to purchase a given quantity of gold, a rate of exchange could be worked out between one country's currency and another's. Now if a country's imports were greater than its exports, it needed additional foreign currency to what it had earned to pay for those imports. This increase in demand had the effect of driving up the price of the foreign currency in terms of its own in the foreign exchange market. Rather than pay this increased price, it would be better for an importer to change his own currency into gold at the fixed rate and then ship this gold to the exporter to pay for the goods received. Therefore, in practice, the exchange rates between the two currencies did not fluctuate outside the cost of buying the gold plus the charge, including insurance, for shipping it to where it was required.

However, this movement of gold out of the country automatically brought certain forces into play which tended to reverse the flow of goods and therefore to correct the deficit. The export of gold could be achieved only by a reduction in the gold reserves of the joint-stock banks held at the Bank of England. This represented a fall in their cash reserves and they were, therefore, obliged to curtail their lending by increasing the rate of interest charged both to the discount market and to industry (see page 404). Moreover, in practice, the Central Bank took appropriate action to protect its gold reserves and support credit restriction, usually by raising the Bank Rate and by open market operations (see page 418). Higher interest rates attracted foreign short-term loans, thereby having an immediate effect of halting the drain on the gold reserves. This, however, was merely a temporary gain. To correct the underlying causes of the balance of payments deficit, exports had to be increased and imports decreased. This was achieved by a sequence of events. Dearer credit led to a policy of contraction by industry. Investment fell, stocks were reduced (some being sold abroad), and the import of raw materials dropped. Unemployment led to reduced income and therefore to a reduced demand for imports. Eventually, too, as unemployment increased, workers would be forced to accept lower wages, thereby lowering the price of British exports. Hence, eventually, the balance of payments deficit would be corrected and the drain of gold stopped.

It can be seen, however, that the restoration of equilibrium, particularly in the twentieth century, was only at the expense of industrial depression and unemployment. Moreover, it often took a long time to achieve. This is because workers are resistant to a decrease in money wages and may accept a reduction only after a long period of unemployment and poverty. Such a painful process occurred between 1929 and 1931, and the result was that the United Kingdom and most other countries abandoned the gold standard.

2. FLUCTUATING EXCHANGE RATES

The method of correcting an adverse balance of payments under the gold standard is, while retaining fixed rates of exchange between one currency and another, to reduce incomes and prices at home by means of a deflationary policy. An alternative method is to maintain incomes and prices at home but to allow exchange rates to fluctuate according to the demand for one's currency. Thus, if country A's exports to B are greater than her imports, the demand for A's currency will increase, for importers in B will be wanting it to pay for those imports. Consequently the exchange rate will move in favour of country A. Similarly, if A's imports are greater than her exports, the exchange rate will move against her. The effect of a fall in the value of the home currency in relation to that of other countries' currencies is to make imports relatively dearer and exports relatively cheaper, the very thing that is required to bring about equality in the values of total imports and total exports.

The great advantage of this method is that the levels of incomes and prices at home remain unchanged, thereby removing one of the causes of industrial depression. Unfortunately, however, fluctuating exchange rates tend to limit considerably the volume of international trade, for an exporter is always apprehensive lest, by the time he receives payment for the goods, the value of the currency in which he is to be paid has fallen, thereby turning his profit into a loss. In addition, the demand for and supply of foreign currencies varies, not only according to the state of trade, but also through the movement of 'hot money' from one country to another by investors who speculate on the future relative values of the currencies. The fact that they transfer money because they expect the value of a currency to fall helps to bring about the very thing they expect, for by so doing they decrease the demand for that currency.

Thus soon after fluctuating exchange rates were adopted in 1931, Britain set up the Exchange Equalisation Fund to buy and sell sterling on the foreign exchange market in order to offset changes in the exchange rate brought about by movements in short-term capital.

3. DEVALUATION

In 1947 most Western countries moved further towards stable exchange rates by joining the Bretton Woods agreement. This set up the International Monetary Fund. Countries agreed to declare an official equivalent of their currency to gold, thus fixing the rate at which it exchanged with the currency of other countries, e.g. the £1 sterling = 2·40 U.S. dollars. They also undertook to vary these rates only in accordance with agreed conditions and within prescribed amounts. Devaluation was said to occur when a country announced a reduction of the value of its currency in terms of gold and other currencies.

Thus, devaluation, like fluctuating exchange rates, works by making imports dearer and exports cheaper. The devaluing country hopes that, as a result of these price adjustments, less foreign currency will be spent on imports and more on her exports. Whether this happens or not depends on the elasticities of demand for imports and exports. Suppose Britain devalued. Prices of imports in foreign currency should remain the same. But in £ sterling, they will rise. Thus, unless demand for imports is absolutely inelastic, the quantity demanded will fall. Hence, *less foreign* currency will be spent than formerly. On the other hand, the prices of British exports in terms of foreigners' currencies will be lower. Moreover, demand for British exports is likely to be elastic, for they will be substituted for the relatively dearer goods of competing exporters. Furthermore, the demand of tourists is likely to be elastic. Thus, *more foreign* currency is earned by Britain. In practice, the demand for imports and exports, taken together, is likely to be sufficiently elastic for devaluation to improve the balance of payments.

Devaluation as a policy is more likely to fail not because of inelasticity of demand for exports but because of inelasticity of supply. If there is already full employment, where are the extra exports to come from? Only from the home market—and this means the government must take away some purchasing power. Worse still, the advantage devaluation has given to exports by making them cheaper might soon be lost. The increased price of imports will cause the cost of living to rise at home. With exports booming, organised labour is in a strong bargaining position. Wages therefore rise in sympathy with prices, and even beyond. Exports are no longer cheap. Devaluation is, therefore, only a once-for-all solution which cannot be regularly repeated.

It should be noted, too, that much of the above analysis applies to a depreciation of the pound sterling even though this happens through the mechanism of the foreign exchange market (as it has since 1972).

4. RESTRICTIVE MEASURES

But we must be careful to note what a failure to devalue really entails. Suppose the United Kingdom is obtaining regularly from the U.S.A. an excess of imports over exports but does not wish to devalue the pound sterling in terms of the dollar. It means that the United Kingdom is obtaining dollars too cheaply, below the price which would be established in a free exchange market. People in the United Kingdom will therefore wish to continue to buy goods from the U.S.A., whereas those in the U.S.A. will not be so willing to buy from the United Kingdom. The result, as with other cases when price is fixed below the market price, is that restrictive measures and controls have to be enforced. But, since controls reduce the volume of international trade, they can, at the best, only be justified after everything possible, short of drastic deflation, has been done to increase exports.

Controls aimed at restricting imports may take various forms:

1. *Import duties and quotas*

Import duties (tariffs) may be levied, though this is not very effective where the demand for the imports is inelastic. A slight improvement on this method is when an import quota is fixed. This means that the government specifies a given quantity of goods which it will permit to be imported over a certain period. Once this quota has been reached no further imports will be allowed.

2. *Exchange control*

The most effective method of restricting imports, from the point of view of reducing expenditure of foreign currency, is to fix a quota, not in terms of volume, but in terms of expenditure. This means that once a period's allotment of foreign currency has been spent, no more imports will be allowed. Such a restriction can be reinforced by other methods of exchange control. Thus a country may regulate the export of capital to countries abroad and limit the amount which persons may spend abroad.

Since the war, the United Kingdom has made an all-out effort to increase her exports, particularly to dollar countries, in order to improve her balance of payments position. When it has been deemed necessary, the government has restricted supplies of certain goods on the home market, given priority of raw materials and capital to firms exporting a large proportion of their output, and provided information services to help firms in their search for markets abroad. Yet, since these methods of increasing exports have proved to be inadequate, other measures have had to be taken. Thus in November, 1967, the pound sterling was devalued in terms of United States dollars from 2.80 to 2.40. Imports, too, have been discouraged by imposing limits to the spending of certain foreign currencies, notably dollars. Firms who wish to import have been permitted to do so only under licence, priority being given to essential goods such as food and raw materials. The foreign travel allowance has also been limited.

The result of these measures is to reduce the volume of trade to less than it would have been were it based solely on relative costs. In other words, the advantages of the division of labour are lost.

5. RECENT INTERNATIONAL MONETARY DEVELOPMENTS

'Managed flexibility' of exchange rates under the Bretton Woods agreement worked tolerably well for 25 years. Its main weakness, however, was that the pressure of exchange adjustment fell almost entirely on debtor nations (who were forced to devalue) rather than on creditor nations (who could have eased part of the burden by re-valuing).

While the United Kingdom and, later, the U.S.A. were frequent 'persistent debtor' nations, Germany and Japan were 'persistent creditor' countries. Both the latter countries, however, proved reluctant to revalue their currencies, fearing that the rise in the price of their exports which this would entail would make them uncompetitive in world markets.

The result was that, in order to maintain the existing exchange rate, the United Kingdom in particular had to deflate her economy whenever balance of payments difficulties arose. To some extent this could be regarded as the just penalty which she had to pay for her inability to prevent prices rising as her economy expanded. Even so, if the major creditor countries had been willing to revalue, the process of 'stop' in the United Kingdom need not have been so drastic. And, as we see below, any weakness in the pound gathered momentum because sterling was held as a reserve currency.

The decisive step was taken in June 1972, when once again sterling came under pressure as the British economy expanded. Now the 'pegged' pound was abandoned; instead the pound was allowed to 'float', its value being arrived at according to the day-to-day demand for and supply of sterling on the foreign exchange market. Originally it was probably intended that the 'float' should be temporary in order to indicate a realistic rate at which it could be re-pegged when Britain entered the Common Market in January 1973. But the pound, together with the Italian lira, continued to float indefinitely. In Britain, the Heath government made it quite clear that expansion of the economy was to have first priority and that the obstacle of maintaining a fixed exchange rate should not stand in its way. Thus a major trading nation threw overboard the Bretton Woods system of international co-operation which had been so laboriously built up over the previous 28 years. Eventually the currencies of other major countries were allowed to 'float'.

Nevertheless, the principle of international co-operation which Bretton Woods embodied is still heeded today and it is hoped that this will eventually lead to a new arrangement being hammered out for the mutual benefit of all countries engaged in international trade.

CHAPTER 15

THE EUROPEAN ECONOMIC COMMUNITY

I. BACKGROUND TO THE E.E.C.

The legacy of wars

The devastation produced by the two World Wars of the first half of the twentieth century convinced statesmen in Western Europe that the cult of nationalism had to be ended in favour of political unity. The original idea was that some form of federation of states should emerge. Thus in 1949 the Council of Europe, based in Strasbourg, was created. This, it was hoped, might form the basis of a European Parliament.

In terms of actual achievement, however, organisations of countries for definite functions proved more fruitful than the Council of Europe with its broad aims. In the economic field, the organisation for European Economic Co-operation was set up in 1948 to administer American aid. It was reconstituted in 1961 as the Organisation for Economic Co-operation and Development (O.E.C.D.) with the aims of liberalising trade, developing nuclear energy for peaceful purposes, stimulating industrial efficiency and co-ordinating aid to developing countries. Co-operation in defence was also achieved through the North Atlantic Treaty Organisation (1949) and the Western European Union (1954).

Supra-national organisations

While all the above organisations involved co-operation, and thus experience in 'give and take' between the nations concerned, they were merely voluntary associations which member nations could join or withdraw from as they chose. Federation implies the handing over of sovereign powers to a supra-national organisation so that policies can be integrated in the interests of the Federal body.

Western European statesmen who supported federation began to see that it could only proceed piecemeal on a functional basis. The first step in this direction was the formation of the European Coal and Steel Community in 1951. This was a supra-national organisation, controlling the whole of the iron, steel and coal resources of the six member countries— France, West Germany, Italy, Holland, Belgium and Luxembourg. The old divisions created by inward-looking national interests were thus broken down.

The success of the E.C.S.C. led to the setting up in 1957 of the Atomic Energy Community (EURATOM, a similar organisation for the peaceful use of atomic energy) and the European Economic Community (E.E.C., an organisation to develop a 'Common Market' between the six member countries). All three communities have now been brought within the E.E.C.

Britain's attitude to the E.E.C.

In spite of the fact that Sir Winston Churchill had been the original advocate of European confederation, Britain, when she was offered membership of E.C.S.C., Euratom and E.E.C., refused to join. She still thought she could go it alone through her links with the Commonwealth and her 'special relationship' with the U.S.A. Not only would joining the E.E.C. have meant a weakening of Commonwealth ties, but Britain was unwilling to forgo the right to follow independent policies in economics and defence. A looser, free-trade area aimed at liberalising trade was more to her liking. Thus, with six other countries, she formed the European Free Trade Area (EFTA). This, it was also envisaged, could be used as a bargaining counter to enable her to be accepted eventually into membership of E.E.C. on terms modified to her own particular interests and attitudes.

Britain applies to join the E.E.C.

Contrary to Britain's expectation, the E.E.C. grew in strength, for the overriding desire of its leaders to make it a success allowed difficulties to be resolved as they arose. Moreover, although trade between the EFTA countries increased as tariffs were reduced, Britain's trade with the E.E.C. increased at a faster rate. In other words, British goods tended to be more complementary to the economy of the E.E.C. countries than they were to those of the EFTA countries. Above all, President De Gaulle began to direct the six members of the E.E.C. towards political union. In this France would play the dominant role—and with a foreign policy which was cool towards the U.S.A. and which sought a *rapprochement* with Russia! Britain, on the other hand, could see that she would have little influence in such developments. Accordingly, in 1961, she opened negotiations for terms upon which she could join the E.E.C.

Negotiations were protracted, largely through the opposition of President De Gaulle, and were even broken off on two occasions. But Britain's application was never withdrawn. De Gaulle retired from politics, negotiations were resumed and terms were arranged which were acceptable to Edward Heath, the British Prime Minister. On 1 January 1973, therefore, the United Kingdom entered the E.E.C.

II. THE INSTITUTIONS OF THE E.E.C.

The Rome Treaty of 1957 created the E.E.C., which includes the E.C.S.C. and Euratom. As already indicated it has political aims—formally stated in the Treaty as 'to establish the foundations of an ever closer union among the European peoples'.

However, while this makes the broad political aim explicit, it has been realised that the objective will only be achieved over a long period as experience is gained through co-operation in specific economic fields.

The essential point to grasp, however, is that the Treaty of Rome set up a 'Community', a Community which, to some extent, is bigger than any one of the other member nations. Moreover, it has a government and institutions, and these have been developed from the old E.C.S.C. When the United Kingdom joined the E.E.C., the general principle was agreed that she should have a position in the institutions equal to those enjoyed by France, Germany and Italy.

There are four main institutions:

(1) *The Commission*

This is the most important organ of the E.E.C. Its thirteen members (two from the U.K.) serve for four years. Once chosen, however, the members of the Commission act as an independent body in the interests of the Community as a whole, and not as representatives of the individual governments that have nominated them.

The Commission is responsible for formulating policy proposals for submission to the Council of Ministers, for promoting the Community interest, for trying to reconcile national viewpoints, and for implementing Community decisions.

(2) *The Council of Ministers*

Each member country sends a cabinet minister (usually the Foreign Secretary) to the Council of Ministers. This is the supreme decision-making body. Its task is to harmonise the policy of the Commission with the wishes of the member governments. Thus while the Commission drafts community policies, they have to be approved by the Council before they can be implemented. Originally it was intended that Council's decision should be on a majority basis, members being given weighted voting strengths. Today, on matters of major importance which affect vital national interests, the rule in practice is that decisions shall be unanimous. Thus one member can veto a proposal affecting what it considers to be a vital interest.

So far, Community decision-making can be said to have been harmonious and successful. This achievement has been possible because of the system by which proposals and compromise plans are exchanged between the Council and the Commission. If the Council becomes deadlocked, the Commission reconsiders the proposal in order to meet some or all of the demands of the opposing countries.

(3) *The Court of Justice*

This consists of ten judges appointed for a six-year term by agreement among member governments. Its task is to interpret the Treaty and adjudicate on complaints, whether from member states, private enterprises or the institutions themselves. Its rulings are binding on member countries, community institutions and individuals.

(4) *The Assembly or European Parliament*

This is a body of 198 members (36 from the U.K.) drawn from the nine national Parliaments. These nominated members sit according to party affiliation and not nationality. The Assembly is consulted on and debates all the major policy issues of the Community, and also examines and approves the Community's budget. It can dismiss the Commission by a two-thirds majority.

(5) *Special Institutions*

Apart from the four main institutions above, there are also special institutions to deal with particular policies, e.g. the Economic and Social Committee, the European Investment Bank, the European Social Fund, the European Monetary Co-operation Fund, etc.

III. ECONOMIC OBJECTIVES OF THE E.E.C.

As we have seen, integration of policies of member countries is the overriding aim of the E.C.S.C., Euratom, and the E.E.C. We shall concentrate on the latter, usually referred to as the Common Market. Integration of overall economic policy is based on two main principles; (1) a Customs Union, (2) harmonisation of particular aspects of policy to produce a Common Market.

(1) *A customs union*

We have to distinguish between a free-trade area and a customs union. The former simply removes tariff barriers between member countries, but at the same time allowing individual members to impose their own rates of duty against outsiders. A customs union goes further. While it has external free trade, it also decides upon the common external tariffs to be levied by all member countries.

The latter is the position regarding the E.E.C. Indeed, a customs union is essential for an integrated Common Market as otherwise goods would enter the Market through low-tariff countries and be resold in the markets of those members who impose higher rates of tariff.

(2) *A Common Market*

In essence the Common Market of the E.E.C. means that goods and factors of production shall move completely freely within the Community through the operation of the price system. Only in this way can the full benefits of the larger market (see later) be realised. The overall aim, therefore, is that trade within the whole of the Community shall be just as free as trade within an individual country.

However, while this is the broad aim there are particular difficulties to be overcome for it to be completely successful. Member countries had developed their own individual taxes, welfare benefits, policies for dealing with monopoly, methods of removing balance of payments imbalances, full employment policies, and so on. If such differences were allowed to persist, they would tend to disrupt the working of the price system because they would give some members of the Community an advantage over others.

We can illustrate by two simple examples. Suppose, on joining the E.E.C., Britain had retained purchase tax on refrigerators compared with no purchase tax on binoculars. This would weight the possibilities of trade against Italy (which has a comparative advantage in producing refrigerators) in favour of Germany (which has a comparative advantage in producing high-grade binoculars). Alternatively, the comparative advantage of some countries may lie in the expertise of the professional services they can provide. Usually this means that such services have to be taken to where the customer is (e.g. know-how regarding property development). There must therefore be mobility of labour within the Market, e.g. for property-developers.

Emphasis has thus been placed on 'harmonisation' policies in order to merge a number of separate economies into one. Thus, when Britain joined, arrangements had to be made for her to bring certain aspects of her economic policy into line with the position already achieved by the original members of the E.E.C.

We shall now outline the most important details of the 'Common Market' policy.

IV. THE AIMS OF COMMON MARKET POLICY

(1) *Common external tariffs (C.E.T.)*

All members will impose tariffs on imports from non-member countries at the same rates. For Britain, adjustment will take place over a four-year period beginning on 1 January 1974.

(2) *Free trade between member countries*

This involves the removal of all duties, quotas and other barriers to free trade between members. Britain will achieve this gradually. Thus tariffs on industrial products will be eliminated over a $4\frac{1}{4}$-year transitional period, the first 20 per cent reduction being made on 1 April 1973.

(3) *A common agricultural policy (C.A.P.)*

Because the demand for agricultural products tends to be inelastic, changes in the conditions of supply can have far-reaching effects on the incomes of farmers. Thus a bumper harvest which lowers the price of foodstuffs generally will result in less total revenue (which is largely farmers' incomes). All countries, therefore, give support to their own farmers. But the means of doing so have differed. Britain has, in the past, followed a 'cheap food' policy, allowing foodstuffs to enter the country free of duty and subsidising farmers by 'deficiency payments' which covered the difference between the market price and the agreed 'guaranteed' price.

C.A.P. works on the basis of maintaining farmers' incomes by high prices on the home market. These are achieved through import levies on imported foods. Three prices are fixed for each product:

(a) a *target price*, which it is estimated will give farmers an adequate return in a normal year;

(b) a *threshold price*, which is used as the basis for assessing levies on imports which will ensure that they do not enter the E.E.C. below this price;

(c) the *intervention price*, at which surplus supplies (e.g. owing to a good harvest or simply over-production through the setting of too high a threshold price) are bought up by various agencies to be disposed of outside the Market. The butter sold to the U.S.S.R. in 1973 is an example.

Obviously C.A.P. confers greater benefits on countries in which agriculture is important (e.g. France) compared with countries which are more dependent on manufacturing (e.g. Germany and the U.K.). We shall return to this problem later.

(4) *Harmonisation of tax systems*

As already shown, some standardisation of methods of taxation is necessary in order to remove any 'hidden' barriers to trade. This applies particularly to indirect taxes. In the E.E.C., V.A.T. is to be the basic form of indirect tax, and it is proposed that eventually it will be imposed by all member countries at the same rates.

No proposals exist for harmonising income taxes, but most countries have adopted the 'imputation' system of corporation tax.

(5) *Free movements of persons and capital*

It is necessary that people and capital should be able to move from one part of the Community to another, just as today they can move from one part of their own country to another.

(6) *Complete monetary integration*

As we saw in Chapter 14, countries can adjust the prices of goods which are traded internationally by varying the exchange rates of their currencies. If this were allowed within the E.E.C. it could enable a member-country to obtain a competitive advantage by depreciating its currency in terms of those of other member countries. It is agreed, therefore, that currencies of member countries are to be kept to a fixed exchange rate with only narrow adjustments. The eventual aim is a common currency system, with one currency in London, Paris, Bonn and Rome, just as there is one currency in London, Cardiff and Edinburgh.

A European Monetary Co-operation Fund, administered by the governors of the central banks, has been set up to intervene in the monetary flows between member countries in order to narrow the margin of fluctuations in currency values and to promote long-run integration.

The United Kingdom was expected to declare the exchange rate for the pound which it would maintain when it entered the E.E.C. At the time the pound sterling was 'floating', and care had to be taken that it was not fixed at an over-valued rate, thereby putting British goods at a price disadvantage compared with those of other member countries. However, the pound continued to float after Britain's entry, though this must be regarded as merely a temporary arrangement.

(7) *A common regional policy*

Just as one nation cannot allow depressed areas to persist, so the E.E.C. is expected to help regions of high unemployment. Northern Ireland and Southern Italy are two such regions. Apart from the establishment of a Regional Development Fund, however, little has so far been done to integrate the various methods of encouraging industry to the problem areas.

(8) *A common transport policy*

By regulating such items as freight rates, licences, taxation and working conditions, the E.E.C. can seek to ensure that transport undertakings compete on an equal footing. Again, any hidden advantages through special freight rates would tend to distort the free movement of goods within the Market.

(9) *Common rules on competition*

With the object of preventing the distortion of competition in trade between member countries, uniform regulations have been introduced to cover price fixing, sharing of markets and patent rights.

(10) *A Community budget*

A Community budget is necessary to meet the costs of administration and to provide funds for operating the main areas of policy which require collective expenditure, for example C.A.P. and Regional policy. Contributions are collected nationally from two main sources—import duties and a 1 per cent V.A.T. Britain agreed to contribute 8·64 per cent of the total budget in 1973, rising to 18·92 per cent over a five-year period.

V. ADVANTAGES OF BELONGING TO THE E.E.C.

The possible advantages which can accrue to countries by forming a Common Market can be summarised as follows:

(1) *Increased possibilities of specialisation*

The extent of the division of labour is, as was shown in Chapter 7, limited by the size of the market. The E.E.C. provides a market of 260 million people, larger than that of the United States. This allows economies of scale to be achieved, especially as regards sophisticated products requiring high initial research expenditure, for example computers, nuclear reactors, supersonic aircraft, and modern defence weapons. Even before she joined the E.E.C., Britain had been forced to combine with other European countries to cover research costs, e.g. with France on the development of the Concorde.

(2) *Increased efficiency through competition in the larger market*

Within the Common Market there are no trade barriers which, in effect, protect inefficient firms. Free trade means that goods and services can compete freely in all parts of the market and that factors of production can move to their most efficient use, not merely within a country, but between countries. Thus our basic economic principle—the maximisation of satisfaction by using scarce resources in their most efficient manner—operates within an economy of 260 million people rather than within one of only 56 million.

(3) A faster rate of growth

Over the last fifteen years, the G.N.P.s of the six original members of the E.E.C. have grown twice as fast as that of the United Kingdom. Indeed, apart from Italy, each of these countries now has a higher G.N.P. per head of the population than the United Kingdom.

It is likely that, to a large extent, this faster rate of growth was the result of the increased economies of scale and competition enjoyed by the Common Market. But it is also possible that the Market generates growth by the mood it engenders.

(4) Political advantages

As already explained, the ultimate objective of the original advocates of European co-operation was some form of political union. A Western Europe which could speak with one voice would carry weight when dealing with other major powers, particularly the U.S.A. and the U.S.S.R. Moreover, the integration of defence forces and strategy would give them far greater security. It is not possible, therefore, to separate the political from the economic advantages, for the two are interlinked.

VI. PROBLEMS FACING THE UNITED KINGDOM AS A MEMBER OF THE E.E.C.

By remaining outside the E.E.C., Britain would have denied herself the possible advantages of being within the larger market. Nor could she have influenced the way in which the Common Market might develop. As a member, however, her views will at least have to be considered.

In defence, Britain is inextricably tied to Western Europe. And, in recent years, although she was outside the E.E.C., her foreign trade was being pulled in that direction. Why then was there so much opposition to Britain's entry? We can pinpoint six major difficulties.

(1) *The C.E.T. could lead to the diversion of trade toward less-efficient E.E.C. suppliers*

The duties imposed by the customs union may allow firms within the Common Market to compete in price with more efficient firms outside.

Suppose, for instance, that the same machine can be produced by both the U.S.A. and Germany but, because the American firm is more efficient, its machine is 10 per cent cheaper than the German. In these circumstances, Britain would, other things being equal, import from the United States. As a member of E.E.C., however, Britain would have to discriminate against the American machine by the appropriate C.E.T., say, 20 per cent. This would make the German machine cheaper, and so trade would be diverted to the less efficient producer.

The main problem this poses for the British concerns foodstuffs, for these have entered Britain duty free. As a result, for instance, dairy produce (particularly butter) from New Zealand has been able to compete with European producers. The imposition of a tariff against New Zealand would alter the pattern of trade in dairy produce.

(2) *The C.A.P. has particular disadvantages for the United Kingdom*

There are four main criticisms of the C.A.P.:

(*a*) The import duties levied on foodstuffs in order to maintain prices for farmers within the Community hits Britain particularly hard. Since she is dependent on imports for one-half of her food supplies, it is obviously to her advantage to obtain them from the most efficient producer.

The C.A.P., on the other hand, could mean that Britain has to switch her imports of foodstuffs to dearer producers within the Market. In doing so she is subsidising, as it were, inefficient methods of farming in other countries.

(*b*) High prices encourage supply by Common Market

countries but not demand, so that over-production (as in the case of butter) can occur.

(c) High food prices hit low-income groups hardest; that is, compared with the old U.K. system of deficiency payments, C.A.P. is regressive.

(d) The distortion of the normal pattern of international trade in foodstuffs may penalise the under-developed nations since these are often food-producers. Thus it could widen the income-gap between the developed and under-developed countries.

(3) *The U.K.'s trade with the Commonwealth has been sacrificed*

Both Britain's former EFTA partners and the under-developed nations of the Commonwealth have been offered the benefits of special association with the E.E.C. Moreover, the import levy against New Zealand dairy products is to be imposed only gradually over a period of 5 years. But exporters of manufactured goods, among whom are Australia, Canada and Hong Kong, will lose the favoured treatment which they formerly enjoyed. Indeed, the C.E.T. will work against them.

In the past, trade has been an important link between the Commonwealth countries, although it must be recognised that the importance of Britain's trade with the Commonwealth has been diminishing over the past twenty years.

(4) *Certain producers will be particularly hit by concessions to Common Market regulations*

In the past, some branches of horticulture (e.g. tomatoes and fruits) have enjoyed a quota protection from Continental producers. This has ended with Britain's entry to the E.E.C. Moreover, it is also proposed that by 1984 territorial waters will be open to the fishing fleets of all member countries. Few concessions have been made to these particular producers.

(5) *Britain's contribution to the Community budget will place a severe strain on her balance of payments*

Originally it was estimated that when Britain bears her full share of the budget it will amount to £300 million a year, with £110 million being returned as aid for the 'assisted areas'.

But even in 1973, Britain's contribution proved to be greater than that estimated at the beginning of the year. One major cause of this was the fall in the values of the dollar and pound sterling. C.A.P. prices were fixed in terms of the dollar and, when this fell in value, farmers' incomes had to be maintained from an increased Community budget.

Britain's loss of foreign currency in this way will be justified only if she can increase the value of her exports as a result of Common Market membership.

(6) *Harmonisation of taxation and the adoption of a common monetary system involves a serious loss of economic sovereignty*

As regards taxation, two examples can be given. (*a*) Protection of agriculture by import duties rather than by deficiency payments means that the consumer pays to maintain Community farmers' incomes rather than the taxpayer. In effect, therefore, the change from subsidies to protective duties is regressive in nature. (*b*) The substitution of V.A.T. for purchase tax also tends to be more regressive inasmuch as the old purchase tax imposed a higher rate on luxury goods.

But it is through the adoption of the common monetary policy that Britain really stands to lose freedom of action over major economic policy. A country which is trading internationally has the option when exports fall in value of either lowering internal costs (the old gold standard mechanism) or lowering the exchange rate (exchange devaluation or depreciation) in order to make its exports more competitive. The latter policy will be denied to Britain under a common monetary policy. The exchange rate will have to be maintained within limits (at present termed 'the snake') which are narrower than the current I.M.F. limits ('the tunnel'). Exports will have to be revived by lowering home prices and this may lead to unemployment. Thus Britain could be a permanent depressed area of the E.E.C. if her goods are not competitive.

Against this, however, some economists might argue that this will present no problem for Britain provided she can hold her inflation in check. And here, the common currency requirement will impose the necessary discipline.

Conclusion

Britain's membership of the Common Market provides the opportunity for an all-round improvement in her standard of living. But the benefits will only be secured if she braces herself to compete in the larger market. Two major problems face her: (*a*) an increase in the rate of capital investment in industry; (*b*) controlling the rate of inflation at home. Both are essential if Britain is to be cost-competitive within the E.E.C. and world markets.

PART V

THE FACTORS OF PRODUCTION
AND THE NATIONAL INCOME

CHAPTER 16

THE FACTORS OF PRODUCTION

A Classification of the Factors of Production

So far we have spoken rather loosely of 'means of production' and 'factors of production'. It is now desirable to look at these terms a little more carefully. We will commence by defining a factor of production as any agent which assists in 'production', used in its economic sense. We have already noted the limitation which arises from this particular concept of production. But we shall see its value in our examination of the national income, for it allows the national output to be calculated either in terms of the rewards that such factors receive (measuring the 'input' of factors), or in the value of the actual output which they produce.

For analytical purposes, however, it is also useful to have some classification of the factors of production, and here we will start from the position of the economists of the eighteenth and nineteenth centuries, the 'Classical' economists, who divided the factors of production into four groups—land, labour, capital and organisation, the reward which each received being labelled respectively rent, wages, interest and profit.

To this classification, there are two main objections. In the first place it is over-simplifying the problem to think that all factors can be separated and put into one of the four distinct compartments, land, labour, capital and organisation. These compartments themselves overlap. Land, used in its popular sense, can be improved and increased in quantity by a capital outlay on fertilisers, drainage and irrigation, while much of the acquired skill of a worker can be regarded as a return to the capital investment which was incurred in training him. Secondly, except as a first approach, it is far too arbitrary and artificial to restrict the factors of production to four types. Any attempt to classify factors according to their qualities must allow for the fact that these vary considerably. An architect is a far different sort of worker from the bricklayer's mate, and the hotel manager from the hotel porter, but the classification lumps them all together under the heading of 'labour' and thereby is inclined to imply that they are all the same. From an economic point of view, one factor is only the same as another in so far as it is a perfect substitute for it or, in other words, if an entrepreneur were indifferent as to which one he used.

In point of fact, however, any classification of the factors of production will come up against difficulties. The main object is to have one that is as simple and useful as possible. Hence the definition of the Classical economists has not been entirely discarded but modern economists have refined it and considered that it can best be done on a threefold basis. Land is retained because its return 'rent' is regarded as an example of any reward which goes to a factor the supply of which is limited over a period of time. On the other hand, 'organisation' is omitted since it consists of two parts, managerial ability and 'risk-bearing'. The first is really only a superior form of labour; the second arises, as we shall see, owing to the possession of certain fixed factors and the return is really in the nature of rent and can be classified as such. Capital and labour are still retained. The accumulation of capital involves forgoing present satisfactions while the fact that its use extends over a period of time creates difficulties in the maintenance of full employment over long periods. Labour has to be treated separately because the human factor gives rise to certain difficulties.

We shall now deal with each of these factors in more detail.

LAND, RENT AND PROFIT

1. *Land*

The term 'land' as used in the popular sense can really be divided into two parts. First, there is the part which it is within the power of man to increase (in the sense that its productivity is increased), by the expenditure of capital on it. Capital investment is represented in the addition of fertilisers, drainage and irrigation schemes, the development of communications, the provision of buildings and greenhouses, and even by reclamation of land from the sea. Secondly, there is that part, the supply of which is a gift of Nature, which is not within the power of man to increase—the amount of sunshine and rain that falls on the land, the particular situation, the supply of mineral deposits. It is of this which economists really speak when they refer to land. Rent, or more precisely 'economic rent', is the return to this fixed element.

It might be asked whether 'land' in the latter sense is really fixed in supply. Admittedly, the distinction between the two parts is often blurred. The expenditure of capital can still today increase 'land' used in its economic sense. Thus, through research, a hardier grade of wheat might be developed which would allow land in higher altitudes previously unused to be put under cultivation. Yet it must be appreciated that there is a limit to total land-space. In large towns today we see the effect of it whenever the rents of the sites nearer the centre are forced up by increased demand. And, while further developments may bring the Sahara and the Polar wastes into economic use, the fact still remains that apart from producing on the moon, eventually we shall be able to go no further and that the total sum of land is fixed. In short, when we add labour and capital to it, we shall be adding them to a fixed factor.

2. 'Economic rent'

The Classical economists, particularly Ricardo, were pre-occupied with this idea of the fixity of land. In their time landlords were a more important social class than they are today and before the Industrial Revolution shared over 20 per cent of the national income compared with considerably less than 5 per cent today. Moreover, at least two-thirds of the workers were employed in agriculture as compared with one-eightieth today, while the dispute as to whether the Corn Laws should be repealed was also bound up with the supply of land. Lastly, the rapid growth of the population in the last half of the nineteenth century seemed to point to the inevitable fact that, since land was limited in supply, population would outrun the means of subsistence.

Their attitude to land and rent was formulated largely by their misguided attempt to explain the value of an article as depending on its cost of production. Land consisted of 'the original and indestructible properties of the soil', land in the economic sense as described above. Such land was a free gift of Nature and fixed in supply because it could not be added to by human agency. But being free, it could not enter into the costs of production. Hence rent, the payment for that land, did not help to determine the price of the good made. Indeed, they said the opposite was true, that the price of the good produced determined the return or rent which was received.

Criticism of Ricardo's theory rests mainly on two points. In the first place, we have his sweeping assumption that the total supply of land is fixed. As we have already seen, other factors, such as transport developments and improved techniques of farming, continually arise and thereby increase the economic use of land. Indeed, in this respect there is little difference between land and the other factors of production, capital and labour, which also increase relatively so slowly that their total supply over a certain period can be said to be fixed (see Chapter 1). Secondly, from the point of view of economics, we are concerned not so much with the total supply of a factor but rather with the alternative uses to which it can be put. Here again land is no different, for it has many alternative uses. In agriculture it can be used to grow many different crops, while if used for building, the buildings can be erected for a variety of purposes. The cost of putting it to one use is the yield that could have been obtained had it been employed in some other way. Hence, in order to secure it for one purpose, a producer will have to pay a sufficient price to attract it from other uses.

But it takes time to transfer many factors of production. Hence, during the 'short period', the supply of certain factors of production is fixed. It is here that Ricardo's views have been used to point out an important general principle—that the return to a factor fixed in supply depends entirely on the price of the good produced by it. Thus, once land is sown with wheat, the return to that land is entirely dependent on the price which the wheat fetches in the market. Similarly, with a farmer who has beef cattle, the return on those cattle is entirely dependent on the price at which beef is selling when the cattle are killed. Again, since the supply of capital equipment, such as a blast furnace, cannot be increased overnight, the return on it is dependent on the present price of pig-iron. Hence Ricardo's concept of rent is but a particular example of a general rule which applies to all factors fixed in supply, and so the term 'economic rent' has since been used as a general term to describe the special nature of this return to all such factors.

Thus the widest and most practical use of the concept of economic rent is really in connection with the distinction between the long and the short periods, and we shall have more to say on this later when discussing 'profit'. Nevertheless, instances do arise which closely correspond to Ricardo's view of land as having certain properties which are inherent and cannot be increased in supply even over the long period by the ordinary process of production. Thus superlative building sites, such as those of the City of London, cannot be duplicated. As the demand for commercial houses within the City increases, so it merely forces up the rents which can be charged for the sites there and their high yield is, therefore, almost entirely a form of economic rent. A similar situation exists with persons who possess a very rare and highly skilled ability, such as certain film stars, renowned surgeons and eminent and fashionable barristers. This ability cannot be duplicated by training others since, very often, their particular quality is unique. Hence their high earnings are once again almost wholly what economists term 'economic rent'.

3. Profit

Existing factors of production have to be combined together to produce goods and services. But first a decision has to be made as to what goods and services shall be produced. As was explained earlier, we may leave it to the State to take the decision or we can let it rest with individuals whose aim in production is to make a profit for themselves.

The early economists named whoever took the decision of what to produce as the 'entrepreneur', and we can use the same term. If the State makes the decision, then the State is the entrepreneur; if a man buys a car and starts a car-hire business with himself as the driver, he also is an entrepreneur. Thus entrepreneurship ranges from the sole trader, through the partnership, joint-stock company (where people buy shares in

the venture), the co-operative society, to the largest of undertakings, such as I.C.I., Unilever, and above all, the nationalised industries.

Here we are concerned with the private enterprise system,
where the entrepreneurs are either alone (as with sole traders)
or in partnership or combination with others (as with the
shareholders of joint-stock companies). With the hope of
making a profit, all these take it on themselves to decide what
to produce. But how is it that a profit can be made? The
answer lies in the difference, already pointed out, between
demand and supply. Whereas demand can vary from one
moment to another, supply can be adjusted only over time. Not
only does the productive process itself take time but, because
the factors of production are immobile, a period must usually
elapse before economic forces can produce their full effect.
Indeed, it was this immobility of the factors of production
which led to the distinction between the 'long' and the 'short'
periods. In the 'long period' all factors are mobile, whereas
in the 'short period' some factors are fixed in the sense that
during this period they can move neither into nor out of a
particular line of production. It must be noted, however, that
in practice it is difficult to draw any absolute line between the
two periods because some factors are fixed for a longer period
than others.

Now since, for the above reasons, it takes time to adjust
supply to changes in demand, the entrepreneur *anticipates*
demand by purchasing or hiring certain 'fixed' factors, such as
land, factory buildings, machinery and managerial staff, and,
together with the 'variable' factors, such as raw materials and
operatives, commences production *in advance*. In doing so,
however, he takes the *risk* that, by the time production is
complete, the demand for his good may have changed. If
demand falls, the price of the good will fall, and he may have
to curtail or cease production. By discharging operatives and
ceasing to buy raw materials, the cost of the variable factors
can be saved immediately the price received for the good does
not cover them. But the fixed factors cannot, by definition, be
transferred elsewhere; the cost of these has been incurred once
and for all for the entire short period. A fall in the price of his
good may therefore result in a loss and even bankruptcy. On

the other hand, if he is right in his estimate of demand, he is likely to receive a reward—profit—for the risk he has taken in assembling fixed factors. This is because, in the short period, no other producer can assemble fixed factors and so increase supply *by increasing productive capacity*. Thus profit arises because certain factors are fixed in supply in the short period. Its size depends upon the price at which the good sells. Profit, therefore, is a form of 'economic rent'. In the long period, of course, other firms can and will, if they see profits are being made, engage factors of production and enter the industry. Their production will increase supply and bring down the price of the good until in the end the profit margin disappears.

Here, however, we must be careful to distinguish the economists' meaning of profit from its everyday meaning. Let us consider the case of the man who starts his own car-hire business. Most people would estimate the profit as receipts minus costs, costs including only the depreciation on the car, expenditure on petrol and oil, taxation, insurance and repairs and the hire of a garage. But the fact that a man works for himself does not mean that there is no labour cost involved. The economist defines 'costs' in the sense of alternatives forgone. Hence, in the case of the man who works in his own business, we must calculate the cost of his labour as being what he could have obtained elsewhere working for somebody else at a fixed wage. A similar allowance must be calculated for the use of the personal capital which the man invests in his own business. Thus, in addition to the costs already mentioned, our car-hire proprietor should consider how much he could earn elsewhere, the interest he could obtain from a different source on the capital invested in his car, and, if he uses his own garage, how much he could let that garage for to another person. Such 'implied costs' must therefore be deducted from profits.

'Profits', then, are receipts less costs of all kinds, including 'implied costs'. They are divided by economists into two groups, 'normal' profits and 'abnormal' (or 'pure') profits. The first, normal profits, is the minimum return which keeps an entrepreneur in a particular industry after *all* the factors have been paid what they could earn in an alternative use. It is the 'long-period' position. Thus, if all firms in the industry are making only normal profits, there is neither a desire by existing firms to move out nor an incentive to other firms to move in. The second, abnormal profits, consists of any additional return remaining to the entrepreneur above normal profit. It is the reward he receives for taking the risk of producing in advance for an uncertain demand, and apart from the special case of monopoly, is due to the immobility of factors in the 'short period'.

CHAPTER 17

LABOUR AND WAGES

1. THE SPECIAL CHARACTERISTICS OF LABOUR AS A FACTOR OF PRODUCTION

LABOUR is the effort made by human beings in the process of production. Nevertheless, as with land, it is not always possible to distinguish clearly between that part of the effort employed which can be attributed entirely to the human element and that part which is still attributable to the investment of capital in the training of the labourer.

The essential thing to note, however, is that, in discussing labour, we are dealing with human beings. Whereas differences in the amount of capital invested in labour results in there being many different kinds of labour, the human element makes the variety of labourers infinite, for human beings, unlike machines, are never exactly the same. Moreover, machines are passive and will respond automatically and precisely to the dictates of an operator. But there is no such automatic and exact response with labour. Psychological factors have to be taken into consideration if we are to obtain the best possible use of this scarce factor of production. This psychological response of labour to varying conditions is significant in economics in a number of ways.

In the first place, when a machine stands idle for any particular reason, it does not deteriorate. Provided it is kept free from rust, it will continue to produce as efficiently as before whenever it is started up again. If the period of idleness is a long one, it may depreciate in value or even become outdated. But the loss is simply the output not produced; that is the only penalty of its being idle. Unemployed labour, however, is different. Not only is there a loss of goods and services, but the factor itself can deteriorate. Few people wish to be idle indefinitely for there is a secret contentment in contributing with

one's fellow-men to the productive effort. Thus an enforced
idleness through the inability to find a job not only involves the
labourer in a loss of earnings, but leads to a feeling of being
unwanted. The difficulty is not overcome by simply giving the
labourer a money grant, even though that grant might itself be
equal to normal earnings. Welfare, which implies happiness
and is really a product of the mind, is not identical with wealth.
Only because an objective measure of welfare cannot be found,
is wealth taken, especially by the government, as the best
indication of welfare. But the difference between the two must
never be forgotten. Thus, in formulating an employment
policy, many economists point out that a small percentage of
unemployment, say 3–5 per cent of the working population,
could increase economic efficiency. It would promote greater
mobility of labour, make it easier to limit wage increases to
increases in productivity, and probably result in more effort
from those in work if only for fear of being discharged for
slacking. Hence total production would be greater than where
there was 'overfull' employment. In short, some unemployment might, in practice, increase total wealth! But would it
increase total welfare? This is the real question which a government must answer when formulating its plans for the
employment of the workers. Since World War II, each government has maintained a high level of employment, the registered
unemployed seldom being greater than 3 per cent of the
working population and often less.

Secondly, labour is particularly immobile. Whilst in the
shifting of machines from one place to another, only transport
costs have to be considered, with labour there is, in addition to
the cost of moving, a psychological barrier to be broken down.
This is the main problem of the immobility of labour, and we
return to it in more detail in Chapter 24.

Lastly, the psychological aspect is important, not only in
finding the labourer employment but also in fitting him into
the actual process of production. For instance, while a
machine is completely passive, a labourer can be miserable,
indifferent and even happy in his work. And the degree of
happiness affects the size and quality of the effort expended.
The organisation and training of labour should ensure that
square pegs are not placed in round holes and that the

intelligence, skill and capabilities of the worker are not wasted. Again, while an entrepreneur can, when varying his expenditure on machinery, expect a corresponding variation in output, this is not so with labour. The response of labour to an increase in the reward offered is not automatic in the sense that a higher reward will lead to a greater effort. It may well be that the increase in wages is not accompanied by any corresponding desire for a higher *material* standard of living. Instead the worker may, as it were, prefer to 'buy' more leisure with his increased wages. When this occurs, the result of an increase in wage-rates may be a *decrease* in the total effort expended. Other methods, such as a straight appeal to his loyalty, may, after a certain stage, be much more effective in inducing the labourer to work harder and for longer hours.

II. THE LABOUR FORCE OF THE UNITED KINGDOM

The contribution of labour to the production of a country depends upon (1) its quantity, (2) its quality.

1. FACTORS DETERMINING THE TOTAL SUPPLY OF LABOUR

Labour, like the other factors of production, is 'scarce' in the sense that its supply is not unlimited. At any one time its quantity is determined by: (i) the size of the population; (ii) the proportion of the population which works; (iii) the amount of work offered by each individual labourer.

1. *The size of the population*

The population of the United Kingdom was discussed in Chapter 3. Numbers obviously set a limit to the total production of a country, but from the point of view of material well-being, production per head of the population and not merely total production is far more significant. Production per head is discussed in an alternative form under 'national income' per head (see Chapter 19). It is governed much more by the quality of the labour force than by its quantity.

2. *The proportion of the total population which works*

The working population of a country is only a proportion of its total population and is determined chiefly by the age distribution, its social institutions and customs and, to a much lesser degree, by the sex distribution and the numbers who can live on unearned income. In the United Kingdom the size of the working population depends largely on the numbers within the 16–65 age-group, for attendance at school is compulsory until reaching 16 years of age, while at 65 years of age (60 years for women) the State provides retirement pensions. Nevertheless, many people go on working beyond the normal retiring age, while the group itself contains a high percentage of married women. The extent to which married women enter paid work rests largely on custom and opportunity, and varies from one place to another and over different periods. Thus in the United Kingdom a higher proportion of married women work than in the U.S.A., while within the United Kingdom, such areas as Dundee, Lancashire and Leicester all show a higher percentage than elsewhere. Similarly, more married women go out to work today than before the war, so that now half the female working population consists of married women, though many of them are only part-time workers.

The sex distribution has only a minor effect on the size of the working population. Equality between the sexes, in so far as it raises the marriage rate, is likely to decrease the working population, while a predominance of females tends towards the same result, since females usually retire from industrial life at an earlier age than men.

It is important to note that not all the potential working population may be employed and it is the task of the Government to see that, as far as possible, unemployment and industrial disputes do not waste a portion of the scarce factor, labour. Similarly, greater equality of wealth and income, achieved largely by taxation, decreases the numbers who do not need to work because they have independent means.

3. *The amount of work offered by each individual labourer*

The amount of work offered by each labourer will vary with the number of hours worked, the intensity of effort applied, and the rate of pay.

Generally speaking, the richer the country, the more leisure it can afford and hence its working week is shorter. For this reason, the United Kingdom has been able to reduce the normal working week from approximately 54 hours at the beginning of the century to an average of 37–40 today. Nevertheless it must be noted that normal working hours can be increased within limits by raising the rate of pay offered and, as we have seen, by incentives of a psychological nature.

Intensity of effort varies with the health, character and psychological attitude of the labourer. The average American, for instance, works much more intensively than the African, while amongst labourers even of the same country the one who is happy in his work will do better than the worker who is not. Welfare schemes, such as pensions, canteens and sports clubs, help to keep the worker contented.

A higher rate of pay makes leisure more expensive, and the tendency is to substitute work for leisure, as, for example, when higher overtime rates are paid. But it can easily happen that higher pay so increases a person's income, that he is able to 'buy' more leisure and work *fewer* hours!

2. FACTORS DETERMINING THE QUALITY OF LABOUR

The average Chinese peasant works much longer hours than any British worker but the value of his output is much less. This is because his labour is, from the economic point of view, inferior in quality. Quality of labour varies according to the skill of the labourer, the tools and machines he has to assist him, and the way he is organised, that is, fitted into the productive process.

Skill depends largely on training. Here, it should be noted that an older working population will normally be more experienced and skilful than a younger one, though the latter may excel in vigour and initiative. Skill today, however, is usually used in conjunction with machines; both represent investment of capital. It is, therefore, difficult to draw any hard and fast line between labour and capital.

Proper organisation of labour is essential if the maximum output is to be secured. Not only must we avoid putting square pegs in round holes, but the principle of the division of labour must be applied whenever it increases output. Even the layout of the factory can economise in the use of labour.

III. PAYMENT FOR LABOUR

According to the form of business organisation in which it is employed and to the occupation, so the method of rewarding labour usually varies. We must first distinguish between: (*a*) persons who work for 'profit', and (*b*) persons who, by selling their labour to somebody else, contract out of the risk that the product of their labour may not be wanted.

1. PERSONS WHO WORK FOR 'PROFIT'

As we have seen, in certain occupations, particularly retailing, farming and professional services, the typical form of business organisation is either the sole trader or partnership. If we asked the owners of these businesses what was the reward for their labour, we would probably be told 'profit'. But here we must draw attention to our earlier analysis of profits. 'Profit' in its general use includes what the entrepreneur could get for his labour (and capital) if it were employed elsewhere and this part of his total profits is really a return to labour. The remainder consists of 'normal' and 'abnormal' profit. The former is the return which is just sufficient to keep the entrepreneur in the industry. The latter is an additional return which arises because, in the short period, other persons cannot enter into competition with him. Abnormal profits are not a part of the reward of labour but are a surplus return for the acceptance of the risks which were involved in the uncertainty of estimating demand. In the long period, as new firms come in, these abnormal profits tend to disappear. Sometimes, however, by profit sharing, bonus and co-partnership schemes, employees do share in the risk-taking function of the entrepreneur, though these schemes are usually introduced as an incentive to greater efficiency.

2. PERSONS WHO SELL THEIR LABOUR
TO SOMEBODY ELSE

Most production is carried on by those entrepreneurs who hire other persons' labour on an agreed contract and over a certain period. They bear the risk of an uncertain future demand, and by so doing shoulder losses or reap profits as the case may be. On the other hand, persons who sell their labour do so in exchange for a fixed salary or wage which they continue to receive until the expiration of their contract, irrespective of whether the good sells at a higher or lower price than was estimated. In short they contract out of the risk involved in producing for a demand that is either not known accurately or which is liable to fluctuate. These contracts can vary as regards their duration, the conditions under which the work is performed, the method of rewarding the work and the actual rate of pay.

Broadly speaking, the method of rewarding the work performed can be based either on the length of time for which the worker is under the direction of the employer or on the results achieved. The first method is known as 'time-rate', the second as 'piece-rate', but it must be emphasised that neither is exclusive of the other. When a worker is engaged on a time-rate basis, the employer has an idea of the minimum standard of achievement he can expect, while if payment is on a straight piece-rate basis, the employer expects a certain minimum output from a worker who is using the capital equipment provided. In fact, most 'payments by results' schemes are combined with a guaranteed minimum wage and often the additional pay per unit of output represents a bonus as an incentive to intensive effort.

Time-rate payments can take the form of either salaries or wages. Salaries are usually paid on a monthly basis and a month's notice terminating the employment is then generally required on both sides. However, in the more important jobs the contract may be for a much longer period, even up to a number of years, the time varying according to the employer's estimate of how long it will take to replace what he considers is a key worker.

With the majority of jobs, however, it is customary for the contract to be for a shorter period. Thus machinists, clerks, shorthand-typists and lorry-drivers generally work on a weekly basis, while casual agricultural labourers and charwomen work by the hour. In many occupations, such as dockers, bricklayers and painters, where the contract period is the day or hour, a minimum number of hours per week is guaranteed. Where persons work by the week or less, we call their reward 'wages', though the term 'wage payments' is generally used comprehensively to include salaries, weekly wages and piece-payments.

Time-rates are usually paid when the quality of the work is so important that it is undesirable to induce the worker to hurry, e.g. train-driving, gardening and farming, retailing; where the work is in the nature of an 'overhead cost' in the sense that a certain amount has to be engaged irrespective of output, e.g. clerical and sales staff; and above all, where the work cannot be easily standardised and measured, that is, where the requirements of the piece-rate method are not fulfilled, e.g. teaching, nursing, police and the Armed Forces. The method, however, suffers from two main drawbacks. In the first place, it provides no additional reward for the more efficient workers. Secondly, close supervision is often necessary in order to prevent slacking.

Piece-rate wage payments are only possible when the output can be distinctly measured and where a given effort always yields a given output. In teaching, for instance, examination passes do not measure the full effectiveness of the teacher's work, and in any case such results are influenced by factors, such as general intelligence, over which the teacher has no control. The same applies to agriculture where the returns to labour are dependent on variations in weather. It is not necessary, however, that each individual's contribution can be assessed. Often, as with the building of motor cars and radio sets, the workers engaged on the task are given as a group so much per unit produced and the total sum is then apportioned amongst them on an agreed basis.

Where piece-rate payments are possible, it is often to the advantage of the employee, the employer and the community in general that they should be instituted. The employee has the satisfaction of feeling that his reward is directly related to his effort and this is particularly true of the quicker and more efficient worker. Moreover, where the payment is to the group, the worker is led to identify himself with the complete task. This provides a sense of achievement and thus overcomes some of the loss of craftsmanship which we noted as one of the disadvantages of the division of labour. Again, he is freed from the irksome restriction of timekeeping and the constant supervision of a foreman. Piece-rates generally bring the worker higher earnings—but without overstrain, since he can choose his own pace. To the employer, payment by results usually achieves a higher output and thus lowers the cost per unit of his overheads. It also makes costing easier, and reduces supervision costs, while the workers often co-operate in improving the organisation. In the long run, therefore, the community benefits from the lower prices which result.

Nevertheless, in the past the trade unions have, for various reasons, been inclined to view piece-rates with disfavour. Sometimes the system has been abused by employers who, as output has increased, have cut the rate paid. In addition, the unions have felt that payment by results puts obstacles in the way of collective bargaining. Thus control is lost over the quantity of labour supplied, while differences in earnings lead to a loss of solidarity. Moreover, if piece-rates are to be fair, they should be adjusted to the different circumstances, such as working conditions and the amount of capital equipment per head provided, which exist from place to place. Yet these local variations in rates make negotiation for standard rates on a national scale difficult. Finally, the unions have found that, in past periods of depression, the system prevents a fair allocation of the limited amount of work available amongst all its members, with the result that many become totally unemployed.

In recent years, too, some employers, e.g. in the car industry, have ended piece-rates. A major disadvantage is that workers resist being shifted from tasks in which they have acquired dexterity (producing high piece earnings) even though the current needs of the factory organisation require such a transfer. In short, employers lose control over their employees, and many prefer to pay high time-rates to obviate this.

3. 'Wage-Rate' and 'Earnings'

It is necessary to distinguish carefully between 'wage-rates' and 'weekly earnings'. The 'wage-rate' refers to the rate of pay for either a normal working week or for the unit of output; the 'weekly earnings' are what are actually received in the pay packet at the end of the week, plus what is paid in income tax and national insurance contributions. Thus where overtime has been worked, earnings will be above the weekly wage rates, while, when a form of piece-rate operates, earnings will vary according to the weekly output and again may be above any guaranteed minimum weekly wage. The Annual Abstract of Statistics shows that whereas average weekly *wage-rates* of manual workers increased by 21 per cent between July, 1970 and December, 1973, average weekly *earnings* increased by approximately 50 per cent.

IV. WHAT FIXES THE LEVEL OF THE GENERAL WAGE-RATE IN ANY PARTICULAR OCCUPATION, INDUSTRY OR AREA?

Before we discuss this question, certain points must be made clear. (i) 'Wages' in this connection refers to the sum of money paid *under contract* by an employer to a worker in exchange for the services he renders. Thus, 'salaries' is included within the definition, while whether rates of reward are on a time- or piece-rate basis is immaterial. (ii) Our examination is of wages in *particular* occupations, industries or areas, and does not refer to any *general level* of wages in the country as a whole. (iii) We must be certain that, in discussing 'occupations', the class includes only persons doing exactly the same sort of work. From the employer's point of view, each worker must be completely interchangeable. It is not considered, for instance, that the driver of a passenger express train and the driver of a local goods train are doing *exactly* similar work, any more than a teacher at a university and a teacher at a primary school are identical. (iv) It is assumed that there is no general unemployment. (v) The explanation is to some extent lacking in precision because, for the sake of simplicity, we avoid a really thorough analysis of the demand for labour, together with the likely effects of the existence of monopoly both in the demand for labour and in the sale of the product. On the other hand, it emphasises the use which can be made of the basic theory of demand and supply in order to analyse the factors influencing wages, the price of labour.

1. The Level of the Wage-Rate in a Particular Occupation

Differences in the wage-rates between different occupations are due primarily to differences in demand and supply.

1. *Demand*

The demand for labour is a 'derived demand', since an entrepreneur wants it, not for its own sake, but because of the contribution it makes to the production of a particular good. How much he is willing to pay for labour, therefore, depends on:

(*a*) *The actual physical addition to production made by the particular unit of labour.* In the short period, the entrepreneur's land and capital equipment are fixed. As increasing labourers are added, therefore, the physical productivity of each additional labourer tends to decrease. Thus one labourer on a small farm would be invaluable, but the farmer is unlikely to rate the additional contribution made by the tenth labourer so highly. Hence, more labourers can be employed the lower the cost of engaging such labour.

(*b*) *The price at which the product sells.* As we saw when discussing the price system, the higher the price obtained for the product, the more an entrepreneur is willing to pay for factors to attract them from other uses. This is because, when engaging a factor, he is interested not so much in its physical productivity, but in what it adds to his receipts, that is, its *revenue productivity*. Thus while an additional labourer may add 10 bushels of wheat to production, the farmer has also to consider the price at which a bushel of wheat will sell before he can decide whether it will pay him to engage that extra labourer. In short, increased demand for a product leads to an increased demand for the type of labour making that product simply because the price at which the product sells has risen. Indeed, it is worth noting here that it is the difference between wage-rates which enables a worker to decide in which occupation he has the greatest relative advantage when choosing his particular line of specialisation (see 'the division of labour').

In the long period, when the proportions of all factors of production can be adjusted, there is no reason why the physical productivity of additional labourers should fall. Here, how-ever, we must recognise that the increased supply of a good, other things remaining unchanged, will lead to a fall in its price so that revenue productivity falls with each additional labourer engaged. Hence we can conclude that in both the short and the long periods, the demand for labour increases as the wage-rate falls.

2. *Supply*

The supply of labour in a particular occupation depends upon:

(*a*) *The number of labourers available.* This is influenced by such factors as the kind of ability required; the degree of training necessary; restrictions on entrance imposed by trade unions and associations; the attraction and repugnance of certain jobs; the influence of custom or the idea of a basic minimum wage; geographical immobility. All these factors are discussed more fully in Chapter 24. Here we need only point to the fact that extra reward is generally necessary to induce more workers to undertake expensive training or to overcome the repugnance of certain jobs. Hence supply increases as the wage-rate increases, though where a high degree of natural ability is called for or there are severe artificial limitations to entering an occupation, supply may be very inelastic.

(*b*) *The quantity of labour offered by each labourer.* Higher rates of pay usually induce a worker to work overtime. But as we have already seen, this is not always so, as a high wage-rate may enable him to maintain his standard of living with less work and he may prefer the increased leisure to additional goods. Normally, however, we can assume that the supply of labour will increase as the wage-rate rises.

The actual wage-rate of an occupation therefore depends fundamentally on the demand for and supply of that particular labour. Generally speaking, differences in wage-rates between occupations of an unskilled nature tend to be eliminated in a comparatively short time, for here supply is fairly easily adjusted. With highly skilled occupations, however, wage differences persist longer, as supply tends to be inelastic except over a very long period.

2. DIFFERENCES IN THE LEVEL OF THE WAGE-RATE BETWEEN INDUSTRIES AND AREAS

When discussing the formation of price in a market, we noted that in time the same price came to be established for the same commodity throughout the market. Indeed, this was used as the basis for our definition of a 'market'. At first sight, it might be thought that the market for labour would at least be the whole of Great Britain and that therefore the wages of workers of the same occupation should eventually be the same both in all industries and in all districts within Great Britain. Thus, for instance, if the aircraft industry is expanding while the motor industry is declining, engine fitters attracted by relatively higher pay in the former move into it until the increased supply in the aircraft industry and the decreased supply in the motor industry establish a common, and therefore an equilibrium, wage-rate where no further movement takes place. In practice, however, differences both between industries and areas persist, owing to the fact that such movements not only take time to effect, but are hampered by the general immobility of labour. We have referred to this earlier when dealing with the depressed areas, and we return to it again in Chapter 24.

V. WHY ARE WOMEN'S WAGES USUALLY LOWER THAN MEN'S?

The Annual Abstract of Statistics shows that in October, 1973 the average weekly earnings (not wage-rate) of manual workers in manufacturing industries was: men over 21 years of age, £41·52; women over 18 years of age, £21·15. Moreover, in each individual industry we find that the average weekly earnings of women are well below those of men. Allowance must be made for the fact that women work on the average only 37·5 hours a week in comparison with a man's 44·7 hours. Nevertheless, this is insufficient to explain the vast difference in their earnings, and so we have to turn to the most important influence on weekly earnings, the actual level of the rate, whether time- or piece-, which is paid. Here we find that women are paid a lower average wage-rate than men. In saying this, however, it must be emphasised that at this stage we are not hinting at the existence of any form of discrimination against women. There is a more basic explanation than that.

Our previous analysis has shown us that the wage-rate paid for each particular occupation depends on demand and supply. The demand for labour varies according to the contribution it makes to production, while the supply consists of the amount of labour offering its services at different prices. What we have to ask, therefore, is: (i) whether there are certain factors which render the productivity of women's labour, and therefore the demand for it, below that of men's; (ii) whether the supply of labour relative to the demand for it is larger for women than for men.

On the demand side, the principal factor which we must note is that women generally are not trained for the better posts where skill is required. A father who finds it difficult to educate all his children will normally give the better education to his sons, while employers are often loath to train a woman for a key position as marriage may well end or interrupt her career. In any case, since many women withdraw from industrial to home life early in their careers, the average age of female employees is lower than that of males and hence their average wage-rate is less because their average level of experience is lower. Thus either through lack of training or inexperience, women fill a much smaller proportion of the skilled jobs than men.

In addition, even where women are working in the same broad occupations as men, we find that for a variety of reasons the productivity of women, at least from the employer's point of view, is below that of men. Not only are men physically stronger, but they are usually considered to be more adaptable and flexible, less prone to absence, less likely to leave a job and more able and willing to work overtime, Sundays and night-shifts. Employers recognise, too, that since most men rather resent having to work under a woman, in the management of subordinates men are more likely to get a better response than women. Some employers even go so far as to assert that the average man is more efficient than the average woman and, in support of that view, point to the fact that even where both earn identical piece-rates men's earnings are generally greater than women's.

Quite frequently, custom and prejudice both play a part in reducing, from the employer's point of view, the productivity of women. The initiative here may be with the employer himself. Thus the State hardly employs any women in the diplomatic service, while many people prefer male doctors, dentists and solicitors or to be served by a man.

We conclude, therefore, that, either in reality or merely in the opinion of employers, the productivity of women even in the same sort of occupation is inferior to that of men and consequently there is a lower demand for their services.

On the supply side we must note that, because most women marry in their twenties and only a proportion continue to work outside the home after marriage, the total supply of female labour is approximately only one-half that of male. In practice, however, this fact has little significance for the simple reason that women are virtually excluded from a number of occupations, either by law (as in underground mining and lead manufacturing) or by virtue of their weaker physical strength (as in the heavy industries, such as iron and steel and shipbuilding) or by reason of custom or prejudice (as in building, taxi-driving and small-machine maintenance). The result is that female labour has to find its way into the smaller number of occupations open to it. We find, for instance, that in textiles, clothing, teaching and the rendering of services generally, there are more women employed than men, while in the distributive trades they are almost equal. The net effect is to swell the supply relative to the demand in those jobs women can perform successfully.

The attitude of women to their wage-rates is also a factor influencing the supply. As most women expect to marry at least within 15 years of commencing work they are less concerned with their earnings during their early working life than men, while even when they are married their earnings are often regarded as being merely supplementary to the basic family income. Hence it can be concluded that women are prepared to offer their services on easier terms than men. Indeed, this attitude to earnings has been one of the causes which has led to the low proportion of women's labour organised into trade unions.

We conclude, therefore, that, on the demand side, employers are usually not prepared to offer so high a price for women's as for men's labour, while on the supply side, women not only have to crowd into the relatively few occupations where they are acceptable, but are in a weak bargaining position relative to employers by virtue of their general attitude towards earnings. Hence, on the average, for purely economic reasons, women earn less than men.

In addition, women may be discriminated against solely on account of their sex. Even in those occupations where they do exactly the same work as men, they may be paid at a lower rate. Until recently, this was true of the Civil Service, local government and teaching, and it still applies to the distributive trades and such industries as transport and engineering. Indeed, even where piece-rates are paid, women often receive a lower rate than men. It is now proposed that equal pay becomes compulsory at the end of 1975.

VI. THE FUNCTIONS OF TRADE UNIONS

In their 'History of Trade Unionism', the Webbs defined a trade union as 'a continuous association of wage-earners for the purpose of maintaining or improving the conditions of their working lives'. Today, however, it would generally be thought that such a definition limits the functions of trade unions too narrowly. Although the protection of the worker and the improvement of his working conditions are still their main functions, they have so developed and extended their influence that today they consult with the government on economic policy, while in addition provision is made for the education, both vocational and cultural, of members.

1. Improvements in the Conditions of Work
by Collective Bargaining

Trade unions arose in the first place in order to strengthen the hand of the workers when negotiating their wages and conditions of work. It is relevant, therefore, to ask: 'Under what conditions and to what extent can a trade union obtain higher wages for its members?' In other words, '*What are the factors which limit the power of a trade union in obtaining permanent wage increases?'*

In answering this question, we can distinguish three overriding considerations which a trade union must bear in mind when negotiating a wage increase, though none is completely distinct from the others.

1. The size of abnormal profits being made

It must be appreciated at the outset that, if wages in an occupation are to increase without any increase in productivity or any reduction in the total employment of the workers concerned, all employers must be making abnormal profits. This follows from our previous discussion regarding 'normal' and 'abnormal' profits. When only 'normal' profit is being made, the employer is receiving just enough to keep him in the business. Hence, if wages increase without any corresponding increase in production, he will eventually be forced out of business. Unless demand is completely inelastic, the amount sold will decrease. (We shall return to this later.)

Abnormal profits can be earned: (*a*) in the short period under perfect competition; (*b*) where there is a monopoly in the sale of the product; (*c*) where the worker is being 'exploited' in the sense that an employer, by virtue of his superior bargaining position, is able to obtain his labour at a wage less than the full value of what the worker produces. It is obvious, therefore, that any advance in wages won by trade unions is likely to be more temporary in the first case than in the last two, for where an industry is highly competitive, profit margins are low and so a rise in the wages of an occupation must, in the long period, force many firms out of business. In such circumstances, therefore, a trade union has to choose between higher wages or less employment. Where, however, abnormal profit persists through imperfect competition, a wage increase is more permanent because it can be secured by cutting into the abnormal profits being earned and no reduction in employment may result. The size of abnormal profits, therefore, puts a ceiling on the wage increase. Trade unions can well learn the lesson from this argument: unless labour has increased its productivity, it cannot conduct successful wage negotiations unless there are profits.

2. The extent to which labour is likely to be unemployed as a result of the wage increase

An increase in wages in a particular occupation or industry will lead to a decrease in the demand for that labour. The factors which determine the elasticity of demand for labour are:

(a) *The possibility of substituting other factors.* How far other factors can be substituted depends upon:

(i) *Physical considerations.* Production can take place only by using two or more factors. As the price of one rises, the others become relatively cheaper, and so the tendency is for the entrepreneur to substitute the cheaper factors for the dearer. Thus when wage-rates rise, entrepreneurs try to replace labour by capital; that is, they install more machinery and labour-saving devices. Such substitution, however, is limited by physical considerations, for some factors are very imperfect substitutes for others. Indeed, sometimes factors have to be employed in fairly fixed proportions, in which case little or no substitution can take place. Hence, where other factors cannot be used in substitution for labour, the demand for labour is inelastic.

It should be noted that the possibility of substitution will tend to be greater the longer the period of time under consideration.

(ii) *The elasticity of supply of alternative factors.* A rise in the wage-rate of the workers of a whole industry will lead to the entire industry demanding the alternative factors in order to substitute them for labour. This increased demand will affect the price of these alternative factors and a higher price will have to be offered in order to attract a greater supply. This will also limit the extent to which substitution is carried out. Thus if the supply of the alternative factor is perfectly elastic, only the physical considerations referred to above will affect the demand for it; if, on the other hand, supply is inelastic, then it is quite likely that the quick rise in its price will soon make it uneconomic to substitute it for labour. Once again, elasticity of supply of the alternative factors will be greater the longer the period of time under consideration.

Where unemployed labour exists, two conditions prevail which make it difficult for the trade union members to obtain a wage increase and yet retain the same level of employment.

These are: (i) a high degree of substitution between the trade union labour and the alternative factor (unemployed labour), particularly if the work performed is unskilled; (ii) an infinite elasticity of supply of the alternative factor (unemployed labour) at least for a time. Hence trade unions are weak in periods of trade depression when there is unemployment.

(b) *The proportion of labour costs to total costs.* This, together with the extent to which substitution can take place, will decide how far the supply curve for the product moves to the left. Where, as in building, labour costs are high, there will be a considerable movement. The opposite will apply where a high proportion of fixed equipment is necessary, as in the iron and steel industry.

(c) *The elasticity of demand for the good.* We drew attention to this when discussing above the limitation on wage increases imposed by the size of abnormal profits. The effect of the rise in the wage-rate will be to decrease the supply of the good at each particular price. Hence market price rises. We have to ask, therefore, by how much this rise in price will reduce the demand for the good. Once again we are back to the practical application of the concept of elasticity of demand. If the demand is very elastic, the quantity of the good demanded will drop considerably and thus the number of workers put off will be considerable. If, on the other hand, demand is inelastic, there will be no great decrease in the quantity demanded. Here the increased wages will be met by the rise in price; or, put in other words, the revenue productivity of labour has risen.

Elasticity of demand tends to be high in export markets for here there are often many alternative sources of supply. Consequently, where an industry sells a high proportion of its output abroad, the ability of the trade union to raise wages is limited.

3. *The strength of the trade union relative to that of the employer*

It is obvious that without any combination labour is in a very weak position. The workers have to bargain individually with an employer who can play off one against the other so that they successively offer their work on inferior terms. Such a situation arises from the fact that, while to the individual worker obtaining employment is probably a matter of dire necessity, the loss of one worker's services is, to the employer, usually of no great concern. Competition for labour amongst employers may eventually force wages up to the value the employer considers the labourer adds to his total revenue. But, owing to the immobility of labour, this may take an exceptionally long time, during which the worker is forced to accept the terms offered. The workers are in a much stronger position when, through their trade union, they can negotiate jointly with an employer. By such collective bargaining they are able to meet the employer's position of a single buyer with their own monopoly, which can lay down the minimum terms upon which any labour whatsoever will be offered to the employer. Here the employer is not faced with merely the slight inconvenience of doing without a few workers who refuse to work on his terms, but has to suffer the loss of all the labour upon which he relies.

The trade union's effectiveness is therefore determined by:

(a) *The strength of its monopoly position.* As we have already seen, a monopoly is strong only so far as it can control supply to exclude competitors. Trade unions exercise this control by: trying to enforce a 'closed shop' policy, aiming at 100 per cent membership; excluding new entrants (who would force down the wage-rate) by apprenticeship or professional requirements or refusal, as in the case of the miners and railwaymen, to admit foreign workers; building up strike funds in order to hold the monopoly together when a strike arises.

(b) *The negotiating ability of its leaders.* When negotiations take place, the rate eventually agreed upon lies somewhere between the maximum wage which the employer can afford and is therefore prepared to pay and the minimum fixed by the trade union. The exact result depends upon the comparative strength and bargaining ability of the two sides, the estimate they put on each other's strength, and how much they can bluff or are prepared to call a bluff.

In practice, trade unions have been so effective in establishing their monopoly strength that many of the employers themselves have joined together in associations to improve their own bargaining position.

2. The Nature of Collective Bargaining

This process whereby workers settled the conditions of employment with employers jointly through the agency of their trade union is known as 'collective bargaining' and with very few exceptions the government has always followed the principle of allowing negotiations by the two sides to proceed on a voluntary basis. For its smooth working, however, certain conditions should be fulfilled. The first is that it must be pursued with good sense on both sides. This is helped considerably if already within the industry there has been built up a tradition of good relations between the employers and the workers. Good sense is further enhanced when there is some accepted objective measure (such as a cost of living index, the wage-rates paid in other grades of work and in other trades, or the profits being made by the industry) to which wage-rates can be linked. Then negotiation from an agreed starting-point is possible, as opposed to a heated wrangle where each side tries to grab the best possible terms by threats based upon its strength in the prevailing economic conditions. Secondly, collective bargaining works better when both sides consist of strong organisations. If all employers in the industry are linked in an association they know that they will not have to face undercutting of wage-rates by outsiders, while when the union can speak for and preserve discipline amongst all its members, the employers know that the agreement will be honoured. Unofficial stoppages damage the reputation of the trade union and in order to avoid them it is essential that there is regular contact between the employer and the union, prompt investigation of grievances at workshop level and that the members understand and follow the procedure for settling disputes.

Thus we come to the third requirement for a smoothly-working system of collective bargaining—that there is an accepted procedure between the parties for dealing with questions as they arise. Such a procedure should, without being so prolonged that it frays patience, exhaust all possibilities of reaching peaceably a mutual agreement. A strike or lock-out should come about only after the procedure has been followed to its finality. We can therefore distinguish two stages in the procedure: (1) negotiation; (2) the settlement of disputes.

1. *Negotiation*

Broadly speaking, the machinery for negotiation falls into three groups.

(*a*) *Voluntary negotiation between the unions and employers' organisations.* Generally the government has left it to the parties concerned to work out their own procedure for negotiation and the settlement of disputes. Today this voluntary machinery covers some 65 per cent of the insured workers of Great Britain. Because the organisation of the different unions varies considerably, so, especially in the older basic industries, the recognised procedure differs according to the particular industry and trade, and, as in the engineering and shipbuilding industries, this procedure may contain no agreement upon arbitration when a wage claim is rejected. Most industries, however, have some national joint council or committee, completely independent of outside assistance, which thrashes out agreements on matters affecting working conditions— wages, hours, holidays, factory conditions, discipline, and the allocation of work amongst the various trades.

(*b*) *Joint Industrial Councils.* The more standard form of voluntary negotiating machinery is through the system of Joint Industrial Councils which were established as the result of a government committee which sat in 1916 under the chairmanship of Mr. J. H. Whitley, M.P., Speaker of the House of Commons at the time. They are composed of representatives of both employers and workers in the industry and their task is to consider regularly such matters as the better use of the practical knowledge and experience of the workpeople, the settlement of the general principles governing the conditions of employment, means of ensuring the workers the greatest possible security of earnings and employment, methods of fixing and adjusting earnings, piece-rates, etc., technical education and training, industrial research, improvement of processes and proposed legislation affecting the industry. Although Joint Industrial Councils are sponsored by the government they are not forced upon any industry and some of the more important industries, such as the iron and steel, engineering, shipbuilding and cotton, which had already developed their own procedure for negotiation, did not form Joint Industrial Councils. Nevertheless, in 1974 there were in existence some 200 Joint Industrial Councils or bodies of similar character.

(c) *Wages Councils*. In some industries and trades, where organisation of workers, or employers, or of both is either non-existent or ineffective, the government has had to depart from the principle of leaving negotiating machinery to be established on a purely voluntary basis. Government interference first started in 1909 when Trade Boards were set up to fix minimum time- and piece-rates for the 'sweated' trades, such as bespoke tailoring, paper-box making, machine-made lace and net finishing, where home-workers were being paid exceptionally low wages. In the course of time these Boards were increased in number and in 1945 were renamed Wages Councils with their powers and scope still further extended. Today (January 1974) there are 49 such Wages Councils in operation covering the clothing, textile, food and drink and metalware industries, together with distribution, catering, road haulage and other services. The Councils are appointed by the Secretary of State for Employment after consultation and are composed of equal numbers of employers' and workers' representatives together with not more than three independent members. Their task is to fix minimum remuneration and conditions regarding holidays and a minimum week, which, if the Minister approves, become the subject of a Wage Regulation Order, enforceable by law. In addition, they may advise the Minister regarding problems affecting labour in the industry.

In agriculture, wages are fixed by machinery, similar to the Wages Councils system, set up by special legislation. Thus, in all, about 20 per cent of insured workers are covered by schemes of statutory wage regulation, as opposed to the 65 per cent where negotiation is on a voluntary basis.

2. *The settlement of disputes*

So far we have discussed the different forms of machinery which are used for negotiating wage-rates, etc., by employers and workers. Where this machinery fails to produce an agreement, it is advantageous if an agreed procedure exists for ending the deadlock.

(a) *Conciliation.* In 1974, the Secretary of State for Employment set up an *independent* Conciliation and Arbitration Service controlled by a Council whose members are experienced in industrial relations. When efforts to obtain settlement of a dispute through normal procedures have failed, the service can offer to provide conciliation if this is acceptable to the parties concerned.

(b) *Arbitration.* The Conciliation and Arbitration Service can, at the joint request of the parties to a dispute, appoint single arbitrators or boards of arbitration chosen from a register of people experienced in industrial relations to determine differences on the basis of agreed terms of reference.

Alternatively, the Terms and Conditions of Employment Act, 1959, allows claims that a particular employer is not observing the terms or conditions of employment established for the industry to be referred compulsorily to the Industrial Court for a legally binding award.

(c) *Inquiry and Investigation.* The Secretary of State for Employment has legal power to inquire into the causes and circumstances of any trade dispute and, if he thinks fit, to appoint a Court of Inquiry with power to call for evidence. Such action however is chiefly a means of informing Parliament and the public of the facts and causes of a major dispute, and is taken only when no agreed settlement seems possible.

The Minister's power of inquiry also allows for less formal action in the setting up of Committees of Investigation when the public interest is not so wide and general.

Neither a Court of Inquiry nor a Committee of Investigation is a conciliation or arbitration body but either may make recommendations upon which a reasonable settlement of the dispute can be based.

3. Trade Union Co-operation with the Government in the Development of Economic Policy

While the improvement of the conditions of work for its members still remains the primary task of a trade union, the time has passed when one union can act independently of others and without reference to government policy. Present-day society is committed to maintaining full employment coupled with freedom of choosing one's kind and place of work. But this can be achieved only by a certain amount of planning by the government. Trade unions are, therefore, faced with two alternatives. Either they can pursue their own policy independently of the wishes of the government and with the possible effect of bringing about a collapse of the free economic system; or they can co-operate voluntarily with the government in its planning schemes, presenting the government's viewpoint to the workers. The trade union movement has chosen the latter course. Accordingly it has a voice in saying how industry can be made more efficient. Indeed, through the National Economic Development Council, permanent arrangements exist for consultation at the national level between the government, the Confederation of British Industry and the T.U.C.

In periods of full employment it becomes almost essential that the government itself should give some lead to the trade union movement regarding a general or national wages policy. Labour is in a strong bargaining position, and the tendency is for each union to exploit the situation in order to obtain wage increases for its own section of workers. Unless such increases are accompanied by increased productivity or can be met by a reduction in profits, such a rise in the money wages of a particular industry will lead to some increase in the price of its goods. Since the expenditure of trade unionists on the particular goods they produce is probably only a very small fraction of their total expenditure, this increase in money wages will represent an increase in real wages (that is, wages in terms of the things they buy) for the particular workers concerned. But for the workers in other industries, the rise in the price of the good represents a decrease in their real wages. The result is that they too ask for wage increases and so we have the spiral of wages and prices chasing one another. Real wages can only rise if prices rise less in proportion than money wage-rates.

Yet, however desirable it may seem, there is a side result to such an increase in real wages. Where the real rate of wages is increased without a corresponding increase in productivity, employers may find that it does not pay them to employ so many workers as previously and so unemployment results. The government may try to prevent this unemployment by undertaking additional expenditure by borrowing; thus the total money income is increased and the same number of men are employed as before. But if output is not increased, this increase in aggregate money income will merely mean that prices rise, and the State's action in preventing unemployment is achieved only because the rate of real wages has not risen. Thus the original purpose of the increase in money wages is defeated (see Chapter 26).

Since World War II, almost all countries have had to exercise central control over trends in wages. In the U.K. voluntary restraint was originally urged upon trade unions, but when this was not forthcoming both the Labour government in 1966 and the Conservative government in 1972 had to take legal powers to limit increases in prices and incomes.

In 1974 the Labour government once more reverted to voluntary agreement as regards wages. Trade unions agreed to limit demands for huge increases in accordance with the terms of the 'Social Contract'.

Here it should be noted that in applying policies of wage increase restrictions, the element of 'fairness' plays a prominent role. There is thus discrimination in favour of lower-paid workers on ethical and social grounds. This means that today not only does the government exercise a considerable influence over the general level of money wages but also that, even as regards relative wages, the demand and supply mechanism is an incomplete explanation.

CHAPTER 18

CAPITAL AND INTEREST

1. THE PROBLEM OF DEFINING 'CAPITAL'

ECONOMISTS differ in what they think should be termed 'capital', but we can start from a point upon which they are all agreed, the contrast between 'capital' and 'income'. Whereas 'income' can be defined as a *flow* of wealth over a period of time, 'capital' is a *stock* of wealth existing at any given moment.

Such a definition of capital coincides roughly with the concept of it held by the man in the street. If such a person were asked what capital he possessed, he would name such assets as the money he held in the bank or had lent to the government, the titles to stocks and shares which he possessed, the house he owned (whether or not he lived in it) and he might even include his car and his wife's jewellery. Similarly a businessman would include the assets of his business—the factory building, machinery, raw materials owned, stocks of finished goods, sums outstanding by debtors to the firm less any sums owing to creditors, and any reserves of money held in the bank. The weakness of the definition, however, is that it makes capital identical with wealth. The businessman includes all the assets of the firm in his definition of capital and, logically, if the everyday consumer includes such items as his house, motor car and jewellery, then he also ought to add in his furniture, carpet-cleaner, gas-stove, billiards table, television set, razor and other goods which render him services over a period. Hence we have to accept a broad definition of capital, emphasising its reference to a stock of goods existing at a particular moment of time (as compared with income, a flow of goods over a period) and modify it, as follows, according to the particular subject under discussion.

First, we have to make an adjustment when we are discussing capital as a factor of production. Capital, in its everyday use, includes all assets in the hands of both producers (entrepreneurs) and consumers. The assets possessed by producers can be classified into three main types. (i) Money reserves, usually referred to as 'liquid' or 'free' capital, since it is available for purchasing any desired form of real capital. (ii) Goods, such as factory buildings, machinery, transport vehicles, raw materials and partly-finished goods which are combined with labour to produce other goods. These are known as *producers' goods* and are not wanted for their own sake in that they do not directly satisfy consumers' wants. (iii) Stocks of finished goods (many of which are *consumers' goods* in that they directly satisfy consumers' wants) which are simply awaiting the final stage in the process of production, delivery to the consumer.

The remaining capital assets are in the hands of consumers and consist entirely of consumers' goods. Many of these goods, such as food and drink, are consumed in a single use, but others, such as a home, car, radio set, furniture and clothing have quite a long life and continue to render services well into the future. Thus, they are sometimes called 'consumers' capital'. With these goods, however, the process of production is complete as they are in the hands of the actual consumer. They cannot, therefore, be considered as 'capital' when we are discussing 'capital' as a factor of production. In this case it is best if we restrict the term to producers' goods, those goods with which the other factor, labour, is combined. Indeed such goods are often referred to as 'capital goods'. Land, inasmuch as it is improved by man by the addition of fertilisers, drainage, buildings and other forms of capital, can therefore be included as a producers' good in this aspect of 'capital'.

The second qualification has to be made when we are estimating 'national capital', for from our original definition certain items have to be excluded. In a closed community, the national capital would consist only of *real* assets which exist within the country, irrespective of whether they are publicly or privately owned. Thus what is sometimes referred to as 'debt capital', such as titles or claims to stocks and shares, money held in the National Savings and other banks, and loans to building societies, would have to be excluded since it is not real capital. In the case of titles to shares in companies, they do *represent* real assets but if, in order to calculate the national capital, we totalled the real assets of companies and the titles to those assets owned by private persons, we should be guilty of double-counting. Similarly, money which is borrowed by the government (the national debt) or money which is held by a bank in a customer's account cannot be included, for they merely represent liabilities and not real assets. In fact this is true of all money in use in the United Kingdom today for it is simply 'token' money and cannot, therefore, be included at its face value (see Chapter 20). If we were to include such acknowledgements of liabilities it would mean that the 'capital' of a country would be increased whenever its national debt or the volume of credit and bank-notes increased!

In the case of a country which conducts economic transactions with other countries, we have to make one adjustment to the above, because we are estimating 'national' and not 'world' capital. Assets, even though they may be merely titles to stocks or shares, held by persons of the United Kingdom in or on other countries have to be included, for they can always be sold for the purpose of importing goods and therefore for satisfying wants. Similarly debts of the United Kingdom to other countries and claims of persons abroad on assets within the United Kingdom have to be subtracted from national capital. During both World Wars the United Kingdom sold many of her foreign assets to pay for the import of goods, and today, because more has been borrowed than has been lent, she is called a net debtor nation. In the same way, because holdings of foreign currency, such as dollars, and reserves of gold can be used to buy goods abroad, they must be included in the 'national capital'.

It would be impossible in practice, however, to calculate all the real assets of a nation simply because many of these assets are consumers' capital. Hence, in calculating national capital, all consumers' capital is excluded, with the exception of one important item, owner-occupied houses. These are given a value in the same way as rented houses, which are included as a producers' good would be.

For the remainder of our discussion we shall use 'capital' in the sense of a factor helping in production; that is, it includes all producers' goods together with stocks of consumers' goods not yet in the hands of the consumer.

2. The Accumulation of Capital

How does capital come into being? The simplest answer and the most fundamental is: by forgoing present consumption. A simple illustration will make this clear. Suppose a Robinson Crusoe, having no possessions but the clothes he is dressed in, is washed ashore on an island. His first concern is to obtain food to eat and he does this by catching fish in the stream with his hands. In order to obtain sufficient fish to provide him with a day's food, he finds that he has to spend fourteen hours catching fish in this way. He realises, however, that with a net the fish could be caught much more quickly and so he sets about making one. He can find the time for this in a variety of ways. Thus he could cut down his daily consumption of fish and make a net in the time saved, though he must be careful not to carry this process to the point of starvation. Or he could spend some of his surplus time, which has so far been employed in making a hut and in sleep, in the making of the net or in catching extra fish to store against a future day which can be spent on the net. In this case he would have the same amount of food but less leisure time. Once the net is made, however, it represents 'producers' goods' or capital equipment and with it the daily requirements of fish can be obtained in two hours. His surplus time has now increased from ten to twenty-two hours, and hence he can enjoy extra sleep, lie in the sun, or make other assets such as a bow and arrow with which to hunt animals, a ladder for climbing trees to pick fruit, and tools for cultivating the ground. In any case, his income has increased and if he adds to his capital, it will continue to increase; but it was only achieved because, in the first place, he was willing to do with less food or less leisure.

One other important point emerges from this illustration. In reducing his consumption of food, Robinson Crusoe could not carry it to the point where he might starve to death. If, owing to a scarcity of fish, it had taken him twenty hours to catch his daily requirements, then he would have found it much more difficult to make his net. In other words, the more plentiful the supply of natural resources, the easier it is to increase income still further. Again, in economics, the maxim holds: 'To him that hath shall be given.' A country with a very low standard of living finds it very difficult to build up the capital which would improve its living standards and it is for this reason that any aid which can be given to poor countries is so valuable. In a modern community, capital has to be similarly accumulated by forgoing current consumption. It is achieved, however, through the division of labour. Certain persons, instead of producing consumer goods, specialise in the production of capital goods. Thus we have some men who build factories, houses and cinemas, others who mine coal, some who produce machinery, transport, bridges and so on. The larger the proportion of the working population devoted to these tasks, however, the smaller will be the current supply of consumer goods available. But when this capital comes into production, the yearly output of consumers' goods will increase. Thus during the nineteenth century the United Kingdom concentrated on building up her supply of capital and during the twentieth century she has reaped the benefit of this in consumption and in the provision for two exhausting wars. It is with the same aim, too, that Russia, China, India and other countries have embarked on 'Five Year Plans'. During this period an all-out effort is made to increase capital—power plants, irrigation projects, factories and machinery—by reducing the production of consumers' goods and by working longer and harder. In some cases this process has been carried so far that it has been extremely painful to the persons concerned in that they have had to suffer a very low standard of living.

3. MAINTAINING CAPITAL INTACT

Robinson Crusoe's net will, as it is used, become broken and worn. Consequently, he must devote a part of his time to making good the deficiencies. This means that he must carry out day-to-day repairs and also start on the making of a new net which will be ready to replace the old one by the time the latter can be repaired no longer. This process of repairing and replacing worn-out capital is known as 'maintaining capital intact'. Some qualification must be made, however, for changes in tastes and techniques. Suppose, for instance, that Robinson Crusoe does not require so many fish per day because he prefers the wild chickens which he has discovered can be kept alive when shut up in pens. Consequently, instead of replacing his large net, he may make a smaller one and with the time saved build the chicken-houses and pens he requires. Or, it may be that he has discovered that the fish can be caught much more quickly by hook and line than by net. Hence, instead of replacing his net, he makes hooks and lines. So long as his capital, given the other factors of production, is providing goods which Robinson Crusoe regards as yielding an equivalent satisfaction as formerly, then we can say that it is being maintained intact.

Suppose, however, that Robinson Crusoe knew that in a month's time he was certain to be rescued from his island. There would then be no point in his making a new net to replace the old one or, so long as it would last the month out, repairing the old net. Instead he could use the time in gathering more fruit or in bathing in the sea. Whichever he preferred, his standard of living would have improved, for either he had more goods to consume or he had more leisure. It must be noted, however, that this improvement in the standard of living due to the process of what is known as 'consuming capital' is only a temporary one. If something happened so that Robinson Crusoe were not rescued at the end of the month then he would have to reduce his consumption considerably while he went through the whole process again of giving up time to making a net.

In a similar way, any community has to maintain its capital intact and this it usually does by having a proportion of its working population specialising in the task of replacing worn-out plant and machinery, replenishing stocks of goods as they run down, and keeping buildings in a state of good repair. Where a country fails to maintain its capital intact, we say that it is living on, consuming, depreciating or running-down its capital.

4. Conclusions

We can see that, in the long run, the standard of living a country enjoys depends very largely on the amount of capital equipment she has relative to the size of her population. Thus both the national income per head and the capital per worker of the U.S.A. are both approximately twice that of the U.K. Nor does our definition of capital equipment take into consideration the consumers' capital in the hands of her people or the 'human capital' which exists in the highly developed skill and training of her workers. A country, therefore, which wishes to effect a permanent improvement in its standard of living must increase its capital equipment.

Under 'Collectivism', the State decides what proportion of productive resources shall be devoted to the accumulation and maintenance of capital. With 'Private Enterprise', however, the decision of whether to produce capital or consumers' goods is left to individual entrepreneurs. The more capital goods that are produced, the fewer consumers' goods will be available and vice versa. Now, as we have seen, capital goods can be produced only by forgoing present consumption, that is, by saving. Under 'Private Enterprise', the people who decide how much to save are not exactly the same people who invest by producing capital goods. Money income is saved, not only by entrepreneurs who withhold some profits ('undistributed profits.') for investment in the business, but also by individuals, who do not spend all their money income. Sometimes entrepreneurs produce capital goods of greater value than intended saving, while at other times they are of less value. When either happens, difficulties arise and so most governments, including that of the United Kingdom, exercise some control. At the same time governments must ensure that investment in capital goods is adequate for maintaining and improving future living standards (Chapter 25).

5. The Rate of Interest

Interest is the return which has to be paid in order to obtain a loan of liquid capital, that is, money. It is usually calculated as an annual rate per cent of the money borrowed. The Classical economists explained the reason for charging interest as follows. Capital is demanded because it is either essential to, or will increase production. On the other hand, because saving, the source of capital, entails forgoing present consumption, a reward is necessary in order to persuade people to overcome the inclination to consume immediately. The higher this reward, the more they will save. Hence the rate of interest is the price which equates the demand for and supply of liquid capital ('loanable funds').

In practice, however, this is far too simple an explanation of how the rate of interest is determined. In the first place, the Classical economists ascribe to the rate of interest a greater influence on the volume of saving than actually takes place in the real world (see page 480). Secondly, it cannot explain the fairly short-term variations in the rate of interest—and it is these short-term variations which are really significant to the volume of investment and hence to the level of employment (see page 481). Thirdly, it assumes that the whole of income saved is eventually lent to entrepreneurs. In this it ignores the fact that many people may, and often do, prefer a part of their assets to be held in the form of money; in short, there is a demand for money in itself solely for its 'liquidity' virtue. It is this aspect which is emphasised by Lord Keynes in his explanation of the rate of interest.

An examination of Lord Keynes's theory, however, would take us far outside the scope of this book. All we can do here is to suggest two major points regarding the rate of interest upon which the reader can reflect. (i) Government policy has today an important influence on the level of the rate of interest (see page 418). (ii) It is unrealistic to speak of *a* rate of interest. There has always been a variety or 'structure' of interest rates. The actual rate charged varies according to: (*a*) the estimate by the lender of the risk of possible non-repayment of the capital; (*b*) the period for which the loan is made. In the case of the former it is obviously much safer to lend to the government than to a gold prospector, while as regards the latter it means that the longer you lend for, the greater inconvenience you are put to should you suddenly need your money.

CHAPTER 19

THE NATIONAL INCOME

I. ITS MEASUREMENT

1. THE PRINCIPLE OF CALCULATION

IN Chapter 1 we touched briefly on the subject of the 'national' income. It was shown that, for a village which used no money and had no connection with the outside world, the year's income was simply the wheat, barley, cattle and wood produced by the villagers in the course of that year. In other words, it was the year's output. The original output might be subject later to a little redistribution. Thus the lord of the manor took some poultry and eggs while the miller retained a portion of the wheat in payment for his services. But this makes no difference to the basic fact that income equals output. It follows, therefore, that we could arrive at the year's income of the village either by totalling the year's output of the farmers or by totalling the income retained by each person of the village during the year. The important fact also emerges that to increase income it is necessary to increase output, for they are simply different ways of looking at the same thing.

If we examine still further this idea of the 'income' of the village, we notice that we have concentrated our attention on income as it is received. But it must be remembered that incomes are also disposed of. The wheat, barley, pigs and wood will be consumed during the course of the year, though perhaps small quantities will be held in reserve, that is, 'saved' against a bad harvest the next year. We could if we wished, therefore, calculate the value of the villager's income by totalling the goods as they were consumed by every villager throughout the particular year, though at the end of the period any net saving, that is, the stock held in reserve less what was started with, would have to be added.

From the above discussion there emerges, therefore, the

important fact that for the village: Income=Output=Consumption+Saving. If we wanted the 'national income' all we would have to do would be to total either the income, or the output, or the consumption plus saving, throughout the year of all the villages in the United Kingdom.

Today our calculation of the national income proceeds on exactly the same principle, though this may be somewhat difficult to perceive. The reason for this difficulty is that our economy is much more complicated. In the first place, persons do not produce goods with the object of directly satisfying their own wants but concentrate instead on producing one good or part of a good which will be exchanged for the goods produced by other people. Secondly, exchanges themselves are not direct but are effected indirectly through the use of money. Thirdly, because there is a far greater variety of goods in comparison with the simple products of the medieval village, it is impossible to total national income in real terms, that is, as so many quarters of wheat, so many head of cattle, so many eggs, etc. Lastly, countries today are not self-sufficient but trade with other countries and since, for some years, exports might not equal imports, adjustments have to be used when calculating national income by the consumption method. All these factors give rise to difficulties which will be considered later. The obvious way of solving the problem of an exchange economy is to measure all values in a common denominator—money— and to express income, output and consumption in money terms. Money income is received either as wages, salaries, profits or rent. If we assume that there is no saving (that is, that people spend all their income each year), then the money income received equals the money value of expenditure on goods and services, which we can call 'money outlay'. Moreover, if there has been no change in the stock of goods, then this money outlay is spent on the year's output. Hence we can say that 'money income' equals the 'money value of output' equals 'money outlay'.

A similar result is arrived at if we look at the problem in the more practical way of studying the trading operations and accounts of firms. Suppose all production is in the hands of a Giant Firm which owns all the land and raw materials and employs all the labour. The Firm's income is made up of the receipts from the sale of its product. Since, however, it owns all the raw materials and land, these receipts are disbursed entirely in the form of wages and profits (assuming that no profits are retained for investment). Thus, once again money income equals the money value of output equals money outlay. Where the production of a nation, however, is undertaken by many firms, each firm has to make payments to the others for materials purchased from them. Here the receipts of each firm are equal to wages +profits +payments to other firms for materials. Were the receipts for each firm to be added now, however, it would not give us the figure of the total national output, for we should have counted the output of each firm, except the one which actually delivered the good to the customer, many times over. What we really wish to total is the share taken by each firm in the production of the goods which make up the national output. These shares, or net output, are equal to receipts less payments to other firms for their materials, and if we take every firm, whether a one-man business, a partnership, a joint-stock company, a public corporation or a government department, and add their net output of goods and services, then we get the national output. Once again, since receipts less payments to other firms for materials equals wages +profits, national output equals national income (the total of all wages and profits and rent), which in turn equals the total of all consumers' expenditure plus any saving.

Thus the principle upon which calculation of the national income is based is a simple one. But, whichever of the three alternative lines of approach is employed, the actual process of calculation is naturally long and complicated, and before we set out the figures arrived at for the national income, output and expenditure, some explanation must be given of certain definitions used and of particular adjustments which have to be made as a result both of government activities and the trade which takes place with other countries.

2. DEFINITIONS USED IN THE CALCULATION OF THE NATIONAL INCOME

1. Production

In Chapter 7 we discussed the meaning of production and showed that any labour was productive which was directed to the satisfying of wants. It was pointed out, however, that for the practical purposes of economics, this definition had to be restricted to only those goods and services which were exchanged against money. This is the definition of 'production' which is used in calculating the national output and it therefore excludes any work which a person does directly for himself or which is not paid for.

2. The services provided by owner-occupied houses

Some consumer goods—tables, television sets, cookers, cars, etc.—render services for many years in the future. They are called 'consumers' capital goods'. Yet it would be difficult to calculate any annual value for the services they render. But one such good—house property—is outstanding in importance. Here the value of the services rendered can be easily calculated, for it is assessed for rating purposes by the Board of Inland Revenue, Hence, in calculating national income, output and expenditure, we include the net annual contribution of owner-occupied dwellings, less expenditure on repairs and maintenance. Where rent is paid to a landlord, it would be included as an income to him similar to a business profit.

3. Depreciation

As a result of the production which takes place in the course of the year, capital is used up, either because of the gradual wearing out of machinery, buildings, etc., or by the running down of stocks. If capital or stocks are not maintained in their original condition then it may be possible for a short time to increase the output of consumers' goods, but eventually there will come a reckoning because such dis-investment cannot go on indefinitely, and there will be a sharp drop in the production of consumers' goods when eventually resources are devoted to restoring capital. Such running down of capital occurred during the war. Machinery, roads, buildings and railway rolling-stock were allowed to deteriorate in order that guns, ships, aircraft, etc., could be built as quickly as possible. After the war, however, these defects had to be made good. Thus houses had to be repaired thereby reducing the number of new houses that could be built, and machinery had to be replaced instead of providing consumers' goods. If no allowance were made for depreciation, national output would have shown a large increase during the war and a decrease after it.

While, however, it is agreed that an allowance should be made for capital appreciation and depreciation, no accurate data is at present available to show the current cost of depreciation of fixed capital. In their profit and loss accounts, companies, when calculating depreciation, are guided by tax advantages and prudence, and so their estimates are on the high side. Consequently the Board of Inland Revenue lays down arbitrary figures for depreciation when calculating tax liability figures which, nevertheless, measure imperfectly the depreciation which actually took place. In view of this lack of accurate data, therefore, the Tables which follow are for Gross National Product, that is, the total output by the nation of goods and services together with net income from abroad. In order to obtain the National Income, we should have to deduct from this what is required to maintain real capital intact. In short, National Income equals the Gross National Product less depreciation.

It should be noted that over a period when the general level of prices is rising, the value of stocks appreciates. This represents a windfall gain to the owners of those stocks, who thus include it in total profits. But it represents no physical increase in stocks, and so must be deducted in reckoning the total of the gross national product.

3. IMPORTANT ADJUSTMENTS TO BE MADE IN CALCULATING THE NATIONAL INCOME

1. *Due to the activities of the State*

(a) *Redistribution of income by the State.* On the income side, calculations are based chiefly on returns of income made by persons for tax purposes. This has two main effects. In the first place, total income includes not only income from wages, salaries, profits and rents but also income by way of civil rights (retirement pensions, family allowances, etc.), and interest on the National Debt. Such income, however, is not a payment for the share the recipients have taken in actual production during the year. It simply represents a transfer of income by way of taxation from one set of persons to another. Hence, when the national income is calculated by totalling all personal incomes, such transfer incomes must be deducted or otherwise double-counting of income would result. The current practice is to isolate these transfer incomes from the other forms of income when preparing the figures of national income, and so no adjustment has to be made in the figures of 'income' shown in Table 23.

The second effect of basing calculations on income tax returns is that it may involve some slight inaccuracy. There is always a certain amount of tax evasion, though this is nothing like so great in the United Kingdom as in some countries. More important is the fact that, where income is below the tax level, returns may not be available or are inaccurate, and so estimates have to be made.

(b) *Indirect taxes and subsidies.* National expenditure has to be calculated in terms of market prices. However, the market prices of most goods and services are inflated beyond their real market prices by the fact that they contain an indirect tax, chiefly V.A.T., imposed by the government. On the other hand, the market prices of some goods, such as Council houses, potatoes, sugar and milk, are deflated below the real cost of the goods by the government subsidies paid, directly or indirectly, to producers. The result is that adjustments have to be made to 'national expenditure at market prices': indirect taxes are subtracted, subsidies added. This gives us 'national expenditure at factor cost' and measures the value of the national expenditure at prices equal to the cost of the factors of production (including profits) used in producing the national output.

(c) *Maintenance of law and order and defence.* If the government did not provide such services as education and health, they would still have to be provided by private enterprise and consumers would spend a part of their income on them. Hence there is no question but that they should be classified as 'consumers' expenditure'. When we come to consider the payments made by the government for police and the Armed Forces we are in a somewhat ambiguous position. Police, for example, not only help pedestrians across the road but also protect factories from theft. In the first case, they are providing a consumers' service, in the second they are merely assisting in the productive process and the cost of their labour has already been included in the price of the good. Thus we should include the former element and exclude the latter from our estimate of the national output. In practice, however, such services cannot be divided and so we treat all government services as directly satisfying consumers' wants, including the actual payments for them in the national output.

2. Due to economic relationships with other countries

The United Kingdom is not a 'closed' community but has dealings with other countries. Thus, on the 'income' side, people receive in the United Kingdom profits, interest and dividends from money invested in companies abroad, while the government receives taxes from certain foreigners. Such receipts increase the national income. Similarly, companies in the United Kingdom have to send profits abroad to any foreign owners of their capital, while some nationals have to pay taxes to foreign governments. Such payments reduce the national income. On balance, however, receipts for 1973 exceeded payments by £1,095 million, and, if the gross domestic product, which only includes incomes received within the country, has been calculated we must add this £1,095 million to obtain the gross national income. Similarly, because this balance can be regarded as representing an output which the United Kingdom receives from a 'foreign industry', it also has to be added on the output side to the total output of the industries of the United Kingdom.

When we deal with the 'expenditure' side, a slightly different adjustment has to be made. Expenditure is not entirely on British goods nor are all British goods sold to residents of the United Kingdom. On the one hand, we buy imported goods and services; on the other, foreigners buy the goods and services exported by the United Kingdom. What we have to do, therefore, when calculating national expenditure, is to deduct the United Kingdom's expenditure on foreign goods and add the expenditure of foreigners on the United Kingdom's exports.

TABLE 23.—*Gross National Income 1973*

INCOME (*before tax*)	£ million	£ million
Income from employment—wages and salaries		42,890
Income from self-employment—professional persons, farmers, sole traders and partnerships		6,244
Profits:		
Companies	8,476	
Public corporations and other public enterprises	2,194	
		10,670
Rent		4,894
Residual error		+589
Total Domestic Income		65,287
Less Stock appreciation		−3,111
Gross Domestic Product		62,176
Net Income from abroad		1,095
GROSS NATIONAL PRODUCT		63,271

OUTLAY (*at market prices*)		£ million
Consumers' expenditure		44,855
Public authorities' current expenditure		13,270
Saving: increases in fixed capital and stocks		14,445
Exports and income received from abroad	21,542	
Imports and income paid abroad	−22,291	
Gross National Expenditure at market prices		−749
		71,821
Factor Cost adjustment:		
Taxes on expenditure	−10,006	
Subsidies	1,456	
		−8,550
Gross National Expenditure at Factor Cost = GROSS NATIONAL PRODUCT		63,271

OUTPUT (*at factor cost*)	£ million	£ million
Production and Trade:		
Agriculture, forestry and fishing	1,876	
Mining and quarrying	868	
Manufacturing	19,103	
Construction	4,429	
Gas, electricity and water	1,939	
Transport and communication	5,460	
Distributive trades	6,122	
Insurance, banking and finance	5,774	
Other services	4,356	
Total Production and Trade		49,927
Public administration, defence, public		
health and education services		7,992
Ownership of dwellings		3,668
Residual error		+589
Gross Domestic Product		62,176
Net income from abroad		1,095
GROSS NATIONAL PRODUCT (at factor		
cost)		63,271

II. THE USES OF NATIONAL INCOME CALCULATIONS

1. ESTIMATION OF CHANGES IN LIVING STANDARDS

The economic progress made by a nation over a fairly long period of time is indicated in a variety of ways. Thus, even if there were no figures available, nobody would deny that today the people of the United Kingdom are materially better off than they were during the Middle Ages. In order to establish the point, we should only have to point to their better houses, the greater variety of their food, their improved mobility by means of mechanical transport and the increase in their leisure and entertainments. But such indications based on observation would provide no exact measurement of the degree to which living standards have improved between two years relatively close to one another. Our calculations of the national income, on the other hand, are fairly accurate and therefore do give us a measure by which progress from year to year can be estimated.

It is not sufficient, however, to take the money national income of two different years and point to the difference as being the increase (or decrease) in the standard of living of the nation. In the first place, what we are really interested in are changes in the *real* national income. This means that, since the national income is measured in money terms, we must take account of any fluctuation in the value of money itself, that is, of any change in the general level of prices. Thus, for 1938, the money value of the Gross National Product of the United Kingdom is shown in the Annual Abstract of Statistics as being equal to £5,175 million, while for 1973 it is shown as being £63,271 million. However, it would be quite incorrect to say that the Gross National Product of the United Kingdom had increased by twelve times over this period, for most of this increase has been due to a fall in the value of money. We need, therefore, some method by which the influence on our calculation of changes in the value of money can be removed.

The principle of the method by which this is achieved is the same as that used for compiling index numbers (see Chapter 20). What happens is that the output of a given year is valued at the prices of a chosen 'base' year, so-called because it is the year on which comparisons are being based. In other words prices are held at the base year level and hence any changes in the values of the national output or expenditure shown do indicate changes in volume. The usual procedure, however, for turning the national income into real terms is to apply the findings of a separately compiled price-index, and indeed this is the only possible method when calculations are being made on the 'income' side. Usually an index of retail prices, such as that compiled by the Department of Employment (see page 377), is used for this purpose as being more relevant than an index of wholesale prices. The important point to note, however, is that the adjustment is made on the index number principle and is therefore subject to all the defects associated with index numbers (see Chapter 20). In particular we have the difficulty which arises because changes occur over time in the composition of output and in the quality of the goods themselves. Should we value a new 1100 c.c. car at the old model's price? Is an air passage to the U.S.A., although it takes fewer hours, to be valued at the price prevailing in the earlier base year? Obviously, the more distant is the base year, the more artificial do our adjustments become.

Even after the figures have been adjusted for price changes, we still, when interpreting these figures, have to bear in mind the fact that the size of the population itself may have varied over the particular period. If we are looking for an indication of economic progress, then the figure should somehow be related to the working population, for we should expect a larger national output the larger the working population. The test of *economic progress*, therefore, must be the changes which have occurred in real national income per head of the *working* population. If we are more concerned with changes in the *standard of living* then it is better to compare changes in the real national income per head of the *total* population.

Even so, having calculated the real national income per head of the population, we must be careful not to assume that it is an *accurate* measurement of changes in the standard of living. In the first place, anomalies result from our adoption of a limited definition of 'production'—to goods and services exchanged against money. Many goods and services are produced for which there is no corresponding flow of money payments. Thus farmers and farm workers consume a proportion of their own produce. Persons grow vegetables in their own gardens or do many jobs for themselves, such as painting the house or repairing the car. Services, such as those of an honorary secretary or a daughter tending a sick mother, are rendered without payment. Above all, the housewife cooks the meals, cleans the house, polishes the windows, washes and mends the clothes and performs many other jobs which, in different circumstances, firms are paid to do. When tasks are performed without money payment they do not enter into national income calculations, but as soon as they are paid for they do. Consequently the national income may rise although there has been no real increase in goods and services. An example will make this clearer. Suppose a dentist has been doing without a receptionist. Then, because of pressure of work, he decides to employ a receptionist-nurse. A housewife, formerly a nurse, accepts the post. To do this, however, she has to send her washing to the laundry, employ a window-cleaner, engage a charlady and go to a restaurant for a midday meal. The result is that the national income rises twice—first, because money is being earned by her in payment for her services, secondly because others are now paid for doing the jobs which she formerly performed herself. In practice, the only difference is that the dentist can work a little more leisurely. Since 1938 there has been an increase in the number of married women in the working population and this accounts for some of the increase in the national income, but we must also remember that it has resulted in some loss of leisure and comfort in the home.

The second reason why figures of real national income per head may fail to give an accurate measurement of changes in the standard of living is that they take no account of the amount of effort involved or of the conditions of work which exist in the production of the national income. Real income per head may remain the same over a number of years, but yet the standard of living may have improved simply because people are working shorter hours. In short, they are taking their increased income in the form of longer leisure. Thus, the increase in national production over the last ten years would have been greater than it actually was were persons not working on the average one hour less per week. Similarly, an increase in national income per head may be at the expense of inferior working conditions, as happened at the beginning of the nineteenth century.

Thirdly, by counting the cost of the public services, particularly of protection and defence, as expenditure by consumers on services rather than as a cost involved in the production of goods which are directly useful, we have the anomaly that bombs, battleships and rifles figure in the national production accounts in exactly the same way as consumers' goods, passenger liners and the tools of the carpenter. Hence, in a period of rearmament, the national income figures remain as high as previously although men are engaged in producing the means of destruction rather than goods and services which improve living standards.

Fourthly, an increase in real income per head may not be

accompanied by a commensurate increase in the general standard of living because it is simply an arithmetic average and tells us nothing about the way the increase has been distributed. A few wealthy persons, for instance, may have absorbed it all, leaving the poor in exactly the same position as they were before. This is what has occurred to some extent in such countries as Saudi Arabia.

Fifthly, the overall national income figure makes no distinction between the production of consumer goods and of investment goods. But only the former determine the present standard of living; investment allows a higher standard to be enjoyed later on. In Russia and China, concentration on the production of investment goods has kept down the people's standard of living.

Finally, since national income figures are based on private costs and benefits, social costs or benefits do not enter into the calculations. Thus the erection of electricity pylons would be included at cost, no allowance being made for the social cost of spoiling the landscape.

2. To Compare the Real National Income per Head of One Country with Another

Today most countries calculate their national income. Even though the accuracy of the figures varies, they do allow useful numerical comparisons to be made. In the matter of foreign aid, for instance, it is helpful to have the answers to many questions. Which are the poor countries? How poor are they? Are their standards of living improving? How rich are the rich countries? Could they afford to give more? Are they making equal sacrifices? Indeed, it may be that national income figures will provide the basis for some future form of international tax. Thus the United Nations Conference on Trade and Development has recommended that a minimum of 1 per cent of national incomes should be given in aid by richer to developing countries.

National income comparisons can also serve somewhat narrower national interests. Because a rich country can sustain a war better than a poor one, they are useful in calculating the strength of potential enemies, estimating the value of alliances, and planning the size and nature of defence expenditure.

Nevertheless, in the actual comparison of the national incomes of two different countries, we are faced with similar, though even greater difficulties to those encountered when comparing a single country's national income for two different years. In the first place, we have to revalue one country's currency in terms of another's. To do this we cannot take the foreign exchange rate between the countries' currencies. This does not represent their relative purchasing power for it depends roughly upon only those goods and services which enter into trade between them. What we have to do is to compare the prices of a 'basket' of actual goods and services of each country and from this calculate the respective purchasing power of one country's currency in terms of the other's. This enables national income estimates to be reduced to a common basis. Mr. Colin Clark, who pioneered work on these lines, used an 'international unit', defined as the average purchasing power of $1 in the United States of America over the period 1925–34. Care must be taken, however, in selecting the basket. The habits and customs of different countries vary considerably. The average Frenchman, for instance, spends a smaller proportion of his income on rent than the average Englishman and he buys wine and coffee instead of beer and tea. Hence in compiling the 'basket' from which the purchasing power of the pound sterling in terms of francs is to be obtained, some adjustments have to be made in the weighting and in the items.

Secondly, we must remember the defects mentioned above in using real income per head to measure the standard of living. But additional snags arise when it is employed to compare the living standards of two countries. (a) Differences in climate and custom lead to differences in requirements. Thus the Englishman has to pay for heating in the winter which the Indian receives free, while the former's suit costs more than the latter's loin-cloth. Both would lead to a higher figure of national income for the United Kingdom as compared with India, but the probability is that there is little difference in the actual satisfaction received. (b) Expenditure on defence appears in the national income in much the same way as expenditure on consumers' goods. But some countries have to spend less per head on defence than others and so, in reality, they are enjoying more consumers' goods than those where defence expenditure is high. (c) The proportion of goods produced which are exchanged against money varies from one country to another. In poorer countries, for instance, housewives would do their own laundry, clean their own windows and even make their own clothes, while in agricultural countries, particularly those where peasant farmers predominate, much of the produce is consumed by the producers. An allowance must, therefore, be made for this in calculating the national income. (d) A difference in the size of income-group leads to differences in the rate at which certain occupations are rewarded. Thus where there are a few rich and a predominating proportion of poor people, as in Egypt, domestic and other unskilled services are very poorly rewarded, while in the United Kingdom, where greater equality in incomes exists, such services are relatively highly paid, thereby producing, in comparision, an inflated national income.

These considerations qualify, but do not invalidate, national income comparisons between different countries. In any case, even if they cannot measure differences in standards of living accurately, they do indicate how large they are.

3. To Calculate the Rate at which a Nation's Income is Growing

Is the national income growing? Is it growing as fast as it should? Are the incomes of other countries growing faster? Is there sufficient investment to maintain future living standards? The answers to these and similar questions can be found by comparing national income figures, though for reasons given above, some caution must be observed.

4. To Assist the Government in the Regulation of the Economy

On many occasions in this book, attention has been drawn to the role which the government must play in order that full use shall be made of the factors of production. Above all, there must be full employment, a term which is discussed in

Chapter 23. For our purposes here, we need only note that, among other things, it involves the maintenance of an adequate level of money income and of foreign exports. The late Lord Keynes in particular showed how total money income was influenced by variations in the levels of consumption, saving and investment. The volume of exports, too, depends largely on the price of the goods and hence it is necessary to keep inflation in check, an object which can be achieved once again by influencing consumption, saving and investment. It is necessary, therefore, that we have reasonably accurate measurements of these three variables and, since the figures we have shown can be still further broken down and reclassified according to the purpose in view, the national income accounts do answer our requirements. In controlling inflation, for example, future expenditure can be estimated more accurately when we know the volume of current expenditure, while, from the figures showing the present production of consumers' goods, it is possible, after applying relevant estimates of changes in investment and exports, to estimate the future volume of available consumers' goods upon which the estimated income will be spent. Incidentally, the national output figures do indicate the importance of the government's role in the economic life of the United Kingdom from year to year, while the expenditure figures indicate the expenditure for which the government is responsible.

In many minor ways, too, national income figures help the government in its work. Thus the fact that the national income can be calculated by three different methods enables the government to cross-check on certain components of it. If, for instance, national income reckoned from the expenditure side is much greater than the national income reckoned from the income side, it may well be that the difference is due to persons understating their income in order to avoid taxation. National income figures therefore provide a further overall check by the income tax authorities.

III. THE MATERIAL STANDARD OF LIFE OF A COUNTRY

It is instructive to conclude this section with a brief survey of the major factors which determine a country's material standard of life. However, since what we mean by 'material standard of life' is capable of having more than one meaning, it is necessary to define it rather accurately.

It is obvious that if a country were prepared to neglect the maintenance of its capital equipment and to spend its foreign assets, it could, over a comparatively short period, have an abundance of consumers' goods, the ultimate aim of production. This, however, would be merely a short-sighted and foolhardy way of increasing material welfare and one which we can ignore here. We must allow for maintaining capital equipment intact. Hence we define the material standard of life of a country as the real national income per head of the population, though we must remember that even this concept is not without its difficulties (pages 351–5). In particular it does not distinguish between expenditure on consumer and investment goods, though only the former determine people's immediate standard of living.

Our survey will have to allow for the fact that few countries these days are economically self-contained. Consequently we have to classify our factors into two main groups, internal and external.

1. INTERNAL

1. *Original natural resources*

It is obvious that 'natural resources' covers such things as mineral deposits, sources of fuel and power (such as coal and hydroelectric supply), climate, fertility of the soil, and fisheries around the coast. It must also be extended, however, to include geographical advantages, such as navigable rivers or lakes and flatness of land, both of which make the development of communications easier.

Variations in national income may take place because natural advantages become exhausted. On the other hand, new techniques may render usable natural resources which were formerly lying idle. Where the economy of a country is predominantly agricultural, variations in weather may produce fluctuations in the national income from year to year.

2. The nature of the people, particularly of the labour force

Factors affecting the quantity and quality of labour have already been discussed. It is obvious that, other things being equal, the material standard of life will be higher the greater the proportion of workers to the total population and the longer the hours those workers are engaged on production.

The nature of the labour force will be affected by the original qualities of the people—their health, energy, adaptability, inventiveness, judgment and ability to organise themselves and to co-operate in production. To these original qualities however must be added the skills that they learn through training and education.

3. Capital equipment

The effectiveness with which the natural resources and the labour force are used depends almost entirely on the capital equipment with which they can be combined. Thus coal and mineral resources need machinery to extract them from the soil, while to get any advantage from a waterfall, a turbine generator must be built. Similarly, the output per labourer can be vastly increased by giving him the right capital equipment. Indeed the biggest single cause of material progress is the addition to capital.

4. The organisation of the factors of production

The available scarce factors of production must be so organised that the maximum production is obtained from them. Such organisation was considered to be so important by the Classical economists that they placed it in a separate category. Today, however, organisation is more usually regarded as being merely a special kind of highly skilled labour. Only 'entrepreneurship', the acceptance of the risk involved in assembling the factors of production for an uncertain demand, is looked upon as being different. However, it is essential that the factors are combined in the right proportions, in the right places and in the right way for production. Have we the correct proportion of machinery to each worker? Is the production of the particular good being carried on in the best possible locality? Could the factors be re-deployed within the factory itself to better advantage? This is the kind of question which has to be answered by the person undertaking the actual task of organising the production of the goods. In view, therefore, of the importance to output of this function, it has been included here under a separate heading.

5. Knowledge of techniques

Technical knowledge is the result of research and invention. Both involve capital expenditure, though it should be noted that the full use of techniques already learned is often held up for want of the necessary capital. Thus before we can harness to our advantage our present knowledge of nuclear energy, much capital development is required. Nevertheless the rapid increase of the standard of living of the United Kingdom over the last hundred years has largely been due to the development of new techniques, such as the steam engine, the internal combustion engine, power from electricity and oil.

6. Political organisation

A stable government promotes confidence and thereby encourages saving and investment in long-term capital projects. Production is therefore greater.

2. EXTERNAL

1. Foreign loans and investments

A net income from foreign loans and investments means that a creditor country can obtain goods or services from debtor countries without having to give goods and services in return. Similarly, where a country has a net deficit on income from foreign assets, goods and services have to be exported to cover it. Material welfare from this source, however, is only likely to fluctuate over a long period.

2. The terms of trade

Fluctuations in the terms of trade are likely to be far more important in changing material welfare in a short period, especially if the country, as with the United Kingdom, has a high level of imports and exports.

By the terms of trade we mean the quantity of another country's products which a nation gets in exchange for a given quantity of its own products. Thus, if the terms of trade move in the nation's favour, it means that it gets a larger quantity of imports for a given quantity of its own exports. This has happened because the prices of goods imported have fallen relatively to those exported. Let us suppose, for instance, that a country exports only cars and imports only wheat. If it exports 10,000 cars at a price of £500 per car, the value of its total exports is thus £5 million. If the price of wheat is £5 a quarter it can import 1,000,000 quarters. Assume now that the price of the cars remains unchanged but that the price of wheat falls to £4 a quarter. The result is that it is now possible to import 1,250,000 quarters of wheat in exchange for the same number of cars. Or the same amount of wheat as previously can be imported but only 8,000 cars need be exported. Thus either an extra 250,000 quarters of wheat or 2,000 cars can be enjoyed at home, not, it should be noted, through any increase in productivity, but simply because the terms of trade have moved in favour of the car-manufacturing country.

3. *Gifts from abroad*

Since the war, the U.S.A. has made grants to various countries for purposes of economic development and defence. Such gifts have had the effect of maintaining or improving the standard of living of the receiving countries. On the other hand, any permanent improvement must come chiefly from a country's own efforts, for gifts from another country cannot be expected to be continued indefinitely.

PART VI

FACILITIES TO EXCHANGE

CHAPTER 20

MONEY

I. THE FUNCTIONS OF MONEY

1. THE DIFFICULTIES OF BARTER

EVEN the early Stone-Age man must have had a surplus of certain goods which he would seek to exchange for others. Thus, if he lived near a river, fish would be offered to his neighbour living in the forest in exchange for wood. This simple form of exchange, a direct swop of one good for another, is known as *barter*.

Barter, however, presents difficulties, particularly as the number of articles exchanged and the variety of people's wants increase. In the first place, it is extremely difficult to find a person who wants what you have to offer and can offer the very thing you want. For example, suppose A has a bicycle and wishes to exchange it for a camera. Now there may be many people who want his bicycle but not one of them has a camera to give in exchange for it. Therefore no deal can take place until A finds a person who not only wants a bicycle, but also has a camera to offer for it.

Secondly, many goods cannot be divided into portions so that they can be exchanged against a variety of goods. Suppose A had a horse to exchange for a fountain-pen, a watch and a bicycle, all owned by separate persons; no deal would take place because there would be no way of dividing up the horse without destroying much of its value.

Thirdly, if you could obtain the goods you wanted only by exchanging them against other goods, it would mean that all your wealth would have to be held in the form of a variety of goods to meet the different demands of the persons who possessed what you wanted. The richer you grew, the more would the difficulty of storage increase, particularly as certain goods deteriorate with keeping. Thus, oxen not only have to be fed, but, if wanted for beef, begin to lose value after three years.

Lastly, in conditions of exchange by barter, there would be no standard unit, no common denominator, for measuring goods. A might be prepared to accept one rifle or one dog or one camera in exchange for his bicycle—the list could be very long. How much simpler it would be for him to be able to state the value of his bicycle in terms of one particular good and for everybody to do likewise! Immediately there would be a simple basis for comparing the value of one good and with that of another.

2. THE INTRODUCTION OF 'MONEY'

Because of the difficulties of barter, men began very early to use one good, *generally acceptable to everybody*, as a go-between to facilitate exchanges. This one good was 'money', though not always in the form of bank-notes or metal coins as we usually conceive of it today. When he led a primarily hunting life, skins were used. In fact, pelts acted as money in Canada in the early days of the Hudson's Bay Company. As they passed to a pastoral life, men kept their wealth in cattle, and so cattle were used as money. Even in certain words today we can discern the close connection between cattle and money. Thus the derivation of the word 'pecuniary' is from the Latin word (money), which itself is derived from 'pecus' (cattle). Later the products of the soil took the form of money—corn, olive oil (around the Mediterranean) and cocoa-beans (Mexico).

But the use of commodities as money has drawbacks. They do not entirely overcome the difficulties of barter. Thus with oxen: (a) they die or deteriorate with keeping; (b) there is no standard quality from one oxen to another; (c) they cannot be used to make very small payments; (d) they are not easy to take a distance in order to settle a debt. So soon precious metals came to be used. As early as Genesis we read that Joseph was sold for 20 pieces of silver, and it was probably the same sort of money which some years later Jacob's sons took with them into Egypt in order to buy corn.

Eventually, in order to have standard units which could be easily counted, the precious metals were coined. Later coins themselves were replaced or added to by paper money, which commenced by being promises to give metal in exchange on demand, but has ended in becoming completely inconvertible.

3. The Functions of Money

We can therefore sum up the functions of money in a modern society in the traditional way under the following four headings.

1. *Money acts as a medium of exchange*

Barter is the only alternative to the use of money in effecting exchanges. But the difficulties of barter which we have discussed would become insurmountable in a modern society, depending as it does on a multitude of exchanges. How, for instance, could we pay a worker who specialised in the spraying of motor cars? If the employer paid him in goods, there would be insufficient variety to satisfy all his wants. Money, on the other hand, is 'a bearer of options'. It can be spent on whatever is available and desirable. The worker will take money for his wages, not because he wants it for itself, but because other persons will accept it in payment for the goods or services he desires.

2. *Money acts as a measure of value and a unit of account*

Money enables us to measure the value we and others put on goods in the same way as a foot-rule enables us to measure the length of things, or as a thermometer measures heat. A price, that is its value in terms of money, is given to a good. By comparing these prices, we can easily see the relative values of different goods, and expenditure of limited income, whether by the nation, the businessman, the housewife, or the schoolboy, can be planned accordingly. Fluctuations in price also indicate whether more or less of a good should be produced. The whole price system depends on the use of money. Moreover, the practice of reckoning all transactions in money and prices facilitates the keeping of accurate accounts.

3. *Money is a standard for deferred payments*

The value of money remains relatively stable over a short period. This means that if a loan of £100 is made now it can be expected that £100 will roughly be the same in value when the loan is repaid, say in three months. Thus loans, and similarly contracts, are usually made in terms of money.

Today, however, the value of money is not so stable, and has been falling over the last twenty-five years. Therefore whilst contracts are still made in terms of money, safeguarding clauses are often inserted to allow for a possible fall in money's value before the completion date. For instance, a builder's estimate for a house may include a clause permitting him to raise the agreed price if costs of materials and wages increase before the house is completed.

4. Money is a store of wealth and a liquid asset

Wealth can be stored in many forms. A man may have the whole of his wealth in goods and, as he uses these goods, so he derives satisfaction from them. But this is not a practicable method of storing that wealth which is surplus to immediate requirements. The goods would just be in the way and would probably deteriorate with keeping. There would always be the possibility of their being stolen, especially if they consisted of such easily carried commodities as precious stones, jewellery, etc. An alternative is to lend the money out or to buy stocks or shares with it. Not only is this more convenient, but the wealth earns further wealth during the period for which it is lent. A snag arises, however, should you wish to buy something in a hurry. If the money is lent to a bank, for instance, seven days' notice is often required before it can be withdrawn. If the money is in the form of stocks and shares you might have to sell them at an unfavourable moment—just when the price is low. Moreover, there is always the inconvenience and trouble of withdrawing or selling your holdings.

For these reasons, people generally find it better to hold at least a part of their surplus wealth in the form of money, i.e. ready cash. It may be kept in a safe or, more usually, in a current account at a bank. Such money is available at any time to be spent on any good or service. It is a liquid asset. The private individual needs a reserve of such money for his everyday purchases. A businessman needs it for the payment of wages, the purchase of raw materials, and so on. An extra reserve may also be kept against an emergency or in order to take advantage of the opportunity to make a purchase on very favourable terms, for it is often the person who has 'ready cash' that secures a bargain. This demand for money *as a liquid asset* is very important and, had we dealt with the rate of interest

in more detail, we should have had to have given it a much
fuller consideration.

II. THE DIFFERENT FORMS OF MONEY

We must now examine in more detail what 'money' consists
of in the United Kingdom today. This can best be done by
classifying such money into three kinds: coin, notes and bank
deposits.

1. COIN

Very early in the history of the United Kingdom, precious
metals, chiefly tin, gold and silver, came to be used as the main
medium of exchange, for they possessed all the chief attributes
of a good monetary unit. They were small relative to their
value and could, therefore, be carried easily. They were easily
divided when that became necessary to pay a smaller debt.
Moreover, they did not wear out quickly or perish or deteriorate
with keeping, while the fact that they could be tested fairly
easily for debasement ensured the same standard of quality
throughout. Above all, because they were scarce and their
supply could not quickly be added to, their value tended to
remain fairly stable. In short, precious metals were used as
money because they were generally acceptable in exchange.

Until such metals were coined, however, they had to be
weighed and tested every time they passed from one person to
another. Coining was therefore undertaken for convenience.
The metals were divided into pieces, each of the same weight
and fineness and usually corresponding in shape, and the value
of the piece was stamped on it. Thus the process of settling
debts was simplified, for payments could now be made by
counting the coins.

Today coins are used for transactions involving only small
sums of money. In fact, copper is legal tender up to the amount
of 20p only, silver coins up to 10p to £5, and above 10p to £20.
(Legal tender is the money which by law must be accepted by
a creditor, or seller of goods, in payment of a debt.) Gold
coins are legal tender up to any amount, but they are no
longer in circulation.

Because silver coins are now made of a cheaper alloy of

copper and nickel, and copper coins of an alloy of bronze, the coins in circulation today have a face value much greater than the actual value of the metal they contain. Therefore, together with notes, they are called '*token money*'.

2. NOTES

In the next chapter we shall see how bank-notes originated, how they came to be used as money, and how the Bank of England was given the monopoly in England and Wales of issuing them. Today, Bank of England notes are issued in denominations of £20, £10, £5, and £1 and these are legal tender up to any amount. Printed on these notes is a promise to pay the sum stated to the bearer on demand, and until 1914 they could be exchanged for gold sovereigns or half-sovereigns. At the beginning of World War I, however, the government allowed the Bank of England to refuse to change its notes into gold and, since then, with the exception of the period 1925 to 1931 when gold bullion only could be demanded in exchange, bank-notes have remained inconvertible.

Bank-notes possess the main attributes of a good monetary unit. Their big disadvantage is, however, that they are so easy for a government to reproduce. Consequently, many governments when in financial difficulties have yielded to the temptation of printing indiscriminately and there has been a consequent reduction in the value of the currency.

3. BANK DEPOSITS AND CHEQUES

A commodity does not have to be 'legal tender' for it to be 'money'. Thus £6 worth of 10p coins is not legal tender, but most people would accept them in payment of a debt. In fact, for a year or so after World War II, the Germans had lost so much confidence in the Reichsbank mark that cigarettes became the chief medium of exchange, being passed freely between one person and another. In this case, cigarettes were money, for any good can be termed 'money' if it is *generally acceptable* in payments of debts. It will be observed, however, that not *all* instruments for settling debts can be classified as money. Stamps, money orders, postal orders, and school dinner tickets do not circulate because they are not *generally* acceptable.

In any case, since they are usually used only once, they do not add greatly to the quantity of purchasing power in existence. But today in the United Kingdom it is only comparatively small transactions which are conducted in cash. For the settlement of large debts, especially in business, cheques are used. A cheque is merely an order to the bank to pay a stated sum of money to the person named or to the bearer of the cheque. This the bank effects by reducing the deposit of the drawer and either paying cash to the person named or crediting his account with the sum stated.

This method of settling debts has the two main merits of convenience and safety. Hence cheques, although not legal tender, are generally acceptable. It means, however, that bank deposits act as money, for as we shall see, they have been 'created' by the banks and are not eliminated by a cheque transaction. What happens is that deposits are merely transferred from one account to another, though in the process they do replace the use of cash in the transaction. Today, approximately 90 per cent in value of all transactions is settled by cheque.

III. THE VALUE OF MONEY

1. What do we Mean by 'the Value of Money'?

The price of a good can, as we have seen, rise or fall owing to changes in the conditions of demand and supply. In other words, its value has increased or decreased relative to other goods. At times, however, it is observed that the prices of all goods generally are rising or falling with little variation in their relative prices. When this happens, the obvious deduction is that it is brought about by some common influence; and so, in order to explain it, we turn to the only thing which is common to all prices—money, in terms of which the value of goods is expressed.

Now when we speak of the value of a good we mean the amount of other goods which will be given in exchange for it.

In practice, the relative values of different goods are usually compared directly by 'pricing' the goods, that is, by expressing their value in terms of a common commodity, money. In doing this, however, we tend to forget that money itself can be valued in terms of goods and services. When, for instance, the prices of goods in general have risen, it means that fewer goods will be given for a unit of money or, in other words, that the value of money has fallen. Similarly, when all prices have fallen, the value of money has risen because its purchasing power, that is the rate at which other goods and services are exchanged for it, has risen. The value of money is thus the reciprocal of the general level of prices and any rise or fall in the general level of prices is equivalent respectively to a decrease or increase in the value of money.

2. The Measurement of Changes in the Value of Money

It seems then that all we have to do in order to measure changes in the value of money is to devise a system whereby variations in the prices of things in general can be recorded. In practice, however, this is far more difficult than appears at first sight. What commodities and services are we going to take as being representative of 'things in general'? Money is used in the exchange, not only of consumers' goods but also of producers' goods, raw materials, labour, buildings, machinery and goods which, although finished, are only a step in the production of the final consumers' good. We have to decide, therefore, whether to measure changes in the prices of only those goods which enter into final consumption, or to include the prices of all the goods and services of whatever kind which are exchanged by the use of money. Since for all people the standard of material welfare is dependent almost entirely on the quantity of finished goods and services which their limited money income will buy, it is more usual to measure the value of money in terms of the retail prices of those goods bought by the final consumer.

From the information which shows the changes over a period of time in the prices of these consumers' goods, a single figure, which gives an immediate indication of how these prices in general have varied, has to be built up. Since, however, money cannot be measured in terms of itself, there is no absolute standard which can be used to express changes in its value. Hence we have to construct what is known as an 'index number', a figure which measures relative changes—the average percentage variation in the prices of goods from one period to another. Nevertheless, as it is relative changes in the price level which are really significant, the measurement of such changes rather than of absolute changes is quite satisfactory. The actual construction of index numbers, however, does present some difficulties largely because certain arbitrary decisions have to be made regarding the definitions and methods to be employed.

At the outset, we have to examine what we really mean by the term 'goods bought by the final consumer', for it is obvious that different consumers, since their incomes and tastes differ, purchase different goods. The £20,000-a-year barrister has a different pattern of spending from his £50-a-week clerk and, if the goods which the clerk buys have not risen in price, the value of money to him has not fallen, although the barrister may be complaining that nearly everything on which he spends his income (his golf, theatre seats, children's school-fees, domestic labour and his wife's luxuries) is costing him twice as much as previously. There is no wholly satisfactory method of solving this difficulty. Later, when we examine the method of constructing the Index of Retail Prices by the Department of Employment, we shall see one way in which the problem has been tackled in practice—by measuring only the changes in the prices of goods usually bought by the family of the man earning under £75 a week.

Having decided on what things to include, we have yet to consider our method of combining the various price changes. Suppose the price of bread has risen by 50 per cent and the price of matches by 25 per cent. Are we then to combine the two by simply averaging these percentage increases and say that the average price level has risen by 37½ per cent? Obviously bread will form a far more important item in the expenditure of the normal person's income than matches and, therefore, in computing the index number, more weight must be given to bread than to matches as an item of expenditure. The first step in 'weighting' is to select for a particular year, the 'base' year, what is considered to be a typical pattern of the way in which the *average* family of the type under consideration spends its total income. This selected pattern is known as a 'basket' and this same basket is used to apply weights to the various items in all other years for which index numbers are calculated. This can, in practice, be carried out by two slightly different methods, though each gives the same result. These methods can be illustrated by comparing prices in a base year, 1970, with those for a later year, 1975.

Suppose that, in 1970, 50p per week is spent on a typical basket of three goods as follows:

	Price, 1970	Quantity bought	Total expenditure (p)	Weight
Bread	10p per loaf	3 loaves	30	60
Matches	2p per box	2 boxes	4	8
Butter	32p per lb.	½ lb.	16	32
			50	100

The same quantity or basket bought at 1975 price would be as follows:

	Price, 1975	Quantity bought	Total expenditure (p)
Bread	15p per loaf	3 loaves	45
Matches	3p per box	2 boxes	6
Butter	40p per lb.	½ lb.	20
			71

Hence the average price level of this particular basket has risen between 1970 and 1975 by 42 per cent and, as the index number of the base year is always 100, the index number for 1975 would be 142.

If a basket is to be truly representative of a consumer's expenditure, however, the number of articles it contains must be as large as possible. In this case it is easier to vary the method of calculating the index by taking the percentage change in price of each item of the basket and then multiplying this change by the 'weight', which is a figure indicative of the relative importance of the item in the basket of the base year. Thus, in our example, when the total of the weights comes to 100, bread would be weighted as 60, matches as 8 and butter as 32. Our calculation of the index would now be as follows:

Item	Price (p)		(a) 1975 as % of 1970	(b) Weight	(c) Weighted relative change
	1970	1975			(a) × (b)
Bread . .	10	15	150	60	9000
Matches . .	2	3	150	8	1200
Butter . .	32	40	125	32	4000
					100)14200
					142

Hence the index number for 1975 of this particular basket is 142.

With this system of 'weighting' by means of a basket of a base year, certain difficulties arise. In the first place, it is obvious that, since different people, even though they may have the same income, have different tastes, they will weight their expenditure differently by buying different baskets of goods. The compiler of the index, therefore, has to decide on an 'average' basket. According to his arbitrary decision, so the index number varies, for a slightly different weighting gives a slightly different index number. It means, too, that the index applies only to the *average* family of a *particular class*. Hence the index moves differently with the 'unusual' family even in the same class and, if it is a working-class family index, it does not apply to families in the high income-groups.

Secondly, the chosen basket is really only applicable to the base year. The further we move from the base year, the more unreal does that basket become. Over a period real income varies and people accordingly rearrange the proportions in which they buy different goods. Thus, as we have seen, as their income increases so people tend to spend a smaller proportion of it on foodstuffs and a larger proportion on luxuries. Changes in tastes also occur independently of changes in income. This is particularly true of seasonal and fashion changes, though tastes change too over the long period, as can be seen by the way in which during recent years men have largely ceased to wear hats. Nor must we forget that the pattern of expenditure will vary as the composition of the average family changes. In addition, people substitute one article for another in their expenditure in order to take advantage of a fall in price and hence relative price changes complicate the calculation of the index. Above all, new items, not produced during the base year to which the basket refers, enter into expenditure, while even the existing items change in pattern and quality. In the 1970s, for example, we had the introduction of cassette recorders, colour television, pocket calculators and new car models. How therefore, can an accurate index be calculated on a basket based, for example, on the year 1960?

The third set of difficulties is concerned with snags that are likely to arise in the actual process of compiling the index. In the first place we must be sure that there is no serious abnormality in the year which we select for a base year as this would distort our basket. Thus abnormally high marriage or birth rates would interfere with the normal pattern of expenditure. Secondly, in the collection of the prices of certain goods, we have to lay down a uniform system and be careful that the price of the good, although the same in money terms, has not changed in some less obvious way. Do we, for instance, have to wait longer in a shop to be served? Are we subject to more standing in buses? Are gift coupons given with certain goods? Such changes disguise what are variations in the real prices of goods.

Thus it can be seen that an index number is merely an indication of relative changes, not in the *general* price level, but in the level of the prices of the particular class of goods chosen. It is not a water-tight device in the sense that it is completely accurate. The further we proceed from the base year, the more inaccurate is it likely to become, for the basket is more liable to change. Moreover, since the normal baskets of different places and countries vary, an index is severely limited in its use when we come to compare the value of money in different places. Nevertheless it does provide us with the best possible approximation of changes in a price level and in order to show in more detail how an index is calculated in practice, we will describe the one most widely-known, the Index of Retail Prices.

3. The Index of Retail Prices

This index is compiled monthly by the Department of Employment and measures changes in the cost of the usual items purchased by an average family where the gross income of the head does not exceed £75 a week. For this reason collective agreements, covering 10 million workers, provide for an automatic 'threshold' adjustment of wage-rates in accordance with changes in this official index.

The government first started to prepare such an index in 1904. This, however, covered only food prices and hence, when at the outbreak of war a measurement of changes in the cost of living became even more desirable, it was decided to widen its basis. Such items as rent, clothes, and entertainment were therefore added and July, 1914 was taken as the base date.

An Index of Retail Prices was introduced in March, 1956. The base date for this is now 15 January, 1974. The weights of the various groups in 1974 were as follows, though each group can be broken down into sections and the sections into items.

Food	253
Alcoholic drink	70
Tobacco	43
Housing	124
Fuel and light	52
Durable household goods	64
Clothing and footwear	91
Transport and vehicles	135
Services	54
Miscellaneous goods	63
Meals bought and consumed outside the home	51
ALL ITEMS	1,000

Weights are found by a continuous Family Expenditure Survey. They are revised in each January, being based on ascertained consumption in the three years ending the previous June, though valued at the current January prices.

Like all other indices, the Index of Retail Prices is sectional, being based on the retail prices of goods bought by the lower-income family, but since such families are overwhelmingly predominant, it is the prices of goods which they buy which are most significant from a cost of living point of view. The methods used for obtaining the various prices have been standardised. Information regarding most of the food items is collected by personal visits to retailers by 200 local offices, spread throughout the country, of the Department of Employment. Five local retailers are chosen, including where possible a local Co-operative Society and a branch of a chain store, from whom prices for each article of food are obtained. For rent and rates, inquiries are made regarding local authority houses and the results are combined with figures for other types of dwellings. The prices of most of the other groups are obtained by inquiry from manufacturers. Except for Bank Holidays, the prices are normally collected for the Tuesday nearest the 15th of each month.

4. The Effects of Changes in the Value of Money

In the United Kingdom since the end of World War II, prices generally have been rising; in other words, the value of money has fallen. The causes of this fall will not be examined until Chapter 26, but it is appropriate here to consider the effects of changes in the value of money, with particular reference to the United Kingdom's post-war situation.

1. *The effect on production*

In the past, periods of falling prices have generally proved somewhat unhappy. During the depression of 1925–33, for instance, prices were falling. Indeed, it is not difficult to perceive the link between falling prices and a depression, though we must be careful to note that the fall in prices is not the *cause* of the depression. In a Capitalist economy, an entrepreneur produces if he expects to make a profit. Now if the price of the good falls before he comes to sell it, he will receive less than he expected, probably less than the costs he has incurred in producing it. A condition of falling prices, therefore, enters into his expectations with the result that he refrains from producing, thereby helping to prolong the depression. In short, it is difficult in a Capitalist economy to maintain full employment over a period when prices are falling.

On the other hand, rising prices have the opposite effect. In such circumstances, the selling price of the good will be even higher than that price upon which the decision to produce was based. The expected profits will therefore be more than justified by 'windfall gains' and this will encourage further investment. Hence full employment is much easier to maintain when prices are rising. Although this is by no means the whole of the story, the condition of rising prices has helped the post-war boom in the United Kingdom.

2. The effect on the National Debt

In periods of rising prices, persons who have borrowed money are in a better position, for in terms of actual goods, they have to repay less in interest and capital. Similarly, when prices are falling, the lenders of money benefit, though in such a situation it might well be that debtors find it beyond their power to repay!

For parallel reasons, rising prices decrease the burden of the National Debt because it means that a smaller proportion of the national income has to be raised by taxation in order to pay persons, often called 'rentiers', to whom the government owes money. This occurs because, while taxation is buoyant, increasing as incomes increase, the money interest on the National Debt remains the same.

For both the above reasons, it seems that at least a stable price level must be aimed at. Indeed, many economists favour a very gradual *rise* in prices (of one to two per cent, for example, every year) in order to stimulate production and investment and to reduce the burden of the government's fixed interest charges. But, although such a solution may appear attractive, in practice it has various ramifications which necessitate a more cautious approach, and final support for it must be given only after careful consideration of other effects, as follows.

3. The effect on the distribution of the national product

Changes in the prices of goods and services have the effect of redistributing the shares which people take of the national product. In the first place, not all prices rise in the same proportion and this hits some people harder than others, according to how they spend their income. More important, however, is the fact that rising prices penalise in particular persons receiving fixed money incomes—people living on pensions or annuities, debenture-holders, landlords who have houses or land rented on a long lease or the rents of which are controlled. As prices rise, such persons become progressively worse off and, in those cases where they are dependent on such fixed incomes, they can only watch helplessly while their real income, and hence their standard of living, continues to fall. Since the largest proportion of such persons consists of retired and disabled persons receiving pensions or drawing on savings, rising prices hit hard that section of the community least able to bear the burden and, in practice, many old people become more and more dependent for the maintenance of their standard of living on belated increases by the government in the rate of retirement pensions. Lastly, wage-earners and, in particular, salary-earners, may lose by rising prices since increases in their earnings often lag behind the price rises. (This is particularly true before a position of full employment has been reached, but afterwards the strong trade unions may secure wage increases which more than compensate for price rises.) On the other hand, persons whose incomes depend on profits tend to gain as prices rise, for usually costs rise less rapidly.

4. *The effect on the balance of payments*

Rising prices in the United Kingdom have the following effects:

(*a*) Exports tend to decline because our goods are relatively dearer in foreign markets.

(*b*) Imports tend to increase because foreign goods are relatively cheaper on the British market.

(*c*) Higher money incomes in the United Kingdom increase the demand for imports *and* tend to decrease exports because the 'soft' home market makes it less vital for manufacturers to seek outlets abroad for their goods.

(*d*) An outward movement of capital may take place if price rises continue, for foreign traders and financiers lose confidence in the pound's maintaining its current rate of exchange.

5. *The effect on industrial relations*

The longer prices continue to rise, the more difficult becomes the government's task of bringing the rise under control. Trade unions eventually ask for a wage-rise each year, or even at more frequent intervals. Claims are usually pitched on the high side, and industrial unrest often results from the failure of employers and trade unions to reach a compromise.

6. *The effect on expectations*

When a condition of rising prices has prevailed for any length of time people begin to base their actions on the assumption that the rise is likely to continue. In such a situation, saving is discouraged for it pays to buy goods now rather than to postpone consumption. The result of such expectations, therefore, is that the increased spending brings the very price rise which was feared; it is an example of 'self-justified expectations'. In practice, therefore, gradual price rises may be difficult to keep in check and we are then in the throes of 'inflation' (Chapter 26), or even 'hyper-inflation'.

CHAPTER 21

FINANCIAL INSTITUTIONS

I. THE NEED FOR FINANCIAL INSTITUTIONS

In Chapter 18 we saw that capital is demanded because of the contribution it makes to production. Hence liquid capital, that is money, is required by producers—manufacturers, traders and the government—for varying periods of time. Such funds of money are provided by persons who not only save a part of their income, but lend all or some of these savings to producers.

For the purposes of assisting saving and of bringing together would-be lenders and borrowers, specialised institutions, some of which were mentioned in Chapter 5, have been established. In short, even in the provision of finance, the principle of the division of labour is applied. Here we shall describe in more detail the work of the more important financial institutions, showing how they are connected and how they facilitate lending and borrowing.

Finance is required for different purposes, by different persons and for varying periods of time. Thus there is a great variety in the institutions providing such loans and in the types of loans arranged. As with goods, markets have sprung up to bring together buyers and sellers.

We shall discuss the subject, however, under the following headings:

    (i) the Money Markets, which deal in short-term loans;
    (ii) the Capital Market, where medium- and long-term capital is raised;
    (iii) the joint-stock banks, which are the major source of working capital, and which exercise a major influence on the system through their ability to create credit;
    (iv) the Bank of England, which exercises overall control on behalf of the government;

(v) the Stock Exchange, which deals in old securities.

None of the Money Markets or the Capital Market have any formal organisation in the sense that buyers and sellers meet regularly in a particular building to conduct business. Instead they are merely a collection of institutions connected, in the case of the Money Markets, by dealings in bills of exchange and short-term loans and, more loosely in the case of the Capital Market, in channelling medium- and long-term finance to those requiring it. The complete structure is shown in a very simplified form in Fig. 25.

Not only are there Money and Capital Markets but, within each, there is further specialisation. This will be illustrated

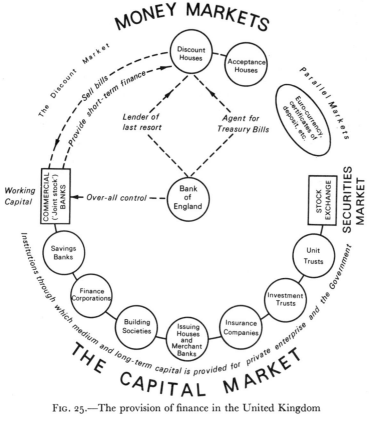

FIG. 25.—The provision of finance in the United Kingdom

later. But, in order to explain: (*a*) the nature of markets in finance; (*b*) how the City of London acquired its expertise; (*c*) how the Bank of England enters into the market, we commence by looking at the traditional London Money Market or, as it would be more precisely described today, the Discount Market.

II. THE DISCOUNT MARKET

The Discount Market is composed of the discount houses and 'running brokers', the acceptance houses or merchant banks, the commercial banks and the Bank of England. All are linked by the various dealings in bills of exchange. We shall show the connection for the commercial bill as used in foreign trade.

During the nineteenth century, the bill of exchange was the accepted instrument for financing trade, both internal and foreign, but since then the cheque system has displaced it for internal use, while in foreign trade it has been replaced by other methods, notably the bank draft and telegraphic transfer by which bank deposits are directly transferred from one bank to another. However, in order to trace the various operations

---

£10,000

Address

25th April, 1974

Three months after date, pay to me or to my order Ten Thousand Pounds, value received.

(Signed) ' Y '

To ' B ',
Address.

Fig. 26.—A commercial bill of exchange

connected with a bill of exchange, let us return to our example on page 268 of the trade in motor cars between a merchant 'Y' in London and an importer 'B' in New York, imagining that the transaction was conducted by this means.

The generally accepted custom of business was that an importer should be allowed a period of grace, usually three months, before payment for the goods would be required. This was arranged as follows. When 'Y' was ready to ship his cars to 'B' he would draw up a bill of exchange for the value of £10,000, as shown in Fig. 26. This would be sent to 'B' together with copies of the shipping documents, such as the bill of lading and insurance certificate, to show that the cars had actually been placed aboard the ship. On receipt of the bill, 'B' would 'accept' it, by writing 'Accepted' and his signature across the face of the bill, and then return it to 'Y'. This acceptance of the bill by 'B' would be the condition for handing over the original bill of lading, the documentary title to the cars.

'Y' could now do one of three things: (i) he could hold the bill until it matured at the end of 3 months; (ii) he might be able, after endorsing it, to get another merchant to take it in settlement of a debt which 'Y' owed; or, (iii) he could sell the bill to somebody, usually a Discount House, having money to spare for the purpose.

1. Discount Houses

The probability is that 'Y' would choose the latter course. So, after endorsing it, he takes it along to one of the eleven Discount Houses operating in the City of London. Here it will be bought at less than its face value, the exact amount paid depending on the length of time it still has to run to maturity, the prevailing official short-term rate of interest (the minimum lending rate), the state of the Money Market, and the opinion of the Discount House as to 'B's' financial standing. Suppose the bill has still three months to run and that the prevailing rate of interest on that class of bill is 8 per cent, the Discount House will pay £9,800 for it. This process is known as 'discounting'. It is obvious that through these arrangements the bill of exchange has advantages to all concerned. The exporter 'Y' can quickly regain liquidity by selling the bill, while 'B' obtains three months' credit, during which time it is probable that he will be able to sell the cars which he has imported.

Discount houses do not usually hold bills for their full currency. Instead commercial bills are assembled in 'parcels' and sold to the commercial banks who like to have so many falling due each day. There are a few 'running brokers' who act as agents in the process of discounting, etc.

In passing, it can be noted that the Discount Houses also buy medium-term British Government bonds which have less than five years to run. In purchasing them, the Discount Houses render a useful function to the government in that: (a) near-maturity bonds of about one year have little appeal to the ordinary investing public when they come on to the market: (b) the collection and concentration of such bonds in a few hands facilitates conversion into a new issue as they mature. Discount Houses also deal in the new short-term instruments e.g. internal bills of exchange, local authority bills and certificates of deposit (see later).

2. Acceptance Houses or Merchant Bankers

If 'B' is a well-known firm of high financial standing, the accepted bill is, from the risk point of view, almost as good as cash. However, as bills are drawn on firms in all parts of the world, it may well be that little is known about 'B's' financial standing. The result is that the Discount House is either chary of discounting the bill or will only do so at a fairly high rate of interest. Nevertheless, the difficulty can be overcome by getting a firm of international repute to 'accept' it. This means that such a firm will make itself responsible for payment should 'B' default when it is presented in July. It is obvious that any firm accepting such a bill must have adequate knowledge of the credit-worthiness of the particular trader upon whom the bill is drawn. Such knowledge was possessed by the Merchant Banks, such as Lazards, Barings and Rothschilds, who commenced as traders but later specialised on financing trade in particular parts of the world. In their capacity of accepting bills, such Merchant Banks are known as 'Acceptance Houses'. They charge a small commission of about ¾ per cent, which is willingly paid by the person wishing to discount a bill because the rate of discount on a 'bank bill', that is one bearing the name of an Acceptance House, is much lower than on a 'trade bill', a bill accepted only by a trader.

In recent years, however, the business of the Acceptance Houses has declined. This has been due to: (a) the diminished use of the commercial bill in trade; (b) the decline of London as the world centre for financing foreign trade, which has resulted from the reduced share of the United Kingdom in world trade and a certain loss of faith in sterling; (c) the increased competition of the commercial banks in the business of accepting bills, largely through the development of the 'reimbursement credit', which works in the following way. 'B', the importer, induces his own bank in New York to secure an acceptance credit for him in London, which means that he can instruct 'Y' to draw the bill on the London branch of his own bank or on a London bank or Acceptance House. The New York bank makes itself responsible for the payment of the bill and so all the London bank or Acceptance House has to do is to satisfy itself as to the financial standing of the New York bank. This simpler procedure means that reimbursement credits can be granted at very low rates of interest.

This decline in their business of accepting bills has increased the importance of the other functions of the Merchant Banks. One such function was noted in Chapter 5—the 'issuing' business connected with the raising of capital by industrial and commercial firms in the United Kingdom. In addition to arranging such issues, the Merchant Banks also underwrite them and arrange for the payment of dividends to the stock-holders as they fall due. They also carry on some domestic banking business and act as trustees and investment advisers to trust funds, pension funds, college endowments, etc. Other functions have resulted from their overseas trading connections. Thus they have important business in the bullion and foreign exchange markets.

Treasury Bills. The operations of the Discount and Accept-ance Houses have been described with relation to the commer-cial bill of exchange, for it was in dealing with this type of bill that they developed. But until recently, Treasury Bills have been the mainstay of the Money Market. A Treasury Bill is really a bill of exchange drawn by the Treasury on itself, usually for a period of three months (91 days). Since such bills are only a short-term loan, they represent the government's cheapest method of borrowing, the interest in February, 1975 being 10 per cent. Treasury Bills are issued only in denominations of £5,000, £10,000, £50,000 and £100,000, and so are primarily for the institutional investors.

3. THE COMMERCIAL BANKS

The Commercial Banks fulfil two main functions in the Discount Market:

1. *They provide funds to the Discount Houses*

The Discount Houses do not themselves possess the huge financial resources necessary to purchase all the bills, commercial and Treasury, which are offered to them. They overcome this difficulty, however, by borrowing money from the Commercial Banks at a comparatively low rate of interest. Then, by discounting at a slightly higher rate, they make a small profit. The banks are willing to lend at a low rate because the loans are of very short duration, often only a day at a time. In this respect, 'money at call' is for the banks very useful, more than compensating for its low yield. Should there be a particularly heavy demand for cash from their ordinary customers, they have an asset which becomes liquid in a day or so. They can therefore economise in cash held in reserve. From the point of view of the Discount Houses, the trouble involved in its daily renewal and the slight risk of its non-renewal is compensated for by the comparatively low rate of interest charged. When the banks are calling in existing loans, money is said to be 'tight', and when lending is expanding, it is said to be 'easy'.

2. *They hold bills until maturity*

The commercial banks can earn a higher rate of interest if they themselves hold both commercial and Treasury Bills for a part of their currency. Indeed, there is no reason why they should not tender for Treasury Bills, though by convention they refrain from doing this. Instead, after the Discount Houses have held the bills for about four weeks leaving them with two months to run, the banks purchase them according to their requirements. In practice, the banks like to have a fairly even amount of bills falling due each day and, with commercial bills, the Discount Houses and Running Brokers perform the additional function of assembling small quantities of bills into 'parcels' corresponding in amount and maturity with the particular requirements of the bank.

The Discount Houses themselves also hold a portion of bills to maturity whereas the Running Brokers do not, acting instead merely as intermediaries for the purpose of holding the bills for a short time while they are sorted into parcels.

4. THE BANK OF ENGLAND

The Bank of England enters into the structure of the Discount Market in two ways:

1. *It is the agency by which the Treasury issues its Treasury Bills*

The issue of Treasury Bills is achieved by one or both of two methods. Government departments, the National Savings Bank, the Exchange Equalisation Account, the National Insurance Funds, and the Bank of England Issue Department, all of whom have funds to invest for a short period, can buy what bills they want at a fixed price, that is 'on tap'. This price is not published.

The Discount Houses and anyone else who wishes to apply (such as Commonwealth and foreign banks) obtain their issue by 'tender'. Every Friday, the Lords Commissioners of the Treasury, acting through the Bank of England, invite tenders for a specified amount of bills, usually between £200 and £300 million. Until 1971, the discount houses tendered as a 'syndicate' at a single rate. As part of the new policy of Competition and Credit Control (CCC), they now compete in their tenders, though they have agreed to 'cover' the whole of the issue.

2. *It is the 'lender of last resort'*

When the Discount Houses are pressed for money because

the Commercial Banks will not renew their 'call money', the Bank of England will lend to them at the 'minimum lending rate', which replaced the old bank rate. It is convenient, however, if we postpone further discussion of this function until the position of the Bank of England as a Central Bank has been considered.

III. PARALLEL MONEY MARKETS

With the traditional sources of finance (particularly the clearing banks) becoming increasingly restricted by the monetary authorities in recent years, there was a ready demand even for short-term funds. Here the City of London has showed its adaptability. Specialist Money Markets developed to meet the specific requirements of particular borrowers and lenders. Indeed, the existence of such markets encourages funds to be lent short-term for they enable lenders to regain liquidity should they so desire.

The following are the most important of these comparatively new markets:

(1) *Inter-bank deposits*

Because money at call and bills of exchange have always been acceptable to the Bank of England as part of the liquidity ratio, clearing banks tended to be connected mainly with the Discount Market.

Until 1971, however, the other banks—Scottish banks, merchant banks, British overseas banks and foreign banks— were not subject to a liquidity ratio. Brokers therefore established a market so that those banks having funds surplus to their immediate requirements were able to lend to those who had immediate outlets for such funds, the rate of interest obtained being higher than in the Discount Market. Now that the non-clearing banks are subject to reserve ratio requirements, the clearing banks also have begun to participate directly in the market.

(2) *Local authority deposits*

Local authorities, which now obtain most of their funds on

the open market, are willing to make use of very short-term money. Brokers now exist for placing such short-term funds from banks, industrial and commercial companies, charitable funds, etc., with the local authority. Such brokers also deal in longer-term local authority bonds.

Today the market is integrated very closely with the inter-bank market as funds from the latter are very often deposited in the former.

(3) *Negotiable certificates of deposit*

Certificates of deposit enable the banks to borrow for periods from three months to five years. They are similar to a bill of exchange drawn on the bank by itself. They have the advantage over the ordinary time deposit in that a bank feels under an obligation to repay the latter to a customer virtually on demand, thereby inhibiting medium-term lending. To the lender, they offer a higher rate of interest, while the market that has developed still provides them with liquidity. This market is largely comprised of the Discount Houses and the banks. It originated in dollar certificates, but sterling certificates of deposit were introduced in 1968 and today comprise two-thirds of the market.

(4) *Euro-currency balances*

Euro-currency deposits are simply funds which are deposited with banks outside the country of origin but which continue to be dominated in terms of the original currency.

The most important Euro-currency is the dollar. As a result of the United States' continuing adverse balance of payments, branches of European banks have built up dollar balances as customers were paid for exports. These balances are offered to brokers in London (where interest rates are higher than can be earned in New York), and are placed mainly with companies or banks (e.g. Japanese) operating on an international scale to finance foreign trade or investment.

While the dollar still dominates the market, other European currencies are now dealt in, chiefly the Deutschmark and the Swiss franc.

(5) *Other markets*

Smaller specialist markets have developed in *Finance House deposits* and *Inter-company deposits*. Thus Finance Houses have obtained funds by issuing bills which are accepted by banks and discount houses. Similarly, in periods of tight credit, firms which are short of finance turn towards other companies which temporarily have funds to spare.

IV. THE CAPITAL MARKET

The unique and complicated machinery of the Money Markets has developed in order to supply trade and the government with the short-term finance each requires. Industry, on the other hand, usually obtains the short-term or 'working' capital it needs (to purchase raw materials, pay workers and maintain stocks) from the commercial banks (to be described later). But the banks hesitate to lend long-term capital (required to finance investment in building and machinery), since they like to keep their assets as liquid as possible. The chief methods of raising such capital have been described in Chapter 5. Briefly, these are: (i) 'ploughing back' the profits of the business or, where a joint-stock company is already in existence, selling additional shares to existing shareholders on bonus terms (a 'rights issue') or to the public; (ii) making use of the services and resources of an Issuing House or Merchant Bank; (iii) applying to the Finance Corporation for Industry (where the amount is above £200,000), or to the Industrial and Commercial Finance Corporation (where the sum required is between £5,000 and £200,000); (iv) negotiating a Stock Exchange 'placing'; (v) arranging a public issue by prospectus. Where capital is required for overseas governments it is usual to leave the flotation of the issue to a Merchant Bank.

Apart from the agencies mentioned above, certain other institutions play an important part in the Capital Market. They do this by collecting the savings of a number of small depositors and reinvesting them in various capital projects. Such 'institutional investors' include:

1. INSURANCE COMPANIES

Insurance companies receive premiums on the various types

of risk insured against. Some of these premiums, such as those received for insuring ships and property, are only held for relatively short periods, having, apart from the profit made, to be paid out against claims. But with one group of insurance, life, endowments, annuities, etc., premiums are usually held for a long time before the final payment has to be made. Hence insurance companies have large sums of money to invest in long-term securities. These investments are spread over British Government and other public stocks, the shares and debentures of various companies, usually in the United Kingdom, property and mortgages. Today 'institutional investors', of which insurance companies are the most important, supply the bulk of savings required for new issues.

2. INVESTMENT TRUSTS

Investors usually try to avoid 'putting all their eggs in one basket' by having an interest in the securities of many different types of enterprise. However, such spreading of risks requires some special knowledge of investment possibilities and, above all, sufficient resources. The small investor can overcome these two difficulties by buying shares in an Investment Trust. This invests its capital over a wide range of companies and, after paying expenses of management, the net yields from its various investments are distributed in the usual way as a dividend on its own shares.

3. UNIT TRUSTS

Unit trusts are a development of the investment trust idea. But they differ in two main respects. First, they are trusts in the legal sense of the term. Trustees are appointed, while the trust deed often limits investments to a specified range of securities. Unit trusts now specialise in their holdings, e.g. metals and minerals, bank-insurance, oil and energy, cross-Channel, capital growth, income, etc. Secondly, the aggregate holding is split into many 'units' of low nominal value. Thus even a small investment covers the whole range of securities. Many unit trusts have schemes linked with assurance, savers subscribing on a regular, usually monthly, basis.

While most of the unit trust funds are used to purchase

existing securities, they do make capital available for new investment, particularly when they take up 'rights' issues by companies whose shares they already hold.

4. SAVINGS BANKS

The National Savings and Trustee Savings Banks provide savings facilities, particularly for persons with a small income. Savings, however, are limited to a total holding of £10,000 per person. The savings deposited are invested in securities prescribed for the trustees, usually government and similar securities.

5. TRUST, PENSION AND TRADE UNION FUNDS

All these accumulate income which is reinvested in government securities, property, shares, etc.

6. BUILDING SOCIETIES

These have a specialised function—the supply of long-term loans on the security of private dwelling-houses purchased for owner-occupation, though sometimes they lend on the security of farms or industrial or commercial premises. Their funds are derived chiefly from money invested in them by the general public, but their shares are not dealt in on the Stock Exchange, being available for cash upon notice. Their liquid reserves are usually invested in Trustee savings.

7. FINANCE CORPORATIONS

The part played by the Industrial and Commercial Finance Corporation and the Finance Corporation for Industry in providing funds for industry has already been described (Chapter 6). There are, however, other somewhat similar corporations, whose funds are subscribed by different sources—the banks, the public and the government—which specialise in particular fields, e.g. the Agricultural Mortgage Corporation, the National Film Finance Corporation, and the Exports Credit Guarantee Department of the Department of Trade.

Capital for small firms may also be provided by the Charterhouse Industrial Development Company and Credit for Industry Ltd, both of which were set up in 1934.

8. Finance Companies

These borrow savings from the public and obtain loans from banks in order to finance hire purchase of both consumer goods and machinery. But when hire purchase has been restricted, many finance companies have switched to financing house purchase. The rates at which they borrow are comparatively high because of the greater lending risks involved, and for a similar reason the rates at which they lend are high. Many joint-stock banks now own a considerable proportion of the equity of certain finance companies, e.g. Mercantile Credit, Lombard Banking, United Dominions Trust.

V. THE DEVELOPMENT OF BANKING IN ENGLAND

1. Early Money-Lending

The practice of banking has its origin in the money-lending business, a fact that is not surprising when it is remembered that the lending of money is still today the main function of a bank. Money-lending itself became possible as soon as men invented and used money as a means of conducting exchanges and storing wealth, and that it was a well-established practice many thousands of years ago can be seen from the fact that, in the Bible, the laws of Moses forbade it (Exodus 22, 25), while later Nehemiah condemned certain Jewish usurers, who, upon lending money to their poorer kinsfolk, exacted pledges of vineyards and even children, and demanded interest (Nehemiah 5, 7–11).

In the commercial centres of Europe during the Middle Ages—Venice, Florence, Amsterdam and Antwerp—the practice of money-lending developed into the business of financing trade, though rulers hard pressed for money or wishing to finance wars also went to the money-lenders for funds. Yet otherwise the business of banking developed very slowly. People, while continuing to make use of the money-lender, nevertheless hated him. This was because borrowing was mostly by persons who had fallen upon misfortune, a circumstance which was not unusual in times when most people lived on the margin of subsistence. To charge interest, often at very high rates, on a loan in these circumstances was considered to be profiteering from other persons' misfortunes. Above all, the Church, basing its doctrine on the teaching of the Old Testament, condemned usury. The views of the Church were expressed in a practical manner in England, for throughout the Middle Ages, the Usury Laws made it illegal to lend money at interest.

During the later Middle Ages, Jews and other merchants from Northern Italy settled in London. Most of them were goldsmiths, dealing in gold and silver, but to this they usually added the business of lending money against security. The Usury Laws were avoided by charging either for the custody of the pledge or else for its redemption. These dealers did their business from benches set up in the street and it is from the Italian word ' banco ' (a bench) that we derive our word 'bank', while from the practice of breaking the bench of any merchant who could not meet his obligations we obtain our word 'bankrupt' and the expression 'to break the bank'. Lombard Street, one of the main banking centres of London, is also named after the 'Lombards', the men who set up business there over 500 years ago.

With the expansion of trade and the development of more capitalistic methods of production, it became necessary to reconsider the morality of charging interest on loans. It was obviously desirable that people who could use the savings of others to conduct trade and hold stocks of goods, such as raw wool and woollen cloth, should be able to do so. A distinction was therefore drawn between the two main reasons for borrowing, the first, urgency of need, the second, using the money in the hope of reaping a reward at a later date. It was held that when money was borrowed for the latter purpose the lender was justified in charging interest. Thus usury was eventually sanctioned by the Church and the legal obstacles to it in England were removed by the repeal of the Usury Laws in 1545, although the maximum rate of interest which could be charged was fixed at 10 per cent.

2. EARLY BANKING

Our present system of banking, however, really began in the middle of the seventeenth century. The growth of trade had given rise to a class of rich merchants, such as those of the Livery Companies of the City of London. These merchants invested some of their wealth in land, but they also desired to keep a surplus fairly liquid in the form of bullion or gold and silver plate. There thus arose the difficulty of finding a safe place in which to store this surplus. In London, many merchants stored their wealth in the vaults of the Tower of London but in 1640, Charles I, who was in financial difficulties, appropriated £130,000 worth of their gold. It is true that he subsequently restored it upon the grant of a loan, but the merchants could foresee that confiscation by the King was quite likely to happen again. So they sought a safer place of custody, and it was to the gold- and silversmiths, who had strong-rooms for the storing of their own valuable goods, that these merchants turned for a safe deposit for their wealth.

Early on, as we have seen, the goldsmiths were in part money-lenders. They now had money deposited with them and very soon they perceived that they could dovetail these two sides of their business. Two factors contributed considerably to this end. The first was that, during the Civil War, much of the gold and silver plate had been melted down into bullion by the gentry to provide funds for whichever side they supported. Thus, after the Civil War, a much larger proportion of the deposits with the goldsmiths consisted of bullion—and such deposits were homogeneous. The goldsmiths saw that their clients left the bulk of their deposits untouched, withdrawing only small sums from day to day to meet their current expenses. Thus the next stage to the goldsmith was obvious—so long as he kept a reserve adequate to meet these everyday calls, there was nothing to prevent his lending out the remainder of the deposit to other clients and charging interest on it.

The second factor which facilitated this development was even more important. The merchant, who deposited his valuables, received from the goldsmith a receipt, which would be produced when he wanted to withdraw them. In time it became customary for these receipts, later known as bank-notes, to be passed from merchant to merchant in settlement of debts. To facilitate this arrangement when the value of the bank-note was not equal to the debt to be settled, persons,

when depositing their wealth, often asked the goldsmith for a
number of bank-notes of varying denominations, the total
being equal to the value of the deposit. This use of the bank-
note as currency to conduct business reduced considerably
withdrawals of gold and silver by depositors. It was therefore
of considerable importance to the goldsmith, for he could now
extend his business of lending money *beyond* the total of the
deposits entrusted to his care by the simple process of writing
out a bank-note, now generally accepted by other merchants,
in favour of any person requesting a loan. In other words,
deposits were 'created'. Of course he would have to be careful
that this process was not carried too far and that he had
sufficient reserve of bullion to meet everyday calls for cash.
The size of this necessary reserve was learnt by experience,
often a bitter one, but, in time, by far the greater proportion
of the goldsmiths' deposits had been 'created' and, in fact,
nearly the whole of the actual bullion deposited with him was
used as day-to-day cash or 'call' money.

3. The Formation of the Bank of England

The formation of the Bank of England in 1694 was a direct
result of the financial need of William III's government in
fighting an expensive war with Louis XIV. Monarchs in the
past had not proved to be good borrowers and the threat of the
Jacobite restoration merely added to the already considerable
risk that money lent might never be repaid. Thus no single
goldsmith was willing to lend money to the government, but a
number of them agreed to share the burden and lent £1,200,000
to William III at a rate of interest of 8 per cent in return for
certain privileges. These privileges were contained in a Charter
which permitted the subscribers to form a joint-stock company
to carry on banking operations in London under the name of
'The Governor and Company of the Bank of England'. In
subsequent years the government borrowed additional sums of
money through the Bank and, in 1708, when its Charter came
up for renewal, an Act was passed prohibiting any other bank
with more than six partners from enjoying the privilege of
issuing notes. In effect, by excluding large rivals, this gave the
Bank of England the monopoly of note-issue among joint-stock

banks. In its early years, therefore, the Bank of England was most unpopular, not only with the goldsmith bankers but also with Jacobite sympathisers who could see that the government, by increasing the number of its creditors, was also creating opposition to the restoration of the Stuarts. But through all the financial vicissitudes and disturbances of the early eighteenth century, especially that of the South Sea Bubble in 1720, the Bank of England remained intact, and as a result emerged with an enhanced reputation inspiring more people to subscribe to it.

4. WEAKNESSES OF THE EIGHTEENTH-CENTURY BANKING SYSTEM

The growing importance of industry and trade outside London throughout the eighteenth century and the difficulty of communications with London led to the establishment of the ' Country Banks '. In this the merchants themselves, often brewers or weavers, were largely predominant, though the banking activity was at first merely a sideline. Many carried out the same functions (the acceptance of deposits, the lending of money and the issue of bank-notes) as the goldsmiths and the more recently formed London specialist bankers, the private bankers. It is estimated that, whereas in 1750 there were not more than a dozen banks outside London, by the end of the century there were close on 400 in the Provinces and 68 in London, the vast majority, since they had no more than six partners, enjoying the right of issuing their own notes.

Nevertheless the structure of the banking system at the end of the eighteenth century was unstable. The history of the period 1775–1825 records a succession of bank failures. In both 1793 and 1797 'runs' on the banks produced many failures, and even the Bank of England's reserves were running low, owing largely to government borrowing in order to finance the war. In 1797, therefore, a Bank Restriction Act had to be passed, suspending cash payments in exchange for notes, and it was not until 1821 that cash payments were resumed. Again, the fall in land values at the end of hostilities in 1815 ruined many farmers, and they were unable to repay the extravagant mortgages which they had borrowed from the banks. The result was that many banks had to close their doors. Lastly, the fall in prices in 1825 brought about the failure of as many as sixty-three country banks.

It was little wonder then that there were frequent demands for a reform of the banking system. The banks as a whole were too adventurous and too small. The size of the earnings of the private banks depended almost entirely on their lending capacity, which in its turn was dependent on the note issue. It was a great temptation, therefore, for the private bankers to increase their note issue and, while many of them showed great restraint and financial wisdom in maintaining an adequate reserve, some cut it too fine. In addition many had not learnt the first principle of banking—not to borrow money for a short period and lend it for a long period. Some critics wanted to see the right of note-issue vested solely in the Bank of England, though others argued that this was not necessary so long as all notes issued were backed by an equivalent in gold and silver. The main weakness, however, arose from the fact that the restriction of the right to issue notes encouraged *small* bankers to set up. Many of these had little or no experience and few had adequate reserves. The result was that, when even a minor or local set-back in trade or industry occurred, they were unable to meet their obligations.

5. THE REFORM OF THE BANKING SYSTEM

The first step, therefore, in the reform of the banking system occurred in 1826 with the removal of the ban on the issue of notes by banks with more than six partners, provided that they had no office within sixty-five miles of London. The same Act, however, qualified this advantage to the private banks by permitting the Bank of England to open country branches in direct competition. This was bitterly opposed by the country banks but nevertheless branches were opened in such towns as Birmingham, Bristol, Hull, Leeds, Liverpool, Manchester, Newcastle and Plymouth. Soon, however, the joint-stock banks claimed the right to open even in London provided they did not issue notes. This claim was opposed by the Bank of England but it was nevertheless sanctioned by statute in 1833. Joint-stock banks, without the right to issue notes, could now be established in London. The first to be set up was the London and Westminster in 1834, and others followed. It represents the beginning of the present-day method of banking, for until then, banks had considered that the issue of notes was an inseparable part of a bank's business. Through the issue of bank-notes, their lending business had been considerably extended, for they were able to 'create' deposits, since depositors used these bank-notes, rather than their actual deposits, to settle debts. The joint-stock banks in London could not use this method of creating money. Moreover, in 1844, the Bank Charter Act still further tightened up on the issue of notes. It said that no more banks were to acquire the right of issuing notes and that if a note-issuing bank stopped payment, or became a joint-stock bank, or amalgamated with another, it would automatically lose its right to issue notes. But for one important development, therefore, the business of the larger banks would have been restricted almost entirely to the mere task of safeguarding deposits and paying them over when required. The development which saved the situation was the 'cheque'.

6. THE ORIGIN AND DEVELOPMENT OF THE 'CHEQUE' SYSTEM

Even by the end of the seventeenth century, customers of banks were beginning to settle debts by writing letters to the bank (the 'drawee'), instructing it to pay money to the person stated (the 'payee'), at the same time debiting the account of the person paying (the 'drawer'). Such a method of settling debts was very convenient to the customer for it saved him carrying around large sums of money and also permitted him to write his instructions for any odd amount. Above all, to the banker it possessed the inestimable advantage that, if the payee were also one of his customers, it would be more than likely that, instead of actually withdrawing the sum authorised, he would merely pay the cheque into his own account. When this took place the deposits held by the bank would not be touched and the transaction could be recorded by a mere book entry. Consequently, when the right of the large London banks to issue notes was withdrawn in 1708, such banks encouraged the development of this cheque system as the way out of their difficulty. From about the middle of the eighteenth century they even issued cheque books to their customers, printing in these books as much as possible of the instructions.

The system was more complicated, however, when the drawer and the payee were customers of different banks. The payee would pay the cheque into his own bank, which would credit his account and then, in order to receive reimbursement, present it for payment with other similar cheques to the drawee (the bank on whom it was drawn). Such a procedure necessitated each bank's holding large amounts of ready money, while clerks had to be employed on the often dangerous task of going round from bank to bank collecting the sums due. In time these clerks hit on the idea of meeting at a suitable coffee-house in order to set off one cheque against another and then pay over only the balance due. The idea was taken up by their employers, the banks, and in 1773 a Clearing House was set up in Lombard Street to carry out the same function. The result was a great saving by the banks in the amount of cash actually used in the settlement of debts. All the cash deposits could now be used as the reserve or 'call' money, and money could again be 'created', not now by the issue of bank-notes, but by the grant of a loan to the borrower. This was done simply by giving him a deposit, that is a credit, in his account, and allowing him to draw on this credit by the usual practice of writing cheques. Later, as each of the member banks of the Clearing House adopted the custom of keeping their accounts and deposits at the Bank of England, it was possible for the daily settlement to be made by a simple book adjustment of their accounts at the Bank of England.

The cheque system developed rapidly during the nineteenth century as one bank after another lost its right to issue notes. The joint-stock banks now came into their own and in 1858 the privilege of limited liability was extended to them. From then onwards there was a steady process of amalgamation and the banking system became centred in London. Today this system is almost synonymous with the 'Big Four' deposit joint-stock banks (Barclays, Midland, Lloyds and the National Westminster), with the Bank of England at the centre.

VI. THE COMMERCIAL BANKS

By far the largest part of the business of the commercial banks today is carried on by the 'Big Four' referred to above. Thus, unlike the systems of other countries, such as the U.S.A., which are composed of a large number of unitary small banks, the United Kingdom has developed a system where there are a few large banks each having a network of branches throughout the country.

This system of branch banking has two main merits. The first is that the larger unit of operation can enjoy the advantages of large-scale production. The second, and more important, is that there is less risk of failure when financial reserves are concentrated in a large bank than where the banking activities for a particular locality are conducted by a small bank. The fortunes of the small bank are tied up with the fortunes of the locality which, especially if the main activity is farming, may be liable to periodic fluctuations. In short, with a large bank, risks are spread geographically. On the other hand, the large unit has to suffer disadvantages on the managerial side, for usually loans of any size have to be sanctioned by Head Office. This is in sharp contrast to the position of the small unit which can grant even large loans on the spot according to its own judgment, based on its knowledge of local conditions.

The capital of the four main banks has been raised on the joint-stock principle. Shares have been bought and the shareholders expect their investment to yield an adequate return. Unlike the Bank of England, therefore, which views its operations in the light of the effect which they will have on the economic system as a whole, the commercial banks exist in order to make a profit. Broadly speaking this profit is earned by borrowing money from persons who are willing to lend it in return for a rate of interest or merely for the convenience of a banking account, and then relending it at a higher rate. In addition, banks carry out many comparatively minor tasks for the benefit of their customers. For some of these, a charge is levied, though many are performed gratuitously with the idea of facilitating the process of borrowing cash.

1. Borrowing

The bank borrows its money from people who have cash surplus to their immediate requirements or who want to retain their money in a safe place. Such cash can be left with the bank on a 'current', 'deposit' or 'savings' account.

To open a current account one has to become a customer of the bank, i.e. a person who has an account in the books of the bank. Before the bank will accept a person as a customer, it requires evidence of his integrity. This is obtained by means of references supplied by two satisfactory persons, preferably persons who themselves are customers of the bank. Money kept in a 'current' account can be withdrawn by the owner on demand, that is, without giving prior notice to the bank. Since it is only on this account that the customer can write cheques, he usually retains in it a sum of money which he considers is sufficient to cover his day-to-day payments plus a surplus for any transaction he expects to make in the immediate future. But, since no interest is received on any sums of money kept in a current account, that money has a 'convenience' return only. Consequently, cash surplus to immediate needs is usually kept in the 'deposit' account, where it earns interest, usually at 2 per cent below the bank's declared 'base rate'. For a variety of reasons large sums of money are kept by persons in deposit accounts. Very often their owners do not wish to undertake the risk, expense or trouble of buying securities. Above all, the money in a deposit account can be recovered fairly quickly, for the bank does not require more than seven days' notice of withdrawal, and even this stipulation may be waived in times of urgency, an appropriate deduction of interest being made.

In order to encourage the small saver, most banks also run Savings Accounts, performing work which is, in principle, very similar to that of the National Savings Bank and the Trustee Savings Banks. A Savings Account may be opened without giving references because, since cheques cannot be drawn on it, the risk from this source is non-existent. Money, cheques, postal orders, etc., may be paid into this account and sums thus deposited earn interest.

Apart from the money saved, the Savings Account is useful

to the customer in that small sums can be withdrawn on demand at any branch of the bank upon the production and signing of the appropriate pass-book.

2. LENDING

Money borrowed in the ways outlined above is lent out at a higher rate of interest, the actual rate depending on the length of time for which it is lent and the bank's estimate of the risk involved. As we have already shown, because most business transactions are now settled by cheque, the actual cash withdrawn from the bank in the course of a day is only a fraction (say, one-tenth) of the value of the money deposited at the bank. The result is that the bank can 'create' money by placing a 'book-entry deposit' in the accounts of persons asking for a loan, for the bank knows that, so long as it keeps a reserve of cash to deposits in the ratio of approximately $1:10$, it will be able to meet all its depositors' normal demands for cash. Thus the whole of the actual cash deposits of lenders can be converted into the essential cash reserve. In this way, for example, a cash deposit by a lender of £100 can be made to serve as the cash reserve for deposits of £1,000, which are brought into being by the simple process of making a book entry crediting the additional sum of £900 to the account of a person asking for an advance of that amount. In fact, not only are advances made by the creation of money in this way, but the method is also used to purchase commercial and Treasury Bills and government securities. Nevertheless, by this 'creation' of money, the bank is taking the risk that, if there is a very heavy demand for the withdrawal of money deposited, it will be unable to meet its obligations. On the other hand, the more money it creates, the further it can extend its business and the larger will be its profits. It is thus torn between the two conflicting aims of enjoying security by having liquid reserves and the making of immediate profit by the expansion of its lending activities. In practice the bank solves the problem in three ways. First, it satisfies itself that it has adequate security for the loan; secondly, it lends for comparatively short periods, generally not exceeding six months; and thirdly, it chooses different types of borrowers and carefully apportions its loans between each to ensure that such loans are for varying periods.

We can best understand a bank's method of working by discussing in more detail the composition of its main assets. For the whole of the London Clearing Banks on Oct. 16, 1974, these were, in order of liquidity:

		Per cent
1. Cash in hand or at the Bank of England		4·4
2. Money at call and short notice	. .	5·0
3. Bills discounted:		
Treasury bills	. . . .	1·3
Other (commercial) bills	. .	3·3
4. Investments	. . . . .	6·5
5. Advances	. . . . .	74·1
6. Certificates of Deposit	. . .	2·8
7. Special Deposits	. . . .	2·5
		100

1. Cash in hand or at the Bank of England

As we have already seen, it is necessary for the bank to retain some cash reserve in order to meet the normal cash requirements of customers together with a surplus for unexpected demands. Usually about half this cash is in its tills, and half at the Bank of England.

2. Money at call and short notice

The lending of money at call (from day to day) and at short notice (up to fourteen days) to the Discount Houses has already been described. The rate of interest charged on these loans varies according to the class of the bill on which they are secured.

3. Bills discounted

As already explained, banks obtain bills from the Discount Houses. These they hold for about two months, arranging their purchases so that each day a certain quantity reaches maturity. At present (February, 1974), the banks earn about 11 per cent on Treasury Bills and 11½ per cent on commercial bills.

4. *Investments*

The investments held by the banks are chiefly long-term British government securities. Their market value on the Stock Exchange fluctuates. 'Gilt-edged' securities may be redeemable many years ahead and even not at all. Thus they are liquid only in the sense that they can be sold freely on the Stock Exchange. An enforced sale, however, would probably involve the bank in a loss.

5. *Advances to customers*

The bank makes advances to the nationalised industries, companies and personal borrowers, charging rates of interest which vary between 2 and 3 per cent above base rate.

Advances are made either by granting a loan or by authorising an overdraft on the current account. With the former method, a loan account is opened in the customer's name and then debited with the amount of the advance, while his current account is credited with the same amount, thus allowing him to draw upon it for his needs. Interest is paid on the whole amount of the loan from the moment it is granted whether it is withdrawn or not. The method is chiefly used, therefore, where a person requires money for a definite purpose, such as for improving a house. If the overdraft method is used, the customer can overdraw his current account to a sum agreed upon by his bank manager, and interest is only paid on the actual amount overdrawn from day to day. This has a great advantage to such persons as traders, farmers and private individuals, who both withdraw and pay in money over a period.

The main object of bank advances is to provide the working capital for industry and commerce. The type of loan preferred is 'self-liquidating' within a period of about six months. A good example of such a loan is one made to a farmer, who borrows at the beginning of the year in order to buy seed, fertilisers and pay wages, and repays the loan when the harvest has been sold. Similarly, a manufacturer may borrow to employ additional labour and raw materials just prior to Christmas in order to increase production. When he receives payment for those goods some time later, the cheque will be paid into his account, thereby enabling him to repay the overdraft.

When making an advance, the bank normally insists on adequate security and for this they will accept insurance policies, government bonds, the deeds of a house, share certificates and the fixed property or stock of a firm. All the same, the bank will not generally grant a loan unless it can see quite clearly beforehand the virtual certainty that the actual money will be coming back. It therefore satisfies itself regarding the integrity and business ability of the borrower, the purpose and time of the loan, and the likely success of the venture for which it is required.

In addition to the above, banks may make 'personal loans' up to £500 without security. These cover the cost of such things as house repairs, domestic equipment, furniture, motor cars, unexpected illness, or the initial expense of fitting out a child for school. The loan is repaid by instalments spread over any period up to 24 months, but the true rate of interest charged is somewhat higher than the normal rate on advances.

Generally banks have refrained from providing long-term capital for firms, leaving this to the agencies in the Capital Market. In recent years, however, they have engaged in financing some long-term capital projects, such as the building of additional factory accommodation. These fixed assets are the security required, although the banks base their lending on their judgment as to whether or not the venture is likely to be successful. It must be noted, however, that although the loans are of a long-term nature, they are generally granted subject to review every twelve months, thereby stressing the fact that bank lending is still essentially for short periods only. Moreover, today, banks are expected to heed the wishes of the government as to the amount of credit they grant, and in the last few years they have often been under pressure to restrict advances, discriminating against loans which are not for essential purposes.

6. Certificates of Deposit

Banks cash and hold until maturity other banks' certificates of deposit.

7. *Special Deposits*

These are the deposits which the commercial banks may be required to deposit with the Bank of England when it is desired to reduce bank lending (see page 420). They earn interest at the current Treasury Bill rate.

In concluding this survey of a bank's assets, it must again be emphasised that the vast majority of such assets are acquired by the 'creation' of deposits. Thus, if it buys a new government security, a bank deposit is merely placed at the disposal of the government; if it is an old government security which is bought, so the person who sells it is credited with a deposit; when it makes an advance to a customer, the bank does so by placing a deposit at his disposal. Hence the 'money' or deposits in a bank represent a liability of the bank to a customer against which the bank holds various assets; assets always equal liabilities.

3. SPECIAL SERVICES TO CUSTOMERS

The main work of a bank is the borrowing and lending of money. In conjunction with this, however, the bank renders customers special services, the most important of which are:

1. *Keeps customers' accounts*

The cheque system benefits both the bank and the customer. Its advantage to the former is that it reduces the use of cash and therefore permits the expansion of business by the creation of deposits; its advantage to the latter is that, compared with cash, it is a much more convenient and safe method for settling debts. Because the bank in the course of its business is receiving and paying out money on behalf of customers, it is necessary for it to keep their accounts, and a statement is forwarded to the customer at regular intervals or whenever he requires it. As a part of this service, whenever a customer has to furnish evidence of his financial standing, the bank will provide a reference.

2. *Receives dividends and interest*

Dividends on shares and interest on stock can be paid directly into the banking account of the owner and the bank will make the necessary credit adjustment. In fact, since the Exchange Control Act, 1947, all bearer securities must be lodged with a bank to prevent individuals from taking and selling them abroad. When they are sold to another person, the bank delivers them direct to the purchaser's bank. The coupons on these bearer securities are submitted by the bank for the interest as it falls due, the amount being credited to the owner's account.

3. *Standing Order payments*

Where regular periodical payments are necessary, as, for example, mortgage repayments to building societies, insurance premiums, ground rents and club subscriptions, the customer can authorise his bank to make them. It is obvious that such payments by the bank save the customer much trouble in remembering when the payments are due and the recipient much correspondence and postage in sending out reminder notices.

4. *Negotiation of investments for customers*

The bank will arrange, through its brokers, for the purchase and sale of investments on behalf of customers. Before purchasing, the customer can obtain through his bank the expert advice of a broker on the securities he favours, but the customer makes the actual selection of the security bought. Savings Certificates and British Savings Bonds will also be purchased by the bank at the customer's request.

5. *Credit transfers*

Where a business has a number of creditors or employees to pay monthly, it can avoid the cost and trouble of writing out separate cheques for each by making use of a credit transfer. Having first ascertained the bank of the creditor and obtained his permission, the firm making the payment prepares a credit transfer form, which instructs his bank to credit the bank of the creditor with the amount stated. Thus the firm has to draw, in favour of its own bank, only one cheque, covering the total of all the payments. The private customer can also settle a number of bills by means of a single credit transfer.

6. *Banker's drafts*

Sometimes cheques are not acceptable in payment of a debt, particularly where the debtor is not known to the payee. A solicitor, for instance, would not hand over the title-deeds of a house against the cheque of a purchaser who was unknown to him. In this case the customer can surmount the difficulty by seeing his bank and writing a cheque in its favour, when the bank will issue a draft, drawn on itself, made payable to the payee. The latter will accept such a draft because it is in effect the cheque of a bank and therefore secure.

7. *Credit facilities*

Where a customer is going away on holiday or business and does not wish to carry a lot of cash with him, he can open a credit account at any branch of his own or other banks. Alternatively, he can become a holder of a credit card such as Access (from e.g. National Westminster) or Barclaycard.

8. *Travellers' cheques*

Where a person is touring or going abroad, travellers' cheques are a convenient method of carrying money. They are bought in units of varying denominations and represent guaranteed cheques of the bank made out in favour of the customer and cashable at any branch of the bank or its agencies either at home or abroad in those countries specified on the back of the cheque. The cheques are signed by the customer when he receives them from the bank and again when he presents them for payment, and the cashier compares the signatures to see that they are the same.

9. *Foreign work*

Banks are a great help to customers having foreign connections. They will 'accept' bills of exchange and, on certain occasions, discount them. They will also obtain and exchange foreign currency.

10. *Safe custody*

The banks have to maintain strong-rooms in which to store their reserves and, subject to there being sufficient space, customers are allowed, free of charge, to make use of these strong-rooms to deposit such valuables as title-deeds to property, life policies, securities, wills, trust deeds, etc. Other valuables, such as jewellery and plate, will be stored if placed in a container.

The banks provide another form of safe custody in the Night Safe. When a person receives money or valuables after the bank has closed, and does not want to keep them in his own safe or take them home, he can put them in a wallet, of which he has the key, and drop the wallet in the night safe of his bank. In the morning either he or the bank will open the wallet and pay the money into his account. It is obvious that this service is of special value to shopkeepers.

11. *Executor and Trustee Department*

A person may appoint his bank to be the sole or joint executor for carrying out the terms of his will. This relieves relatives and friends of much work and has the advantage, besides that of efficiency and the availability of expert knowledge, of having an executor with a continuous existence. Thus there is no possibility of the executor's dying before the person making the will, with its accompanying confusion.

The bank will also act as a trustee under settlements, trusts, and deeds of covenant.

12. *Income Tax Department*

The bank will act as an agent for the preparation of income tax returns, seeing that the customer's case is presented correctly.

Thus it can be seen that in the course of their work, the banks perform many functions valuable not only to their customers but to the community at large. People who have cash surplus to their requirements can, because the bank lends it out to persons who wish to borrow, obtain a return on the money. In this way much of the working capital is supplied to industry and commerce. The banks also supply cash for the day-to-day working of the community and this often means moving it from the place where it is paid in (e.g. the shopping centre of a town) to the place where it is paid out (the industrial area of the town). Lastly, the government makes great use of the banks as agents for the implementation of policy, relying on them, as the occasion demands, to put into effect regulations controlling the exchange of foreign currency or requests to grant credit freely only to certain types of borrower, e.g. exporters.

VII. THE BANK OF ENGLAND

1. Its Development as a Central Bank

The Bank of England, established by Act of Parliament in 1694, remained a joint-stock company until nationalisation in 1946. The whole of its capital stock is now owned by the State and its affairs are regulated by a Court of Directors, consisting of a Governor, a Deputy-Governor and sixteen Directors appointed by the Crown, though not more than four of the Directors can be full-time officers. The members of the Court are distinguished men in financial, industrial and commercial affairs, and it is usual for the full-time members to be professional bankers with experience of work in the Bank of England.

Nationalisation in itself, however, made little difference to the actual practice of the Bank. Although it started as a private enterprise, it had always been closely in touch with the government of the day. From its very beginning it was a principal lender to the government and in the middle of the eighteenth century it took over the actual management of the National Debt. The government, in its turn, let it be known by various actions that it had set the Bank in a privileged position. Thus, throughout the eighteenth century, the Bank enjoyed a monopoly of joint-stock banking, while, by the Bank Restriction Act of 1797, the government protected the Bank's gold reserve in a moment of acute financial crisis. The position of privilege was carried one step further in 1833 when Bank of England notes were made legal tender, but the most important step was taken in 1844 when, by the Bank Charter Act, the note issue was vested, for all practical purposes, exclusively in the hands of the Bank of England.

This association between the government and the Bank became even closer during the century and it was generally recognised that the Bank could always be relied upon to pursue that course which was considered to be in the best interests of the country, although that course might not be in its own interests from the point of view of making profits. In practice the Bank took those measures calculated to forward the monetary policy of the government of the day, though, of course, this policy varied from time to time, according both to circumstances and the political party in power. Whilst the United Kingdom was on the gold standard, the Bank of England, by regulating the Bank Rate and by open market operations (see later), could reinforce the automatic action of that system. After the United Kingdom left the gold standard in 1931, management of the monetary system became even more important, and this was achieved by close consultation between Treasury officials and the Court of the Bank. In short, the Bank of England had ceased to be a mere profit-making concern. Instead it had developed into a Central Bank—the bank which is responsible for regulating the credit structure of a country in accordance with government policy.

The discussion of the functions of the Bank of England (which follows) will clarify and enlarge on its position as the Central Bank of the British monetary system.

2. Its Functions

1. *It issues notes*

The effect of the Bank Charter Act, 1844, was to consolidate the note issue in the hands of the Bank of England. Today, except for a few Scottish and Northern Ireland banks who enjoy a limited right to issue notes, the Bank of England has a complete monopoly. The object of the Bank Charter Act was to prevent the over-issue of notes, and so it laid down that notes could be issued only against the gold held by the Bank, except for £14,000,000 of notes which could be issued against securities. This latter issue, known as the Fiduciary Issue, was subsequently increased from time to time. When in 1939 the gold reserves of the Bank were transferred to the Exchange Equalisation Account under Treasury control, the £300 million fiduciary issue ceased to be relevant, for no notes could be issued against that gold. Hence the fiduciary issue is now secured against Treasury Bills. Today (November, 1974) it stands at just over £5,000 million. Indeed, the current practice is for the note issue to be increased whenever the country's cash demand requires it, e.g. at Christmas and holiday time.

2. *It acts as banker to the government*

The banking business of the government is transacted by the Bank of England. All government revenue is paid into the Exchequer Account (also known as the Consolidated Fund) kept there, and expenditure, after the necessary authorisation by the Comptroller and Auditor General has been given, is also made out of this Account. The Bank also keeps the accounts of the separate government departments.

In the same way, however, as a joint-stock bank performs ancillary services for its customers, so the Bank of England does the same for the government. Such services include:

(*a*) *Management of the National Debt.* By the middle of the eighteenth century the government's debt to the bank had increased from the original sum of £1,200,000 to nearly £12,000,000. At the same time the National Debt stood at £72,000,000, and when, in 1752, Pelham decided to convert this National Debt in stages from 4 to 3 per cent by the issue of Consolidated stock ('Consols'), the task was entrusted to the Bank of England. Since that date, the Bank has managed the whole of the National Debt except that controlled by the National Savings Bank. It arranges new issues and conversions, records transfers and pays the interest on the stock to the holders as it falls due. As regards short-term borrowing, the Bank sells Treasury Bills on the instructions of the Treasury.

(*b*) *Cash assistance, by means of 'Ways and Means' advances if the Exchequer Account goes temporarily 'into the red'.*

(*c*) *Adviser to the government on general financial matters.* Besides advising in foreign exchange policy, the Bank also gives the government advice on the likely economic effects of its financial policy. In this matter, however, it must be noted that the

Treasury has the last word and is responsible to Parliament for whatever decision is arrived at.

3. *It acts as banker to the joint-stock banks*

The next most important customers of the Bank of England are the joint-stock banks. The London clearing banks hold about half their cash reserve at the Bank of England, and they use the Bank very much as a private customer uses his bank. In particular, they:

(*a*) draw notes and coin from their balances at the Bank as required;

(*b*) set off the net payment which has to be made to other banks as a result of the day's clearing by drawing on the balance held at the Bank of England;

(*c*) take advice on financial matters from the Bank.

4. *It manages the Exchange Equalisation Account*

The Exchange Equalisation Account was set up in 1932 in order to smooth out temporary fluctuations in the value of sterling in terms of other currencies, which arose through the inflow or outflow of short-term speculative foreign capital (known as 'hot money'). The initial capital of the Account was provided by Treasury Bills, but in September, 1939 the whole of the gold and foreign exchange resources of the country were concentrated in the Account and have remained there ever since.

Prior to 1939, the Account operated as follows. Suppose there were a movement of capital from New York to London. This would increase the demand for sterling and the value of sterling would rise above the desired level. Hence the Account entered the market by selling pounds (obtained through the sale of its Treasury Bills) in exchange for gold and foreign currencies. Later, when the price of the pound tended to move downwards, the Account would sell its accumulated gold and foreign currencies for sterling, which was reinvested in Treasury Bills until required again.

Today, in order to maintain some stability in the sterling

rate of exchange, the task of the Account is to buy or sell sterling as demand and supply vary in the foreign exchange market.

5. *It protects the gold and dollar reserves*
   (a) It determines the 'minimum lending rate' (see p. 420).
   (b) It administers foreign exchange control. Under the Exchange Control Act, 1947, the Treasury can control payments out of sterling into other currencies. The administration of this control rests with the Bank of England. The task is performed chiefly by issuing regulations to the joint-stock banks. Thus a bank is restricted in the amount of sterling it can exchange for foreign currency on behalf of a customer.
   (c) It arranges loans from other central banks to strengthen the United Kingdom's reserves.

6. *It has financial responsibilities internationally*
   (a) The Bank of England maintains close contact with the central banks and monetary authorities of other countries, chiefly with the aim of bringing greater stability to international monetary affairs.
   (b) It provides banking services for the central banks of non-sterling countries, e.g. holds and manages their holdings of sterling.
   (c) It participates in the work of certain international financial institutions, such as the Bank for International Settlements, the International Monetary Fund, the International Bank for Reconstruction and Development, the European Monetary Agreement.

7. *It manages the monetary system of the country in accordance with government policy*
   It is fundamental to recognise the position of the Bank of England as the Central Bank of the monetary system of the United Kingdom. Thus, although it performs the other and varied functions already mentioned, its most important function is that of controlling the commercial banks in such a way as to

implement the monetary policy decided upon by the government.

Where people (entrepreneurs and private persons) can obtain credit on relatively easy terms, the demand for goods (both producer and consumer goods) will normally increase. If there is unemployment, this is a good thing, for the economy will expand and idle resources be put to work. If there is already full employment, the supply of goods cannot be expanded, and prices rise.

The Bank of England, therefore, has frequently to adjust the cost and supply of credit to the prevailing economic situation. This it does by the following methods:

(i) *The minimum reserve assets ratio*

The foundation of the policy by which the supply of credit is controlled rests in the ability of the Bank of England to dictate to the banks and other lending institutions the minimum liquidity ratio which they shall maintain.

Each bank is required to observe a minimum reserve ratio (at present $12\frac{1}{2}$ per cent) of 'eligible reserve assets' to 'eligible liabilities'.

'Eligible reserve assets' comprise:
  (a) balances with the Bank of England, other than special deposits;
  (b) Treasury Bills;
  (c) company tax reserve certificates;
  (d) money at call with the London money market;
  (e) local authority bills eligible for re-discount at the Bank of England;
  (f) commercial bills eligible for re-discount at the Bank of England (up to a maximum of 2 per cent of eligible liabilities);
  (g) British government securities with one year or less to go to reach final maturity.

'Eligible liabilities' refer broadly to net bank deposits (excluding foreign currency deposits and deposits having an original maturity of over two years).

(ii) *Open market operations*

While the minimum reserve assets ratio provides the base for monetary policy, marginal adjustments to the money supply can be made by 'open market operations'.

This works on the basis that any reduction in the eligible reserve assets held by the banks will, with a liquidity ratio of $12\frac{1}{2}$ per cent, cause a reduction of total deposits by eight times, and vice versa. A weapon of monetary policy which can therefore be used is to vary the banks' holding of liquid assets.

This the Bank of England achieves by buying or selling government securities in the open market. Suppose, for instance, it sells long-term securities. The increase in the supply offered lowers their price until the total offering has been bought by the banks or by their customers. But cash will be necessary to pay for them, and so the banks' cash balance at the Bank of England falls. In other words, the liquid reserve assets held by the banks are reduced and, if previously they were fully lent, they will be forced to squeeze their advances.

Or the Bank of England may put the pressure on the short-term end of the market by varying the size of the Treasury Bill offer at the weekly tender. Inasmuch as these bills are bought initially outside the banks, the cash balances of the bank's customers are likely to fall and hence, also, the cash of the banks.

(iii) *Funding*

A deliberate policy of converting government short-term debt into long-term debt is known as 'funding'. It is achieved by open market operations as described above over an extended period. What happens is that the Treasury Bill offer for tender is reduced, the government raising the finance it requires by selling medium and long-dated securities instead. This reduces the banks' supply of liquid assets.

(iv) *Special deposits*

More fundamental changes in the supply of credit can be effected through calls for 'special deposits'.

This policy originated in 1960. Banks are required to deposit with the Bank of England a given percentage of their total eligible liabilities. These special deposits do not count as part of their liquid assets, though they earn interest at the current Treasury Bill rate.

The weapon of 'special deposits' has certain advantages:

(a) The percentage of special deposits called for can be sufficiently high to make it difficult for the banks to maintain their 12½ per cent liquidity ratio.

(b) When the banks are put on a tight rein in this way, marginal adjustments by way of open market operations and funding become more effective.

(c) The reduction in the banks' liquidity is achieved without the dislocation of large scale funding operations.

(d) The banks cannot afford to sell investments provided the Bank of England stays out of the market. The impact of special deposits must then eventually result in the banks' having to reduce 'advances' to customers.

(v) *Requests*

The Bank of England may request the banks to limit their lending generally or simply to restrict loans to certain types of borower, e.g. exporters, and deny them to others, e.g. property developers. In the past, the banks have always heeded these requests. But they have not liked them, for often it may mean refusing excellent credit-worthy borrowers who have turned to, and found funds from, other competing institutions, such as merchant banks and finance companies.

(vi) *Directives*

By section 4(3) of the Bank of England Act, 1946, the Bank of England can, if so authorised by the Treasury, issue directions to any banker for the purpose of ensuring that effect is given to its requests and recommendations. So far this power has not had to be used, the banks preferring to heed the requests of the Bank of England, rather than being forced into obeying them.

(vii) *Minimum lending rate*

The policy connected with 'minimum lending rate' (which replaced the old Bank Rate in 1972) springs directly from the fact that the Bank of England is 'a lender of last resort'. When the commercial banks are hard pressed for cash, they call in their loans to the Discount Houses. The Discount Houses have, however, used this money in discounting bills for merchants and could not therefore fulfil their obligations to the banks. Without assistance, the banks would be unable to repay their creditors, especially as the number demanding the return of their money deposited with the banks would increase as the news of a possible failure spread. The Bank of England, backed by the government, is not prepared to stand by and watch the ruin and financial chaos which would result through this general loss of confidence in financial institutions. It does not lend direct to the banks but it comes to their aid indirectly by providing the Discount Market with cash. This it does by discounting for them the first-class bills of exchange which the Discount Houses hold or by lending money against such bills for a minimum of seven days. The rate of interest at which the Bank of England will lend is known as the 'minimum lending rate' and is above the discount rates ruling in the market. Consequently, when the Discount Houses have to resort to such borrowing, they are involved in losses. Hence the Discount Houses reduce the possibility and extent of such losses by discounting bills only slightly below the minimum lending rate.

Minimum lending rate is normally announced on a Friday at $\frac{1}{2}$ per cent above the average rate of discount for Treasury Bills. Movements in the rate are still regarded as indications of government intentions regarding the future movements of interest rates generally.

In practice, the Bank of England does not rely solely on one weapon when carrying out its monetary policy. Each is far more effective when used in conjunction with the others.

VIII. THE SECURITIES MARKET: THE STOCK EXCHANGE

1. ORIGIN

In the same way that organised *produce* markets were set up for buying and selling such commodities as wheat, tea, wool, and cotton, so an organised market was eventually established for buying and selling 'securities', that is, claims to loans or shares. This market is the Stock Exchange, and although there are exchanges in most of the larger cities of the United Kingdom, the London exchange is by far the most important and henceforth will be referred to as 'the Stock Exchange'. A glance at the financial page of any daily newspaper will reveal the nature of the securities dealt in. They consist chiefly of British Funds (Government stock and the stock of the nationalised industries), Dominion and Foreign Government stock, Corporation stock (issued by local authorities, such as the Greater London Council, or by public utility undertakings, such as the Metropolitan Water Board), and the stocks and shares of all types of industrial and commercial companies.

It was not until the second half of the seventeenth century that a recognisable stock market began to function, although joint-stock companies had existed for a hundred years, the first in England being the Russia Company, 1553. The stock of these companies was dealt in on this early market, and additional dealings took place in government-sponsored lottery tickets, in seamen's pay tickets and, above all, in loans contracted by Charles II and James II from the goldsmiths. A large part of the money borrowed by them was never repaid and this formed the nucleus of the National Debt of £644,000, officially recognised in 1688 when it was incorporated by William III. Since that date the National Debt has, despite variations in its importance, largely been the mainstay of the Stock Exchange.

The early Stock Exchange had no settled premises or formal organisation. The business was at first conducted in the old Royal Exchange, but owing to pressure from the other merchants who found the stock brokers too noisy, the business was moved, chiefly to 'Change Alley', where it was conducted in the open street and in the various coffee-houses there, particularly Jonathan's Coffee House. Dealings in British Government securities, however, continued to be conducted in the Rotunda of the Bank of England and dealings in foreign stocks in the Royal Exchange.

The first settled premises were established in 1773 and, over the door, were inscribed the words 'The Stock Exchange', showing that it was now a formal institution. The present site in Capel Court was occupied in 1801, and in 1803 the first Official List of prices, which is today still issued by the Stock Exchange, appeared.

2. MEMBERSHIP

The Stock Exchange is privately owned and the 'proprietors' are the members who between them hold the shares which originally provided the capital necessary to purchase freehold the site on which the Stock Exchange stands and to erect the buildings and later extensions. Today the affairs of the Stock Exchange are controlled by an elected Council, consisting of forty-six members.

To be accepted as a member, a person must have experience, an unblemished financial reputation, and considerable capital. Any prospective member must serve at least two years on the floor of the House or in a broker's or jobber's office, and pass an examination. After gaining his experience and if he still wishes to take up membership, it is necessary to pay £1,000 into a 'Nomination Redemption Fund', pay an entrance fee, and make an annual subscription. In addition two members of the House have to give an assurance of his good character.

Members are either 'brokers' or 'jobbers', but they are not allowed to act in both capacities at the same time.

The *stock broker* acts as the agent for the public, receiving and executing business according to the instructions of his clients and giving them advice regarding their investments. He earns a living by drawing commission on the business he transacts but he is not allowed to advertise. In effect, he acts as the link between the investing public, who wish to buy and sell securities, and the *jobber*, the actual dealer and 'wholesaler' who buys and carries a stock of securities in order to resell them later. The difference between broker and jobber may best be shown by an example.

Mr. A, any member of the public, wishes to buy 200 25p ordinary shares in Unilever Limited. He therefore phones or writes to his broker (or to his bank manager who will contact the broker who acts for the bank), giving him the necessary instructions. He will either name the maximum price at which he will buy or instruct the broker to buy at the lowest price possible. The broker will then leave his office and go to the 'House' in order to carry out these and other instructions which he has received. He finds his way to that part of the 'House' occupied by the jobbers who specialise in the leading industrial ordinary shares. The broker approaches a jobber and inquires the price of Unilever Ordinaries, but he does not say whether he wishes to buy or sell. Suppose the jobber replies: 'Two-seventy-five,, two-eighty'. This indicates that he is prepared to buy at 275 pence and to sell at 280 pence. The difference between the two prices is known as the 'jobber's turn' and is the normal source of the jobber's profit, the size of spread depending on the jobber's estimate of the risk involved in dealing in that particular security. The broker can accept the price, try to get the jobber to lower his price or else move on to other jobbers in the hope of doing better. Let us suppose that he considers 280 pence satisfactory. He then informs the jobber that he wishes to buy 200 shares, the bargain is struck, and both broker and jobber make notes in their dealing books. The broker, having arranged the deal, sends to Mr. A, or to the bank acting for him, a contract note as follows. A transfer and contract stamp is affixed.

BOUGHT by order of: THE NATIONAL WESTMINSTER BANK LIMITED

On Account of:	Amount	Security	Price	Consideration	Transfer Stamp	Contract Stamp	Commission divisible with the Bank	Total
'A' Esq.	200	Unilever Co. Ltd. Ordy. £1 units	280p	£560.00	£12.00	30p	£8.40	£580.70

The transfer and contract stamp represents revenue charged on all transfer deeds (except British Government stocks). Commission charged by the broker is $1\frac{1}{2}$ per cent of the purchase price, except on small transactions when the rate works out a little higher. Transfer stamp is charged only on purchases. All bargains have to be settled on the next 'Account Day' which usually falls fortnightly on a Tuesday, though Government and Municipal stock is 'for cash', meaning that settlement is immediate.

3. ITS ECONOMIC FUNCTIONS

There is a widespread view that brokers and jobbers are merely parasites who have created a market in securities simply in order that they might make money by speculating at the expense of the public. Such a view, however, merely reveals ignorance of the real functions of the Stock Exchange. It is true that the facilities offered by the Stock Exchange do provide openings for speculation. The fortnight's grace allowed before settlement is made enables anyone who buys securities at the beginning of the period a fortnight in which to find the money to pay for them. Thus he can buy securities at the beginning of the 'Account', sell them again within fourteen days and take the profit (or loss), without ever having put up any money. A speculator who buys securities because he thinks the price will rise before settlement day is said to be a 'bull'. He is thus an optimist, buying shares, not because he wants to keep them, but because he hopes to sell them at a profit. On the other hand, a speculator who is a pessimist is known as a 'bear', and he sells securities he does not possess at the beginning of the Account period because he expects the price to fall before the time for settlement. If the price of these securities does fall, he will make a profit because he can buy them at the lower price. Sometimes, if a person's credit stands high with his broker or if he can put up security, he may be permitted to 'carry over' his commitments from one Stock Exchange Account to the next. Such a transaction is known as a 'contango'.

The difficulty concerning speculation is that both optimism and pessimism are contagious and the market becomes extremely susceptible both to panic and over-confidence. Indeed, the effect of the initial outlook, whether of optimism or pessimism, is to cause prices to take the very direction in which they were expected to go. For instance, persons who expect the price of securities to rise bid for those securities, *thereby* sending up their price. The result is that, particularly in the past, there have been numerous speculative booms and slumps, when stocks and shares were written up and down, not with any real change in the legitimate expectation of income from them, but with waves of confidence or mistrust which swept over the great financial centres of the world. Two such booms ended with the South Sea Bubble (1720) and the Wall Street Crash (1929). More recently the London Stock Exchange suffered a severe decline in 1974.

We must not forget that speculation may have certain advantages. Expert professional operators, such as the jobbers, tend to steady prices through their function of holding stocks. This also permits securities to be bought and sold at any time, thereby making securities more liquid. The great difficulty occurs in distinguishing harmful speculation from genuine investment, for with all investment there is a certain element of risk involved. In any case the magnitude of the speculative business must not be over-estimated. The majority of business represents genuine investment conducted on behalf of investment trusts, insurance companies, pension funds, building societies and private individuals. Indeed the latter often have to come to the market to sell securities in order to pay death duties.

The truth is that, for the following reasons, an organised market in securities is an indispensable part of the mechanism of a Capitalist economy where such property is privately owned.

1. *It provides the link between those citizens who wish to sell securities and those who wish to buy*

Organised markets, where persons who wish to sell are brought into touch with persons who wish to buy, exist for such commodities as cotton, wool, cocoa, rubber and tin. The Stock Exchange is a similar market, except that the commodity dealt is in securities. Not only does much of the money subscribed come from small investors in amounts of less than £500, but the ordinary man in the street has an interest in the Stock Exchange since insurance, pension and trade union funds are invested there.

2. It facilitates borrowing by the government and industry

Under Collectivism, the State decides how much to save and invest. Saving is 'forced' by some form of taxation, while investment is achieved by the direct allocation of men and machinery to specified capital projects—factories, hydro-electric plants, irrigation schemes, etc. Under Capitalism, however, decisions regarding saving and investment are left to private individuals. Some people, instead of keeping their assets in the form of money, will wish to lend it for a return to finance government borrowing or private enterprises. It must be pointed out, however, that, apart from the method of a 'placing' or 'introduction' through a firm of stockbrokers, the Stock Exchange does not find the money for new issues. This is the work of the 'Capital' or 'New Issues' Market described in Chapter 5.

But a person lending money is always interested in the terms on which he can 'regain liquidity', that is, get his cash back. (The government, for instance, is explicit on this point when borrowing by means of the National Savings Bank, for it emphasises the generous terms on which deposits can be withdrawn.) Similarly, if people are to be encouraged to lend to industry and the government by the purchase of securities, they must be satisfied that they will subsequently be able to sell easily those investments which they no longer wish to hold. Such an assurance is afforded to any holder of a fairly well-known security, for through the Stock Exchange, he can find a ready and immediate buyer.

Thus, indirectly the Stock Exchange encourages savers to lend to the government or to invest in industry and thereby performs a very valuable function. Indeed, if a new issue receives a Stock Exchange quotation, the chances of its success are considerably enhanced.

3. Through the jobbers, it helps to even out short-run price fluctuations in securities

Whilst the jobber himself may often speculate, in the short run he acts as a buffer to offset the effects on price of specula-tion by outsiders. This is because his job is not merely 'matching' a buyer with a seller but rather of acting as a

wholesaler and holding a stock of securities. Since he specialises
in dealing in certain securities, he obtains an intimate knowledge of them. Thus when the public is pessimistic and selling,
he may be more optimistic in his outlook and consider that the
drop in price is not likely to continue. He therefore takes these
securities on to his book. Similarly, when the public is rushing
to buy, he will, when he considers the price has reached its
zenith, sell from his stocks. The effect in both cases is to even
out the fluctuations in price, for in the first case, he increases
his demand as supply increases, and, in the second, he increases
supply as the demand increases.

4. *It advertises security prices*

The publication of current Stock Exchange prices enables
the public to follow the fortunes of their investment and to
make sensible decisions to buy or sell.

Indirectly, too, these prices assist industrial development to
be directed into the right channels. A rise in the price of the
shares of an industry, particularly a new industry, such as
photo-copiers, indicate rising profits or expectation of future
profits. This will enable existing firms to borrow easily and
therefore to expand, while other manufacturers will be directed
towards the industry. The increased production which
eventually results will be to the advantage of the public.

5. *It protects the public against fraud*

The Stock Exchange List of securities is a guarantee that
securities listed are honest and reputable. Permission to deal
is only given to members if the Council has no doubts on
this score, and it may be withdrawn if any doubts arise about
the conduct of a company's affairs. Moreover, the Council
insists on a high standard of professional conduct from its
members. Nevertheless, should any member default, the
investor is indemnified out of the Stock Exchange Compensation Fund.

6. *It acts as a 'barometer' of the economic prosperity of the country*

Future changes in the level of economic activity are fore-
shadowed by general movements in the prices of securities.
The impact of political events on the economy is also often
indicated in this way.

PART VII

GOVERNMENT FINANCE

CHAPTER 22

GOVERNMENT FINANCE

I. GOVERNMENT EXPENDITURE

In Chapter 2 we noted the various reasons why the government of the United Kingdom interferes in the economy of the country. Broadly speaking, such intervention is necessary in order to offset the disadvantages which are inherent in a pure Capitalist economy. Many of the spheres in which control is exercised, and the various means by which the desired ends are achieved, have already been considered. Thus we have discussed: rent control, instituted when abnormal conditions make the free operation of the price system undesirable; the nationalisation of certain industries, carried out when it is thought that such industries are better operated by the government than by private enterprise; the control of factory location in order to mitigate the disadvantages which arise from the concentration of industry; the regulation of the international trade of the United Kingdom so that, while the advantages of the international division of labour are secured, British nationals receive, over a period, as large a quantity of imports as possible in exchange for a given quantity of exports. Nevertheless, although the spheres of government control are many, the same general reason applies to each—that intervention is necessary because it is considered that the free operation of the price system under Capitalism fails to secure the most desirable results.

Similarly, the Capitalist system may also break down because the free operation of the price system fails to provide certain essential services for the people as a whole. What services are to be regarded as 'essential' is really a matter of personal opinion and therefore, since there is no objective test, the decision is eventually a political one. The *laissez-faire* economists of the later eighteenth century considered that a country could achieve its greatest prosperity by having as little intervention by the State as possible. Thus Quesnay, the French economist of the period, lays it down as a maxim that 'the surest guardian of internal and external commerce, the most exact and the most profitable to the Nation and the State, lies in the unlimited freedom of competition'. Nevertheless these economists recognised that the security of the nation from outside attack and the maintenance of law and order internally were functions so vital that they could not be left to private enterprise and that, therefore, the State must be responsible for the provision of the Armed Forces, the police and courts of law. Adam Smith was prepared to add to these functions that of providing 'public institutions and public works' chiefly for 'facilitating the commerce of the society and for promoting the instruction of the people'. Thus the State was recommended to maintain good roads, bridges, canals and harbours, to protect trade, to maintain the coinage and to provide education and religious instruction. He was nevertheless careful to point out how the expenses of all these services could be almost wholly recovered from tolls, fees and levies paid by those using them!

As the nineteenth century progressed, it became obvious that the State would have to control, supplement or replace private enterprise in these and other spheres. Private enterprise had proved to be inadequate in providing roads, education and fire-brigade services. Moreover, public health was suffering because of defective sewerage and the lack of pure water supplies. Finally, the individual required protection in his activities both as a consumer and as a producer. Hence the State, largely by delegating the duties to a variety of local authorities, made itself responsible for the provision of roads and sanitary services (such as sewerage and the collection or disposal of refuse), supplemented the efforts of voluntary agencies where educational facilities were inadequate, and provided officials to check weights and measures, inspect premises used for the storage of food and to enforce the regulations regarding conditions of work in factories and shops.

The twentieth century has witnessed a further extension of State activities. From late Tudor times it had been recognised that destitute persons should be provided with a minimum standard of life out of public funds, though in practice the minimum meant little more than the bare essentials necessary to maintain life. In the course of time, however, this minimum has been raised, and today it is generally considered that every citizen is entitled to a number of benefits which can be grouped together under the general heading of 'social security'. Such benefits include insurance against unemployment, industrial injury, sickness and old age, and medical and health services whenever they are needed. In fact, to this objective of an adequate minimum standard of life has been added the aim of equality of opportunity. Whether or not the fulfilment of such an aim, however desirable, is possible, is largely a matter for conjecture. What does happen, however, is that, in so far as inequality of opportunity arises through inequality of income, the State plays a part in removing it. This it does by redistributing income from rich to poor, granting family allowances to parents with family responsibilities, and providing an education, directly, and indirectly by means of scholarships and money grants, to every person according to his own particular capabilities, thereby ensuring that a person's education is not limited solely by lack of money.

We see, therefore, that expenditure is incurred, by central and local governments, both in providing services and in exercising control. Yet not only has such government expenditure increased over the last fifteen years, but a new method has been instituted in planning it. The method is based on a recognition of the fact that the national income is limited and that therefore spending in one direction can be achieved only at the expense of spending elsewhere. Thus if the government spends a larger part of the national income on defence, less will remain with the people for their own personal consumption, thereby leading to a reduction in their standard of living. On the other hand, the government must remember that, if such a reduction is too drastic, the result may be to so lower the will of the people to resist aggression that all the expenditure on the material means of defence is of no avail. Similarly, too large an expenditure on the social services at the expense of defence expenditure may denude the country of the wherewithal to defend itself from attack—and social security is dearly bought if it is at the price of national security. The result is that the actual amounts spent in each direction represent as it were a compromise between competitive desires. Once again we are back to the problem of scarcity discussed in Chapter 1.

Hence expenditure must be considered and planned in order to obtain the best possible value from it. In practice the government not only plans its own expenditure but allocates the whole of the national income between personal (or private) expenditure and government (or public) expenditure. Indeed it goes further than this, for the State, having a continuous existence, must see that economic progress is maintained and that future living standards are not endangered by excessive consumption in the present through too little of our resources being devoted to replace and improve existing capital.

To be successful, this allocation of the national income between private and public consumption and between private and public investment must be based on adequate information and made only after careful calculation. In the last few years, statistics collected have increased in quantity and improved in quality. The result is that, towards the end of every financial year, the government can review the expenditure of resources during the past year, estimate the needs and difficulties of the coming year and state proposals regarding the allocation of resources for that year. Upon these calculations the Chancellor of the Exchequer bases his budget.

SUMMARY OF OBJECTIVES OF GOVERNMENT EXPENDITURE

Government expenditure 1973–4 was £20 million. Fig. 27 shows how this was divided among the different categories.

Here it is convenient to classify, in summary form, the various objectives of government expenditure, showing which items help towards the achievement of each objective. Local government expenditure will be considered later in this section.

1. *National security*

Through the central government, payment is made for the training and maintenance of the Army, Navy and Air Force and the supply of the necessary equipment to them by the Ministry of Defence.

2. *Maintenance of internal law, order and security*

This objective requires a police force for the protection and the help of citizens, a system of justice through the judges and the Courts, and adequate fire-fighting services. The cost of these is borne both by the central and local governments.

3. *Social security*

Social security, as already shown, includes a minimum standard of life and greater equality of opportunity. Therefore under this heading we can group insurance against unemployment, sickness, and old age; the health services; the food and housing subsidies; family allowances; education and educational grants.

4. *Provision for economic security and progress*

In different parts of this book, consideration has been given to various instances of expenditure under this heading. Thus, as part of its policy for full employment, the government pays for the retraining and moving of labour. Again, with the object of boosting production in certain branches of agriculture, it grants subsidies. We must also note how, in order to protect the individual in his economic activities, the government exercises control by inspection of factories and the testing of weights and measures.

Moreover, it is likely that, in times of unemployment, when the State itself promotes additional public works schemes to stimulate employment, such government expenditure will increase, while we may find that, with a few nationalised industries, such as the railways, working deficits, for which the State will have to accept liability, may be a regular yearly occurrence.

5. *Miscellaneous*

Under this heading we group those activities which do not fit easily into any of the previous categories. These items include interest payments on the National Debt, expenditure on and grants to colonies, the maintenance of foreign relations abroad through the Foreign and Commonwealth Office, and the protection of British citizens and rights abroad through the Consular services.

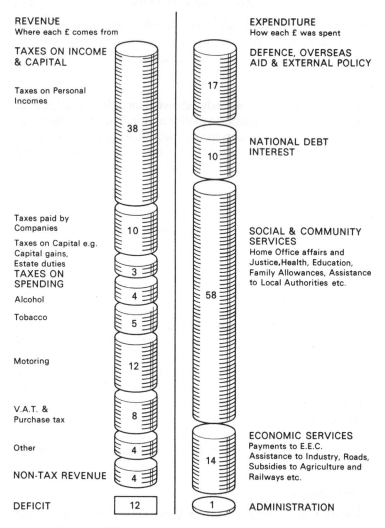

REVENUE
Where each £ comes from

TAXES ON INCOME
& CAPITAL

Taxes on Personal
Incomes

38

Taxes paid by
Companies

10

Taxes on Capital e.g.
Capital gains,
Estate duties
TAXES ON
SPENDING

3

Alcohol

4

Tobacco

5

Motoring

12

V.A.T. &
Purchase tax

8

Other

4

NON-TAX REVENUE

4

DEFICIT

12

EXPENDITURE
How each £ was spent

DEFENCE, OVERSEAS
AID & EXTERNAL POLICY

17

NATIONAL DEBT
INTEREST

10

SOCIAL & COMMUNITY
SERVICES
Home Office affairs and
Justice,Health, Education,
Family Allowances, Assistance
to Local Authorities etc.

58

ECONOMIC SERVICES
Payments to E.E.C.
Assistance to Industry, Roads,
Subsidies to Agriculture and
Railways etc.

14

ADMINISTRATION

1

FIG. 27.—How the Government collected and spent each £ of revenue 1973–4

436

II. GOVERNMENT BORROWING
AND REVENUE

To provide for its expenditure on the various goods and services mentioned above, the government has to obtain money. Broadly speaking this is achieved by: (i) borrowing; (ii) receiving revenue from State-owned property; (iii) charging for certain of the goods and services produced; (iv) taxation.

1. BORROWING: THE 'NATIONAL DEBT'

The government has to borrow money from time to time. These loans, which are for varying periods, comprise what is known as the 'National Debt', and in 1974 amounted to £38,500 millions.

1. *Short-term loans*

Whereas government expenditure is incurred fairly evenly throughout the year, revenue comes in irregularly, most of it being received towards the end of the financial year. The government makes up the difference by borrowing, largely through the issue of Treasury Bills and by Ways and Means advances from the Bank of England. This short-term government debt is known as the 'floating debt' and consists today of a much larger proportion (17 per cent) of the total National Debt than pre-war. This is because, in order to borrow as cheaply as possible, the government has increased its issue of Treasury Bills.

2. *Long-term loans*

As a general rule, current expenditure, that is regular expenditure on everyday needs, should be financed out of regular yearly income. (The main exception to this is when a government deliberately budgets for a deficit to stimulate employment and covers the deficit by borrowing. We shall return to this later.) On the other hand, with capital expenditure (that is on projects such as schools, housing estates, roads and bridges), the full benefit of which will extend far into the future, it would be unfair to throw the whole burden on the taxpayers of one particular year. It is therefore permissible and desirable to furnish such expenditure by long-term borrowing, for by this means the cost of the project can be spread over the years during which benefits are received. Similarly, if a war is to be fought without incurring inflation, people must be willing to save much of their income and lend these savings to the government in order to cover its huge war expenditure.

All loans are usually classified as either 'funded' or 'unfunded' debt. Strictly speaking, the former consists of perpetual debt, where the government gives no definite date for the repayment of the principal (such as $2\frac{1}{2}$ per cent Consols and $3\frac{1}{2}$ per cent War Loan), though sometimes it specifies a particular date after which it *may* repay. The 'unfunded' debt is that part which the government is bound to repay by a certain date, and includes the floating debt, medium- and long-term stock (such as Exchequer Stock and National War Bonds), together with British Savings Bonds and Savings Certificates. These strict definitions, however, are not always followed in practice. The operation of converting floating debt into long-term debt is known as 'funding'. Hence sometimes all debt other than the 'floating debt' is known as 'funded' debt.

2. REVENUE FROM STATE-OWNED PROPERTY

This is a comparatively minor source of income, being derived mainly from rents on Crown Lands and the interest on sundry loans.

3. CHARGES ON GOODS AND SERVICES

For some of the goods and services which the government provides, a specific charge is levied on the persons receiving them. Thus charges for medical prescriptions and dental treatment, the national insurance contributions and the costs imposed by the Courts in civil litigation all help to pay for the respective benefits. In the same way, local authorities receive income directly from many of the services provided. For example, they charge entrance fees to swimming baths, hire out the Town Hall for concerts and dances, and levy fines for the late return of library books.

4. TAXATION

Very seldom, however, do such charges defray the whole cost of the service. In fact, for the majority of services provided by both the central government and the local authorities, no charge is levied directly and specifically on persons as they receive them. Today, for instance, all persons benefit alike from the protection afforded by the Armed Forces and the police and from such communal services as education, parks, roads and bridges. Wherever income does not cover expenditure the difference has to be made up by the appropriate authority and this is usually obtained by taxation (Fig. 27).

III. OBJECTS OF TAXATION

Throughout the nineteenth century and indeed well into the twentieth century, the approach to the problem was both simple and direct. Expenditure was estimated and, following proposals submitted by the Chancellor of the Exchequer, taxes were imposed to meet the cost. Broadly speaking local authorities still operate along these lines today and, in a large measure, the reason for the imposition of taxation by Parliament is to defray the cost of the necessary services which are provided by the government.

Particularly during the last thirty years, however, it has been recognised that the problem of raising revenue is much more complex. In the first place, many of the objects of government expenditure can be furthered by co-ordinating with the expenditure particular methods of raising the money needed. Thus the national security may be promoted not only by maintaining Armed Forces but also by fostering the development within the United Kingdom of certain industries vital in time of war. For this reason customs duties may be levied, not only to raise revenue, but to protect industries, such as agriculture and chemicals, from foreign competition. Similarly, the object of a more equitable distribution of wealth and income can be achieved by the type of tax imposed. As we shall see, death duties help to remove inequalities in the ownership of wealth, and income tax and progressive surtax to reduce inequalities in income.

Secondly, care must be taken that, so far as is possible, the taxes imposed do not have the effect of making the already limited national income still smaller. Thus, a high income tax may reduce people's incentive to work, while a high tax on profits may lead firms to adopt an over-cautious or limited policy of development and expansion.

Thirdly, the government can regulate particular taxes in order to secure ends which it considers desirable and which might not be achieved by the mere operation of the price system. We have already drawn attention to the way in which the government can impose tariffs in order to stimulate vital home industries and protect 'infant' industries (page 259). Similarly value-added tax on certain articles can be varied with the same aim in view. Thus V.A.T. on petrol was increased in 1974 in order to reduce expenditure on imported oil. Nor must we forget that one reason for taxing tobacco and spirits is to reduce their consumption in order to avoid the evils of excess.

Above all, as we shall see in Chapter 25, the relationship between expenditure and revenue can be used as one of the weapons in the fight against cyclical unemployment, the main reason before the war why our national income was much smaller than it need have been. The specific measures taken by the government will depend upon the actual level of employment in existence at the particular moment. For instance, when there are idle resources still available, a programme of expansion must be followed. This may involve direct action by the government, such as the initiation of a special public works policy; or it may be set in motion more indirectly by fiscal and monetary measures, such as a 'budget deficit' or a lowering of the rate of interest. But once full employment has been achieved, the government must beware lest inflation at home produces complications. Inflation, by putting increased monetary spending power in the hands of consumers, stimulates the demand for imports and releases fewer goods for export and may therefore lead to an external deficit. Or, if wages rise in sympathy with the general rise in prices, exports may be priced out of foreign markets, with resulting unemployment in the export industries. Here the government must adopt measures, such as a 'budget surplus', to curb the

rise in prices and to achieve stability at the full-employment
level. The latter is the problem which has persistently con-
fronted the United Kingdom since the war, and we return to
it in more detail in Chapter 26.

Thus we can summarise the purposes of taxation as follows:

(1) to pay for the goods and services produced by the State,
either to meet the whole cost or else to make up the
deficit where receipts do not cover expenditure;

(2) to achieve a more equitable distribution of wealth and
income, thereby reinforcing the effect of the social
benefits;

(3) to exert restraint on moral grounds;

(4) to regulate the economy of the country in order to secure:

    (a) the development of the vital industries;

    (b) the protection of the 'infant' industries;

    (c) the movement of the factors of production from
one industry to another;

    (d) the bolstering-up of employment in certain regions
in order to reduce the shock of structural unemployment;

    (e) the full employment of resources without the evils
of inflation;

    (f) an adequate and steady growth of the national
income.

IV. PRINCIPLES OF TAXATION

Before examining particular taxes in order to see how far
they achieve the above objects, it is useful to consider certain
general principles which the Chancellor of the Exchequer
should bear in mind when deciding what taxes to impose. We
cannot do better than to follow the four maxims which Adam
Smith considered should apply to taxes in general, and the
quotations are from his *Wealth of Nations*.

1. ABILITY TO PAY

'The subjects of every State ought to contribute to the
support of the government as nearly as possible in proportion
to their respective abilities.' Here we should note that, owing to
changes in the social outlook, the interpretation of 'ability'

has changed considerably with time, and particularly since 1776 when Adam Smith was writing. Today we should say that, as far as possible, there should be *equality of sacrifice* between individuals. This involves calculating the tax according to both the size of income and family responsibilities. We will look a little more closely at the former.

The Poll Tax, 1380, an annual tax of one shilling (equivalent to one week's wages today) levied on every member of the household over fifteen years of age, was unjust because, as the same sum was imposed on rich and poor alike, it took a higher proportion of income away from the poorer people. It was, therefore, what economists term today a *regressive* tax and was one of the causes of the Peasants' Revolt in 1381. Similarly, taxes on such commodities as beer and tobacco are regressive, since the poor spend a greater proportion of their income on them than the rich.

There is an improvement on such a tax when it is *proportional*, that is, when it takes away a certain proportion of one's income. In this way, the person with a large income pays a greater sum in tax than a person with a smaller income.

Even so, a proportional tax does not achieve equality of sacrifice. The man with an income of £20,000 per annum is still doing very well, even after a tenth of it has been taken in tax, compared with a man whose income is only £400 and who yet has to pay a similar proportion in taxation. To achieve greater equity it must be *progressive*, that is, take a higher proportion of income from the higher income groups. Later we shall see how 'ability to pay' is worked out along these lines in the way incomes and estates are taxed.

2. CERTAINTY

'The tax which each individual is bound to pay ought to be certain and not arbitrary. The time of payment, the manner of payment, the quantity to be paid, ought all to be clear and plain to the contributor and to every other person.' In short, taxes should be simple to understand, difficult to evade, and equitable in the sense that all persons similarly placed should pay the same tax. Generally speaking, all British taxes fulfil these requirements. In some countries, however, taxes, and particularly those on income, are widely evaded.

3. CONVENIENCE

'Every tax ought to be levied at the time, or in the manner, in which it is most likely to be convenient for the contributor to pay.' The P.A.Y.E. method of collecting income tax was invented partly to suit the convenience of the taxpayer, partly to avoid bad debts, and partly to make the tax more difficult to evade by the falsification of returns.

4. ECONOMY

'Every tax ought to be so contrived as both to take out and to keep out of the pockets of the people as little as possible over and above what it brings into the public treasury of the State.' By this Adam Smith meant that a tax should not be: (a) expensive to collect; (b) harmful to the production of a good (save in special circumstances); (c) irksome to the people, in that it exposed them 'to much trouble, vexation, and oppression'; (d) a dis-incentive to effort. No doubt if Adam Smith were writing today, he would place much more emphasis on the last point, since high rates of direct taxation figure much more prominently in our present system.

It will be obvious that, for certain taxes, there may be some conflict between these principles. Thus the allowance for varying family and other responsibilities, when calculating a person's income-tax liability, brings into conflict, by making the tax more complicated, the principles of 'ability' and 'certainty'. Similarly, increasing marginal tax rates on high incomes act as a dis-incentive to effort. In such cases, the Chancellor must use his judgment to strike a balance, having regard to the main object of the tax.

V. THE STRUCTURE OF TAXATION

Taxes are usually classified according to the method of payment into direct and indirect taxes.

1. *Direct taxes* are those where the person pays his tax direct to the revenue authority, either the Board of Inland Revenue or the local authority. Such taxes can be classified as:

(*a*) taxes on income—income tax, surtax and corporation tax;

(*b*) taxes on capital—capital transfer tax, capital-gains tax;

(*c*) other taxes—chiefly stamp duties, motor-vehicle duties and local rates.

2. *Indirect taxes* are those paid on the importation or purchase of certain goods and services. The importer or manufacturer pays the tax, although as far as possible its burden is 'passed on' to the final consumer by being included in the selling price. Hence there is usually no direct contact between the final purchaser and the taxation authority, the Department of Customs and Excise.

Indirect taxes can be classified into:

(*a*) customs duties on goods imported from abroad, e.g. cameras, watches, cars, wireless valves, televisions tubes;

(*b*) excise duties on home-produced goods and services, e.g. beer, spirits, matches and mechanical lighters, betting;

(*c*) the value-added tax (V.A.T.) now imposed on most goods and services.

Generally speaking, direct taxes are taxes on income or capital, and the individual's tax liability is personally assessed. On the other hand, indirect taxes are taxes on outlay, no personal assessment being made of tax liability. Exceptions are the stamp duty (which is payable on financial documents such as receipts and deeds transferring property), and the motor-vehicles duty, both of which are outlay taxes.

VI. THE MERITS AND DEMERITS OF THE PRINCIPAL DIRECT TAXES

1. INCOME TAX

British taxes on income score heavily in making for equality of sacrifice. This is achieved by the allowances which are given for family and other responsibilities and progressive rates of income tax. The following example makes this clear.

Case 1. Single man. *Sole income:* earnings, £2,000 p.a.

Allowances: personal (single man) 625

Taxable income 1,375

Taxation at 33 per cent = £453·75

The total tax of this man is nearly ¼ of his income.

Case 2. Married man, 1 dependent child under 11 years.
Income: earnings, £2000

Allowances: (a) personal (married man) . . . 865
(b) child's 240

Total allowances 1,105
Taxable income 895

Taxation at 33 per cent = £295·35

The total tax of this man is just over ⅐ of his income.

For taxable income above £4,500, income tax is levied at rates which become progressively higher. Thus taxable income above £20,000 p.a. is taxed at 83 per cent. In addition, investment income between £1,000 and £2,000 is subject to a surcharge (in addition to income tax) of 10 per cent, and above £2,000 of 15 per cent. Income tax, therefore, possesses the further advantage of being very effective in redistributing income in favour of the poor. This redistribution effect can be seen by studying Table 25.

Apart from the two advantages already mentioned, income tax has a particular attraction from the point of view of the Chancellor of the Exchequer in that the yield from it is fairly certain and can be calculated fairly accurately in advance. With many other taxes this is not so. Capital transfer tax, for instance, depends largely on the number of the wealthier

TABLE 24.—*The Distribution of Personal Income, before and after Tax, 1971*

Range of income before tax £	Number of incomes (thousands)	Total income (£mln.)		Percentage of income retained
		Before tax	After income and surtax	
420–499	883	406	399	98·2
500–999	5,965	4,459	4,001	89·7
1,000–1,999	10,016	14,531	12,305	84·7
2,000–9,999	4,446	12,691	9,759	76·9
10,000 and over	59	918	383	41·7

people who die in the course of the year. Similarly, the yield from indirect taxes, as we have already seen, may be influenced considerably by the elasticity of demand for the good, and although experience in the levying of such taxes has provided information which enables reasonable predictions to be made, such predictions are still liable to a wide margin of error. From the returns of income each year, however, the Board of Inland Revenue does obtain the approximate numbers falling within each income group so that the effect on the total tax received of varying the rate of tax can be calculated accurately. The calculation, nevertheless, is subject to two main qualifications. The first is that money incomes may vary in the course of the year owing to inflation or deflation. With the former, the Chancellor of the Exchequer obtains a larger money tax return than he budgeted for; with the latter he receives less. The second is that a big increase in the rate of income tax may make people feel disgruntled at the fact that, over a certain income, much of the reward of their effort is taken by the government. The result, therefore, may be that they do less work than formerly, preferring in effect to take their income in the form of additional leisure (which is not taxed), rather than in money received from work (which is taxed heavily). Whether this does happen or not depends on many considerations. Very often a person is not free to vary his income, simply because it is derived from a pension, government stock or debentures. More important, he may be in a regular job and receiving a fixed weekly wage or monthly salary, in which case, since his basic income is fixed, any variation in his effort would be shown chiefly in the amount of overtime he is prepared to work. It may, however, show itself in the fact that the person is unwilling to move to a higher job because he feels that the additional reward, once income tax has been deducted, does not compensate him for the effort and expense needed in training for the new job or for the extra responsibility involved. Thus no general rule can be stated about the effect on incentive of a high rate of income tax. In recent years, boxers, when they have moved into a high sur-tax group, have confined their efforts to one or two fights a year. On the other hand, in addition to the points already considered, it may well be that a higher income tax may cause people to work harder—simply because they wish to maintain their standard of living. This is especially true where a person has commitments which he cannot avoid, such as mortgage repayments and fees for the education of his children. What is certain is that a high rate of income tax increases the advantage of 'fringe benefits'—a company car, expense lunches, etc.

In addition to the dis-incentive to effort and initiative which may result, a high rate of income tax has other disadvantages. In the first place, it induces people to evade payment of the tax. This is achieved in a variety of ways. If, for instance, a person can avoid keeping records of his business transactions, there is no means, apart from a comparison with other persons in a similar business, by which the Board of Inland Revenue can check his profits. Certain accounts have to be kept by law, while the payment of cheques in and out of a banking account does yield an indication of the profit likely to have been made by a business. But the keeping of such records can be avoided by doing business only through cash transactions. Similarly, when income tax is high, companies and persons working on their own account are encouraged to incur high expenses in the course of business. A businessman, for instance, might be prepared to travel second-class rather than first-class if the whole of the difference in the fare, say £2, would accrue to him. In actual fact, however, since his income for the year would be increased by £2, at a 50 per cent tax rate, £1 would have to be paid to the Board of Inland Revenue. He might, therefore, decide that, since he would be saving for himself only £1, he may as well enjoy the extra comfort of travelling first-class.

Secondly, a high marginal income tax rate may have the effect of reducing the extent to which the principle of the division of labour is applied. Let us, by way of illustration, imagine a writer whose books are so successful that his income exceeds £40,000 per annum. This means that today any additional income is taxed at 83 per cent. Any spending has to be made out of his income after it has been taxed and so, to spend another £1, he has to earn £6. The result might well be that, instead of employing his time writing books, he prefers to spend it in doing jobs for himself, such as mowing the lawn, cleaning his car, or painting his house—jobs which otherwise he would be pleased to pay somebody else to do.

Lastly, a high rate of income tax may encourage the spending rather than the saving of personal capital. When income tax and investment surcharge amount to 98 per cent, the spending of £1,000 of one's capital involves the loss of only £2 income each year supposing it had been invested to yield 10 per cent. Similarly, income tax may discourage people from saving, for it has to be paid on nearly all savings apart from Savings Certificates, Save As You Earn, and the first £40 interest from National Savings. Thus at 33 per cent income tax, the rate of interest received on 9·5 per cent British Savings Bonds is reduced to 6·3 per cent, which may not be enough to compensate for the postponement of present satisfaction to a later period.

2. Corporation Tax

A tax, in some form or another, on the distributed profits of *companies* has been in operation continuously since April 1st, 1937. In 1965 the profits tax was replaced by a corporation tax, now (1975) 52 per cent of the profit of companies. Shareholders pay further income taxes on profits distributed as dividends.

Apart from the revenue raised by means of it, the corporation tax is advantageous in that it falls on persons who are usually in the higher income groups. In fact, in times of full employment and rising prices, a tax on profits is necessary if the workers, through their trade unions, are to restrain their demands for wage increases, for they are not content to forgo the use of their strong bargaining position while they see dividends increasing.

Yet a high tax on profits cannot be said to be very satisfactory. From the point of view of certainty of yield it is defective. The yield varies because the amount of profit depends largely on the state of trade, which in the past has been liable to fluctuate considerably. Secondly, the tax has the effect of stifling enterprise. The inducement of reaping a higher profit is necessary if persons are to invest their money in the ordinary shares (as opposed to debentures) of the less certain enterprises. Yet should the enterprise succeed, much of this inducement is swallowed up by the tax on profits. In other words, when the business wins through, the government takes a share of the reward; when the business fails, however, the government loses nothing. The result is that it induces investors to play for safety. Moreover, in addition to damping down the incentive to enterprise and expansion, a high profits tax reduces the resources available to the firm for 'ploughing-back' into the business—something which is particularly serious for the small firm.

Fourthly, a high profits tax may lead to inefficiency and high expense accounts, for, in a sense, both can be discounted at the expense of the tax, since both lead to a reduction in profits. Thus the cost of sports fields, advertising and high directors' fees will probably be borne initially by a reduction in the profit distributed and thus eventually in part by a reduction in tax. And, lastly, a high profits tax on businesses in the United Kingdom increases the relative value of the shares of companies abroad. Hence investors abroad are more likely to subscribe to the promotion and development of companies outside the United Kingdom.

3. Capital Transfer Tax

Capital Transfer Tax replaced Estate Duty in 1974. It applies to lifetime gifts as well as to legacies, though the former generally bear only half the latter's rate of tax. The rates of duty are progressive, varying according to the size of the transfer. The transfers pay 10 per cent in the £15,000 to £20,000 band, and this increases to 75 per cent above £2 million.

The object of levying capital transfer tax is primarily to raise revenue, but in so doing it is very efficient in bringing about a redistribution of wealth. It is advantageous, too, in that, when it takes place through death, it is not likely to lead to so great a dis-incentive to effort, being based, as it were, on 'past' rather than on present effort. Moreover, if revenue were not raised by capital transfer tax, it would merely mean that it would have to be raised in other ways, probably by a higher rate of income tax. Most people would prefer to pay the tax on their estate rather than forgo present income—a surmise borne out by the fact that few people are willing to insure their lives, by payment of regular premiums during their lifetime, for a sum sufficient to cover capital transfer tax at death.

Yet capital transfer tax is not a buoyant tax, for in bringing about a more equal distribution of wealth, it gradually eliminates those estates which yield the largest revenue. In short, it is possible to 'kill the goose that lays the golden egg'. For instance the tax on capital transfer of £1 million is now nearly £600,000. But as wealth becomes more equally distributed, that £1 million may be held by 10 persons each transferring £100,000. Tax on this is £28,250 and therefore the total revenue received, if those people die in the course of the year, is £282,500.

It should be noted that capital transfer tax is a capital tax. This has significance with regard to government action to combat inflation. As we shall see, in such circumstances the government aims at increasing saving, either voluntarily or, if this does not materialise, compulsorily by means of increased taxation. Such saving, however, to be effective must be out of *present* income. Hence a capital tax, such as capital transfer tax, cannot be used with this aim in view, for the revenue raised comes from saving which has already taken place (unless people were spending their capital).

Minor objections can also be stated. Thus the fact that capital transfer tax may have to be paid by sale of agricultural

land and estates results in an artificial increase in the supply
of that type of land on the market, thereby depressing its value.
Again, some estates may be hit very hard over a few years
when a family is subject to a large number of deaths, as often
occurs, for instance, when the person inheriting is a brother,
sister or cousin of the deceased.

4. CAPITAL-GAINS TAX

A tax is now levied on capital gains realised on all assets held
for more than a year at a flat rate of 30 per cent. Owner-
occupied houses, private motor cars, and goods and chattels
sold for not more than £1,000, are excluded.

VII. THE MERITS AND DEMERITS OF INDIRECT TAXES

The chief disadvantage of direct taxes is that, when the rate
of tax is high, there is a dis-incentive to effort. Hence, because
at the present time a very large amount of revenue has to be
raised by the government, it is necessary to impose alternative
taxes. Today nearly one-half of taxation revenue is obtained
by means of 'indirect' taxes levied on goods and services.
Usually, as with value-added tax, the tax is imposed on an
ad valorem basis, i.e. as a proportion of the value of the good or
service; sometimes, however, as with the tax on cigarettes, it
is a 'specific' tax, i.e. a fixed sum on an article irrespective of
its value.

As we have seen, indirect taxes comprise customs duties,
excise duties and value-added tax. Customs duties may be
levied for a variety of reasons. Some are imposed with the
main object of raising revenue. On the other hand, as the
history of the tariff shows, duties may be placed on goods
coming into the United Kingdom as a means of regulating
international trade (see pages 257–60).

Excise duties and value-added tax (which will be considered
separately later) are levied chiefly with the object of raising
revenue, though, when we consider the evil effects of the reduc-

tion of the tax on gin in the eighteenth century, we cannot but note that excise duties can be used for regulatory purposes. Apart from the high proportion of revenue that is raised by them and the value they have in regulating the economy, indirect taxes have other advantages. Since, in the first instance, payment is to be made by the importer or the 'producer' of a good or service, the number of people on whom the Customs and Excise officials have to keep check is comparatively few, although V.A.T. has increased the numbers. Hence indirect taxes are difficult to evade and simple to collect. Moreover, when the tax is raised, extra revenue begins to come in immediately. A change in the tobacco tax or petrol tax usually operates within a day or two of its announcement. Thus such taxes are useful when the Chancellor of the Exchequer does not wish to wait six months or a year for his revenue, as would happen were he to try to obtain it through an increase in the income or profits tax. On moral grounds too, it is widely considered that some taxes should be paid by all persons, even the poor, so that everybody can feel that they are bearing some responsibility for the cost of running the State. The basis of this argument is that when people pay taxes they are more interested in seeing that the money raised is spent economically, while, since they are sharing in its cost, they will be more likely to take an interest in the process of government.

The main disadvantage of indirect taxes is that, since the rich man and the poor man pay the same rates of tax, they are regressive and therefore represent a heavier burden for the poor man. To this extent, therefore, they work in the opposite direction to the direct taxes, which are imposed particularly with the aim of redistributing income more equitably. Moreover, the number of articles on which selective high rates of tax can be imposed for the purpose of raising revenue is limited. As we have seen, the demand for such a good to be taxed should be inelastic. The largest single class of good which has this characteristic is the necessities, but to impose taxes on necessities would be manifestly unfair to persons with very low incomes. Hence the Chancellor of the Exchequer is forced to exclude them from V.A.T. and find goods having an inelastic demand upon which to impose special rates of tax. He therefore chooses the 'conventional luxuries'—tobacco, alcohol, motoring. The result is that today these three items provide one-quarter of all taxation.

Moreover, this comparative restriction of the revenue-raising indirect taxes to the three commodities above carries with it a certain amount of injustice, for the person whose tastes lead him to spend much of his income on either or all of these has to bear a larger share of indirect taxation than a person who takes his pleasure in ways that are not taxed. Thus the person who eats fruit instead of smoking, drinks tea instead of beer, and who walks, digs his garden, reads and listens to the wireless instead of taking a car trip in the country makes a reduced contribution to the revenue through indirect taxation. There may be a possible defence of such discrimination on moral grounds, but in any such case a defence involves personal opinions. The simple fact is that the discrimination arises simply because these three sources yield well.

Lastly, a rise in the rate of tax on goods which figure to a considerable extent in the everyday expenditure of the worker will raise his cost of living. Thus, in periods of full employment, such increases are likely to lead to demands for higher wages, and to this extent, therefore, the tax may have an inflationary effect.

Value-added tax (V.A.T.) replaced purchase tax and the selective employment tax in 1973. It is levied on most goods and services at a specified rate of the 'value added'. The principle is shown in Fig. 28. This assumes that there are four stages in the production of a table. Each large rectangle represents the receipts of the producer at the given stage. After the tree-grower, however, each person's receipts contain a sum for materials 'bought-in' (an input) from the previous producer. What is left represents the money value of what the producer adds at his stage of production. Tax is collected on this value-added portion. Thus, if V.A.T. were 10 per cent and the retailer could sell the table at £10, the purchaser would be charged £1·00 V.A.T., making a total purchase price of £11·00. When the retailer had been invoiced for the table by the manufacturer, he would have been charged V.A.T. of 80p. Thus the retailer merely sends 20p (the

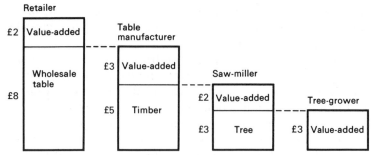

FIG. 28.—The principle of 'value-added'

difference between £1·00 and 80p) as tax to the Customs and Excise. Similarly, others would pay tax as follows: table-manufacturer 30p; saw-miller 20p; tree-grower 30p. The total V.A.T. paid by the four is thus £1·00.

Some goods, e.g. food, coal, gas, electricity, the construction of buildings, books, newspapers, public transport fares, medicines on prescriptions, etc. are zero-rated. This means that the final seller charges no V.A.T. *and* can re-claim any V.A.T. invoiced by intermediary producers. Other goods, for example rents, loans and medical services, are 'exempt'. Here no V.A.T. is charged by the final seller, but any V.A.T. paid by an intermediary, for example for building repairs, cannot be reclaimed.

Apart from harmonising with the E.E.C. indirect tax system, the main merit of V.A.T. is that it is broader-based than the old purchase tax. Because the latter was applied to a comparatively narrow range of goods, for example cars and consumer durables, the yield did not increase proportionately with consumer spending. Moreover, since V.A.T. covers most forms of spending, it does not distort consumer choice to the extent of the old purchase tax (see later). Finally, by zero-rating exports, exporters were given some encouragement by V.A.T. because they paid Selective Employment Tax (the tax it replaced) equally with home-market producers.

On the other hand, it can be argued that a general tax on spending is regressive, for it hits those on lower incomes hardest. This is tempered somewhat, however, by zero-rating goods which can be regarded as necessities.

VIII. LOCAL GOVERNMENT FINANCE

For a variety of reasons, many of the tasks of government are delegated by Parliament to the local authorities in the United Kingdom. Sometimes it is felt that more economy will be observed in the expenditure of money if that money is raised where it is spent. Moreover, many students of political science approve of the arrangement because, through local government, more people are permitted to participate directly in government. In fact, they go further and consider that the personal contact of the local inhabitants and the officials of the local authority promotes confidence in matters of government generally. Above all, government by a locally elected body, for its own particular area, enables variations to be made according to differences which exist, from one area to another, in needs and circumstances. Thus, it not only renders direct advantages but helps to avoid the tendency towards bureaucracy of the Central Government.

In England and Wales the Local Authorities consist mainly of the counties and the county districts. The county authorities are responsible for the provision of such services as education, fire brigades, police, parks, the maintenance of roads and bridges, town and country planning, the welfare of the aged and handicapped, the protection of children and young persons, and libraries. The county districts are chiefly 'health authorities', responsible for refuse collection and disposal, drains, sewerage, the suppression of nuisances, certain duties regarding infectious disease, street scavenging, vermin destruction, the inspection of shops and food, and housing and planning applications. In addition, they provide amenities such as baths, swimming baths, wash-houses, libraries, museums, cemeteries, civic restaurants, entertainment, parks and open spaces, transport, and information centres. It is their task, too, to levy and collect the rates, a portion being paid over to the county authority.

THE REVENUE OF LOCAL AUTHORITIES

For capital development, the local authorities can borrow

money. This they can do through the Public Works Loan Board or by issuing their own stock.

Current expenditure should be covered by current revenue which, as Table 26 shows, is obtained in three main ways.

TABLE 25.—*Current Income of Local Authorities in the United Kingdom 1972–3*

	£mln.	Percentage
Trading income, rents and interest .	2,900	35
Central Government grants . . .	3,135	38
Rates	2,180	27
	8,215	100

1. *Sale of goods and services*

For its 'trading services', such as housing estates, entertainments, civic restaurants, water supply, burial grounds and cemeteries, allotments, baths and wash-houses, charges are often levied to meet the cost, or part of the cost. Roughly the principle is that persons who make use of such services should bear a larger share of the cost than those who do not. Thus fees are charged for admission to swimming baths and wash-houses, for the hire of the local town hall and the tennis courts in the parks, while rents are levied on houses and allotments.

2. *Central Government grants*

The Central Government makes grants towards the cost of local authority expenditure. The reasons for this are:
   (i) to assist and encourage the local authorities in the provision of adequate services which are considered to be of national or semi-national importance, e.g. education, fire brigades, police, housing, highways and bridges;
   (ii) to exercise some control, through the power to refuse money grants, over the standard of efficiency of those services;
   (iii) to help the poor authorities, and thereby to seek to remedy a major defect in the rating system—grants given for this reason are known as 'rate support grants';

(iv) to offset the failure of the rate yield to keep pace with inflation by transferring some of the burden to general taxation;

(v) to provide for a special emergency, e.g. floods.

3. Rates

The difference between expenditure and income from charges and government grants has to be made up by rates. The rate is a tax which is levied by the local authority on the value of the land and buildings occupied. What happens is that all land and buildings within the area are given a 'rateable value' which is assessed by the Board of Inland Revenue and is roughly equal to the annual letting value of the property less upkeep expenses. By totalling all the rateable values in its area, the local authority can arrive at its own gross rateable value. Suppose, for instance, that this gross rateable value is £2 million. If then the amount which has to be raised by the rates for the year is £10mn., the local authority levies a rate of 50p in the £. This means that a person, whose house is rated at £140, would pay £70 rates each year, usually by half-yearly instalments of £35. A portion of the rates has to be given to the County Councils to cover the cost of the services which they provide.

The chief advantage of the rating system as a form of tax is that it provides a fairly stable yield, for it does not vary a great deal with the state of trade. Moreover, since it is the occupiers of the land or buildings who are responsible for paying the rates, it is difficult to avoid payment and relatively easy for the local authority to collect. Above all, the rates represent a tax reserved for the local authorities, for the Central Government has refrained from 'poaching' on it.

Nevertheless the rating system has certain disadvantages. Rates themselves may be regressive. Thus a person may occupy a large house paying high rates, not because he is wealthy but because he has a large family, while no differentiation is made between a business which is doing well and one which is doing badly. Secondly, it has led to inequalities over the country between one district and another. Often the authorities who have the largest amount of rates to raise because of rehousing necessities and so on have a very low gross rateable value. Thirdly, anomalies have arisen because since 1929 agricultural land and buildings have been exempted from rate liability. Fourthly, because the rateable value is increased when the property is improved, e.g. by a garage or central heating, it militates against desirable improvements. Lastly, the revenue from the rates is inflexible and rigid. This operates against go-ahead local authorities who would prefer a more progressive form of tax, yielding a larger amount, in order that they can finance their more ambitious schemes of improvement. Moreover, since rateable values are only adjusted periodically, the rate yield does not automatically rise with inflation.

PART VIII

FULL EMPLOYMENT

CHAPTER 23

FULL EMPLOYMENT: A SURVEY
OF THE PROBLEM

As we explained in Chapter 1, economics is concerned with the relationship between unlimited wants and the scarce means of production. Because the means of production are scarce, it is necessary that they be put to their most effective uses. If this does not happen, then there is not complete 'economic efficiency', or, put in another way, the standard of living is lower than it need be. Of course, when some of the means of production are not put to any use whatsoever but are allowed to stand idle, then it is obvious that there is 'economic *in*efficiency'. Since this is an aspect of the economic problem which so far has largely been ignored, this section attempts to give an elementary explanation of why, on occasions, factors of production are not fully employed. It must be remembered at the outset, however, that the subject is very complex and so the explanation which follows is merely a very sketchy summary which can best be regarded as a first approach to a more thorough and advanced study. This caution applies particularly to the chapter on cyclical unemployment.

1. Why 'Full Employment' is usually concerned with Labour

When speaking about unemployment we are usually thinking of one particular factor of production only, labour. We must remember, however, that in periods of trade depression, not only labour, but other factors of production, such as machinery and buildings, are also standing idle or at least are working at less than full capacity. But labour, as we have already pointed out, is a peculiar kind of factor in that, whilst standing idle, it not only fails to produce but deteriorates mentally, morally and then physically. The man who is out of a job for a long time loses his self-respect and feels that he is of no further use to the community. Eventually he ceases to have confidence in his ability to do even that particular job for which he has been trained, while later there may even occur a lack of desire to work. Moreover, the longer the worker remains unemployed, the more difficult does he find it to obtain work, for employers, when filling vacancies, prefer the recently unemployed. Hence, in what follows, we shall keep to the usual connotation of unemployment, assuming that it refers exclusively to labour. Unemployment therefore means that persons, capable of and willing to work, are unable to find suitable paid employment in the production of the goods and services needed in the community. The problem which we analyse here does not include 'voluntary' unemployment, through strikes, lock-outs, idleness and other causes. Similarly, we must treat as a separate problem the case of persons who, either through low physical or mental capacity, must be classified as 'unemployable', though the existence of conditions of full employment obviously lowers the standard at which the handicapped become 'unemployable'.

The seriousness of the problem of unemployment is obvious when it is pointed out that over the period 1921–38 the average unemployment rate among insured workers in the United Kingdom was 14·2 per cent. At no time were less than one million insured workers unemployed, while in 1932 the number rose to 2,813,042, a rate of 22·1 per cent. Moreover, between both industries and localities, the rate varied. Thus, in 1932, the unemployment rate in the shipbuilding industry was 62·1 per cent, while in the tobacco industry it was only 8·7 per cent. As regards localities, we can compare the unemployment rate in 1934 for Redhill (Surrey) of 2·0 per cent with a rate for Blaina (Monmouthshire) of 75·5 per cent. The net result was that if not actually unemployed, the fear of being so was a spectre which haunted the lives of most workers during the inter-war years.

2. Types of Unemployment

On account of the 'perishable' nature of labour, the problem of unemployment is not solved by giving the unemployed a 'dole' even if it were almost equal to normal earnings. The unemployed worker must be found a job which he can accept.

Our immediate task is to discover the reasons why jobs have ceased to exist.

The first thing that we notice is that there is no single cause of unemployment. However, for the sake of simplifying our analysis we can classify the different causes under five main headings, though it must be noted that the existence of one type has an influence on the others. Thus, where cyclical unemployment exists, seasonal and casual unemployment become much more acute, for employers have no need to pay 'retaining' wages or to find alternative employment between the main working periods. Similarly with structural unemployment, the transfer of labour to other areas or occupations does depend on there being an unsatisfied demand for labour elsewhere, a situation which is rare when general cyclical unemployment prevails.

1. *Normal or transitional unemployment*

Unemployment of this kind arises in a variety of ways. In many industries temporary stoppages of work occur when there is a change-over to new methods of production while short periods of not working quite frequently come about when people change their jobs. Moreover, a high rate of employment is often accompanied by a high rate of labour turnover, many workers finding it easy to 'flit' from one job to another. Seasonal labour, a feature of such industries as building, agriculture and seaside catering, is another form of 'normal' unemployment. Under this heading, too, we can include unemployment resulting from 'blind-alley' jobs performed by juveniles, for such work often proves only temporary.

2. *Frictional unemployment*

This is the type of unemployment which arises chiefly through the general immobility of labour. Such immobility leads to the situation where, while a deficiency of labour exists in some occupations or places, in others there persist pockets of unemployment because the unemployed workers are not of the right sort or are unable or unwilling to move to the area where there is a labour shortage. While such a situation occurred only rarely in the inter-war years, it has become more significant in the post-war years, for there has been little unemployment of a cyclical nature. Thus today there is a shortage of unskilled labour in London and the south of England compared with the north of the country.

3. *Structural unemployment*

In some ways this can be regarded as a more severe form of frictional unemployment. Since, however, it occurs through permanent and long-term changes in the structure of the national economy, it must be put in a separate category. Attention was drawn to this type of unemployment when considering the disadvantages of the localisation of industry. Industries, often of dominating importance in a particular area, can decay owing to the invention of substitutes, the loss of overseas markets, changes in the tastes of consumers at home or the exhaustion of mineral resources. Labour refuses to move to other districts, while new industries fail to come in to take the place of the decaying ones. The result is that areas exist where the level of unemployment is well above the national average.

4. *Cyclical unemployment*

Since industry assumed its modern form at the end of the eighteenth century, the volume of economic activity and hence the level of employment has, in nearly all the industrial countries, proceeded in a series of fairly regular waves, periods of boom alternating with periods of depression. This feature is generally referred to as the 'trade cycle', and it is possible to distinguish fairly regular characteristics applying to each complete cycle. Here we note three:

(*a*) The length of the cycle ranges between 5 and 11 years, averaging in Great Britain about 8 years.

(*b*) In Great Britain, the trade cycle is felt more acutely in two groups of industries, the export and the heavy constructional industries. The first suggests that the trade cycle is international in character, a fact which we now know to be true; the second indicates that it is closely connected with a falling-off in the demand for producers' goods.

(*c*) Prices, particularly of raw materials at first and of producers' goods later, fall in the recession and rise in the boom.

This rise is due partly to the use of less efficient plant and labour as output expands, but much more to the temporary shortages in machinery, skilled men and raw materials during the short period when those factors cannot be attracted from other uses. The rise is fairly gradual until the position of full employment is reached when retail prices as well begin to rise considerably.

5. *Persistent general unemployment*

Between the two World Wars cyclical fluctuations became much more serious. In the trough of the depression, the number of unemployed in the United Kingdom was between two and three million, but even at the crest of the wave there still remained approximately one million unemployed persons. In short, the boom worked itself out before it proceeded far enough to remove this hard core of one million unemployed. An explanation of this form of unemployment is therefore a part of the theory of the trade cycle.

3. THE MEANING OF A 'FULL-EMPLOYMENT' POLICY

The seriousness of unemployment needs no emphasis for those persons who can remember the economic conditions of the inter-war years. Indeed, the stress which all parties, Conservative, Labour and Liberal, place on a full-employment policy is a measure of the priority which they give to a solution of the problem. In May, 1944, even while the war was still being fought, the Coalition Government, in making its post-war plans, issued a White Paper which specifically stated: 'The Government accepts as one of its primary aims and responsibilities the maintenance of a high and stable level of employment after the war.'

Maintaining 'a high and stable level of employment', however, formulates the object in terms too general. A more specific definition is necessary in order to know when to apply remedies and to measure their success. But before we state this, two essential features of the policy must be underlined.

In the first place, emphasis must be placed on finding jobs for the unemployed rather than on merely giving them unemployment insurance while they are not working. As Lord Beveridge says: 'The greatest evil of unemployment

is not physical but moral, not the want which it may bring
but the hatred and fear which it breeds.' Hence unemployment insurance must be regarded as only a first-aid measure to
offset the damaging effects of unemployment. But until he is
working again, neither the wishes of the worker nor the
criterion of economic efficiency are fully satisfied.

Secondly, full employment must be achieved in conjunction
with the preservation of the essential liberties of the citizen.
This means, among other things, that there is freedom among
individuals to choose their own employment, to associate
together in trade unions and to manage their own personal
income. Such freedoms, however, do make the task of achieving
full employment more difficult. Thus with frictional and
structural unemployment in particular, the freedom of the
worker to choose his employment means that the State is pre-
cluded from directing workers to take up particular jobs in
specified places. As we shall see later, the government is
expected to move labour by offering a carrot rather than by
wielding the big stick. Similarly, the freedom of the workers
to unite in trade unions and to engage in strike action makes
it more difficult for the authorities to keep in check inflation
resulting from demands for wage increases, while, by leaving
individuals free to make their own decisions as to how much
of their income they save, the government has to adopt round-
about methods to ensure that the monetary demand for goods
is adequate to maintain full employment.

Full employment does not mean that there is literally no
unemployment at all and that each person fit and free to work
is employed every day of his working life. As we have seen,
there are always likely to be some persons unemployed because
of seasonal difficulties. Much more important, however, is the
fact that, in a progressive society, changes in the demand for
labour between one industry and another and one area and
another occur through the introduction of new methods and
techniques of production and through changes in the pattern of
consumption. In the resulting change-over there is frequently
some time-lag, with consequent transitional unemployment.
Finally, since we have no direct control over demand for our
exports, some structural unemployment may occur when this
falls. Lord Beveridge suggested that if total unemployment is

no more than 3 per cent of the working population it would still be consistent with full employment. Until recently, the U.K. has usually had an unemployment rate below this.

Some economists have argued that a slightly higher unemployment rate would have advantages. First, the greater difficulty involved in obtaining a job would induce those in employment to work harder. Secondly, because organised labour was not in quite such a strong bargaining position, it would make it easier to restrain the demand for wage increases of an inflationary nature. Thirdly, it would provide a pool of unemployed labour which would allow industries which are expanding to do so more easily. Although such economists consider that a larger national income would result, it is hardly a policy with which any government is likely to agree, for it fails to eliminate one of the main curses of unemployment—that for certain workers the period of unemployment is long. Full employment, as envisaged by Lord Beveridge, entails the existence of more jobs than there are workers to fill them, while for those workers who are unavoidably out of work the period of being unemployed is short.

4. CONCLUSIONS

The brief survey above shows that, if we exclude normal unemployment, the problem of unemployment can be considered in two distinct sections, divided according to difference in cause. On the one hand we have unemployment which results from changes in demand and the immobility of labour; on the other, we have that which is associated with the trade cycle. Both will be considered in the following chapters.

Normal unemployment, as its name suggests, is partly unavoidable, though we must be certain that it is kept to a minimum. For workers who are merely stood off for a short period or who are not working through changing jobs, the grant of unemployment insurance benefit is the most appropriate measure. With seasonal workers, too, the period of unemployment is limited in duration and so financial help to offset its damaging effects seems the most suitable course. In both cases, however, the position is much easier when there is an overall situation of full employment in the economy.

The problem of 'blind-alley' occupations can be tackled

by the development of apprenticeship schemes. Casual unemployment has now been largely eliminated by requiring registration of workers and the adoption of schemes guaranteeing minimum weekly wage payments. Both measures have been introduced with success in the docks. It is worth noting, too, that the installation of expensive machinery which must be kept fully employed has quite often had the indirect effect of 'decasualising' labour.

We now turn to a consideration of the two main causes of unemployment, the immobility of labour and the trade cycle.

CHAPTER 24

THE IMMOBILITY OF LABOUR

1. What do We mean by 'Immobility'?

OUR study of the price system has shown that, where the demand for the good of a particular industry or occupation expands, the price of the good rises and hence employers can offer a higher wage to attract workers from other industries, chiefly from those where demand has fallen. It must be emphasised, however, that this theory does assume that there is no immobility of the factors of production, that is, that there are no obstacles hindering their smooth transfer. The fact is, however, that such obstacles do exist and they are more pronounced the shorter the period under consideration. Land, for instance, may be specific, that is limited to one particular use, while real estate, though it may be put to many different uses, is almost impossible to transfer from one place to another. Capital equipment may be similarly specific or nearly so, while with labour, the factor in which we are particularly interested here, immobility is produced by psychological as well as by physical factors.

2. The Causes of the Immobility of Labour

Immobility of labour may be of an industrial, occupational or geographical nature. By industrial immobility we mean the existence of obstacles to the movement of labour between different industries where this may not necessitate any change of occupation or area. Today such immobility is relatively unimportant.

A study of occupational mobility is concerned with those factors other than the wage offered, which influence the movement of labour from one occupation to another. On the one hand, we have real obstacles to such mobility in the form of the cost of training; the lack of the requisite degree of natural ability necessary for certain jobs; trade union regulations and prejudices regarding apprenticeship, the employment of foreign and coloured workers, the division of particular jobs between various crafts and so on; and ignorance, perhaps through lack of guidance when leaving school, of the demand for labour of a particular kind. On the other hand, we have to consider the psychological attitude of workers to different jobs. Some jobs, such as mining, are unpleasant, while others, such as the ministry, teaching and the arts, offer rewards above the monetary return. With the former, an increase in the rate of pay in the occupation may not attract workers to it, while with the latter, a relative decrease in pay may not induce them to seek some other employment. Alternatively, in some occupations such as the law, art and acting, entrants are consistently over-optimistic of success, so that a number of unemployed frequently exist in each, resulting in what we have called 'frictional unemployment'. Finally, many workers who would otherwise be willing to move to a new locality feel that they are too old to start learning a new job.

Geographical immobility occurs when there are obstacles to the free movement of labour from one area to another within the same occupation. Once again both real and psychological obstacles have to be considered. Real obstacles include the capital cost involved in moving a home and the possible loss of earnings for a short interim period: immigration quotas fixed by governments and, to a lesser degree, local prejudices against foreign workers; the present-day difficulty of finding housing accommodation. Probably more important, however, are the psychological factors—reluctance to leave friends and associations, dislike of interrupting the children's education. Nor must we rule out the possibility that many people fail to move because they are ignorant of relatively better conditions in other parts of the country.

In addition to the more or less permanent obstacles described above, other difficulties exist from time to time. Thus today we have the shortage of houses, an ageing population which is more reluctant to change occupation or area, and a high rate of income tax which reduces the wage differential between occupations.

3. GOVERNMENT ACTION TO REDUCE THE IMMOBILITY OF LABOUR

Immobility of labour gives rise to frictions which prevent the price system from working smoothly. Theoretically the price system should move those workers who become unemployed to other jobs. The fall in the price of a good through a decrease in demand, and the consequent fall in the demand for the workers producing it, will lead to a relative deterioration in their wages. On the other hand, wages should rise where demand is buoyant (assuming that demand is adequate throughout the economy as a whole). This change in relative wages should have two effects: (a) a movement of workers from low-wage to high-wage industries; (b) a movement of industries from high-wage to low-wage areas.

While these movements might eventually occur, in practice the time they would take is so long that the free operation of the price system proves to be highly unsatisfactory. Labour cannot move easily from one industry to another because of occupational immobility; it does not move out of the depressed areas because of geographical immobility. Industry does not move into the depressed areas because the unemployed workers do not have the necessary skills, or because the saving in wage costs is not sufficient to offset the higher costs of being separated from main markets or losing other advantages of localisation. Indeed, national wage agreements may mean that there is little difference in the wage rates which have to be paid between one area and another. This elimination of wage differentials undermines the forces which set the price system in motion.

However, before examining the precise nature of the action which might be taken, three considerations of a general nature, each of which makes transfer easier, should be noted. The first is that a shift of only a small percentage of the workers in a particular occupation or given area may be all that is necessary to effect the required adjustment in the pattern of production. Thus the shift need be just a marginal one and so will affect only those workers who are the least reluctant to move. Secondly, it is not always necessary for there to be a transfer of the redundant workers direct to the new occupation or locality where they are required. Instead, the movement may proceed gradually in a series of 'ripples'. This is more likely to occur in occupational transfer; for example, the shop-assistant becomes a clerk, the clerk develops into a shorthand-typist and the shorthand-typist takes over as secretary. Thirdly, in both occupational and geographical immobility, there are outward and inward obstacles to mobility, and the proposed remedies must take account of each.

The government's first task must be to improve occupational mobility. Entry into certain occupations should be made less difficult. Here the government can give information on opportunities in other industries and occupations and use its influence to persuade trade unions to modify their regulations concerning the length of apprenticeship to be served and the maximum number of apprentices who can be taken on in a year.

But the main objective must be to ensure that people are trained in the new skills required by light engineering as opposed to heavy industry. The government has set up some 40 Government Training Centres to provide courses in skilled trades for the unemployed. Wage-related financial benefits are given, together with travel and lodging allowances. In practice, however, the unemployed have been slow to avail themselves of these courses. It is also hoped that lump-sum redundancy payments introduced in 1966 will encourage workers to change jobs when their particular skills are no longer required. In the longer period, the problem can be tackled by seeing that school-leavers are adequately advised on career prospects and by ensuring that recruits to the expanding industries are fully trained. As regards the latter, the Industrial Training Act, 1964, provided for industrial training boards to review training in their respective industries, to pay grants for approved courses, and to impose levies on employers to spread the cost.

Obstacles to geographical mobility are more difficult to overcome. Where a whole area is 'depressed', the government can give first aid by placing its contracts there and awarding it priority for public-works programmes—schools, trunk roads, new hospitals, etc. In the long period, however, it must take measures which will on the one hand encourage the outward movement of workers, and on the other induce firms to move in to employ those workers who find it difficult to move.

The first group of measures—'taking workers to the work'—

consists of granting financial aid towards the cost of moving, providing information on prospects in other parts of the country, and removing artificial barriers, such as the shortage of housing accommodation. At present, workers who maintain dependants at home can draw a boarding allowance for twelve months. Free fares to a place of work away from the home town can also be given, and if it is necessary for a worker to buy a house, a part of the solicitors' and agents' fees can be met.

The second policy—'taking work to the workers'—is now regarded as the real long-term solution. It avoids forcing workers to move out of areas to which they are attached, relieves the growing congestion in the Midlands and South-East England, and prevents depopulation of districts in the North, with the loss of 'social capital' which this involves. Above all, moving unemployed workers and their families out of depressed areas reduces spending in the area, the incomes of retailers, for instance, falling. Thus the region becomes still further depressed.

On the other hand, it must be remembered that this may involve firms in higher costs. Their desire to establish plant in the South-East is to secure advantages of localisation, such as a supply of skilled workers or close contact with customers on the Continent.

To move young expanding firms into the depressed areas, the government may use either the carrot or the big stick. So far it has concentrated on the former, though there has been some oblique compulsion through planning requirements.

The carrot must compensate firms for the extra costs incurred by virtue of an inferior location. The Industry Act, 1972, extended the areas where preferential assistance is given by the government to encourage industrial development (Map 6).

There are three different categories of Assisted Area: *Special Development Areas*, where the need for jobs is most acute, *Development Areas* and *Intermediate Areas*. All these areas are suffering from the same sort of problems, though in varying degree. The extent of the financial help available for new industrial projects in the different categories of area varies according to need.

A firm re-locating in one of the Assisted Areas is eligible for a wide range of financial incentives, the most important of which are:

(1) *Regional Development Grants* as follows:

	Plant, machinery, and mining works (%)	Buildings (%)
Special Development Areas	22	22
Development Areas	20	20
Intermediate Areas	—	20

These new grants are not limited to projects creating employment, and so will be available to help with improvements and modernisation. In addition, they are not treated as reducing the capital expenditure which qualifies for capital allowances for tax purposes.

(2) *Removal grants* of up to 80 per cent for certain costs incurred in moving to a Special Development Area or Development Area.

(3) *Loans at favourable rates or interest relief* for projects which reduce unemployment.

(4) *Government factories* for sale or to rent on favourable terms.

(5) A *Regional Employment Premium* of £1·50 per week for adult male employees in a manufacturing establishment in a Special Development Area or Development Area, with lower rates for women and young persons.

(6) *Help for transferring key workers* essential to setting up a new plant.

All the above are in addition to the investment incentives available to manufacturing and service industries throughout the whole country. These include a 100 per cent first-year depreciation allowance for investment in plant and machinery, and a 40 per cent tax allowance on new industrial buildings.

The Department of Industry also controls three Industrial Estates Corporations which supervise over fifty government-

Map 6.—The Assisted Areas, 1973

sponsored industrial estates in England, Wales and Scotland. Similar schemes operate in Northern Ireland, where much use is made of advertising the advantages of the region—a plentiful supply of labour, recreational facilities for workers, lower living costs, etc.

Through its planning powers the government can indirectly use some compulsion. Consent of the local planning authority is necessary for any new building or addition to an existing building. Where this involves the creation of industrial floor-space of more than 1,500 square metres (1,000 in South-East England), an industrial development certificate is also required from the Department of Industry to the effect that the proposal is consistent with the proper distribution of industry, especially as regards the level of employment in the region. These certificates are generally freely available in the Intermediate Areas and are not necessary in the Special Development Areas or Development Areas. Similar controls now operate for office development of over 1,000 square metres in the South-East England region.

In the dispersal of industry the government has set an example whenever possible. Thus the Department of Health and Social Security is centred in Newcastle, and branches of the Department of Inland Revenue have been moved to Wales. The official Location of Offices Bureau provides information about the advantages of areas seeking to attract new office development.

Regional planning

While development area policy deals with special districts needing extra help, the whole country is now divided into ten regions (eight for England and one each for Scotland and Wales), for each of which there is planning on a broad scale as regards the distribution of labour, the diversification of industry and the rate of growth. Primary responsibility, not only for national economic planning but for regional development, lies with the Department of Industry. In 1972 a Minister for Industrial Development was appointed, responsible for the private sector of industry generally and also for industrial development in the Assisted Areas.

The Department's regional organisation has also been strengthened. *Regional Industrial Development Boards* have been set up in the seven regions requiring most assistance. These Boards advise generally on applications for selective financial assistance for the development of industry in their regions.

Each region still has an Economic Planning Council and an Economic Planning Board. The first consists of people with industrial, commercial and local government experience or who are associated with the universities, etc. Its task is to help in the formulation of regional plans, having regard to the region's resources, and to advise on the regional implications of national economic policies. The second, the Board, consists of civil servants from the main government departments concerned with regional planning. Its task is to help the Council in formulating plans and to co-ordinate the work of the various government departments concerned. As far as possible, the members are brought together in one building.

Present policy seems to be moving away from the idea of help to districts towards planning for larger areas, each with a sound infrastructure of public amenities and a much broader-based industrial structure.

CHAPTER 25

CYCLICAL FLUCTUATIONS

1. THE IMPORTANCE OF TOTAL MONETARY DEMAND

IT has been possible to explain unemployment in particular localities or occupations in terms of the ordinary demand and supply analysis. Broadly speaking, this unemployment was caused by imperfections in the price mechanism in the particular market owing largely to the immobility of labour. In order to explain *general* unemployment, however, it is necessary to break with this analysis of particular markets and to speak in general terms. National income must be looked at as a whole and we have to refer to consumption, saving, investment, wages, entrepreneurs, etc., in broad terms.

In a strict Capitalist economy, the decision whether or not to produce rests with entrepreneurs. Usually they produce in advance for an estimated demand, but only if they expect receipts from the sale of the product to at least cover the costs (including normal profit) incurred by them in employing the necessary factors of production.

Now when we were discussing the national income, it was shown that there was a circular flow of money—incomes paid out in wages, profits, rents and interest return to producers in payment for the goods and services on which they are spent. If, for instance, I buy a table, my expenditure becomes the wages of the carpenter and of the man who cut the tree, the income of the person who planted and grew the tree, and so on. In short, my spending of a part of my income on a good also represents at one and the same time earning by the person who sells. Indeed, it was because of this fact that we were able to calculate the national income by approaching it from both the expenditure and income sides. Spending is therefore necessary for earnings. If goods are not sold, incomes are reduced and entrepreneurs, who have usually paid out on wages, raw materials, etc., in advance, do not obtain the receipts they

1

expect. Hence they cut down on production and factors of production become unemployed.

We can see, therefore, that production and employment depend upon the fact that incomes received are retained in the circular flow of income by spending. This spending, however, occurs in three main ways. First there is the spending of private persons on consumer goods. Secondly, there is the money borrowed by entrepreneurs and spent on capital goods or on the holding of stocks; this type of spending is more usually called 'investment'. Thirdly, there is spending by the government. In a closed economy, the total of this spending, which we can refer to as 'total monetary demand' is, as we have seen, equal to national income. If total spending is reduced, there is thus a drop in total monetary demand and therefore in the national income. Hence the level of employment is very closely linked with the size of total monetary demand and, for the sake of simplicity, we will assume that it moves in the same direction and proportionately to it. Our next task is to discover how an increase or decrease in total monetary demand can occur.

Only a part of the incomes received is spent on current consumption, that is, on consumer goods. The remainder of the incomes is saved. Saving is therefore defined as income less consumption. It can be undertaken by private persons; by companies which do not distribute the whole of their profits amongst shareholders; and by the government, which can obtain a budget surplus by receiving more from taxation than it spends on the goods and services it currently provides. It is probable, however, that saving by companies or by the government will be used directly to finance investment. Indeed, that is the object of those companies which 'plough back' their savings to maintain and extend their plant, while similarly a budget surplus helps to pay for government investment. But private persons who save out of their income are not usually concerned directly with spending those savings on investment goods. This is done by entrepreneurs who seek to borrow these savings in order to buy capital goods. Thus the decision to save and the decision to invest are, in this case, taken by two different sets of people impelled, as we shall see later, by entirely different motives. Hence it may easily happen that the desire to save and the desire to invest do not match. Only if the money saved by private persons is borrowed by entrepreneurs to spend on investment will it be retained in the circular flow of income. Where investment is less than saving, there will be a fall in total monetary demand (Fig. 29). The national income is less and hence the level of employment will fall. Where borrowing for investment exceeds saving, additional money will be brought into the circular flow of incomes, increasing total monetary demand. This means that there is a rise in national income and so, if there was previously a less than full employment situation, more people will now be employed (see 'inflation', later).

Cyclical unemployment is brought about largely by changes in the relationship between saving and investment and hence in the size of total monetary demand. Thus, before we can give an explanation of what causes these cyclical fluctuations, we must examine a little more closely the factors which influence saving and investment.

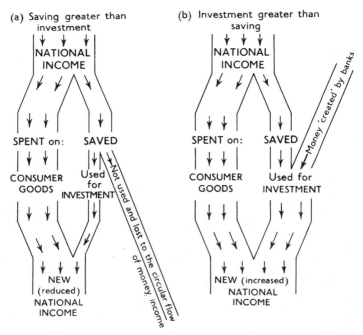

FIG. 29.—Relationship between saving, investment and the national income

2. SAVING

1. *Saving by private persons*

In 1973, personal saving accounted for approximately 30 per cent of total saving. Such saving is influenced by a variety of factors, which include: (*a*) the rate of interest offered; (*b*) the psychological desire either for power or security; (*c*) the availability of institutions, such as the National Savings Bank, Building Societies, Investment Trusts, Unit Trusts, Insurance Companies, making for convenience in saving; (*d*) the stability of the government; (*e*) government activities, such as propaganda to increase saving, or, on the other hand, high taxation (particularly a high capital tax) and an inflationary policy, which decrease saving; (*f*) the hardness of hire-purchase terms; (*g*) the distribution of wealth in the community, the wealthy person being able to save a greater proportion of his income than the poor; (*h*) the rate of invention of new consumer goods; (*j*) the size of the national income, which affects the overall ability of persons to save. It is the latter which is of chief importance when dealing with the trade cycle since it is the factor which is most likely to alter in the short period.

2. *Saving by companies*

Not all company profits are distributed each year amongst shareholders. Some are retained, that is remain 'undistributed', either to be 'ploughed back' into the business or to be held as liquid reserves for maintaining dividends in the event of some unforeseen contingency, such as a trade recession, a strike, an increase in profits tax and so on. Hence, because such saving is usually for the purposes of reinvestment, it is unlikely to be affected by the rate of interest which reserve funds would earn. Rather it will depend almost entirely on the size of profits being made. In the first place, a profit is necessary to effect any saving whatsoever; secondly, the greater the profits, or prospect of profits, the greater will be the desire to invest. Other factors which will influence a company's decision to save are the rate of tax on distributed profits and the extent to which it thinks that it will be able to obtain funds for expansion on the capital market. It should be noted that, in 1973, company saving was about 44 per cent of total saving.

3. *Saving by the public sector*

In the public sector, saving is achieved by the central government, local authorities and public corporations. Any surplus of central government revenue over expenditure represents a net saving by the government except in so far as that revenue was obtained by means of a capital tax, such as death duties. Saving can also take place when, for instance, the receipts from National Insurance contributions exceed the benefits paid out. The same principle applies to local authorities. Public corporations, like companies, save out of current surpluses to provide for future expansion. Public sector spending and saving is largely determined by government policy, political and economic. As we shall see, the budget surplus or deficit is a weapon for regulating the level of total monetary demand.

3. INVESTMENT

By investment we mean spending on the production of new capital goods, such as houses, factories and machinery, or on the holding of additional stocks. Hence it does not include the purchase of existing paper securities such as bonds, shares and debentures, though new securities will probably be issued to cover most of the investment.

Now an entrepreneur will only invest if he thinks that the yield, in the form of eventual profit, will justify such investment. He has, therefore, two main considerations in mind: (a) the cost of such investment; (b) the expected yield from the investment. The cost of investment is represented by the cost of borrowing money to finance it, that is, by the rate of interest (chiefly that on debentures). Hence a low rate tends to stimulate investment, and a high rate to discourage it. On the other hand, the yield on the investment good will depend largely on the demand for the consumer good it produces, and hence the entrepreneur is chiefly concerned with estimating future demand for these consumer goods. In forming his opinion he is most likely to commence from a position regarding which he does possess some definite knowledge, that is, the present demand for those goods. If that demand is buoyant and has remained so for a fairly long period, he will probably view the future optimistically. On the other hand, if the present demand is low and has shown itself resistant to attempts to increase it, the future, to say the least, will appear somewhat gloomy. But since the current demand for goods, that is, the level of consumption, depends chiefly on the current level of income, we can say that the volume of investment depends, on the one hand, on the rate of interest and, on the other, on the present level of income. In practice, the expectations of entrepreneurs have a far greater influence on the level of investment than the rate of interest, especially when it comes to reviving investment.

In short, therefore, both saving and investment depend upon the size of total monetary demand, that is, the national income. Consequently the problem resolves itself into one of maintaining a total monetary demand which is just adequate for producing full employment. Allowance must be made, of course, for increases in national income as the new investment goods increase the supply of consumer goods, for monetary demand would have to be increased accordingly to prevent prices falling.

In practice, the attainment of this aim is much more difficult than it appears. In the first place, as we have already noted, decisions to save and invest are often taken by two distinct sets of persons. Secondly, the level of investment tends to fluctuate violently. Once total monetary demand begins to fall, the adverse influence it has on entrepreneurs is both contagious and, because investment is reduced still further, cumulative. Thus an initial fall (or rise) in investment is multiplied. (By how much, is outside the scope of this book.) In this way, the down-swing of the trade cycle occurs. Thirdly, control is complicated by the fact that the United Kingdom is so dependent on international trade.

4. COMPLICATIONS ARISING FROM INTERNATIONAL TRADE

Goods and services, produced in the United Kingdom and exported, generate income at home and therefore add to monetary demand. On the other hand, goods produced abroad and imported into the United Kingdom generate no such incomes at home. Instead, the money spent on them goes to foreign producers. It is therefore lost to the circular flow of income at home, thereby reducing total monetary demand. We can see, therefore, that if the value of exports equals the value of imports, income generated by producing exports is matched by that spent on imports, and monetary demand at home has not been altered by international trade. If, however, exports exceed imports in value, monetary demand will be increased. Similarly, if imports exceed exports in value, monetary demand will be decreased.

The United Kingdom, which is so dependent on international trade for maintaining her high standard of living, is thus vulnerable to unemployment through a possible fall in her exports. This could occur for three main reasons:

(a) a relative increase in the price of British goods;
(b) a relative decrease in incomes abroad;
(c) the erection of trade barriers by foreign countries.

The first represents a contraction of demand due to a rise in price. As we have seen, there are measures (e.g. depreciation) which the United Kingdom can herself take to correct the disequilibrium. But the remedies for the other two causes of the fall in her exports *may* be outside her own direct policy.

Suppose, for instance, that the United Kingdom has a total monetary demand just sufficient for full employment. Now one of her major customer countries suffers severe unemployment. As a result, demand for British exports falls. There is a balance of payments deficit and total monetary demand falls. What has happened, therefore, is that Britain has 'caught' unemployment from abroad.

Alternatively, the fall in demand for British exports may be the result simply of countries abroad erecting trade barriers by tariffs, quotas, etc. This is usually done to protect the home market. But, as regards the United Kingdom, the result is the same—unemployment.

It can be seen that a country finds it easier to maintain full employment when it has a favourable balance of payments. Unfortunately, when the depression occurred in the 1930's, countries tried to secure such a balance by imposing restrictions on trade. In the event, this 'beggar-my-neighbour' policy was disastrous. It led to an all-round (and cumulative) contraction of international trade and the loss of its advantages.

How then can the United Kingdom make her full-employment policy less vulnerable to fluctuations in international trade? Broadly speaking, her choice can be along one of two lines. The first, known as bilateralism, means that the United

Kingdom selects the countries with whom she trades, offering to buy the exports of those countries if they likewise agree to take imports from her to an equivalent value. In addition to ensuring that imports are at least matched by exports, such a policy could easily be advantageous to the United Kingdom by allowing her to discriminate in her trade. She would select those countries that she considers would be more likely to achieve their own full employment and thus to maintain their demand for her exports. In addition, if the United Kingdom were the major importer of their produce, it might even be possible for her to drive favourable price bargains.

Such a system suffers, however, from most of the disadvantages of barter, especially that of finding a 'double coincidence' of wants. As an examination of the pattern of the United Kingdom's international trade shows, no one country's imports from her are exactly balanced by exports to the United Kingdom of an equivalent value. Hence, bilateral trading agreements would seriously restrict international trade, and it seems pointless to follow a policy for improving material welfare through full employment if such gains are lost by reducing international trade.

The alternative to bilateral trade is multilateral trade, where every country buys goods where they are cheapest and sells its exports wherever it can, each country's currency being freely exchangeable one with the other. This is the system which operated, until the depression, under the gold standard. It is the system most favourable to the United Kingdom, which depends for her high standard of living on international trade. Its big disadvantage, however, is the one already noted—that it can be used by certain countries for their own ends irrespective of the fact that, in the process of achieving full employment at home, other countries are impoverished.

The effective working of a multilateral trading system depends, therefore, on the fulfilment of three conditions: (a) that all participating countries endeavour to maintain effective demand for imports by following a full-employment policy at home; (b) that no one country seeks to maintain a favourable balance of payments position with the rest of the world in order to foster employment at home; (c) that countries do not frequently vary their international economic policy, e.g. by changes in tariffs and exchange rates, for this upsets the long-term production plans of other countries.

In order to produce the international stability necessary for multilateral trade, various schemes have been propounded. The most important of these was the International Monetary Fund Agreement (Bretton Woods) to which the United Kingdom adhered until 1972. As we have already seen (Chapter 14), this system of 'managed flexibility' has, for the time being at least, ceased to operate.

5. An Explanation of the Trade Cycle

We are now in a position to attempt a very brief explanation of the main features of the trade cycle. Let us start from the top of the upswing, when the boom is at its peak. Throughout the upswing, total monetary demand has been expanding. As we have seen, such an expansion can be brought about by: (a) an increase in investment without any corresponding increase in saving; (b) an increase in consumption (that is, a decrease in saving), investment remaining unchanged; (c) an excess of exports over imports; (d) a government budget deficit. The break in the boom and the beginning of the downswing is due to the fact that total monetary demand ceases to expand and then contracts, which may itself be due to a reversal in any one or more of the above relationships. We will discuss each in turn.

A fall in the level of investment is the most likely reason for the boom to end. Especially when the population is not expanding very rapidly, it is likely that a point will be reached where demand remains fairly steady, and so we must expect investment to fall back to the position where it is sufficient for replacement purposes only and not for providing also for an expanding production of consumer goods. In short, additional fields of investment, irrespective of whether they have arisen from an increased demand, the invention of new techniques, or the development of new industries, gradually become exhausted. Again, investment may fall simply because entrepreneurs take a less optimistic view of the future. Normally this will occur through a slackening-off in the increase in demand, but when the rate of investment is high, the confidence of entre-preneurs is particularly vulnerable to even minor set-backs. Lastly, a rise in the rate of interest may reduce investment. Such a rise is most likely to occur through the deliberate action of the government, which considers that the boom will go too far and lead to inflation.

A decrease in the proportion of income consumed may occur owing to the increase in income as the boom proceeds and also to the fact that, during a boom, a greater proportion of the national income tends to go to profits whose recipients save a larger proportion of income than wage-earners. If the lower consumption is not matched by an increase in investment, then total money income falls. A similar result will occur if the government maintains a budget surplus, for then its saving will be in excess of its spending, that is consumption. Moreover, a country so dependent on foreign trade as the United Kingdom has to watch its balance of payments. If, for instance, the trade depression has already reached the chief buyers of its exports, their falling income will cause them to buy less from the United Kingdom. The United Kingdom, however, may continue to import at the previous rate. Imports therefore exceed exports, producing a deflationary effect. Thus it is possible to 'import' a depression.

Once the downswing has commenced it tends to be cumula-tive. Falling expenditure in one sector leads to a reduced expenditure elsewhere. Thus an initial decrease in investment leads to an even greater fall in income, and the pessimistic expectations of entrepreneurs justify themselves. Consequently the drop to the bottom of the depression is a sharp one. The very low expectations of entrepreneurs outweigh any reduction in the rate of interest aimed at restoring investment. Indeed, a rise in the rate of interest is much more effective in breaking a boom than a fall is in halting a depression.

Eventually, however, the bottom is reached and total monetary demand begins to expand. Investment may increase simply because replacements to fixed capital cannot be post-poned any longer, while, as people become poorer, a larger proportion of income will be 'consumed'. Government expenditure is likely to be maintained and probably increased, during the depression. Any rise in expenditure in one part of the economy will stimulate expenditure elsewhere and so the gradual climb back to greater prosperity, the upswing, begins. Thus we see that both the boom and the depression contain the 'seeds of their own destruction'. Nevertheless, it is the duty of the government to take what steps it can to maintain a full-employment level of money income.

6. Government Action to Eliminate Cyclical Unemployment

Our previous analysis shows that, in order to eliminate cyclical unemployment, total monetary demand must be maintained at that level which will just produce full employment. (As we shall see later, an expansion beyond that point merely leads to inflation with its various disadvantages.) For two reasons, the government must assume responsibility for maintaining the desired level of total monetary demand. In the first place, only the government has the knowledge and overall control to make possible the regulation of the economy, and if the government does not assume this responsibility, the private-enterprise system is doomed to failure. Secondly, the announcement by the government of its firm intention to maintain full employment would eliminate much of the uncertainty regarding future economic conditions and thereby remove one of the major influences which tend to produce variations in total monetary demand.

As we have seen, in a closed economy, total monetary demand is made up of spending on consumer goods + spending on producer goods. But this spending may be done by private persons, by entrepreneurs and by the government, the present-day tendency being for the proportion spent by the government to increase. Hence, since it is only over its own spending that the government has direct control, it is necessary, for the purposes of examining government policy, to decide exactly by whom the money is spent. We say, therefore, that total monetary demand consists of private spending on consumer goods + private spending on producer goods (investment) + government spending. If government spending remains constant and private

spending on producer goods increases without any corresponding increase in the proportion of income saved, total monetary
demand will increase. Similarly, if the proportion of income
saved decreases and there is no corresponding decrease in
investment, then once again total monetary demand will
increase. For both cases, too, the converse is true. Hence, in
order to maintain total monetary demand at the desired level,
the government can act on all or any one of these three variables, consumption, investment and its own spending.

Dropping the assumption of a closed economy means that we
have to allow for the effect of a surplus or deficit in our balance
of payments (our current account with foreign countries) on
total monetary demand. As we have seen, an excess of U.K.
exports over imports, both visible and invisible, increases total
monetary demand in the U.K. Similarly, an excess of U.K.
imports over exports has the opposite effect. Thus, for a
country engaging in international trade, we have the important
equation:

Total Monetary Demand = Consumption + Investment
+ Government spending + Balance of Payments
(Surplus +, deficit −).

It is obvious, therefore, that a country can more easily
maintain full employment when it has a favourable balance of
payments. But, as emphasised above, any temptation to
secure, by artificial means, a surplus on its balance of payments
simply to achieve full employment at home, must be resisted. That
policy merely leads to retaliation and international poverty.
The government must concentrate its action on the other
three variables.

In order to take such action, however, the government must
know with reasonable accuracy what total monetary demand
should be in order to produce full employment and also the size
of the variables comprising it. In short, statistics have to be prepared analysing the various components of total monetary
demand. It further assumes that the government has sufficient
knowledge (*a*) to forecast future possible changes in these variables, and (*b*) to control them. In other words, the government
needs expert economic advisers. Both requirements usually
entail the setting-up of special administrative machinery.

Today, in the United Kingdom, the work of preparing the statistics is performed by the Central Statistical Office, the main results of whose work, from our point of view, are published annually in the Blue Book on National Income and Expenditure. The expert planning is performed by the Economic Section of the Treasury which works very closely with the Chancellor of the Exchequer.

The first task is to prepare a budget showing what the estimated yearly value of production is likely to be if all the resources of the country were fully employed. The figure arrived at would be a fundamental datum, the limit to total production set by the resources themselves. In the words of the late Mr. Ernest Bevin it is a 'human budget'.

The next step is to estimate expenditure for the year, breaking down such expenditure into the four variables described above —consumption, investment, government spending and the balance of payments surplus or deficit. We are now in a position to see whether total expenditure, that is total monetary demand, is sufficient to sustain production at the full-employment level during the coming year. If expenditure were less than the estimated value of production, then it would provide a warning of future unemployment; if it were greater, it would give a warning of approaching inflation. The problem of adjusting the two can be tackled by influencing consumption, investment and government spending.

The volume of consumption depends chiefly upon the level of income. It is, therefore, a 'dependent variable', for it is only as the government is successful in varying the level of total monetary demand by other means that the level of consumption itself will be affected. It is possible, however, for the government to influence the other factors which help to determine the proportion of income which is spent. Thus it is probable that this proportion would be increased by a more equal distribution of income. On the other hand, the government can encourage saving by means of propaganda, the development of savings institutions, the restriction of hire-purchase facilities and the taxing of expenditure through indirect taxation.

Like consumption, the volume of investment is, as we have seen, chiefly dependent on the level of income, for it is this which has the chief effect on the expectations of entrepreneurs. Nevertheless, pressure can be brought to bear on the other factors which influence investment. Moreover, such pressure is likely to be more effective in varying investment than in dealing with consumption, for any change in the latter often entails an alteration in long-term habits. Above all, the government is more likely to prefer raising investment to increasing consumption as the means of combating a depression, owing to the future advantages derived by a community from increasing its stock of capital goods. When increased investment is desired, the rate of interest may be reduced, though if the expectations of entrepreneurs are very low, a reduction in the rate of interest has little effect on the volume of investment. The government may also exhort entrepreneurs to invest and may even stimulate them into doing so by means of tax reliefs, subsidies, etc., though it should be borne in mind that the vigour and determination with which the government pursues its policy of increasing total monetary demand will probably have by far the greatest effect on the response of entrepreneurs. To decrease the volume of investment, the rate of interest is usually raised, though the effectiveness of this is doubtful. Thus the government may have to resort to physical controls on the volume and purposes of investment.

This brings us to a consideration of government expenditure. Here the important thing to note is that, unlike consumption and private investment which depend on many other variables, government spending is directly under its own control. Thus it is this item which the government can most easily control and which, it is now generally agreed amongst economists, should be varied in order to influence total monetary demand.

When it is desired to expand monetary demand, the government may make itself responsible for extra investment, paying for such investment by means of borrowing. Reliance on this policy alone, however, faces two difficulties. The first is that if full employment continues for a long period, desirable investment projects, such as the development of roads and bridges, tend to be postponed in view of the possibility of their fulfilling the purpose of increased government investment later. The second is that eventually the projects for such investment may be of little social benefit.

These considerations mean that varying public investment as a means of adjusting monetary demand is restricted in its use. Fortunately we have a much more flexible weapon— budgetary policy.

A budget policy involves looking at our ordinary budget in a new light. Instead of considering it as the means by which revenue is raised in order to balance government expenditure, it must be regarded as the means whereby taxation is adjusted in order to vary private consumption. Taxation represents an appropriation by the government of a part of private incomes. The amount so appropriated is retained in the circular flow of income only in so far as it is spent by the government. Hence, if taxation is greater than government spending, there will be a budget surplus and total monetary demand will be reduced. On the other hand, if taxation is less than government spending, more spending power will be left in the hands of consumers and monetary demand will increase.

This provision for adequate monetary outlay by means of appropriate adjustments in the relationship between govern- ment expenditure and receipts enables the national product to be divided between private and communal uses according to their relative priorities. There are certain tasks which can be undertaken better by the State than by private enterprise, and the government must decide on the proportion of the estimated national product to be devoted to the communal needs, such as defence, justice, social welfare, health and other essential services, for which it provides. The rest of the national product can be left to private demand. Here the price system will decide what shall be produced. Taxation must then be adjusted, not to balance the budget, but according to how far it is thought that private demand is excessive or inadequate. If there is full employment, an excessive private demand will cause resources to be drawn from the communal production to which the government has given priority, and so taxation must be increased. If, on the other hand, the outlay left to private demand after the government has finished spending is inadequate to employ fully that part of production left to it, then more purchasing power must be left with private consumers by reducing taxation. The resulting deficit in government expenditure and income would be financed by borrowing. Such budget deficits might be offset by surpluses in the good years, but even if this did not occur and an increase in the National Debt resulted, the disadvantages would be far outweighed by the gains, both economic and social, resulting from full employment.

It must be remembered, however, that a public works programme or a 'budget deficit' policy take a certain amount of time to become effective. They are particularly suitable when a fall in outlay can be predicted fairly accurately. If the fluctuation in demand comes suddenly, however, prompt steps must be taken to arrest its development. This means that the policy outlined above must be supplemented in a way which puts extra purchasing power quickly into the hands of consumers. Among suggestions which have been made to achieve this are varying the size of the national insurance contribution according to the level of unemployment and lowering the rates of V.A.T.

'Budgetary' policy for full employment is not without its problems. The danger of inflation, probably the major problem, will be considered in the next chapter. Taxation, too, has other uses besides that of adjusting total monetary demand But the policy does present a means whereby full employment can be maintained while still leaving a large section of the economy to be operated under the private-enterprise system. Thus the main advantages of that system—the efficiency which springs from the profit motive, individual choice, the accurate measurement of consumers' wants and the provision for those wants—are retained.

CHAPTER 26

INFLATION

1. THE BACKGROUND TO A GENERAL RISE IN PRICES

AT any one moment, the price of goods in general depends upon: (a) the supply of goods available for sale; (b) the amount of money being offered against that supply. If the supply of goods decreases and the amount of money offered against the reduced supply remains the same, prices in general will rise. Similarly, if the supply of goods remains fixed and the amount of money offered against this fixed supply of goods increases, again prices in general will rise. It should be noted that this is merely a statement of fact, not of cause.

The first situation, a decrease in the supply of goods available against a fixed purchasing power, may come about through such natural causes as widespread harvest failure, earthquake, flood, drought and fire. But it may also be due to abnormal circumstances, such as war, internal political unrest or labour disputes. Lastly, a country, such as the United Kingdom, which engages in a vast amount of international trade, may find that, owing to a deterioration in its trading position, more goods have to be exported or fewer imported, leaving relatively fewer on the home market. Such a deterioration may result from a worsening of the terms of trade or from a drop in invisible earnings due to the sale of foreign assets.

In practice, however, rising prices are much more likely to occur for the second reason, an increase in the amount of money offered against a fixed supply of goods. Hence our analysis of a rise in the general level of prices will be confined to this particular situation, especially as it is the one existing in the United Kingdom today. This involves a re-examination of total monetary demand to see how it affects, not the level of employment, but the general price level.

2. THE MEANING OF 'INFLATION'

1. *The Movement of Prices when Total Monetary Demand is below the Level Required for Full Employment*

In the upswing of the trade cycle, until the point of full employment is reached, the increase in total monetary demand is matched by additional output. To begin with, therefore, prices can be expected to remain fairly steady. As the upswing proceeds, they will probably start to rise. This comparatively slight rise could be due to: the use of less efficient plant and labour as output expands; increased costs because of temporary shortages or 'bottlenecks' in machinery, skilled labour and raw materials, whose supply is relatively inelastic; a rise in money wages as a result of trade union pressure following the improved position of labour. (Similarly, for parallel reasons operating in the opposite direction, prices can be expected to fall somewhat during the downswing.)

2. *The Movement of Prices when Total Monetary Demand Rises beyond the Level Required to Produce Full Employment*

When total monetary demand rises beyond the level required to produce full employment, there is a distinct change in the situation. Whereas before this point was reached, an increase in total monetary demand produced an increase in output as more factors of production ceased to be unemployed, now output cannot be further increased because the point of full employment has been reached. Instead an increasing total monetary demand is being offered against a fairly fixed quantity of goods. Total monetary demand is therefore greater than the value of production at current prices. Hence prices rise.

But this may not be all. People may expect further rises to occur, and so they hasten to spend their money, often from their savings, thereby bringing about the very thing they fear. The steady price rise now develops into a more rapid one. Once this occurs a dangerous situation has arisen, for the rise in prices may even reach a point where the government is powerless to arrest it. Money loses its value so rapidly that people refuse to hold it, changing it into goods immediately it is received in order to forestall a further price rise. This is what happened in Germany in 1923 and in Hungary and Greece after World War II. Owing to its rapidly falling value, people in these countries completely lost confidence in the paper money in current use until then, and so such money became valueless. These extreme cases of inflation are generally referred to as 'runaway' or 'hyper-' inflation.

When speaking about 'inflation', therefore, it is necessary to distinguish between an economy which has a very steadily rising price level and one where the rate at which prices are rising has become uncomfortable, not only because of the disadvantages of rising prices, but also because the rise is likely to gain momentum. Such a position is likely to occur once full employment has been reached, for then any increase in total monetary demand will be offered against a fixed quantity of goods. In other words, an inflationary situation exists where the level of total monetary demand is in excess of that required to buy the full employment output at current prices. Specific measures must be taken forthwith to get the rise in prices under control.

3. The Causes of Inflation

An expanding monetary demand arises, as we saw in Chapter 25, because there is insufficient saving to finance investment, the difference having to be made up by the creation of credit. But in order to understand what measures should be taken to combat the inflation, it is necessary to delve a little deeper by inquiring how this disparity between saving and investment originated.

Briefly, it can come about in three ways:

(a) an increase in investment without a corresponding increase in saving;

(b) an increase in consumption (that is a decrease in saving) without a corresponding decrease in investment;

(c) an increase in *government spending* without a corresponding increase in taxation.

All three situations have played their part in producing Britain's post-war inflation. Both private producers and the government have increased investment in machinery, factories and houses, roads and bridges, the nationalised industries, and so on. On the other hand, consumers, especially after suffering from the austerity of the war period, desired to enjoy more goods, and so they spent, not only out of their current incomes but even out of accrued savings, the result being that current net saving decreased. Finally, the government has exceeded the proceeds of current taxation and borrowing, as it has tried to provide at one and the same time for defence, the preservation of law and order, increased social benefits, loans to local authorities and investment in the nationalised industries.

4. GOVERNMENT ACTION TO REMEDY INFLATION

In the same way as inflation may originate either on the demand or supply side, so the government is able to tackle it from both angles. Thus, although the inflation may have been brought about by an increase in total monetary demand, it may be partly offset by an increase in the output of goods, achieved by means of improved techniques and more intensive working of labour and machinery. Hence the government asks people to increase their effort by working overtime, extra shifts, etc., and sometimes it augments these exhortations with specific policy, as, for example, by reducing income tax to provide an incentive. Of course, in a position of full employment, the government has little room for manoeuvre along these lines and so it has to think chiefly in terms of reducing the excess spending power.

Broadly speaking, measures can be classified into three main groups—direct control, monetary and fiscal. Under the first group we include both exhortation and control. The government encourages people to save their money instead of spending it. To this end it has provided attractive methods of saving, such as Savings Certificates, Premium Savings Bonds and British Savings Bonds, and granted concessions regarding income tax for National Savings. On the other hand, at times, in order to reduce consumption, hire-purchase terms have been made more stringent and the banks have been asked to restrict advances. Sometimes controls have been even more direct. Thus, as regards investment, until 1959 any amount over £10,000 had to be approved by the Capital Issues Committee.

Monetary policy is aimed at varying the cost and availability of credit. The first is achieved by raising the rate of interest. First, by increasing the cost of borrowing it tends to discourage investment. Secondly, by increasing the reward, it may encourage saving. The availability of credit is varied by restricting the lending powers of the banks and hire-purchase companies.

The third remedy is for the Chancellor of the Exchequer to budget for a surplus of revenue over expenditure. Such a surplus may be achieved either by a reduction in government expenditure or by an increase in taxation, though in practice the latter method is generally used. In effect what the Chancellor says is that if people will not save some of their income voluntarily, he will take it from them by taxation. Thus the budget surplus 'mops up' some of the excess spending power and this the government uses to cover its own investment.

5. The Inflationary Effect of Wage Increases

In a position of full employment, the initial impulse given by an increase in spending power may be supplemented and even replaced by the effect of demands for wage increases. Indeed, some economists have gone so far as to call this a 'cost' or 'wage-induced' inflation in order to distinguish it from the first cause. It operates in the following way. In conditions of full employment, as have occurred in the United Kingdom since 1940, labour, particularly that labour organised through trade unions, is in a strong position. Since the main object of a trade union is to redistribute income in favour of the worker, claims for increased wages are put forward in spite of the fact that there has been no corresponding increase in productivity. Such claims are usually granted. The current existence of excess spending power means that people are willing to bear the increase in prices which results from higher wages. Above all, the increase in the wage packet represents directly in itself an increase in money spending power. We are in the situation where 'supply creates its own demand'. Even indirectly, however, spending power is increased. Wage-earners, as a rule, spend a larger proportion of their income than salary-earners and people living on profits. Hence, as they begin to take a higher proportion of the national income through the granting of wage claims, so more is spent.

Increased wages, however, result in higher prices, thereby giving rise to further wage claims. In practice, this puts the government on the horns of a dilemma. If wage claims are refused, strikes result, dependent workers also become unemployed, and output decreases (itself a cause of inflation). On the other hand, the granting of a wage increase to one section of the workers leads to additional claims by the rest. And so the spiral continues, wages and prices chasing each other upwards. In an attempt to check this type of inflation, the government has, in recent years, followed two main lines of policy. The first has been a plea to the trade unions to moderate their demands for wage increases. In fact, at times, exhortation by the government has been backed up by a general 'wage-freeze' policy, though in effect this 'incomes policy' has still not proved really successful. The second method has been to control the prices of essential goods and often to keep down their prices to an artificial level by means of subsidies. By preventing a rise in the cost of living, it is hoped to remove the cause of demands for wage increases.

We see then that the achievement of full employment brings its own difficulties. In the first place, a government has to keep a closer watch on the possibility of inflation, especially in the case of the United Kingdom, which is so dependent on international trade. Inflation not only renders the price of her exports too high for world markets but the excess spending power leads to an excessive home demand for goods which should find their way to the export market and also for imports from abroad. Hence balance of payments problems arise.

Secondly, it must solve the problem of collective bargaining, for the indiscriminate and irresponsible use of this right may easily produce an inflationary spiral. Thus the co-operation of trade unions must be sought and the government must use its moderating influence on both sides.

Lastly, the government must ensure that the more important investment projects are the ones which have first call on the limited supply of capital. This problem arises because of the changed conditions produced by full employment. Until this position is reached, any investment project is beneficial in that it provides income which, by being spent, encourages further investment elsewhere. With full employment, however, capital itself is fully employed and we cannot afford to waste it on useless enterprises. The rate of interest does help to sort out the more worthwhile investment projects from the indifferent ones, but even so internal policy may have to be reinforced by physical controls.

CONCLUDING OBSERVATIONS

Our survey of the problem of full employment, although brief, has thrown into relief certain points which are fundamental to the solution of economic problems today. The first is that policy is more difficult to apply effectively when there is complete freedom of individual choice and action throughout the economy. This does necessitate some degree of control, but basically the people of the Western World still consider that such compulsion should be kept to a minimum.

This, however, brings us to our second point—that, in the solution of the 'economic problem', co-operation is essential. We have seen, for example, that such co-operation must be observed by the individual worker for effective production through division of labour, and by trade unions in periods of full employment. Internationally, too, there must be economic as well as political co-operation. Thus, in foreign trade, each country must consider the effect its policies will have on the well-being of others. It must not, for instance, deliberately take measures to 'export' unemployment in periods of depression. Above all, the rich countries can do much to help the poorer raise their standards of living by giving the invaluable initial capital equipment, etc., which they need.

Lastly, it will be observed that there is usually no one hard-and-fast solution to a particular problem. The result is that economists quite often disagree. But there are justifiable reasons for this. Economic facts are difficult to establish and hence economists may base their recommendations on different data. More important, however, is that matters of policy often involve 'moral judgments' and are, therefore, strictly within the province of the politician. All the economists can do is to point out the results of alternative lines of action and then leave it to the politician to decide. It is this which lies behind an observation attributed to Sir Winston Churchill that, whenever he asked England's six leading economists a question, he got seven answers—two from Lord Keynes!

INDEX

Acceptance houses 386–8
Accountability 93
Accounts 404, 409
Acrylics production 226
Advertising 15, 66
costs saved by monopolies 179
to aid product differentiation 177
Aerospace industry 219
Age distribution 34–8
Agricultural Mortgage Corporation 80
Agricultural Revolution 44
Agriculture 41, 42, 44–5
Common Agricultural Policy (in E.E.C.) 289–90, 294–5
difficulties of division of labour 56
marketing produce 161–2
revival in South West England 248
Aircraft industry 219–21
nationalisation plans 221
(see also Civil aviation)
Annual reports of nationalised industries 98
Arbitration 332
Assets 335
eligible reserves 418
included in national capital 337
of nationalised industries 98
Assisted Areas 473–5
Associations 175
of professional people 176
Atomic Energy Commission 284
Average age of population 36

Balance of payments 271–82, 380
correction of deficit 274–81
effect of money value changes 380
Bank Charter Act (1844) 401
Bank for International Settlements 417
Bank-notes 370, 398, 413
Bank of England monopoly 414
Bank of England 389–90, 413–21
as banker to joint-stock banks 416

development as central bank 413–14
directives 420
formation 398–9
functions 414–21
government banker 415–16
international responsibilities 417
Bank Rate (see Minimum lending rate)
Bank Restriction Act (1797) 399, 413
Banker's drafts 411
Banking
development 395–402
eighteenth-century weaknesses 399–400
invisible earnings 270
reform 400–401
Banks 386–90
advances to customers 407–8
borrowing by 404–5
Clearing House 402
commercial 388–9, 403–13
deposits 370
inter-bank deposits 390
lending by 405
origin of term 396
special services 409–13
Barlow Report (1939) 234
Barter 365
'Bears' 124, 425
Beveridge, Lord William 465, 466
Bilateral agreements 258, 484–5
Bills of exchange 384–5, 388–9
as bank assets 406
Birth control 30
Births 24
1801–1911 26
1911–1973 28–9
1941 to present 30–32
male/female ratio 39
projections 33
(see also Infant mortality; Population)
Black Death 21

503

Job satisfaction 310–11
in nationalised industries 91
Jobbers 423–4, 427–8
Joint Industrial Councils 330–31
Joint-stock companies 75–82
types 78–82

Keynes, John Maynard 342, 358, 501
King, Gregory 22

Labour 301
Adam Smith's definition 102
amount of work done 312–13
as factor of production 309–11
direction 466
division (see Division of labour)
in United Kingdom 311–13
nature 360
payment 314–18
percentage employed in small firms 64
productive 103
psychological effects of unemployment 461–2
quality 313
specialisation 9–10
Labour markets 117
Labour mobility 38
(see also Immobility of labour)
Labour relations
in motor industry 218, 219
in shipbuilding industry 222
Laissez-faire 45
(see also Capitalism)
Land 301, 302–3, 336
Leisure 313
'Lender of last resort' 390, 421
Liabilities 418
Limited liability 75
Living standards 19
changes 351–5
Loans
foreign 270, 361
from banks 405
personal 408
restrictions by Bank of England 420
to government 437–8
(see also Borrowing)

Local authority bills 386
Local authority deposits 390–91
Local government 19
charges for services 456
employees 46
finance 455–8
loans from central government 456
revenue 455–6
Lombards 396
London
explanations for population growth 244–5, 246
population overflow to southern towns 248
special planning arrangements 238
Luxury goods 15

Machinery (see Mechanisation)
Mail order firms 112–13
Maintenance of goods 108
Malthus, Rev. T. R. 22
Managerial economies 60–61
Managers
diseconomies in nationalised industries 92
effects of scale 67
Marketing Boards 150, 173
(see also Commodity markets)
Markets 116–25
influencing location of industry 230
organised 121–5
perfect and imperfect 120–21
world-wide 117
(see also Commodity markets; Produce markets)
Marriages 29, 31
Mass production 52
(see also Economies of scale)
Mechanisation 59
as a means of increasing income 7
in agriculture 44
in coal mines 46
Medieval economy 5–6
Medium of exchange 129
Merchant banks 80, 386–8
Middlemen 114–16
Migration 24